LIBRARY AND INFORMATION SCIENCE

A GUIDE TO KEY LITERATURE AND SOURCES

LIBRARY AND INFORMATION SCIENCE

A GUIDE TO KEY LITERATURE AND SOURCES

MICHAEL F. BEMIS

facet publishing

Published by Facet Publishing,
7 Ridgmount Street, London WC1E 7AE
www.facetpublishing.co.uk

Facet Publishing is wholly owned by CILIP: the Chartered Institute of Library
and Information Professionals.

First published in the USA by the American Library Association, 2014.
This UK edition 2014.

British Library Cataloguing in Publication Data
A catalogue record for this book is available from the British Library.

ISBN 978-1-78330-002-0

Printed and bound in the United Kingdom by Lightning Source.

To my colleagues, the librarians of the world,
this work is respectfully dedicated.

Come, and take choice of all my library, and so beguile thy sorrow.

Shakespeare, *Titus Andronicus,* 4.1, 1594

CONTENTS

ACKNOWLEDGMENTS

NO AUTHOR CAN CLAIM TO CREATE A WORK SUCH AS THIS SINGLE-handedly. Many wonderful folks have invested their time and effort on my behalf, and I would like to express my appreciation for their contributions to the finished product you now hold before you. Any errors or omissions are my responsibility alone, but credit for a job well done is rightly shared among the following list.

To Jill Bemis, my loving and faithful wife of many years, for her organizational abilities and for keeping me on task. To Nathaniel Bemis, our son, for his encouragement and faith in the Old Man. To Jenni Fry of ALA Editions for her assistance with Endnote software. To Josh Hadro and Margaret Heilbrun at *Library Journal* for helping me to acquire review copies of LIS material. To Chris Rhodes, acquisitions editor at ALA Editions, for his initial interest in my book proposal and for his continuous encouragement, good cheer, and sage advice. To the entire staff at the St. Catherine University Library, St. Paul, Minnesota, for all the assistance they have lent me during the course of this project.

I would be remiss if I did not also make mention of the North Pole Restaurant in Newport, Minnesota, owned and operated by Mary, David, and Brian North. The many fine meals served by a friendly and efficient staff helped fuel long days and nights of plowing through library science literature.

INTRODUCTION

I WROTE THIS BOOK FOR A SIMPLE REASON: I NEEDED A CURRENT ANNO-
tated bibliography of library science but couldn't find one. My goals were twofold: to
collect as much of the available information sources regarding various aspects of the
profession as reasonably possible and to then organize them in a logical fashion. It is my
fervent hope that my colleagues will find this to be a useful work as they conduct research
in our field of endeavor.

Written specifically with working librarians in mind, this volume should also appeal
to library students, library educators, and to a lesser extent bibliographers in general. Of
course, anyone wishing to survey the current landscape of library literature should find
this book helpful.

Books and print periodicals are the focus of this annotated bibliography. Electronic
journals, websites, and databases also receive attention, but to a much lesser degree. Print
works with a copyright date of 2000 to, generally, early 2012 make up the bulk of this
volume, although some classic LIS titles are featured in special "Historic Interest" sidebars. A case in point is the one in chapter 22, which discusses the *ARBA Guide to Library
Science Literature* and its several annual supplements. Readers are directed to this resource
should they desire to locate professional material for the period 1970 through 1999.

I enlisted OCLC WorldCat, local library collections within Minneapolis/St. Paul (most
notably the LIS collection at the library of the College of St. Catherine, which supports
a library school there), and review copies from publishers along with their websites and
catalogs to find suitable material for inclusion in this volume. Emphasis is on usefulness
and practicality for the working librarian—thus the many "how-to" manuals, handbooks,
and other materials that may be employed for on-the-job use.

ENTRIES

There are two types of entries herein. Full annotations include complete bibliographic
information, such as title, author/editor, publisher, and date of publication, as well as
ISBN or ISSN, as appropriate, and a URL for websites, along with commentary on the

work at hand. Citations include just the bare-bones bibliographic data and are listed under the heading "Further Resources." In either case, entries follow the provisions set forth in *The Chicago Manual of Style*, which for the past century has been widely regarded as the standard of manuscript preparation. The specific criteria I used to select a particular resource for either the full treatment or the more concise listing appear below. It should be noted that there were some resources reviewed that, in my professional opinion, met few or none of these standards and therefore were not listed at all. Fortunately, the level of quality of library literature is quite high overall.

Resources that met the following four criteria include full bibliographic data as well as commentary:

Timeliness of information. Reflects current trends, issues, or historical perspective.

Authority of resource or author qualifications. Clearly indicates who the author is, what organization(s) he or she is affiliated with, and if the work had sponsorships.

Professional standing. Is quoted widely and often cited in lists of references, bibliographies, or works cited in other resources examined during primary research. Primary and secondary sources were clearly listed.

Special features. Contains special features that are unusual or particularly helpful (e.g., tables, diagrams, step-by-step instructions, case studies, historical context).

Resources that did not merit annotation are nonetheless applicable to the specific chapter topic and provide supplementary or alternative information not covered by the annotated entries. A further benefit of listing these additional resources is that it allows for the inclusion of much more material and gives the reader a sense of where publishing activity is most prevalent. It probably comes as no surprise, for example, that the chapter covering information technology is one of the largest in this book.

For annotated entries, the thrust of the notes is to survey the work's contents and the aims of the author/editor. Although many annotated bibliographies attempt to be evaluative or critical, I contend that a particular work's usefulness is ultimately up to the reader. It is not a bibliographer's place to dictate what should or should not be read. (Nonetheless, if I considered a work to be wholly inappropriate or poorly executed, I excluded it from this listing.)

Readers will note that the majority of the entries are for narrative works. Some reference titles are included, but they form a minority. Not only does this avoid unnecessary duplication, it allows more space for LIS titles not reviewed elsewhere. Dictionaries and encyclopedias of library and information science are covered pretty comprehensively in *American Reference Books Annual*, published by Libraries Unlimited.

SPECIAL FEATURES

Chapters appear in alphabetical order by title, each one covering a specific aspect of library science, such as cataloging and classification, collection management, readers' advisory, and so on. Each chapter begins with several representative Library of Congress subject headings. I recognize that this book is not comprehensive. Readers who wish to find further titles on a particular topic may use these headings to locate still more material on WorldCat and local library electronic card catalogs.

Each chapter is subdivided by format: books, periodicals, websites (a category that includes online-only articles), and databases (if applicable). Sidebars are scattered throughout the book. "Historic Interest" sidebars mention classic but out-of-print titles that are too important to be ignored. "FYI" sidebars alert readers to sources of information which, though on the whole are outside the scope of this work, may nevertheless contain material pertinent to the subject of library science.

Finally, two appendixes list and comment on professional organizations, the first for ALA subunits and the second for international and regional library associations.

1

ADMINISTRATION AND MANAGEMENT

◆ BOOKS

1 Allan, Barbara. *Project Management: Tools and Techniques for Today's ILS Professional.* London: Facet, 2004. ISBN: 978-1-85604-504-9.

Allan draws on her experience in managing a wide variety of library projects to create this textbook for practitioners and students on implementing IT systems, setting up websites, and managing projects. Topics include project life cycles, planning, implementation, evaluation, funding, and partnerships. Text includes illustrations, examples, and case studies.

2 Applegate, Rachel. *Managing the Small College Library.* Libraries Unlimited Library Management Collection. Santa Barbara, CA: Libraries Unlimited, 2010. ISBN: 978-1-59158-917-4 (print), 978-1-59158-918-1 (e-book).

Just what the title says: "The purpose of this book is to give men and women who direct libraries at small colleges the tools and ideas they need to be effective managers" (p. 3). Applegate does a commendable job of doing exactly that. The book's dozen chapters are organized into four broad sections: "Thinking about Managing," "People and How They Fit Together," "Core Responsibilities of Managers," and "Supporting Teaching, Research and Service." This is an excellent overview of the duties and responsibilities of the job for those new to it or who simply aspire to reach it some day.

3 Brooks, Sam, and David H. Carlson, eds. *Library/Vendor Relationships.* Copublished simultaneously as *Journal of Library Administration* 44, no. 3/4, 2006. New York: Haworth Information Press, 2006. ISBN: 978-0-78903-351-2.

This compilation examines the relationship between libraries and those organizations that supply the goods and services used to help their patrons. The irony of for-profit companies supplying materials and equipment to nonprofit libraries is not lost on the contributors as they examine both the authorization and transaction processes. Topics include a review of database markets, book vendor efficiencies, collaboration in standards development, fostering productive relationships, and online support services. Charts and graphs are a strong complement.

4   Brophy, Peter. *Measuring Library Performance: Principles and Techniques.* London: Facet, 2006. ISBN: 978-1-85604-593-3.

As Brophy explains in his preface, "Without clear and reliable information about what is happening within an organization and in its interactions with its customers and suppliers, it is impossible to make well-founded decisions to guide future development or even to monitor the effects of decisions that have been made in the past" (p. xv). Well said. The purpose, then, of this volume is to give the reader the tools necessary to effect the opposite outcome. This is accomplished with clearly written text, helpful charts and diagrams, and three appendixes covering data collection methods, analysis of data, and presentation of results. The book's fourteen chapters cover such aspects as user satisfaction, social and economic impacts, and benchmarking. Each chapter concludes with a list of additional resources and a bibliography.

5   Carson, Paula Phillips, Kerry D. Carson, and Joyce S. Phillips. *The Library Manager's Deskbook: 102 Expert Solutions to 101 Common Dilemmas.* Chicago: American Library Association, 1995. ISBN: 978-0-83890-655-2.

101 common management issues and their proposed solutions are organized in a question-and-answer format; they cover topics such as workplace security, personnel issues, supervision, personality conflicts, lead workers, liability, leadership, and sexual harassment. The authors use Total Quality Management tools in combination with professionalism to provide a process to create answers to other management problems.

6   Cohn, John M., and Ann L. Kelsey. *Staffing the Modern Library: A How-to-Do-It Manual.* How-to-Do-It Manuals for Librarian 137. New York: Neal-Schuman, 2006. ISBN: 978-1-55570-511-4.

The authors base their staffing process on Michael Milgate's "lean" manufacturing concepts as used to measure and manage the drivers of business success. They stress the necessity for library managers to establish staff competencies that are aligned with library mission and goals. Focus is changed from a task-oriented to a competency-based approach to providing library services through revamping position descriptions and assignments. Sample checklists, examples, worksheets, and illustrations are provided, along with an annotated bibliography. Appendixes contain sample behavioral and competency-based job descriptions and core and technical competencies for librarians, children's collection librarians, and music librarians.

7   Cravey, Pamela J. *Protecting Library Staff, Users, Collections, and Facilities: A How-to-Do-It Manual.* How-to-Do-It Manuals for Librarians 103. New York: Neal-Schuman, 2001. ISBN: 978-1-55570-392-9.

This is a pragmatic step-by-step guide to dealing with security issues including staff and patron safety, securing facilities, and safeguarding collections. The book covers overall security concerns, general collection and special collection safeguards, staff and patron physical safety during normal activities and special events, and electronic files and systems protections.

8   Curran, Charles, and Lewis Miller. *Guide to Library and Information Agency Management.* Lanham, MD: Scarecrow Press, 2005. ISBN: 978-0-81085-115-3.

Like any good identification manual, this "field guide" to library management attempts to point out the various "species" one is likely to encounter, in this case, opportunities, workplace issues, success/failure, and topics both routine (budgets, office politics) and unique, as in—ahem—"fraternizing" with one's coworkers. Flashes of humor frequently sparkle between the lines of drier dialogue. In reference to the aforementioned possibility, the authors state that such shenanigans cannot be hidden: "Listen up, lovebirds; it's on the bulletin board. Everybody knows! No one doesn't know. You are busted!" (p. 327). For the most part, this is nitty-gritty hands-on advice, much of it not to be found in garden variety management tomes, which are frequently long on theory but short on practice. The gist is nicely summed up in the introduction: "to fill . . . the cracks between information about managerial principles and the processes required to carry them out" (p. ix). Special features include "Your Turn" text boxes, in which library managers describe real-life episodes and how they were handled. End-of-chapter bibliographies point the way for further research.

9 Curzon, Susan Carol. *Managing Change: A How-to-Do-It Manual for Librarians.* Rev. ed. How-To-Do-It Manuals for Libraries 145. New York: Neal-Schuman, 2005. ISBN: 978-1-55570-553-4.

This is, indeed, a how-to-do-it manual. Each chapter begins with the words "How to," as in "How to Conceptualize Change" and "How to Prepare the Organization for Change." All this is under section 1, "Managing Change Successfully." Particularly appealing is the step-by-step outline presented at the beginning of each chapter. Curzon almost literally leads the reader by the hand through the process, then wraps up everything neatly with concluding remarks and a "Quick Check" box that states "review Chapter X and answer the following questions." She then shifts gear for section 2, "Practicing Change Management," looking at such scenarios as "Adjusting to the budget cut" and "Improving poor service at reference," which are basically a series of case studies. Overall, this is an easy read and a thorough treatment of the subject matter.

10 Diamond, Tom, ed. *Middle Management in Academic and Public Libraries.* Westport, CT: Libraries Unlimited, 2011. ISBN: 978-1-59884-689-8 (print), 978-1-59884-690-4 (e-book).

Contributors look at the many roles middle managers play in today's modern library, in addition to such topics as creating a leadership development program, managing cross-collaborations,

managing changes in library services, and developing managerial skills in academic and public libraries. Attention is also paid to colleagues and cross-functional teams, integrating technology, and career ladder steps.

11 Disher, Wayne. *Crash Course in Public Library Administration.* Crash Course Series. Westport, CT: Libraries Unlimited, 2010. ISBN: 978-1-59884-465-8.

This crash course for librarians in rural or small urban areas covers local government and its services, public administrators, organizational design, power and politics, budgeting, planning, human resources, communications, teams, problem solving, facilities management, communities, policies, and working with councils, boards, and commissions. Principles and key subjects are from a public library perspective.

12 Dougherty, Richard M. *Streamlining Library Services: What We Do, How Much Time It Takes, What It Costs, and How We Can Do It Better.* Lanham, MD: Scarecrow Press, 2008. ISBN: 978-0-81085-198-6.

As any business executive can tell you, time is money. In this era of static or (more likely) shrinking budgets, doing more with less is of paramount importance. As Dougherty points out in his preamble, "Saving the time and conserving the energy of busy library staff so that their attention can be focused on priority services and activities is what this [book] is all about." Essentially, an efficiency expert presents his case for how libraries can, in fact, do more with less. This is fairly technical stuff, full of work flow analysis forms and the like. Fortunately, the author writes in plain English, and what he says makes perfect sense. The basic idea is that instead of working harder, librarians should be working smarter.

13 Driggers, Preston F., and Eileen Dumas. *Managing Library Volunteers.* 2nd ed. Chicago: American Library Association, 2011. ISBN: 978-0-83891-064-1.

The authors discuss volunteer service library programs, volunteer recruitment, training and development, awards and recognition, rules and disciplines, and record keeping. Practical advice, tips, sample job descriptions, application forms, parental permission slips, sign-in sheets, check-lists, a survey, and more are provided in this updated edition. A bibliography, illustration credits, and index are included.

14   Dudden, Rosalind Farnam. *Using Benchmarking, Needs Assessment, Quality Improvement, Outcome Measurement, and Library Standards: A How-to-Do-It Manual with CD-ROM.* How-to-Do-It Manuals for Librarians 159. New York: Neal-Schuman, 2007. ISBN: 978-1-55570-604-3.

Dudden assumes that the reader has little or no knowledge of benchmarking, statistics, or mea-surement tools. She first reviews management theory, assessment, measurement, and evalua-tion before covering needs assessment, quality improvement, benchmarking, performance, and outcomes in part 2. In the final part, question-naire design, statistical analysis, and communica-tion techniques are illustrated with manageable steps, workbooks, and real-life examples. The accompanying CD-ROM contains reproducible workbooks, standards, templates, sample reports, surveys, and more.

15   Elliott, Donald S., Glen Holt, Sterling W. Hayden, and Leslie Edmonds Holt. *Measuring Your Library's Value: How to Do a Cost-Benefit Analysis for Your Public Library.* Chicago: American Library Association, 2007. ISBN: 978-0-83890-923-2.

The authors show how to complete a cost-benefit analysis for a service offered by a library. The book begins with an introduction to cost-benefit analysis, fundamentals, important considerations, and preparation. Much of the book is devoted to measuring library benefits through identify-ing and sampling library users, preparing survey instruments, determining library costs, and eval-uating return on taxpayer and donor investments. The first appendix is a cost-benefit analysis that

looks at a patron's willingness to purchase books rather than borrow them from a library. Other appendixes cover sampling cardholders, survey instruments, calculating and reporting survey response rates, and technical insights for project consultants. A glossary and index are included.

16   Evans, G. Edward. *Performance Management and Appraisal: A How-to-Do-It Manual for Librarians.* How-to-Do-It Manuals for Librarians 132. New York: Neal-Schuman, 2004. ISBN: 978-1-55570-498-8.

Evans covers employee performance reviews, set-ting performance standards, training, appraising, coaching, and applying disciplinary actions. The three sections cover preparation, appraisal meth-ods, and appraisal forms for academic and public libraries. The companion CD contains Microsoft Word and PDF sample forms and instructions.

17   Evans, G. Edward, and Patricia Layzell Ward. *Leadership Basics for Librarians and Information Professionals.* Lanham, MD: Scarecrow Press, 2007. ISBN: 978-0-81085-229-7.

Organized into three sections ("Background," "Developing Leadership Skills," and "The Expe-rience of Leadership"), nine chapters detail such topics as teamwork, strategic thinking, and acquiring political skills. Text boxes are liber-ally sprinkled throughout, with headings such as "Keep In Mind" and "Check This Out," which reference both print and online documents that reinforce points made in the narrative. This is a good introductory text for those contemplating being an agent of change or those already in this position but unsure how to proceed.

18   Evans, G. Edward, and Patricia Layzell Ward. *Management Basics for Information Professionals.* 2nd ed. New York: Neal-Schuman, 2007. ISBN: 978-1-55570-586-2.

This is a standard LIS textbook, albeit a very useful one. Its underlying principles are that "management is the accomplishment of things with, through, and for people" and that "good managers are made, not born" (p. xx). Twenty chapters are organized under four broad categories: "Background, Knowledge, and Skills," "Managing Resources," "Career Development," and "Your Future." Among the many helpful features are a plethora of text boxes, with headings such as "Consider This," "Check This Out," and "Reflect On."

19 Giesecke, Joan. *Practical Strategies for Library Managers.* Chicago: American Library Association, 2001. ISBN: 978-0-83890-793-1.

Giesecke used her experience as dean of libraries at the University of Nebraska to develop this practical guide for beginning managers. Descriptions and analyses of organizational problems cover meetings, planning strategies, supervision, and business theories. The tips for working with irrational or nontraditional employers are practical and straight to the point.

20 Gordon, Rachel Singer. *The Accidental Library Manager.* Medford, NJ: Information Today, 2005. ISBN: 978-1-57387-210-2.

The book title reflects the fact that many librarians are thrust into management positions unexpectedly. For the most part, this resource is concerned with practical stuff: "The following pages focus on using your library skills, background, and training to become a more effective library manager, as well as on learning when thinking like a librarian might actually be a hindrance in your management position. You will find ideas on how to become a better and more effective manager, and ideas on what to avoid" (p. xiii). Of special note are verbatim responses from two online surveys conducted for library managers in 2003 and for library support staff in 2004. These comments are quite revealing and give an accurate snapshot of everyday workplace issues. To cite just one example from the manager survey: "It is frustrating that not everyone understands that if you are going to collect a paycheck, it's necessary to perform the job duties for which you are employed" (p. 59). The other side of the coin is illustrated by a respondent from the support staff camp: "He was a despot. He would

time your breaks to the minute. He was a bureaucrat through and through, and cared more for rules than humans" (p. 147). Likewise remarkable is chapter 11, "Theories of Management," which catalogs no fewer than thirty-two modes of thinking about this subject, from "Benevolent Neglect" to "Total Quality Management."

21 Green, Ravonne A., ed. *Library Management: A Case Study Approach.* Oxford: Chandos, 2007. ISBN: 978-1-84334-349-3.

The type of intensive analysis known as the case study is here applied to library problems. Part 1, "The Case Study as Research Tool," consists of three chapters written by Green that outline the basics of performing a case study. Part 2 consists of actual examples of case studies written by students of Valdosta State University that represent "dilemmas that these students have faced or cases that were reported to them by practicing librarians" (p. 73). This is a slender volume but a useful one.

22 Grover, Robert J., Roger C. Greer, and John Agada. *Assessing Information Needs: Managing Transformative Library Services.* Westport, CT: Libraries Unlimited, 2011. ISBN: 978-1-59158-797-2 (print), 978-1-59158-798-9 (e-book).

The gist of this book is that any library should understand the community in which it is situated and customize services according to the needs of the users. The authors provide an overview of information needs and discuss libraries in society; knowledge systems in society; a theoretical framework for community analysis; gathering data for decision making; lifestyles; community analysis; information needs of individuals, groups, and agencies; planning information services; and implementation issues. Each chapter begins with an overview and includes issues and recommendations, a summary, and references. Educational attainment for six communities, case study chronology, and case study survey questions are contained in the appendixes. A selected bibliography and index conclude the book.

23 Hallam, Arlita, and Teresa R. Dalston. *Managing Budgets and Finances: A How-to-Do-It Manual for Librarians and Information Professionals.* How-to-Do-It Manuals for Libraries 138. New York: Neal-Schuman, 2005. ISBN: 978-1-55570-519-0.

Part 1 defines what a budget is, how and when to formulate a budget, and how to monitor a budget. The chapter on monitoring explains requisitions, encumbrances, purchase orders, approving and paying invoices, accounting systems, and reconciling statements. Part 2 looks at special financial management library topics including outsourcing, protecting library property, capital projects, RFPs, and contracts. The final part looks at alternative library funding and covers both sources and grants. Sample library accounting forms and a sample RFP are included.

24 Halstead, Deborah D., Richard P. Jasper, and Felicia M. Little. *Disaster Planning: A How-to-Do-It Manual for Librarians,* with Planning Templates on CD-ROM. How-to-Do-It Manuals for Librarians 129. New York: Neal-Schuman, 2005. ISBN: 978-1-55570-486-5.

Broken into three parts, the manual begins with an overview of disaster planning, expands by listing types of disasters and ways to deal with the calamity in question, and finishes with an annotated list of web-based resources. The accompanying CD-ROM provides information on vendors, a disaster-planning database with links to national agencies, checklists, templates, and other quick reference tools.

25 Hernon, Peter, ed. *Shaping the Future: Advancing the Understanding of Leadership.* Westport, CT: Libraries Unlimited, 2010. ISBN: 978-1-59884-615-7.

In the first part of the book, contributors looked at managerial leadership in academic and public libraries, leadership theories, library leaders' perspectives, and research skills. Part 2 is an examination of managerial leadership in the information professions curriculum, students, faculty, and accreditation. Case study methods, student case studies, scenario planning, and student scenario plans written by doctoral students are scrutinized to explore leadership in library services.

26 Hernon, Peter, and Joseph R. Matthews. *Listening to the Customer.* Westport, CT: Libraries Unlimited, 2011. ISBN: 978-1-59884-799-4 (print), 978-1-59884-800-7 (e-book).

The authors believe the customer is the answer to using limited resources effectively and efficiently and gaining community support. The book covers listening to and valuing customer comments, obtaining staff buy-in, methodologies for gathering voice-of-the-customer, methodologies and the presentation of data, methodologies and analyzing study findings, and unstructured and unsolicited approach methodologies using social search engines, blogs, message boards, and more. The various methods presented are geared toward serving customers and providing leadership within communities in the future.

27 Hernon, Peter, Ronald R. Powell, and Arthur P. Young. *The Next Library Leadership: Attributes of Academic and Public Library Directors.* Library and Information Science Series. Westport, CT: Libraries Unlimited, 2003. ISBN: 978-1-56308-992-3.

The authors examine Association of Research Libraries, Association of Colleges and Research Libraries, and public library directors' qualities through a literature review and extensive interviews with directors. The results from an analysis and comparison of qualities show that managers, LIS students, and LIS graduates need appropriate support to obtain upper-level director positions. A leadership assessment and strategies for acquiring preferred qualities are also provided.

28 Hickey, Damon D., and Bob Pymm. *Learn Library Management.* Library Basics 6. Lanham, MD: Scarecrow Press, 2003. ISBN: 978-0-81084-885-6.

This easy-to-read workbook covers basic management principles for libraries and other information agencies through real-life examples. The authors look at managers and their roles, environment, strategic planning, operational planning, human resources, effective teams, and financial management as applied to library operations.

29 Horton, Valerie, and Bruce Smith, eds. *Moving Material: Physical Delivery in Libraries.* Chicago: American Library Association, 2010. ISBN: 978-0-83891-001-6.

Edited by the director of the Colorado Library Consortium and the delivery services coordinator for the South Central Library System in Wisconsin, this book looks at current practices, service models, physical delivery services, and the future of physical deliveries for libraries. Topics include outsourcing deliveries; vendor selection and contracts; material routing; and costs related to picking up, sorting, and delivering library materials. A glossary of common shipping terms in a handy reference guide excerpted from the Messenger Courier Association of the Americas. The bibliography includes several unpublished documents and press releases about current physical delivery options.

30 Hughes, Kathleen M., ed. *The PLA Reader for Public Library Directors and Managers.* New York: Neal-Schuman, 2009. ISBN: 978-1-55570-684-5.

Created under the auspices of the Public Library Association (PLA, a subunit of the American Library Association), this work of seven parts divided into thirty-two chapters is a collection of "key articles, culled from the pages of *Public Libraries* and from chapters of bestselling PLA books" (p. v). Designed to be a quick read for time-strapped library leaders, most chapters are pretty concise (fewer than ten pages) and concern such nitty-gritty topics as staffing, communication, and dealing with consulting services. The aim of the volume is to "provide the best information to help public library managers and directors more effectively and successfully lead their libraries" (p. v).

31 Hurlbert, Janet McNeil, ed. *Defining Relevancy: Managing the New Academic Library.* Westport, CT: Libraries Unlimited, 2008. ISBN: 978-1-59158-419-3.

This book is summed up in the first paragraph of the introduction: "Connection. Competition. Collaboration. These three words define management of college libraries today and in the future. They also describe the contents of the chapters in this book, which focus on planning for the multiple directions that must be considered and effectively acted on by college library managers" (p. ix). Eighteen chapters, each written by an academic librarian in some managerial/administrative capacity, cover all the bases: changing demographics of users, brick-and-mortar issues, information literacy on campus, promotion of the library, and so on. Each chapter concludes with a short bibliography.

32 Jones, Patrick. *Running a Successful Library Card Campaign: A How-to-Do-It Manual for Librarians.* How-To-Do-It Manuals for Librarians 119. New York: Neal-Schuman, 2002. ISBN: 978-1-55570-438-4.

Jones provides fifteen library card case studies with sample brochures, press kits, ads, handouts, strategic plans, budgets, meeting minutes, and best practices for successfully running a library card registration drive. Case study sites include Houston, Philadelphia, Chicago, Los Angeles, Long Beach, Durham County, Jefferson County, and Birmingham. The final chapter contains easily reproducible applications in English and Spanish, reports, postcards, posters, and letters.

33 Kahn, Miriam B. *Disaster Response and Planning for Libraries.* 3rd ed. Chicago: American Library Association, 2012. ISBN: 978-0-83891-151-8.

Disaster can strike at any time under a variety of circumstances. Kahn explains how to respond to a disaster, how to recover and resume normal operations, what to do to prevent a disaster from occurring in the first place (as our parents used to tell us, an ounce of prevention is worth a pound of cure), planning for disasters, and preparing response and recovery procedures. The how-to-do-it material is intended to help librarians write their first disaster plan or update an existing plan. The appendix contains forty-three checklists and forms along with a directory of associations, organizations, and companies familiar with disaster planning. A bibliography and index are included.

34   Kingma, Bruce R. *The Economics of Information: A Guide to Economic and Cost-Benefit Analysis for Information Professionals.* 2nd ed. Library and Information Science Series. Westport, CT: Libraries Unlimited, 2001. ISBN: 978-1-56308-816-2.

This close examination of cost, benefits, markets, information as a public good, externalities, monopolies, uncertainty and risk, commodity versus public good, pricing, time, resource sharing, digital information, and network economic fundamentals is for library managers and library services students. Chapter topics are illustrated with examples from library services such as interlibrary loan, digitization projects, and more, with chapter questions and summaries.

35   Laughlin, Sara, Denise Sisco Shockley, and Ray Wilson. *The Library's Continuous Improvement Fieldbook: 29 Ready-to-Use Tools.* Chicago: American Library Association, 2003. ISBN: 978-0-83890-859-4.

Brainstorming, cause analysis, cause-and-effect diagrams, consensograms, fishbowl charts, top-down modular design, Gantt charts, histograms, nominal groups, and scatter diagrams are just a few of the continuous quality improvement tools within this guide devoted to improving library services. Each quality management concept discussed includes step-by-step instructions, hints, cautions, tricks, and library examples.

36   Laughlin, Sara, and Ray W. Wilson. *The Quality Library: A Guide to Staff-Driven Improvement, Better Efficiency, and Happier Customers.* Chicago: American Library Association, 2008. ISBN: 978-0-83890-952-2.

Call it what you will: total quality management, continuous quality improvement, or whatever, it all boils down to getting more bang for your library bucks, which are in ever shorter supply these days. In this slender tome it is called *process improvement*, and the advice is based on several years' worth of work on the part of the authors, who have acted as consultants to libraries in many states, preaching the gospel of efficiency. As stated in the foreword, "The sharp-eyed will recognize the influence of W. Edward Deming in this approach—his notions of continuously assessing and improving systems work for libraries just as well as they do for manufacturing plants" (p. v). Some of the discussion gets pretty technical, with mathematical equations and busy diagrams, but don't let this put you off. Cutting out time-wasters makes life more pleasant for staff and patrons alike.

37   Lee, Sul H., ed. *Repackaging Libraries for Survival: Climbing Out of the Box.* New York: Routledge, 2011. ISBN: 978-0-41569-743-9.

Sponsored by the University of Oklahoma Libraries, the essays in this book were originally presented at the "Climbing Out of the Box: Repackaging Libraries for Survival" conference held March 4–5, 2010, in Oklahoma City. Discussion revolved around how academic libraries can continue to provide services and resources while planning for future diversity and economic changes and challenges. Change is inevitable. Libraries need to move to a position of forethought and planning rather than one of service and collection acquisition response to patron research, teaching, learning, and technology requests. The material presented here first saw print as a special issue of the *Journal of Library Administration*.

38   *A Library Board's Practical Guide to Finding the Right Library Director: The Detroit Suburban Librarians' Round Table Succession Planning Committee.* Chicago: American Library Association, 2009. ISBN: 978-0-83898-349-2.

This slender thirty-six-page book walks library boards through the process of hiring a library director. It shows how to consider variables, set goals, and work as a team to obtain optimum results from the search process.

39 Lubans, John, Jr. *"Leading from the Middle," and Other Contrarian Essays on Library Leadership.* Beta Phi Mu Monograph Series. Santa Barbara, CA: Libraries Unlimited, 2010. ISBN: 978-1-59884-577-8.

A collection of fifteen years' worth of columns that originally appeared in the pages of *Library Leadership and Management* (see entry 115) has been revised for this book. The "contrarian" in the title stems from the author's nontraditional view of leadership. Again and again, he shows the limiting nature of the command-and-control model used in a majority of organizations, which basically means that the person at the top gives the orders and the loyal underlings are expected to march in lockstep as they carry them out. Lubans's view is one of true empowerment, in which everyone in the organizational hierarchy is not only allowed but expected to contribute opinions, ideas, and suggestions. Quite simply, the author argues for a democracy within the library, rather than a dictatorship.

40 Matthews, Joseph R. *The Evaluation and Measurement of Library Services.* Westport, CT: Libraries Unlimited, 2007 ISBN: 978-1-59158-532-9.

Matthews provides a variety of tools to measure customer service and patron outcomes in this comprehensive overview of library evaluation tools. This four-part manual covers the evaluation process and models, methodology concerns, evaluation of library services, and evaluation of the library. Evaluation of library services is covered in depth for library users and nonusers, physical collections, electronic resources, reference services, technical services, interlibrary loan, bibliographic instruction, and customer service. A library usability analysis tool and name and subject indexes complete the book.

41 McGhee, Marla W., and Barbara A. Jansen. *The Principal's Guide to a Powerful Library Media Program.* 2nd ed. Santa Barbara, CA: Linworth, 2010. ISBN: 978-1-58683-526-2 (print), 978-1-58683-527-9 (e-book).

Although the intended audience for this book is administrators of elementary schools, colleagues contemplating a career transition from, say, a public or university institution to a grade school library or media center will find much of use in this book written by a former elementary school principal and a librarian. In short, "The book provides school leaders with a working knowledge of how to appropriately support the program so that library professionals and their classroom counterparts can practice their expertise, creating a synergistic effectiveness that far exceeds the capabilities of any one person, department or program" (p. xxvi). Best practices, roles and responsibilities of the library media specialist, and continuous quality improvement within the school are all given due attention. This slender volume contains much food for thought to help the school library improve learning outcomes for children. A CD contains checklists, worksheets, and other blank forms for implementing the ideas contained within the book itself.

42 Moniz, Richard J., Jr. *Practical and Effective Management of Libraries: Integrating Case Studies, General Management Theory and Self-Understanding.* Chandos Information Professional Series. Oxford: Chandos, 2010. ISBN: 978-1-84334-578-7.

This book covers such diverse topics as employee motivation, communication, and decision making. The appendix contains a sample "Annual Plan," which lists priorities broken down by timeline and success indicators.

43 Moore, Mary Y. *The Successful Library Trustee Handbook.* 2nd ed. Chicago: American Library Association, 2010. ISBN: 978-0-83891-003-0.

Moore offers practical and proven advice to library trustees on their roles and responsibilities.

Topics covered include relationships, meetings, advocacy, policy development, strategic planning, programs, services, employee evaluations, budgets, liabilities, and fund-raising. Appendixes provide ALA's Resolution on the USA PATRIOT Act and Related Measures That Infringe on the Rights of Library Users, Useful Websites for Library Trustees, Freedom to Read statement, and Library Bill of Rights. An index provides easy access to all topics.

44   Moorman, John A., ed. *Running a Small Library: A How-to-Do-It Manual.* How-To-Do-It Manuals for Librarians 149. New York: Neal-Schuman, 2006. ISBN: 978-1-55570-549-7.

Moorman covers budgeting, policies and procedures, staffing, buildings, planning, governing boards, Friends groups, and community partnerships for college, special, public, and school libraries. Written from the perspective of a solo librarian, the book provides detailed tasks for adult and youth services, collection management, ordering, cataloging, circulation, weeding, computer systems, and integrated library systems. Appendixes present state library agencies, book and periodical vendors, library furniture and supply vendors, automation vendors, and professional organizations.

45   Morris, Betty J. *Administering the School Library Media Center.* 5th ed. Library and Information Science Series. Westport, CT: Libraries Unlimited, 2010. ISBN: 978-1-59158-685-2 (print), 978-1-59884-894-6 (e-book).

Morris thoroughly covers media centers from a historical perspective, leadership and partnerships, functions, programs, budget, staff, facilities, media selection, technology, acquisitions, administration, and outside influences. Charts, tables, and illustrations highlight key information. The appendixes include a state directory of school library media center agencies, directory of associations and agencies, directory of selected library furniture and supply houses, key documents from ALA websites, the Association for Educational Communication and Technology

Code of Ethics, and a Citizen's Request Form for Reevaluation of Media Center Materials.

46   Nakamura, Margaret, and Larry Osborne. *Systems Analysis for Librarians and Information Professionals.* 2nd ed. Library and Information Science Text Series. Westport, CT: Libraries Unlimited, 2000. ISBN: 978-1-56308-693-9.

This revised edition applies basic systems analysis techniques, which are widely used in the business world, to library environments. The authors focus on practical, easy-to-follow steps to manage system projects successfully. Topics include identifying and defining problems, analyzing and displaying data, designing and selecting systems, installing and implementing systems, and overall project management. The appendixes include brief case studies and a Java program used to determine sample size.

47   Nelson, Sandra S. *Implementing for Results: Your Strategic Plan in Action.* PLA Results Series. Chicago: American Library Association, 2009. ISBN: 978-0-83893-579-8.

Another excellent volume in the Public Library Association's Results series, this addition to the roster "is the manual you will need to transform your strategic plan from dream to reality" (p. ix). Practical stuff here: material is broken down by task, which is then further refined in step-by-step fashion. Nineteen work forms along with detailed instructions help simplify the process.

48   Nelson, Sandra S. *The New Planning for Results: A Streamlined Approach.* Chicago: American Library Association, 2001. ISBN: 978-0-83893-504-0.

Nelson's system of steps shows librarians how to prepare, imagine, design, build, communicate, and implement a library operation plan within four to five months. One-third of the book consists of appendixes that cover, in detail, individual processes used to create and implement a library operations plan through service, clientele, community, and partnership analysis.

49 Nelson, Sandra, Ellen Altman, Diane Mayo, and Public Library Association. *Managing for Results: Effective Resource Allocation for Public Libraries.* Chicago: American Library Association, 2000. ISBN: 978-0-83893-498-2.

The authors use step-by-step processes in this examination of how to manage and reallocate staff, collection issues, facilities, and technology to meet the demands of library programs and materials. Appendixes include in-depth material on the planning cycle, gap analysis, analyzing numerical data, library scans, resource allocation, in-library use of materials, document delivery, and material availability measures.

50 Nelson, Sandra, and June Garcia. *Creating Policies for Results: From Chaos to Clarity.* PLA Results Series. Chicago: American Library Association, 2003. ISBN: 978-0-83893-535-4.

Library staff need clear and up-to-date procedures to be able bring order out of the daily chaos wrought by patrons and their problems, which can include unattended children, pornography on public computers, nonresident library card requests, and items found in returned books. This step-by-step guide addresses five major areas of library policy: development, issues, inventory, assessment, and implementation.

51 Nicholas, David, and Eti Herman, eds. *Assessing Information Needs in the Age of the Digital Consumer.* 3rd ed. New York: Routledge, 2009. ISBN: 978-1-85743-487-3.

Contributors use results of several research projects to provide a framework grounded in theory but practical in execution to conduct an information needs analysis. They provide a systematic look at information needs and a framework for identifying, evaluating, and comparing information services and system designs. The six sections of the book address what information needs are, why we undertake information needs assessments, a framework for evaluating information needs, the determinants of information needs and practices, collecting data, and information needs analysis. This revised edition includes a

web log analysis, focus group interviews, I-player concepts, and a discussion of the digital information user.

52 O'Connor, Steve, and Peter Sidorko. *Imagine Your Library's Future: Scenario Planning for Libraries and Information Organizations.* Chandos Information Professional Series. Oxford: Chandos, 2010. ISBN: 978-1-84334-600-5.

The future arrives whether we want it to or not. This book attempts to answer this question: Do we want to simply allow things to happen to our libraries, or do we want have a say in the matter? Scenario planning is one way to help shape the future before it gets here. The preface draws a clear distinction between this and strategic planning. The former is "an imaginative process, creating stories of the different futures from which each organization, their users and staff may choose. Strategic planning, on the other hand, is an administrative tool, often formulaic, allocating resources with which to meet the chosen future" (p. xi). Ten chapters cover the basics of scenario planning, models of predicting the future, design and implementation, and a series of case studies of libraries where scenario planning was carried out. The book is well illustrated with charts, diagrams, and graphics and concludes with a short bibliography.

53 Prentice, Ann E. *Managing in the Information Age.* Lanham, MD: Scarecrow Press, 2005. ISBN: 978-0-81085-206-8.

"What has worked in the past will not necessarily work in the future," the author states in her introduction (p. 2). As today's manager well knows, that future keeps coming at us ever faster. This book attempts to provide a road map to running a library in the hyperkinetic era in which we live. Text is broken down into three sections. Part 1, "Living and Working in the Information Age," puts things into historical context. Part 2, "Management: Putting Theory into Practice," details just that. Part 3, "Managing the Organization," takes a holistic look at groups of people. Prentice states, "In writing this text, I have described current management concepts and structures and then shown how one can go from there to deal with today's problems" (p. 5). Each chapter concludes with a generous bibliography.

54 Pugh, Lyndon. *Managing 21st Century Libraries.* Lanham, MD: Scarecrow Press, 2005. ISBN: 978-0-81085-185-6.

Pugh warns in his introduction that "organizations and the people who work in them suffer from the debilitating consequences of over management" (p. x). His solution is to encourage, through the pages of this slim volume, "a small outbreak of anarchy in the interests of organizational health" (p. ix). As the reader might guess, libraries fall squarely under the "organizations" heading. The lead message is: don't be afraid to experiment. Specifically, Pugh lists some examples (redeploy existing talents, tinker and patch, challenge long-held assumptions) and goes on to expand on how to implement such possibilities.

55 Rubin, Rhea Joyce. *Demonstrating Results: Using Outcome Measurement in Your Library.* PLA Results Series. Chicago: American Library Association, 2006. ISBN: 978-0-83893-560-6.

There is a favorite saying among administrative types: "If it can't be measured, it can't be managed." This is a handbook on how to use measurement as a tool of management. Chapter 1, "The What, When, and Why of Outcome Measurement," lays the foundation. Subsequent chapters cover design and implementation aspects. As with other books in the Results series, a generous helping of appendixes containing worksheets and sample forms, a glossary, and bibliography make this a useful book. Again, as with its companion volumes, emphasis is on the practical stuff library managers deal with on a daily basis.

56 Sheldon, Brooke E. *Interpersonal Skills, Theory and Practice: The Librarian's Guide to Becoming a Leader.* Westport, CT: Libraries Unlimited, 2010. ISBN: 978-1-59158-744-6.

Sheldon focuses on interpersonal communication and emotional intelligence attributes needed to become a leader in the library profession on a local, national, or international level. Topics include leadership theories, management functions, understanding your leadership potential, listening, small-group dynamics, motivation, conflict, creating a positive climate for changes, and leadership development plans.

57 Singer, Paula M., and Gail Griffith. *Succession Planning in the Library: Developing Leaders, Managing Change.* Chicago: American Library Association, 2010. ISBN: 978-0-83891-036-8.

We have all read the statistics and heard the dire predictions about the graying of the profession and the imminent wave of retirements. Whether this is a gradual process (at the time of this writing, the economic fallout from the "Great Recession" has no doubt delayed many a planned retirement) or comes in a tidal wave of departures, the fact remains that at some point librarians would like to stop making a living and start having a life. That's where this volume comes in. The first sentence of the first chapter sums it up: succession planning is all about "having the right people in the right place and the right times to do the right things" (p. 1). That doesn't happen by accident. Chock full of blank forms, charts, and tables, the seven chapters of this slender but informative book walk readers through the steps necessary to ensure continuity of operations. Covering more than just the tip of the personnel pyramid, the authors also discuss how to motivate and retain valued workers at all levels of the library hierarchy. Noteworthy is the chapter "Additional Stories of Library Succession Planning and Development Programs," which reads like mini–case studies of how seven public libraries are wrestling—and largely succeeding—with these issues.

58 Smallwood, Carol, ed. *Library Management Tips That Work.* ALA Guides for the Busy Librarian. Chicago: American Library Association, 2011. ISBN: 978-0-83891-121-1.

Contributors tackle the daily details and duties faced by library managers. Topics covered range from the manager's role and time management through emergencies, staff accountability, coordination, and more. "Running a Library" covers collections, unreturned materials, nontraditional users, multiple sites, merging multiple services points, weeding, and grant project management. "Information Technology" includes blogs, Google Apps, SharePoint collections, virtual tools, session control, Facebook, and wikis. Staffing topics are managing multiple generations, librarians with young children, mentoring graduate assistants, new employee orientation, discrimination, underperformance, and staff shortages. The final part of the book covers board meetings, partnerships, small-town presence, statistics, and funding.

59 Stueart, Robert D., and Barbara B. Moran.
Library and Information Center Management. 7th ed. Library and Information Science Text Series. Westport, CT: Libraries Unlimited, 2007. ISBN: 978-1-59158-408-7.

This standard textbook on the subject has been in print for over thirty years. Although the book has been expanded with each new edition (now encompassing twenty chapters and almost 500 pages), the goal has been constant: "The book focuses upon the complex and interrelated functions common to all organizations and is intended specifically for managers and future managers of services and staffs. The purpose of separating and individually discussing the functions that make up the management process is to examine the various threads in the fabric of what managers actually do" (p. xxiii). Seven comprehensive sections cover planning, organizing, human resources, leadership, and other important topics and make use of numerous charts, diagrams, and tables. Especially helpful are various text boxes with headings such as "What Do You Think?," "Try This!," and "What Would You Do?" that give both LIS students and current practitioners real-world situations that help translate theory into practice.

60 Toor, Ruth, and Hilda K. Weisburg. *Being Indispensable: A School Librarian's Guide to Becoming an Invaluable Leader.* Chicago:

American Library Association, 2011. ISBN: 978-0-83891-065-8.

There is some overlap between this and the similarly titled *Simply Indispensable: An Action Guide for School Librarians* (see entry 1455), but the latter volume has to do primarily with advocating attention to the school library, whereas this book is more about visibility, that is, getting the rest of the school hierarchy to recognize how important the media specialist's role is. As succinctly stated in the introduction, "Too many school librarians have not been proactive in their buildings, and there has been an ongoing disconnect between what *you* know you do and what administrators and teachers think you do" (p. ix). Ten chapters cover understanding your school's mission, knowing who your stakeholders are and what they want, and, to use an overused but in this case apt expression, thinking outside the box, all of which are intended to result in the school librarian becoming "a visible, vital presence in your building" (p. 114)—which is where the "indispensable" part comes in. Bonus: Each chapter concludes with a "Key Ideas" summary of preceding contents.

61 Tucker, Dennis C., and Shelley Elizabeth Mosley. *Crash Course in Library Supervision: Meeting the Key Players.* Crash Course Series. Westport, CT: Libraries Unlimited, 2007. ISBN: 978-1-59158-564-0 (print), 978-0-313-09700-3 (e-book).

This crash course is designed for first-time library supervisors, to help get them up to speed quickly. Topics include settling in, getting to know the staff, managing personnel, hiring and firing, performance reviews, Friends of the Library, volunteers, board members, customers, key people in the community, and making changes. Real-life examples, tips, and pitfalls to avoid are also discussed.

62 Wilkinson, Frances C., Linda K. Lewis, and Nancy K. Dennis. *Comprehensive Guide to Emergency and Disaster Preparedness and Recovery.* Chicago: American Library Association, 2009. ISBN: 978-0-83898-548-9.

The authors present step-by-step instructions for pre- and post-disaster planning for libraries. Case studies, photographs, diagrams, and examples are used to highlight critical disaster recovery points. The series of model recovery plans, resources, and contact lists in the appendixes are particularly helpful to any library team drafting or updating its emergency plan.

63 Winston, Mark, ed. *Leadership in the Library and Information Science Professions: Theory and Practice.* Copublished simultaneously as *Journal of Library Administration* 32, nos. 3/4. New York: Routledge, 2001. ISBN: 978-0-78901-415-3.

Library administrators and staff must develop new skills and adapt to sometimes overwhelming patron demands in these fast-paced, technology-driven times. The book focuses on how librarians can become effective leaders through knowledge and competencies. Ideas covered include crisis and opportunities, recruitment theories, financial resources, and leadership in various realms (e.g., diversity, women, times of change).

64 Woolls, Blanche. *The School Library Media Manager.* 4th ed. Library and Information Science Series. Westport, CT: Libraries Unlimited, 2008. ISBN: 978-1-59158-643-2 (print), 978-1-59158-928-0 (e-book).

Woolls's textbook on library media center administration emphasizes the library media specialist role in teaching reading, assessment of student learning, librarian leadership roles, and the influence of information technologies on media center services and programs. Appendix topics include writing a technology plan, sample letter of application, questionnaire, presentation of a five-year long-range plan, volunteers, ALA Intellectual Freedom policy statements, publications list, budget information for grant applications, and a sample letter to a legislator.

ADDITIONAL RESOURCES

65 Allan, Barbara. *Supervising and Leading Teams in ILS.* London: Facet, 2006. ISBN: 978-1-85604-587-2.

66 Booth, Andrew, and Anne Brice, eds. *Evidence-Based Practice for Information Professionals: A Handbook.* London: Facet, 2004. ISBN: 978-1-85604-471-4.

67 Bremer, Suzanne W. *Long Range Planning: A How-to-Do-It Manual for Public Libraries.* How-To-Do-It Manuals for Librarians 40. New York: Neal-Schuman, 1994. ISBN: 978-1-55570-162-8.

68 Curzon, Susan Carol. *Managing the Interview: A How-to-Do-It Manual for Hiring Staff.* How-To-Do-It Manuals for Libraries 47. New York: Neal-Schuman, 1995. ISBN: 978-1-55570-160-4.

69 Dadson, Emma. *Emergency Planning and Response for Libraries, Archives and Museums.* London: Facet, 2012. ISBN: 978-1-85604-808-8.

70 Davis, H. Scott. *New Employee Orientation: A How-to-Do-It Manual for Librarians.* How-To-Do-It Manuals for Libraries 38. New York: Neal-Schuman, 1993. ISBN: 978-1-55570-158-1.

71 Dorner, Daniel G., G. E. Corman, and Phillip J. Calvert. *Information Needs Analysis: Principles and Practice in Information Organizations.* London: Facet, 2014. ISBN: 978-1-85604-484-4.

72 Fiels, Keith M., John M. Cohn, and Ann L. Kelsey. *Planning for Automation: A How-to-Do-It Manual for Librarians.* How-To-Do-It Manuals for Libraries 25. New York: Neal-Schuman, 1992. ISBN: 978-1-55570-120-8.

73 Fortriede, Steven Carl. *Moving Your Library: Getting the Collection from Here to There.* Chicago: American Library Association, 2010. ISBN: 978-0-83890-994-2.

74 Fortson, Judith. *Disaster Planning and Recovery: A How-to-Do-It Manual for Librarians and Archivists.* How-To-Do-It Manuals for

Libraries 21. New York: Neal-Schuman, 1991. ISBN: 978-1-55570-059-1.

75 Fouty, Kathleen G. *Implementing an Automated Circulation System: A How-to-Do-It Manual.* How-To-Do-It Manual for Librarians 43. New York: Neal-Schuman, 1994. ISBN: 978-1-55570-175-8.

76 Gersitz, Lorraine. *Managing the Circulation Process: A How-to-Do-It Manual for Librarians.* How-to-Do-It Manual for Librarians. New York: Neal-Schuman, 1992. ISBN: 978-1-55570-138-3.

77 Giesecke, Joan, and Beth McNeil. *Fundamentals of Library Supervision.* 2nd ed. Chicago: American Library Association, 2010. ISBN: 978-0-83891-016-0.

78 Hakala-Ausperk, Catherine. *Be a Great Boss: One Year to Success.* ALA Guides for the Busy Librarian. Chicago: American Library Association, 2011. ISBN: 978-0-83891-068-9.

79 Hansel, Pasty J., ed. *Managing Overdues: A How-to-Do-It Manual for Librarians.* How-To-Do-It Manuals for Libraries 83. New York: Neal-Schuman, 1998. ISBN: 978-1-55570-291-5.

80 Hernon, Peter, and Ellen Altman. *Assessing Service Quality: Satisfying the Expectations of Library Customers.* 2nd ed. Chicago: American Library Association, 2010. ISBN: 978-0-83891-021-4.

81 Hernon, Peter, and Robert E. Dugan. *An Action Plan for Outcomes Assessment in Your Library.* Chicago: American Library Association, 2002. ISBN: 978-0-83890-813-6.

82 Huber, John. *Lean Library Management: Eleven Strategies for Reducing Costs and Improving Services.* New York: Neal-Schuman, 2011. ISBN: 978-1-55570-732-3.

83 Intner, Sheila S., and Peggy Johnson. *Fundamentals of Technical Services Management.* Chicago: American Library Association, 2008. ISBN: 978-0-83890-953-9.

84 Jacob, M. E. L. *Strategic Planning: A How-to-Do-It Manual for Librarians.* How-To-Do-It Manuals for Libraries 9. New York: Neal-Schuman, 1990. ISBN: 978-1-55570-074-4.

85 Low, Kathleen. *Recruiting Library Staff: A How-to-Do-It Manual for Librarians.* How-To-Do-It Manuals for Libraries 94. New York: Neal-Schuman, 1999. ISBN: 978-15-557-0355-4.

86 Marek, Kate. *Organizational Storytelling for Librarians: Using Stories for Effective Leadership.* Chicago: American Library Association, 2011. ISBN: 978-0-83891-079-5.

87 Matthews, Joseph R. *Strategic Planning and Management for Library Managers.* Westport, CT: Libraries Unlimited, 2005. ISBN: 978-1-59158-231-1.

88 Mayo, Diane, and Jeanne Goodrich. *Staffing for Results: A Guide to Working Smarter.* Chicago: American Library Association, 2002. ISBN: 978-0-83890-826-6.

89 McCune, Bonnie F., and Charleszine Nelson. *Recruiting and Managing Volunteers in Libraries: A How-to-Do-It Manual.* How-To-Do-It Manual for Librarians 51. New York: Neal-Schuman, 1995. ISBN: 978-1-55570-204-5.

90 Metz, Ruth F. *Coaching in the Library: A Management Strategy for Achieving Excellence.* 2nd ed. Chicago: American Library Association, 2011. ISBN: 978-0-83891-037-5.

91 Montgomery, Jack G., Eleanor I. Cook, Patricia J. Wagner, and Glenda T. Hubbard. *Conflict Management for Libraries: Strategies for a Positive, Productive Workplace.* Chicago: American Library Association, 2005. ISBN: 978-0-83890-890-7.

92 Nelson, Sandra S. *Strategic Planning for Results.* PLA Results Series. Chicago: American Library Association, 2008. ISBN: 978-0-83893-573-6.

93 **Orcutt, Darby, ed.** *Library Data: Empowering Practice and Persuasion.* Westport, CT: Libraries Unlimited, 2009. ISBN: 978-1-59158-826-9 (print), 978-1-59158-827-6 (e-book).

94 **Osborne, Robin, ed.** *From Outreach to Equity: Innovative Models of Library Policy and Practice.* Foreword by Carla D. Hayden. Chicago: American Library Association, 2004. ISBN: 978-0-83893-541-5.

95 **Owens, Irene, ed.** *Strategic Marketing in Library and Information Science.* Copublished simultaneously as *Acquisitions Librarian* 28. Binghampton, NY: Haworth Information Press, 2002. ISBN: 978-0-78902-143-4.

96 **Pantry, Sheila.** *Managing Stress and Conflict in Libraries.* London: Facet, 2007. ISBN: 978-1-85604-613-8.

97 **Pantry, Sheila, and Peter Griffiths.** *Managing Outsourcing in Library and Information Services.* London: Facet, 2004. ISBN: 978-1-85604-543-8.

98 **Roberts, Sue, and Jennifer Rowley.** *Managing Information Services.* London: Facet, 2004. ISBN: 978-1-85604-515-5.

99 **Rowley, Jennifer.** *Being an Information Innovator.* London: Facet, 2011. ISBN: 978-1-85604-671-8.

100 **Singer, Paula M., and Laura L. Francisco.** *Developing a Compensation Plan for Your Library.* 2nd ed. Chicago: American Library Association, 2009. ISBN: 978-0-83890-985-0.

101 **Stanley, Mary.** *Managing Library Employees: A How-to-Do-It Manual.* How-To-Do-It Manuals for Libraries 161. New York: Neal-Schuman, 2008. ISBN: 978-1-55570-628-9.

102 **Stueart, Robert D., and Maureen Sullivan.** *Developing Library Leaders: A How-to-Do-It Manual for Coaching, Team Building, and Mentoring Library Staff.* How-To-Do-It Manuals for Libraries 172. New York: Neal-Schuman, 2010. ISBN: 978-1-55570-725-5.

103 **Stueart, Robert D., and Maureen Sullivan.** *Performance Analysis and Appraisal: A How-to-Do-It Manual for Librarians.* How-To-Do-It Manuals for Libraries 14. New York: Neal-Schuman, 1991. ISBN: 978-1-55570-061-4.

104 **Swan, James.** *Working Together: A How-to-Do-It Manual for Trustees and Librarians.* How-To-Do-It Manuals for Libraries 24. New York: Neal-Schuman, 1992. ISBN: 978-1-55570-096-6.

105 **Sweetman, Kimberly Burke.** *Managing Student Assistants: A How-to-Do-It Manual for Librarians.* How-To-Do-It Manuals for Libraries 155. New York: Neal-Schuman, 2007. ISBN: 978-1-55570-581-7.

106 **Thenell, Jan.** *The Library's Crisis Communications Planner: A PR Guide for Handling Every Emergency.* Chicago: American Library Association, 2004. ISBN: 978-0-83890-870-9.

107 **Traw, Jeri L., and the College Libraries Section, Association of College and Research Libraries.** *Library Web Site Policies.* Clip Notes 29. Chicago: American Library Association, 2000. ISBN: 978-0-83898-088-0.

108 **Trotta, Marcia.** *Supervising Staff: A How-to-Do-It Manual for Librarians.* How-To-Do-It Manuals for Libraries 141. New York: Neal-Schuman, 2005. ISBN: 978-1-55570-524-4.

109 **Tunstall, Patricia.** *Hiring, Training, and Supervising Library Shelvers.* Chicago: American Library Association, 2010. ISBN: 978-0-83891-010-8.

110 **VanDuinkerken, Wyoma, and Pixey Anne Mosley.** *The Challenge of Library Management: Leading with Emotional Engagement.* Chicago: American Library Association, 2011. ISBN: 978-0-83891-102-0.

111 **Weingand, Darlene E.** *Administration of the Small Public Library.* 4th ed. Chicago: American Library Association, 2001. ISBN: 978-0-83890-794-8.

112   Winston, Mark D., ed. *Leadership in the Library and Information Science Professions: Theory and Practice.* New York: Haworth Information Press, 2001. ISBN: 978-0-78901-415-3.

📖 PERIODICALS

113   *Journal of Library Administration.* Florence, KY: Routledge/Taylor and Francis Group. Frequency: Eight issues per year. ISSN: 0193-0826 (print), 1540-3564 (online). URL: www.informaworld.com.

The purpose of this journal is laid out in nononsense terms on the inside back cover of each issue: under the heading "Aims and Scope" it is clearly stated that the *Journal of Library Administration* "is the primary source of information on all aspects of the effective management of libraries," which "administrators need to efficiently and effectively manage their libraries. The journal seeks out the most modern advances being made in professional management and applies them to the library setting." Each issue has a theme, for example, "Climbing Out of the Box: Repackaging Libraries for Survival" (Vol. 51, no. 1, January 2011). As one might expect, articles in this issue cover the various aspects of funding (or lack thereof) during the "Great Recession" years and how libraries have responded. Highly academic, all articles begin with an abstract and conclude with a bibliography, with generally straight text in between.

114   *Library Leadership and Management (formerly Library Administration and Management).* Chicago, IL: American Library Association. Frequency: Four issues per year. ISSN: 1945-8851. URL: www.ala.org/llama.

This official journal of the Library Leadership and Management Association, a subunit of ALA, has had quite a makeover of late. First came the name change, then, with the Winter 2010 issue, it became an online-only publication (the print incarnation ran for twenty-three years). The "Editor's Desk" column describes this publication as focusing on "assisting library administrators and managers at all levels as they deal with day-to-day challenges," with "in-depth articles that address a wide variety of management issues and highlight examples of successful management methods used in libraries; features, including interviews with prominent practitioners in libraries and related fields; and columns with practical advice on managing libraries" (Vol. 23, no. 4, Fall 2009, p. 159). This is a long-standing and well-regarded publication in the field of library management.

115   *Library Management.* Westport, CT: Emerald Group. Frequency: Nine times per year (irregular double issues). ISSN: 0143-5124. URL: www.emeraldinsight.com/products/journals/journals.htm?id=lm.

This journal focuses on articles of interest and value to senior managers and academics within the library and information professions. Topics include strategic environment, HRM/HRO, cultural diversity, information use, managing change, quality management, leadership, teamwork, outsourcing, automation, library finance, performance measurement, and data protection and copyright.

116   *Performance Measurement and Metrics.* Westport, CT: Emerald Group. Frequency: Three issues per year. ISSN: 1467-8047. URL: www.emeraldinsight.com/products/journals/journals.htm?id=pmm.

This journal is devoted to measurement of the performance of library and information services. Topics include quantitative and qualitative analysis; benchmarking, measurement, and the role of information in enhancing organizational effectiveness; quality techniques and quality improvement; methods for performance measurement and metrics; using emerging technologies; and setting standards of services or service quality.

✿ WEBSITE

117 *Leads from LLAMA.* Chicago: Library Leadership and Management Association, American Library Association. URL: www.llama .ala.org/llamaleads/.

This blog features news and information for the Library Leadership and Management Association (LLAMA, a subunit of ALA) members. Features include recent comments, links, WordPress documentation, editors desk, and archives, which allow members access to information of awards, conferences, and other resources of interest to library leaders.

ARCHITECTURE

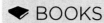

❖ BOOKS

118 Baule, Steven M. *Facilities Planning for School Library Media and Technology Centers.* 2nd ed. Worthington, OH: Linworth, 2007. ISBN: 978-1-58683-294-0.

This practical and useful guide on all aspects of library media and technology lab facilities includes a review of curriculum and educational needs. Baule presents various floor plans; suggests schematics for elementary, middle, and high school library media centers; and lists detailed specifications for shelving, storage spaces, and furniture. Checklists can be used to track progress and keep construction on schedule.

119 Bazillion, Richard J., and Connie L. Braun. *Academic Libraries as High-Tech Gateways: A Guide to Design and Space Decisions.* 2nd ed. Chicago: American Library Association, 2001. ISBN: 978-0-83890-792-4.

Rather than the dictum "Form follows function," this work posits that the two united in a happy marriage create a most pleasant space on the college or university campus. As the authors state in their preface, "Librarians are justified in insisting that design factors must complement efficient operation of the building. There is no reason why a functional library cannot also be an attractive building" (p. viii). Emphasis here is on hard-won practical knowledge, as in "A high-grade commercial carpet constructed of solution-dyed nylon with a low, narrow loop may be expected to last at least fifteen years with regular cleaning" (p. 117). Topics covered include planning and design of academic libraries, selection of furnishings and equipment, and occupying and commissioning a new building, illustrated with black-and-white photographs and line drawings. Each chapter concludes with a list of references cited in text in addition to a bibliography of additional material at the end of the book. Special features include two appendixes, on ATM (asynchronous transfer mode) networking and building design and on electronic teaching and learning facilities.

120 **Brown, Carol R.** *Interior Design for Libraries: Drawing on Function and Appeal.* Chicago: American Library Association, 2002. ISBN: 978-0-83890-829-7.

Blueprints, architectural drawings, and color and black-and-white photos highlight library architecture and interior designs in this slender book for architects and librarians. Brown covers planning phases of a library building project, basic interior designs, furnishings, signage, materials (including finishes and colors), specialty spaces, lighting, and acoustics. The appendixes provide interview questions for obtaining information from library staff and a directory of contributors. A bibliography and index are included.

121 **Bryan, Cheryl.** *Managing Facilities for Results: Optimizing Space for Services.* PLA Results Series. Chicago: American Library Association, 2007. ISBN: 978-0-83890-934-8.

"Doing more with less" have always been watchwords for budget-minded librarians, but during the recession of 2008–2010 stretching dollars was paramount for one and all. The premise of this book is that it is cheaper to take a current space and find a new use for it, whether for expanded services or new programs, than it is to renovate or expand the library itself. Although that may seem obvious, it is also easier said than done. This book takes readers logically through the "repurposing" planning process by breaking a project down into a series of manageable tasks and steps (Task 1, Step 1.1, Step 1.2, etc.). Special features abound: "Milestones" sections at the beginning of each chapter read "By the time you finish this chapter you will know how to," followed by a bulleted list. A case study of a hypothetical library presents a real-world feel to how this process plays out. Boxes labeled "Level of Effort Note" relate how challenging or time consuming a particular issue may be to resolve. No less than twenty-three work forms with accompanying instructions simplify the decision-making process. This volume is designed to be used in conjunction with others in the PLA Results series.

122 *Building Blocks for Planning Functional Library Space.* Lanham, MD: Scarecrow Press, 2001. ISBN: 978-0-81084-136-9.

First published by the Library Administration and Management Association, an ALA subunit, this revised edition provides formulas to answer the question "How much space do we need?" The formulas allow for every conceivable element of a library building. Specifications for computer workstations and visual examples of complex configurations are included.

123 *Building Blocks for Planning Functional Library Space.* 3rd ed. Chicago: American Library Association, 2011. ISBN: 978-0-81088-104-4.

Besides providing detailed formulas to calculate the square footage required for every possible element of a library building, this new edition adds up-to-date specifications for computer workstations along with visual representations of complex configurations. This book is for librarians and managers to consult after a decision has been made to build but before the architectural plans are drawn up.

124 **De Laubier, Guillaume, Jacques Bosser, and James H. Billington.** *The Most Beautiful Libraries in the World.* New York: Harry N. Abrams, 2003. ISBN: 978-0-81094-634-7.

Art book publisher Abrams has here produced a coffee-table tome of sumptuous color photographs, many of which are gatefolds, the effect being one of *Playboy* for book lovers. Text is minimal, but with shots of volumes bound in leather and gold leaf sitting on shelves of carved mahogany, who cares? This work appeared originally in French, which explains the Eurocentric selection of libraries, although the United States is represented here by the Boston Athenaeum, Library of Congress, and New York Public Library. Although the book as a whole is really just an excuse to drool over repositories that most of us would want to die and be buried in, Librarian of Congress James H. Billington makes some cogent comments in his foreword, reminding us that, being more than a mere edifice complex, these cathedrals of the printed word are a marriage of architecture and literature. Well said, sir.

125 Feinberg, Sandra, and James R. Keller. *Designing Space for Children and Teens in Libraries and Public Spaces.* Chicago: American Library Association, 2010. ISBN: 978-0-83891-020-7.

Children and young adults represent the future not only of our country but of our profession, so it behooves us to ensure that areas of the library devoted to their age brackets be both functional and inviting. *Designing Space* helps today's library planner in this task by not just presenting the bricks and mortar but also examining financial, political, and administrative considerations. Written by a librarian with over three decades of experience, including overseeing two renovation/expansion projects, and an architect of similar vintage employed as director of library planning and design at VITETTA Architects and Engineers, this work is intended to give readers a "presentation of ideas that will be helpful to library and design professionals in the quest to improve the quality of services for young people in libraries and other public places" (p. ix). There are black-and-white photos throughout and an eight-page section of color plates. Special features include lists of questions to ask at the conclusion of each chapter (helps to avoid overlooking important considerations) and a references section.

126 Lushington, Nolan. *Libraries Designed for Kids.* New York: Neal-Schumann, 2008. ISBN: 978-1-55570-631-9.

Physical-needs assessment, children's area organization, designs, lighting, graphics, furniture, and equipment are all included in this book on remodeling or planning a new children's library, along with a chapter on quick fixes and common mistakes. The information about traffic flow, access to material, line of sight, and ease of use shows how to organize and supervise the facility efficiently. Photos and two case studies of library redesigns illustrate how design planning is implemented. A glossary and an annotated list of readings, suppliers, and architects are given in the appendixes.

127 Martin, Ron G., ed. *Libraries for the Future: Planning Buildings That Work.* Chicago: American Library Association, 1992. ISBN: 978-0-83890-597-5.

Though somewhat dated, this collection of papers from the Library Administration and Management Library Buildings preconference of 1991 still contains valuable and relevant information, since basic principles, such as the building planning process, remain stable over time. Topics covered include producing a building program statement, selecting an architect, and such nitty-gritty details as a primer on architectural symbols and specifications. No photographs, but plenty of charts, diagrams, and line drawings nicely illustrate points made in the text.

128 McCabe, Gerard B., and James R. Kennedy, eds. *Planning the Modern Public Library Building.* Libraries Unlimited Management Collection. Westport, CT: Libraries Unlimited, 2003. ISBN: 978-0-31332-155-9.

Helmed by a pair of library building consultants, this collection of twenty essays covers building planning from a management perspective. The individual authors cover topics usually absent from standard handbooks, such as landscape architecture, involving the local community in the decision-making process, and applying retail technology solutions to library operation problems. The book concludes with a helpful annotated bibliography that reviews materials relating to planning, designing, and building public libraries. An appendix provides a "Pre-qualification Form for Library Furniture Manufacturers."

129 Mulford, Sam McBane, and Ned A. Himmel. *How Green Is My Library?* Westport, CT: Libraries Unlimited, 2009 ISBN: 978-1-59158-780-4 (print), 978-1-59158-781-1 (e-book).

"Green buildings" are structures that are energy efficient and environmentally friendly, among other attributes. Here the authors take an in-depth look at what it's all about as far as the physical library building is concerned. Definitions (e.g., LEED, which stands for Leadership in Energy and Environmental Design), checklists, sample project forms, and a model process for planning and facilitation are provided. Glancing through the index shows several suggestions for projects to implement—from something as simple as having dimmer switches installed to more complex projects such as gray-water plumbing systems and shared facilities.

130 Sannwald, William W. *Checklist of Library Building Design Considerations.* 4th ed. Chicago: American Library Association, 2001. ISBN: 978-0-83893-506-4.

As the title indicates, this is a collection of checklists covering everything from initial planning of a new library building to the groundbreaking and dedication ceremony. From a practical standpoint, it is the embodiment of the admonition that "an ounce of prevention is worth a pound of cure." Indeed, as Sannwald himself points out in the preface, the whole point of the detailed questionnaires is to "make sure that the building design team in the evaluation and programming of spaces overlooks no element of the building" (p. vii). Each chapter covers a major aspect of the planning/building continuum, which is then broken down into subcategories. Chapter 2, for example, "Library Site Selection," contains individual checklists for such factors as location, accessibility, and environmental issues. Although very useful, not to mention popular, as evidenced by numerous previous editions, this work is not a substitute for state and local codes of building regulations, but rather a supplement to them. It is an excellent defense against those who like to play the "gotcha game."

131 Woodward, Jeannette. *Countdown to a New Library: Managing the Building Project.* 2nd ed. Chicago: American Library Association, 2010. ISBN: 978-0-83891-012-2.

As Woodward points out in her introduction, "No one knows better than members of our profession

that the absence of information is at the root of many problems. Therefore, this book will outline the kinds of information needed to embark upon a building project" (p. x). Representative chapter titles include "The World of Architects and Contractors," "Environmental and Human Needs," "Technology and Modern Building Infrastructures," and "Security and Safety." New to this updated edition is an emphasis on "green" buildings and flexible designs. Several features are effective in getting main ideas across, especially "Tips and Tales from the Trenches," which are verbatim excerpts from conversations with colleagues regarding projects that have gone well or gone south. Example: "We have a sophisticated lighting system that we don't use. All we really wanted was an on-off switch" (p. 94). That kind of real-world warning can save time and money, not to mention headaches, for first-timers facing a building or expansion project. Likewise, a "Resources" section at end of each chapter lists pertinent organizations, associations, agencies, and the like that can be contacted for additional information. The book is illustrated with black-and-white photos.

ADDITIONAL RESOURCES

132 Bolan, Kimberly. *Teen Spaces: The Step-by-Step Library Makeover.* 2nd ed. Chicago: American Library Association, 2009. ISBN: 978-0-83890-969-0.

133 Crosbie, Michael J., and Damon Douglas Hickey. *When Change Is Set in Stone: An Analysis of Seven Academic Libraries Designed by Perry Dean Rogers and Partners, Architects.* Chicago: American Library Association, 2001. ISBN: 978-0-83898-136-8.

134 Erikson, Rolf, and Carolyn B. Markuson. *Designing a School Library Media Center for the Future.* 2nd ed. Chicago: American Library Association, 2007. ISBN: 978-0-83890-945-4.

135 Khan, Ayub. *Better by Design: An Introduction to Planning and Designing a New*

Library Building. London: Facet, 2008. ISBN: 978-1-85604-650-3.

136 Leighton, Philip D., and David C. Weber. *Planning Academic and Research Library Buildings.* Chicago: American Library Association, 2000. ISBN: 978-0-83890-747-4.

137 McCarthy, Richard C. *Managing Your Library Construction Project: A Step-by-Step Guide.* Chicago: American Library Association, 2007. ISBN: 978-0-83890-931-7.

138 Piotrowicz, Lynn M., and Scott Osgood. *Building Science 101: A Primer for Librarians.* Chicago: American Library Association, 2010. ISBN: 978-083891-041-2.

139 *Redesigning the College Library Building—2011.* New York: Primary Research Group, 2011. ISBN: 978-1-57440-162-2.

140 Watson, Les, ed. *Better Library and Learning Space: Projects, Trends and Ideas.* London: Facet, 2012. ISBN: 978-1-85604-763-0.

☁ WEBSITES

141 AIA Architect Finder. http://architectfinder.aia.org.

Administered by the American Institute of Architects, this free-access database allows the user to search for architectural firms by geographic area (country, state, city, or ZIP code) or by firm name. Drop-down menus allow filtering by type of project envisioned (example: highlighting "libraries" from the list displays only firms that specialize in that type of construction) and service rendered, such as bid evaluation or cost estimating. Each firm displayed has a gray arrow to its left; when clicked, "firm overview" appears, listing applicable projects, photos of completed projects (if any), contact info, and other information. Links at page bottom provide a wealth of data on contract documents, contract language, and other details. This source provides quick and no-cost way to find and compare design firms

---

THE LATEST NEW LIBRARIES **FYI**

Some general-interest professional journals regularly run feature articles about newly constructed/expanded/renovated libraries. For example, every year since 1977, *American Libraries,* the official membership magazine of the ALA (see entry 833), has run an April "showcase" article on the most notable new buildings erected in the United States. *Library Journal* (see entry 839) does a similar spotlight feature that runs annually in its December issue.

---

as a first step in deciding who will build your library's showpiece.

142 "Building Libraries and Library Additions: A Selected Annotated Bibliography." www.ala.org/ala/professionalresources/libfactsheets/alalibraryfactsheet11.cfm.

One in a series of fact sheets prepared by ALA, this handy guide lists print and electronic sources broken down by library type (public, academic, etc.), in addition to a section on general resources. Included is a section of resources on planning specialized spaces within a library (children, teens, older adults, etc.).

143 Clearinghouse of Professional Information: Facilities Planning Resources. www.sols.org/links/clearinghouse/facilities/index.htm.

Produced by Ontario Library Service North, this site is intended to provide "links to a variety of resources to support libraries in planning and assessing their facilities." Topics include general resources, building projects, joint-use facilities, and environmentally friendly facilities.

144 **"Planning and Building Libraries."** www
.slais.ubc.ca/resources/architecture/index.htm.

As noted in the introduction to this online annotated bibliography, "This site has been created
for librarians, architects, design consultants, and
students interested in all aspects of planning and
building libraries. The site provides an outline of
key resources that are available online." Architectural standards, barrier-free design, lighting,
and many other subjects are covered. A Canadian site, it leans heavily toward libraries of that
nation, but it is sufficiently international in scope
to be of interest to most seekers of facilities information. Though regularly updated, most recently
in 2005, it is unfortunate that many of the hyper-
links are broken, thus reducing its usefulness.

145 **"The Seven Deadly Sins of Public Library
Architecture."** www.urbanafreelibrary.org/about/
affiliations/presentations/sevensins/sevensins.pdf.

As noted in the introductory paragraph, this is an
outline of a program presented by Fred Schlipf
and John Moorman at the Public Library Association national conference in Kansas City in
1998. Although lacking the visuals and details
of the presentation itself, this list is nevertheless
food for thought regarding some of the more

egregious examples of how *not* to design and
build a public library. Most of these items, while
deserving further commentary, are nevertheless
self-explanatory in nature. Ordering information
is given for purchase of audio tapes of the presentation.

146 **Whole Building Design Guide, "Libraries."**
www.wbdg.org/design/libraries.php.

Administered by the National Institute of Building
Sciences, a nonprofit, nongovernmental organization whose mission is to solve building-related
problems, this website is offered to provide "government and industry practitioners with one-stop
access to up-to-date information on a wide range
of building-related guidance, criteria, and technology from a 'whole buildings' perspective."
Although the site is meant mainly for architects
and other building professionals, librarians involved in planning construction projects would do
well to consult this resource, especially for such
segments as "Emerging Issues," which discusses
new technologies making their way into daily
library life, and "Relevant Codes and Standards,"
which contains links to the web page for the
Americans with Disabilities Act, among others.

■ LC SUBJECT HEADINGS

(1) Archives—Societies, etc.
(2) Information Science—Societies, etc.
(3) Library Science—Societies, etc.

ASSOCIATIONS

 BOOKS

147 Connor, Jennifer. *Guardians of Medical Knowledge: The Genesis of the Medical Library Association.* Lanham, MD: Scarecrow Press, 2000. ISBN: 978-0-81083-470-5.

Connor has made excellent use of published literature, oral histories, old memoranda, letters, journal articles, interview transcripts, and archival documents to trace the history of the Medical Library Association (MLA) in the United States, from its conception as a resource for libraries to its current role as a national professional organization dedicated to improving and updating medical knowledge through an exchange of duplicate materials and best practices. This analysis of MLA's origins, its dominant medical culture, and its intricate network of physician leaders includes over 100 sources, which are listed in the useful "Bibliographic Essay."

148 Meinhold, Alexandra, ed. *World Guide to Library, Archive, and Information Science Associations.* 3rd ed. IFLA Publications 142–143.

Berlin: Walter De Gruyter, 2010. ISBN: 978-3-11022-637-9.

This handbook includes more than 600 comprehensive profiles of information agencies, societies, and institutions from over 130 countries. Internationally active associations are listed alphabetically in the first half. In the second part, national associations are sorted by country, then listed alphabetically within each nation heading. Indexes of associations, official journals, officers, and subjects are included.

@ ADDITIONAL RESOURCES

149 Beecroft, Kathryn, ed. *CILIP: The Chartered Institute of Library and Information Professionals Yearbook 2014.* London: Facet, 2012. ISBN: 978-1-85604-709-8.

150 Bluh, Pamela, ed. *Commemorating the Past, Celebrating the Present, Creating the Future: Papers in Observance of the 50th Anniversary of the Association for Library Collections and Technical Services.* Chicago: American Library Association, 2007. ISBN: 978-0-83898-431-4.

151 Dawson, Alma, and Florence M. Jumonville, eds. *A History of the Louisiana Library Association, 1925–2000.* Baton Rouge: Louisiana Library Association, 2003.

152 Hodges, Terence Mark. *The Southern Chapter of the Medical Library Association: A Fifty Year History, 1951–2001.* Nashville, TN: Southern Chapter of the Medical Library Association, 2001.

153 Jones, Plummer Alston. *North Carolina Library Association: Centennial Handbook, 1904–2004.* Charlotte: North Carolina Library Association, 2004.

154 Killian, Stephen B. *The Wilkes-Barre Law and Library Association: One Hundred Fifty Years of Community Service: A Sesquicentennial History.* Wilkes-Barre, PA: Wilkes-Barre Law and Library Association, 2000.

155 Richmond, Robert W. *Shining the Light: A Centennial History of the Kansas Library Association.* Hutchinson: Kansas Library Association, 2000.

156 Scarborough, William Saunders. *Cincinnati Law Library Association.* Memphis, TN: General Books, 2010. ISBN: 978-1-15449-357-3.

157 Van de Klundert, Merle. *Turn Back the Pages: A History of the Dunedin Public Library Association, 1890–2005.* Dunedin, New Zealand: Dunedin Public Libraries Association, 2006. ISBN: 978-1-87713-993-2.

📖 PERIODICALS

158 *AASL Hotlinks.* Chicago: American Association of School Librarians, American Library Association. Frequency: Twelve issues per year. URL: www.ala.org/aasl/aaslpubsandjournals/aaslhotlinks/aaslhotlinks/.

Hotlinks is the e-mail newsletter of the American Association of School Librarians (AASL, a subunit of ALA). It covers upcoming association events, news from AASL, continuing education programs, web resources, new products,

services, summaries of articles from AASL's print and online journal, and other articles on topics of interest to school librarians.

159 *ALCTS Newsletter Online.* Chicago: Association for Library Collections and Technical Services, American Library Association. Frequency: Four times per year with ongoing updates. URL: www.ala.org/ala/mgrps/divs/alcts/resources/ano/index.cfm.

The online quarterly published by the Association for Library Collections and Technical Services (ALCTS, a subunit of ALA), *ALCTS Newsletter Online* covers forums and events, liaison reports, interest groups, council actions, committees, and projects and provides a calendar of events for the association. Recurring features include "From the Editor," "Looking Ahead," and "News."

160 *ALCTS Paper Series.* Chicago: Association for Library Collections and Technical Services, American Library Association. Frequency: As approved. URL: www.ala.org/ala/mgrps/divs/alcts/resources/papers/index.cfm.

Published irregularly by the Association for Library Collections and Technical Services (ALCTS, a subunit of ALA), the *ALCTS Paper Series* is a theme-based collection of topical, time-sensitive papers on library collection and technical services. Institutional repository, managing electronic serials, models for managing electronic resources and services, the future of descriptive cataloging rules, and more are covered.

161 *College and Research Libraries.* Chicago: Association of College and Research Libraries, American Library Association. Frequency: Six times per year. ISSN: 0010-0870. http://crl.acrl.org.

Published bimonthly, *College and Research Libraries* is the official journal of the Association of College and Research Libraries (ACRL, a subunit of ALA). Topics include all fields in the interest and concern to academic and research libraries. Articles are peer reviewed. Recurring features include "Letters to the Editor" and "New Publication Reviews."

162 *College and Research Libraries News.* Chicago: Association of College and Research Libraries, American Library Association. Frequency: Eleven times per year. ISSN: 0099-0086. http://crln.acrl.org.

College and Research Libraries News is the official newsmagazine of the Association of College and Research Libraries (ACRL, a subunit of ALA). Recurring columns include "Internet Resources," "Internet Reviews," "Preservation News," "Washington Hotline," "Grants and Acquisitions," "People in the News," and "New Publications." Other regular features are "Scholarly Communication," "Job of a Lifetime," and "The Way I See It."

163 *Public Libraries.* Chicago: Public Library Association, American Library Association. Frequency: Six issues per year. ISSN: 0163-5506. www.ala.org/pla/publications/publiclibraries/.

The official journal of the Public Library Association (PLA, a subunit of ALA) contains industry news, PLA and ALA updates, and column and feature articles that offer strategies and ideas to cope with the ever-changing needs of library communities and patrons. Each issue usually includes feature articles, "Verso" opinion pieces, "Tales from the Front," "News from PLA," vendor announcements, and reviews of professional literature. Past issues are available in PDF format.

164 *RUSA Update.* Chicago: Reference and User Services Association, American Library Association. Frequency: Four times per year with ongoing updates. www.rusa.ala.org/rusaupdate/.

This quarterly newsletter published by the Reference and User Services Association (RUSA, a subunit of ALA) includes posts from the RUSA director and president along with coverage of RUSA-sponsored events. Also covered are updates from RUSA committees, scheduled events, RFPs, nominations for achievement awards and travel grants, standards and guidelines, calls for papers/presentations, and other items of interest to RUSA members.

165 *YALSA E-news.* Chicago: Young Adult Library Services Association, American Library Association. Frequency: Twelve times per year. www.ala.org/yalsa/products&publications/yalsapubs/enews/.

This monthly e-mail newsletter published by the Young Adult Library Services Association (YALSA, a subunit of ALA) is for members only and is sent directly to each member's in-box. *YALSA E-News* is sent on the second Tuesday of each month and offers information on YALSA, its members, and its committees.

✎ ADDITIONAL RESOURCES

166 *Nebraska Library Association Quarterly.* Lincoln: Nebraska Library Association. Frequency: Quarterly. ISSN: 0028-1883. URL: www.nebraskalibraries.org/nlaq.html#subs.

167 *PNLA Quarterly.* Mercer Island, WA: Pacific Northwest Library Association. Frequency: Quarterly. ISSN: 0030-8188. URL: www.pnla.org/quarterly/index.htm.

168 *Texas Library Journal.* Waco: Texas Library Association. Frequency: Four times per year. ISSN: 0040-4446. URL: www.txla.org/tlj/.

☁ WEBSITES

169 *ALA Connect.* Chicago: American Library Association. URL: www.ala.org/ala/mgrps/communicate/alaconnect/index.cfm.

This site is designed specifically for ALA members to conduct official business, such as might be necessary for participants in divisions, round tables, and committees. Nonmembers are allowed entry but have restricted access. Some of the tools available are blog posts, online documents (like wiki pages), a calendar, polls, a chat room, a discussion board, and images. Members are able to select which of the 1,500 active groups they want to join, set up easy access to group information through an individual "My ALA Groups" account, and track upcoming events through "My Connect Calendar." Since professional networking is also part of the mix, one might think of this site as LinkedIn for librarians.

170 *American Library Association Handbook of Organization.* URL: www.ala.org/aboutala/governance/handbook/.

Founded in 1976, ALA is the nation's oldest and largest organization representing information professionals. Available online only since 2009, the *Handbook* contains links for a staff directory, headquarters and office locations, policies, details regarding organizational units, awards information, and a general reference section (membership statistics, scholarships available through ALA, etc.), among other useful information.

171 *Interface.* URL: www.ala.org/ascla/interface/.

Interface is the official online publication of the Association of Specialized and Cooperative Library Agencies (ASCLA, a subunit of ALA). Regular columns include the president's message, ASCLA announcements, official acts of the various units of ASCLA, and upcoming conferences and meetings. Article topics focus on the latest developments in the field of specialized and cooperative library activities.

LC SUBJECT HEADINGS

(1) American Library Association—Awards
(2) Information Science—Scholarships,
        Fellowships, etc.
(3) Library Science—Awards
(4) Library Science—Scholarships, Fellowships, etc.
(5) School Libraries—Awards—United States

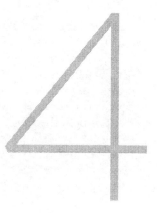

4

AWARDS AND RECOGNITION

 BOOKS

172 Carr, Jo Ann, ed. *Leadership for Excellence: Insights of National School Library Media Program of the Year Award Winners.* Chicago: American Library Association, 2008. ISBN: 978-0-83890-961-4.

This is a critical examination of the National School Library Media Program of the Year (NSLMPY) Award winners' visions for the future of school library media programs. Case histories, best practices, and methods of integrating school library resources into the curriculum to attain student success are a few items to be found here. Entries are a few pages long and cover objectives, leadership roles, contributions to student achievement, funding, and evaluation. A postscript about the NSLMPY method for building school library media programs, an appendix of NSLMPY winners' websites, a bibliography, and an index complete the volume.

FYI

ALA AWARDS

Curious about what accolades ALA bestows on worthy members of the profession? The *Awards Manual of the American Library Association* would seem to be a logical place to look, but this is actually a policies and procedures manual spelling out who does what, and so forth; the most recent edition can be accessed freely via a link on the ALA home page (www.ala.org). For a rundown of actual ALA awards, consult the *American Library Association Handbook of Organization* (see entry 171).

173   Hilbun, Janet W., and Jane H. Claes. *Coast to Coast: Exploring State Book Awards.* Santa Barbara, CA: Libraries Unlimited, 2010. ISBN: 978-1-59158-735-4.

The authors provide information about state book award programs, organizations that bestow awards, award purposes, nomination criteria, and who selects the winners. Interviews of authors, publishers, booksellers, and award program coordinators are used to analyze and compare awards and to illustrate how winning a particular award affects people personally and professionally.

174   Treviño, Rose Zertuche, ed. *The Pura Belpré Awards: Celebrating Latino Authors and Illustrators.* Chicago: American Library Association, 2006. ISBN: 978-0-83893-562-0.

Part 1 covers Latino author and illustrator awards along with biographical sketches. Part 2 contains booktalks for the author award books and activities for the illustrator award books. Each entry contains the name of the author or illustrator, title, publisher, copyright, story synopsis, and a statement from the award winner.

☁ WEBSITES

175   Association for Library Collections and Technical Services. Awards and Grants. www.ala.org/ala/mgrps/divs/alcts/awards/index.cfm/.

The Association for Library Collections and Technical Services (ALCTS) and its sections employ juries that are composed of peers to honor librarians and information professionals for outstanding and potential achievement in serials, cataloging, acquisitions, published scholarship, preservation, and general technical services librarianship. December 1 is the deadline for all award nominations. There are five award categories: Writing/Publishing, Innovation, Personal Achievement, Achievement for Newer Professionals, and For Professionals in Developing Countries.

176   Library Leadership and Management Association. Awards and Grants. http://ala.org/llama/awards/.

The Library Leadership and Management Association (LLAMA), a division of ALA, offers four major library awards: The LLAMA/IIDA Library Interior Design Award honors excellence in library interior design and promotes examples of extraordinary design and innovative concepts. The LLAMA ALA/AIA Library Building Award is for excellence in library architectural design by an architect licensed in the United States for any worldwide library. The LLAMA John Cotton Dana Library Public Relations Award honors outstanding library public relations, whether a summer reading program, a year-long centennial celebration, fund-raising for a new college library, an awareness campaign, or an innovative partnership in the community. The LLAMA/PRMS PR Xchange Best of Show Awards are given to the best individual pieces of public relations materials produced by librarians within the past year.

177 Young Adult Library Services Association.
Awards, Grants, Stipends, and Scholarships.
www.ala.org/yalsa/awardsandgrants/
yalsaawardsgrants.

Young Adult Library Services Association (YALSA) members can apply for grants or awards that recognize an individual or group for outstanding contributions to either YALSA or the profession of young adult librarianship. YALSA also offers grants for summer reading, teen summer internships, and several scholarships, stipends, and fellowships. Annual awards and grants include these:

- Baker and Taylor/YALSA Conference Grants
- BWI/YALSA Collection Development Grant
- ABC-CLIO/Greenwood/YALSA Service to Young Adults Achievement Award
- MAE Award for Best Literature Program for Teens
- Frances Henne/YALSA/VOYA Research Grant
- Great Books Giveaway Competition
- YALSA Writing Award
- Midwinter Paper Presentation
- YALSA Presidential Citation

LC SUBJECT HEADINGS

(1) Children's Librarians—United States—Biography
(2) College Librarians—United States—Biography
(3) Librarians—United States—Biography
(4) Library Administrators—United States—
         Biography
(5) Young Adult Services Librarians—United
         States—Biography

BIOGRAPHY, AUTOBIOGRAPHY, AND MEMOIR

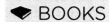

BOOKS

178 Akey, Stephen. *Library.* Alexandria, VA: Orchises Press, 2002. ISBN: 978-0-91406-191-5.

Akey recounts his years attending library school and then working in a public library in Brooklyn, New York. The characters and situations described are often humorous and all too frequently encountered in any large public library. This is an insider's look at how bureaucracy and an urge to please everyone in a dumbed-down society have eroded the professionalism and intellectual role of librarians and libraries.

179 Ali, Amjad. *Libraries and Librarians of the World.* New Delhi: Ess Ess, 2006. ISBN: 978-8-17000-482-0.

This book is divided into two parts: libraries and librarians. Famous libraries and librarians of the world are listed in alphabetical order within their respective sections for ease of reference.

180 Beck, Clare. *The New Woman as Librarian: The Career of Adelaide Hasse.* Lanham, MD: Scarecrow Press, 2006. ISBN: 978-0-81085-106-1.

Beck details the controversies surrounding Adelaide Hasse, from her significant contributions to librarianship to her role in helping to shatter the glass ceiling as a woman working in a then male-dominated profession. Hasse spent twenty-one years at the New York Public Library before the trustees fired her, partially because of her personality and partially because of her possible involvement with a growing female union force within the library. She was best known for her work with government publications and her outspokenness on major issues in the nascent profession of librarianship in the early 1900s. Hasse was an editor for *Special Libraries* (see annotation at entry 1539) and also the first librarian for America's first think tank, the Brookings Institution. This is a thoughtful analysis of the woman and her place in American library history.

181 Benoit, Gaetan M. *Eugène Morel: Pioneer of Public Libraries in France.* Duluth, MN: Litwin Books, 2008. ISBN: 978-0-97786-178-1.

Eugène Morel, who died in 1934 at the age of sixty-five, was an eminent public library pioneer in France. This biography covers his years working to bring the French professional library organization into closer alignment with British and American national library organizations while encouraging libraries to employ women. Morel was interested in all aspects of librarianship, and this critical study shows the impact his work had on French libraries.

182   Fine, Leon J., ed. *Harvey's Keepers: Harveian Librarians through the Ages.* London: Royal College of Physicians of London, 2007. ISBN: 978-1-86016-299-2.

This is a listing of the obituaries and biographies of thirteen Harveian Librarians from 1654 to 2007: Christopher Merrett, Walter Charleton, Richard Tyson, William Munk, Frank Payne, Norman Moore, Arnold Chaplin, Archibald Gilpin, Charles Dodds, Charles Newman, Gordon Wolstenholme, Christopher Booth, and Ian McDonald. The appendixes contain a timeline of the Royal College of Physicians Library and extracts from the Burmarsh Trust Deed.

183   Gorman, Michael. *Broken Pieces: A Library Life, 1941–1978.* Chicago: American Library Association, 2011. ISBN: 978-0-83891-104-4.

Michael Gorman has led a long and illustrious career in librarianship. Among his accomplishments, he has served as editor of the Anglo-American Cataloging Rules, 2nd edition (AACR2) and as ALA president and has written books about the profession he has been involved in for some four decades. Here he recounts the early and middle years of his career. Periods touched on include time spent at Finchlet Catholic Grammar School, Hampstead Public Library, library school, the British Library, and the University of Illinois.

184   Kister, Kenneth F. *Eric Moon: The Life and Library Times.* Jefferson, NC: McFarland, 2002. ISBN: 978-0-78641-253-2.

Kister relies on interviews with Moon, his family, friends, and colleagues to present this story of a progressive, radical librarian's career of fifty-plus years. Aspects covered include Moon's early years growing up in Southampton, his entrance into the profession of librarianship, defending home and country in the Royal Air Force during World War II, and attending Loughborough University. This story continues with his many and varied positions in British, Canadian, and U.S. libraries. Close attention is given to Moon's work on reviving *Library Journal*, remaking library journalism, and reforming ALA. Notes, a bibliography, and index are provided. To follow Moon's life is to follow the main course of Anglo-American librarianship from the 1950s into the 1990s.

185   McEldowney, W. J. *Geoffrey Alley, Librarian: His Life and Work.* Wellington, NZ: Victoria University Press, 2007. ISBN: 978-0-86473-534-8.

McEldowney uses the biography of Geoffrey Alley, New Zealand's first national librarian, to track the development of New Zealand's national library system from the Carnegie Corporation's initial support for public libraries to the establishment of the National Library of New Zealand. Alley's life, contributions, and connections illustrate the social and political context in which the present library networks evolved. A list of illustrations, bibliography, and index are included.

186   Miller, Marilyn, ed. *Pioneers and Leaders in Library Services to Youth: A Biography Dictionary.* Westport, CT: Libraries Unlimited, 2003. ISBN: 978-1-59158-028-7.

Miller compiles ninety-seven biographical essays of pioneers and leaders from the late nineteenth century to the recent past who significantly improved public and school library services to children and young adults. Each entry contains information on the subject's year of birth, year of death, family background, educational pursuits, professional career, contributions to librarianship, and bibliography.

187   Seaver, Barry William. *A True Politician: Rebecca Browning Rankin, Municipal Reference Librarian of the City of New York, 1920–1952.* Jefferson, NC: McFarland, 2003. ISBN: 978-0-78641-634-9.

Until her retirement in 1952, Rebecca Browning Rankin supervised the New York Municipal Reference Library. Her thirty-two-year career as a librarian, author, and radio commentator is the main focus of this illuminating biography. Rankin served as president of several library organizations, including the Special Libraries Association. There are chapters on the Municipal Reference Library, the Special Libraries Association, civic education, publications and policies, pensions and committees, international affairs, and the creation of the municipal archives. Notes, bibliography, and an index are included.

188   Webb, Terry. *Re-membering Libraries: Essay on the Profession.* Jefferson, NC: McFarland, 2000. ISBN: 978-0-78640-871-9.

Webb, former dean of the Guggenheim Library at Monmouth University, looks back over his career through a series of fifteen essays and previously unpublished papers. Overarching topics are management, libraries, and the library profession. The collection is a hodgepodge of personal anecdotes, reflections, reminiscences, puns, and analogies. Works cited and an index are included.

189   Wiegand, Wayne A. *Irrepressible Reformer: A Biography of Melvil Dewey.* Chicago: American Library Association. 1996. ISBN: 978-0-83890-680-4.

This is the definitive book on Melvil Dewey—his life, accomplishments, and difficulties. Known for his Decimal Classification system for libraries, Dewey was also a founder of ALA and the Lake Placid Club. Wiegand takes readers through his years at Amherst College, Columbia University, the New York State Library, and the University of the State of New York. He also explores the traits that made Dewey's personality difficult, his inability to control himself around women, and his thoughts on race and religion. This is a fascinating read about an influential pioneer in librarianship and library services in the United States.

ADDITIONAL RESOURCE

190   Sherman, Jill. *Melvil Dewey: Library Genius.* Publishing Pioneers Series. Edina, MN: Abdo, 2009. ISBN: 978-1-60453-761-1.

(1) Burnout (psychology)
(2) Information Science—Vocational Guidance—
         United States
(3) Librarians—Employment—United States
(4) Librarians—Psychology
(5) Librarians—Vocational Guidance—United
         States
(6) Library Employees
(7) Library Science—Psychological Aspects
(8) Library Science—Vocational Guidance—
         United States

CAREERS AND EMPLOYMENT

 BOOKS

191 Bacon, Pamela S., and Tamora K. Bacon.
*Library Lifesavers: A Survival Guide for Stressed
Out Librarians.* Westport, CT: Libraries Unlimited,
2009. ISBN: 978-1-59158-768-2 (print), 978-0-
313-39123-1 (e-book).

THRIVE is an acronym developed by the Bacon
sisters to help librarians remain calm and productive under stressful circumstances: T (Take
action); H (Hurry no more); R (Read and regain
control); I (Inspire yourself and others); V (Visions . . . past, present, future); E (Exercise your
mind and body). Divided into six themes, each
chapter begins with a question and includes practical solutions and hands-on activities. Many of
the lifesaver tools are reproducible documents.

192 Dority, G. Kim. *Rethinking Information
Work: A Career Guide for Librarians and Other
Information Professionals.* Westport, CT: Libraries
Unlimited, 2006. ISBN: 978-1-59158-180-2 (print),
978-0-313-09065-3 (e-book).

Dority covers several routes for creating, revis-
ing, and improving your librarian career through
traditional, nontraditional, and independent
paths. A majority of the book is spent examining self-knowledge, creating your professional
portfolio, growing your career, and thriving on
change. The step-by-step exploration of careers
and career choices reflects the flexibility needed
to grow and advance in the profession. Tables,
exercises, tips, worksheets, lists, and recommended bibliographic resources provide structure, guidance, and goal identification.

193 Doucett, Elisabeth. *What They Don't Teach
You in Library School.* Chicago: American Library
Association, 2010. ISBN: 978-0-83893-592-7.

Doucett covers unwritten rules and information
helpful to know before getting your first job as
a librarian, when you are new on the job, and as
you gain some experience. Each chapter contains
a brief description of the topic, why the reader
should care, main discussion points, and suggested readings. Topics include problem patrons,
confrontations, teamwork, marketing, trends,
facilities, and financial matters.

194   Gordon, Rachel Singer. *What's the Alternative? Career Options for Librarians and Info Pros.* Medford, NJ: Information Today, 2008. ISBN: 978-1-57387-333-8.

Somewhat similar in topic and scope to *A Day in the Life: Career Options in Library and Information Science* (see entry 200), this volume takes a different tack in that, rather than looking at specific nontraditional LIS careers, it examines fields and areas of endeavor. For example, chapter 2, "Organizations Serving Libraries and Librarians," sees vendors, library associations, and library schools as opportunities to work outside the field while still utilizing the bibliographic skills pertinent to the vocation. Having a business of one's own, information technology work, bookstores, publishing, and writing also receive appropriate coverage. Text boxes are sprinkled throughout, in which individuals in nontraditional LIS jobs give a first-person rundown about their jobs, although much more concisely than in the title referenced earlier. There are eleven chapters altogether, four appendixes—"Finding Nontraditional Positions," "Alternative Careers Survey," "Web Sites," and "Resources"—and a bibliography of journal articles and books for further research.

195   Lawson, Judy, Joanna Kroll, and Kelly Kowatch. *The New Information Professional: Your Guide to Careers in the Digital Age.* New York: Neal-Schuman, 2010. ISBN: 978-1-55570-698-2.

As the field of librarianship continues to evolve, the literature concerning it evolves along a parallel path. Increasingly, emphasis is being placed on the technological and information management aspects of our profession, and this volume has been cast from that mold. Careers in records management, social computing, and information policy are a few examples of nontraditional fields that this book presents to the reader. Eight chapters follow a standard format, each containing the following subheadings: "Introduction," "Skills and Abilities," "Professional Roles," "Occupational Outlook," "Salary Information," "Profiles—Perspectives of New Professionals," "Careers in Information Analysis and Retrieval: At a Glance," "Resources for

Further Information/Exploration," "Education and Training," and "References." A chapter titled "Planning for Your Career in Information" offers helpful information about the job search process. Special features include text boxes sprinkled throughout the text with such headings as "Key Words to Know" (short glossaries of technojargon and other newly minted terminology).

196   Neely, Teresa Y., ed. *How to Stay Afloat in the Academic Library Job Pool.* Foreword by Camila Alire. Chicago: American Library Association, 2011. ISBN: 978-0-83891-080-1.

Contributors offer practical advice for finding a position as a college or university librarian. After a brief overview of entry-level positions, the material moves into the nuts and bolts of finding openings, applications, interviews, and job offers. Topics cover how to read a job ad (e.g., seeing the obvious, and reading in between the lines), compiling an application packet, phone interviews, in-person interviews, salary negotiations, and more. A list of contributors and index are included.

197   Newlen, Robert R. *Resume Writing and Interviewing Techniques That Work: A How-to-Do-It Manual for Librarians.* How-To-Do-It Manuals for Libraries 148. New York: Neal-Schuman, 2006. ISBN: 978-1-55570-538-1.

This revised How-to-Do-It book is divided into three sections: writing a winning resume, reviewing successful sample resumes, and interviewing successfully. Newlen includes a list of action verbs used to enhance a resume and work history indexes geared toward the library profession.

198   Perez, Megan Zoe, and Cindy A. Gruwell, eds. *The New Graduate Experience: Post-MLS Residency Programs and Early Career Librarianship.* Westport, CT: Libraries Unlimited, 2010. ISBN: 978-1-59158-886-3.

Articles contain research and reviews of U.S. and Canadian residencies along with residents' and program coordinators' perspectives on post-MLS programs and careers. Contributors explore new approaches to recruitment, mentoring, and retention of new librarians. Vacancy announcements, survey instruments, interview scripts, and mentor criteria forms are included, and each chapter has bibliographic reference lists.

199   Sellen, Betty-Carol, ed. *What Else You Can Do with a Library Degree: Career Options for the 90s and Beyond.* New York: Neal-Schuman, 1997. ISBN: 978-1-55570-264-9.

Contributors present fifty-plus success stories of librarians in nontraditional settings. Occupations that are a good fit for those with LIS backgrounds include publisher, writer, bookseller, book reviewer, provider of products and services for libraries, consultant, freelance worker, company owner, association professional, and corporate employee. Private investigator, art dealer, archivist, and computer workshop presenter are some of the unique occupations mentioned. Although the sixty-two first-person narratives predate the ever-expanding technological changes from the past decade, contributors recognize that having an MLS does not limit career opportunities. A list of organizations for independent information professionals, contributors' information, index, and editor information are included.

200   Shontz, Priscilla K., and Richard A. Murray, eds. *A Day in the Life: Career Options in Library and Information Science.* Westport, CT: Libraries Unlimited, 2007. ISBN: 978-1-59158-364-6.

Options indeed. No fewer than ninety-five, to be specific. That number represents the total chapters in this volume, each written by a contributor, embodying myriad career possibilities within the library science sphere. As one might expect, many of these are nontraditional gigs, such as "learning resource center director" and "knowledge manager." The vast majority, though, would fall under the umbrella phrase *special librarian,* and the list is quite lengthy—"special materials cataloger," "law librarian, private law firm," and so on. Each of these chapters follows a standard format: a paragraph or two of personal background on the person holding down the job, a section

on what a typical workday is like, pros and cons of the assignment, and, especially interesting, a section titled (generally) "How would I get a job like yours?" that discusses qualifications, typical number of job openings, geographic location, and other relevant information. Each four- to five-page essay concludes with a short bibliography for further research. Written in the first person, the tone is conversational, which gives the reader a "you are there" feel. Overall, this is an excellent introduction to the many—not to mention unexpected—career paths an MLS/MLIS degree can prepare you for.

201   Smallwood, Carol, ed. *The Frugal Librarian: Thriving in Tough Economic Times.* Chicago: American Library Association, 2011. 978-0-83891-075-7.

Creative and resourceful ideas from contributors focus on sharing resources, maintaining core functions, finding supplemental funding, and developing grassroots support during these recent years of shorter hours, tighter budgets, and scare resources. Topics cover helping patrons' job searches, librarian survival tips, grants, programming, sharing resources, management decisions, on-the-job success, staffing, and professional development. A list of contributors and index are included.

202   Smallwood, Carol, ed. *Pre- and Post-retirement Tips for Librarians.* Chicago: American Library Association, 2011. ISBN: 978-0-83891-120-4.

This anthology helps librarians prepare for retirement and beyond. Pre-retirement topics discussed include retirement options, four steps to a better retirement, how to retire graciously, and basic elements and helpful tips for social security benefits. Once retired, librarians must consider income in retirement, developing a spending plan, investment activities, learning to be frugal, and maintaining, repairing, and protecting credit. These librarians now have time to explore new roads, which may include following a dream, going back to school or work, or volunteering. Additional topics include health insurance, the

logistics of downsizing, the potential for reloca-
tion, and continued financial planning.

203 Toor, Ruth, and Hilda K. Weisburg. *New
on the Job: A School Library Media Specialist's
Guide to Success.* Chicago, American Library
Association, 2006. ISBN: 978-0-83890-924-9.

This hands-on guide covers getting the job,
finding your way, getting organized, reaching
students and teachers, dealing with principals,
advocacy, planning, technology, ethics, and standards. There are appendixes of essential resources
and jobbers and vendors. A glossary and index
are included.

204 Tucker, Cory, and Reeta Sinha, eds. *New
Librarian, New Job: Practical Advice for Managing
the Transition.* Lanham, MD: Scarecrow Press,
2006. ISBN: 978-0-81085-851-0.

As is suggested by the title, this book has been
written for the novice librarian. In the words
of the introduction, it is designed to "demystify
libraries and librarianship for new professionals" and seeks to "provide practical knowledge
in all the major areas of librarianship and an
overview of the professional skills necessary to
perform effectively in each" (p. v). Readers may
sarcastically reply that that is the whole reason
for attending library school in the first place,
but, as we all know, there is much that remains
untaught in the classroom, and of the material
that is taught, much is long on theory and short
on real-world implications. Be that as it may, this
handy guide to the everyday life of the information professional is a compact and concise read.
The text is organized around four themes. Part
1, "Getting Started," examines the transition
from graduate school to the profession, finding
the right fit between candidate and job opening, and then getting comfortable in one's new
library environs. Part 2, "Library Departments,"
is basically a guided tour through the various
functional units of today's facilities—reference,
collection development, technical services, and
so on. Part 3, "Career Advancement," is all about
moving ahead in one's chosen career, and part
4, "Survival Skills for Your First (or Fifteenth!)

Year" covers such pertinent topics as time management, office politics, and the ever-changing
technology scene. This is great primer for the
newbie and a refreshing refresher for the veteran.

205 Watson-Boone, Rebecca. *A Good Match:
Library Career Opportunities for Graduates of
Liberal Arts Colleges.* ALA Research Series.
Chicago: American Library Association, 2007.
ISBN: 978-0-83890-941-6.

Watson-Boone surveyed librarians who gradu-
ated from eight liberal arts colleges from 1962 to
2000 to gain insight on career choices, what life
and work are really like for LIS professionals, and
how the profession has changed over forty years.
This a reprint of the 2000 edition.

206 Woodward, Jeannette A. *A Librarian's
Guide to an Uncertain Job Market.* ALA Editions
Special Reports. Chicago: American Library
Association, 2011. ISBN: 978-0-83891-105-1.

In this slim volume, Woodward provides tips,
guidelines, and steps to recession-proof your present job. Subjects covered include preparing for
the worst, dealing with sudden job loss, moving
on, first impressions, applications, resume com-
position, and successful interviews. This special
report will help librarians survive career crises
and pursue jobs with confidence.

ADDITIONAL RESOURCES

**207 Born, Judy, Sue Clayton, and Aggie
Balash, eds.** *Community College Library Job
Descriptions and Organizational Charts.* CJCLS
Guide 4. Chicago: American Library Association,
2000. ISBN: 978-0-83898-119-1.

208 Bridges, Karl, ed. *Expectations of
Librarians in the 21st Century.* Libraries Unlimited
Library Management Collection. Westport,
CT: Greenwood Press, 2003. ISBN: 978-0-31332-
294-5.

209 de Stricker, Ulla. *Is Consulting for You? A
Primer for Information Professionals.* Chicago:

American Library Association, 2008. ISBN: 978-0-83890-947-8.

210 Griffiths, José-Marie, and Donald W. King. *A Strong Future for Public Library Use and Employment.* Chicago: American Library Association, 2011. ISBN: 978-0-83893-588-0.

211 Hawks, Melanie. *Life-Work Balance.* ACRL Active Guide 1. Chicago: American Library Association, 2008. ISBN: 978-0-83898-478-9.

212 Jackson, Andrew P., Julius Jefferson Jr., and Akilah S. Nosakhere, eds. *The 21st-Century Black Librarian in America: Issues and Challenges.* Lanham, MD: Scarecrow Press, 2012. ISBN: 978-0-81088-245-4.

213 Kane, Laura Townsend. *Straight from the Virtual Stacks: A Firsthand Guide to Careers in Library and Information Science.* Chicago: American Library Association, 2011. ISBN: 978-0-83890-865-5.

214 Kane, Laura Townsend, ed. *Working in the Virtual Stacks: The New Library and Information Science.* Chicago: American Library Association, 2011. ISBN: 978-0-83891-103-7.

215 Myburgh, Sue. *The New Information Professional: How to Thrive in the Information Age Doing What You Love.* Oxford: Chandos, 2005. ISBN: 978-1-84334-087-4.

216 Newlen, Robert R. *Writing Resumes That Work: A How-to-Do-It Manual for Librarians.* How-To-Do-It Manuals for Libraries 82. New York: Neal-Schuman, 1998. ISBN: 978-1-55570-263-2.

217 Pantry, Sheila, and Peter Griffiths. *Your Essential Guide to Career Success.* 2nd ed. London: Facet, 2003. ISBN: 978-1-85604-491-2.

218 Ruddock, Bethan. *New Professional's Toolkit.* London: Facet, 2012. ISBN: 978-1-85604-768-5.

219 Smallwood, Carol, and Melissa J. Clapp, eds. *How to Survive as a Solo Librarian.* Lanham, MD: Scarecrow Press, 2011. ISBN: 978-0-81088-213-3.

220 Trotta, Marcia. *Successful Staff Development: A How-to-Do-It Manual.* How-To-Do-It Manuals for Libraries 55. New York: Neal-Schuman, 1995. ISBN: 978-1-55570-180-2.

221 Walster, Dian. *Managing Time: A How-to-Do-It Manual for Librarians.* How-to-Do-It Manuals for School and Public Librarians 12. New York: Neal-Schuman, 1993. ISBN: 978-1-5557-0127-7.

222 Watson, Margaret. *Building Your Portfolio: A CILIP Guide.* 2nd ed. London: Facet, 2010. ISBN: 978-1-85604-714-2.

223 White, Gary W., ed. *Help Wanted: Job and Career Information Resources.* RUSA Occasional Papers Series. Chicago: American Library Association, 2003. ISBN: 978-0-83898-222-8.

📑 PERIODICAL

224 *Library Worklife: HR E-news for Today's Leaders* (replaced *Library Personnel News, LPN*). Chicago: Allied Professional Association, American Library Association. Frequency: Twelve issues per year. ISSN: 1550-3534. URL: http://ala-apa.org/newsletter.

This electronic newsletter focuses on career advancement, certification, human resources, practice, pay equity, recruitment, research, and work/life balance for library workers. Articles may be based on news, trends, or research. Librarians are encouraged to submit scholarly articles, news, noteworthy events, and individual profiles for publication.

7

CATALOGING AND CLASSIFICATION

BOOKS

225 *American Book Publishing Record Annual (ABPR), 2011.* 2 vols. Amenia, NY: Grey House, 2012. ISBN: 978-1-59237-941-5.

This basic resource contains complete data on MARC records for approximately 73,000 books that are either published or distributed in the United States. These records originate from the Library of Congress. Title, author, edition, copyright date, Dewey numbers, LC classification numbers, LC control numbers, ISBN, price, binding, and distribution are provided for each entry. Bibliographic data are organized by Dewey Decimal classification (for nonfiction), adult fiction, and juvenile fiction. Author, title, and subject guide indexes are provided for easy cross-referencing. The gap between annual editions may be filled with a subscription to *American Book Publishing Record Monthly*, also available from Grey House (see entry 292).

226 Chan, Lois Mai. *Library of Congress Subject Headings: Principles and Application.* 4th ed. Library and Information Science Series. Westport, CT: Libraries Unlimited, 2005. ISBN: 978-1-59158-154-3.

The consensus among book reviewers seems to be that this is the go-to resource for anything related to Library of Congress subject headings (LCSHs). The fact that it is now in a fourth edition would bear that out. Chan provides a comprehensive look at this schema with an introduction to the LCSH classification and a brief history of its development, then guides readers through the general principles, structure, and format of this system. Application of LCSHs to MARC records is also covered. New to this edition is a chapter on faceted application of subject terminology (FAST), a LCSH-based controlled vocabulary for electronic resources. The appendixes include Library of Congress bibliographic records with MARC 21 coding, free-floating subdivisions, names of persons, floating topical subdivisions, general reference sources used in established headings, and MARC 21 coding for subject information.

227   Chan, Lois Mai, and Edward T. O'Neill.
*FAST: Faceted Application of Subject
Terminology: Principles and Application.*
Westport, CT: Libraries Unlimited, 2010. ISBN:
978-1-59158-722-4.

FAST reworks the Library of Congress subject headings (LCSHs) so that they are easier
to understand and apply while cataloging. The
authors provide information regarding organization, metadata encoding, and an introduction to
FAST structure before moving into specific usage.
Detailed cataloging information, examples, and
prototypes are provided for topical headings,
geographic headings, chronological headings,
proper names as subject headings, and form and
genre headings. Extensive information on FAST
application, derivation of FAST headings, authority records, authority control, and faceting LCSH
classifications into FAST concludes the book.

228   Curras, Emilia. *Ontologies, Taxonomies and
Thesauri in Systems Science and Systematics.*
Chandos Information Professional Series. Oxford:
Chandos, 2010. ISBN: 978-1-84334-612-8.

Curras focuses on the conceptual structure of the
thesaurus. A brief historical discussion on the
various structures and structuring principles sets
the stage for the deeper discussion of ontologies
and taxonomies. Chapter titles include "From
Classifications to Ontologies," "Taxonomies and
Thesauri as Knowledge," "Thesauri in (Cladist)
Systematics," and "Thesauri in Systems Theory."
A list of figures, author index, and subject index
are provided.

229   Durrance, Joan C., and Karen E. Pettigrew.
*Online Community Information: Creating a Nexus
at Your Library.* Chicago: American Library
Association, 2002. ISBN: 978-0-83890-823-5.

This scholarly work explores how librarians can
provide access to a timely and relevant online
community information network. The authors
found that, not surprisingly, members of the
general public use and organize community
information quite differently from information
professionals. In response, the authors attempt to

reconcile the traditional Dewey Decimal/Library
of Congress classification systems with so-called
folksonomies and also recommend best practices.
A literature review and methods section are particularly useful to librarians who are considering
establishing a community information network
at their own facilities.

230   Eden, Bradford Lee, ed. *Twenty-First
Century Metadata Operations: Challenges,
Opportunities, Directions.* New York: Routledge,
2011. ISBN: 978-0-41568-969-4.

Downsizing, reorganization, and retooling of
both professional and support staff are common
discussion topics among library administrators.
Contributors to this volume provide practical
examples of revamping operations to move from
an analog to digital environment. They discuss
how to assist catalogers and other staff with
standard MARC catalog adaptations, non-MARC
metadata, and ways to outsource redundant activities. This book was published as a special double
issue of *Cataloging and Classification Quarterly*.

231   Fletcher, Jain. *Collection-Level Cataloging:
Bound-with Books.* Third Millennium Cataloging
Series. Westport, CT: Libraries Unlimited, 2010.
ISBN: 978-1-59158-543-5.

Bound-with books is a cataloging term referring
to unrelated printed material bound together
as a single unit. Not surprisingly, this can cause
classification problems. Fletcher demystifies the
challenges inherent with this type of material
through illustrations, photographs, and examples
that highlight bound-with book backgrounds,
early approaches, existing guidance, unique
compilations, best practices, and collection-level
cataloging. Ten full-length sample records with
individual fields and a drawing depicting a
bound-with book with a diagram showing how
to catalog each individual item are easy-to-follow
how-to-do-it examples.

232   Foundation, Joanna F. *Subject Headings
for School and Public Libraries: Spanish and
English.* An LCSH/Sears Companion. Bilingual 4th

ed. Westport, CT: Libraries Unlimited, 2012. ISBN: 978-1-59158-638-8.

Foundation's manual is the only resource that provides both English and Spanish authorized and reference entries. This assists librarians in applying Library of Congress subject headings, Canadian subject headings, and Sears subject headings. Most of the approximately 30,000 headings are cross-referenced, and many have MARC codes listed to simplify entering information into a computerized catalog.

233   Hart, Amy. *The RDA Primer: A Guide for the Occasional Cataloger.* Westport, CT: Libraries Unlimited, 2010. ISBN: 978-1-58683-348-0 (print), 978-1-59884-747-5 (e-book).

This slim book traces the development of resource description and access (RDA) to reflect changes to the Anglo-American Cataloging Rules (AACR2) introduced in 1978 to construct catalogues and bibliographic lists. Hart discusses the need for changes, the impact on other cataloging systems, bibliographic relationships, and how to merge various techniques into one model. A comprehensive index highlighting key terms and RDA concepts and a four-page works cited section are included.

234   Haynes, Elizabeth, and Joanna F. Fountain. *Unlocking the Mysteries of Cataloging: A Workbook of Examples.* Library and Information Science Text Series. Westport, CT: Libraries Unlimited, 2005. ISBN: 978-1-59158-008-9.

Haynes and Fountain introduce the topic of cataloging by looking at the objectives of cataloging, Ranganathan's five laws of library science, key items needed to get started, and general information about MARC. Students and librarians complete 150 exercises in description, classification subject analysis, and MARC 21 entries. The appendixes include selected genre terms and MARC records for selected exercises. There is a title index and index to exercises in numerical order, type of material, rules by title, and rules by number. There is a companion website for students with a password-protected section for instructors who adopt the book for courses.

235   Hsieh-Yee, Ingrid. *Organizing Audiovisual and Electronic Resources for Access: A Cataloging Guide.* 2nd ed. Library and Information Science Series. Westport, CT: Libraries Unlimited, 2006. ISBN: 978-1-59158-051-5.

Hsieh-Yee's updated guide to Anglo-American Cataloging Rules includes basic topics such as organizational principles, cataloging, sound recordings, video recording, computer files, interactive multimedia, Internet resources, and cataloging in the changing information environment. Additional materials include print and online cataloging standards, web resources on cataloging and metadata, recommended readings, and author/title and subject indexes.

236   Intner, Sheila S., and Jean Weihs. *Standard Cataloging for School and Public Libraries.* 4th ed. Westport, CT: Libraries Unlimited, 2007. ISBN: 978-1-59158-378-3 (print), 978-1-59884-819-9 (e-book).

This extensively revised edition of an old standby, a fairly comprehensive examination of Anglo-American Cataloguing Rules, is not for the novice cataloger, although it may be used as a textbook for cataloging classes (for a less intimidating text, an excellent primer is *Beginning Cataloging* by the same authors; see entry 251). The authors cover special applications of AACR2-98, subject authorities, Sears subject headings, Library of Congress subject headings and classifications, Dewey Decimal classifications, and MARC formats. Cataloging exercises with answers are included in the appendix. A selected bibliography, glossary, and index are also included.

237   Kaplan, Allison G. *Crash Course in Cataloging for Non-Catalogers: A Casual Conversation on Organizing Information.* Crash Course Series. Westport, CT: Libraries Unlimited, 2009. ISBN: 978-1-59158-401-8.

This crash course helps librarians without formal training in this area catalog collection materials in a professional manner. The practical and nontheoretical presentation is easy to follow and includes what you need to know about classification, subject and key word headings, descriptions, MARC and automated systems, local cataloging problems, and information organization. This book includes bibliographical references and an index for easy lookup.

238 Karpuk, Deborah J. *Kidzcat: A How-to-Do-It Manual for Cataloging Children's Materials and Instructional Resources.* How-To-Do-It Manuals for Libraries 160. New York: Neal-Schuman, 2008. ISBN: 978-1-55570-590-9.

The author provides illustrative exercises with answers to help librarians work through the steps needed to catalog board and picture books, sound recording, DVDs, electronic games, series books, websites, and other children's materials. Discussion includes cataloging descriptions, authority control, automation systems and retrieval, MARC, subject headings, and classifications. Brief commentaries on local policy issues, outsourcing, and future directions help keep collections organized, accessible, and manageable.

239 Lubas, Rebecca L., ed. *Practical Strategies for Cataloging Departments.* Third Millennium Cataloging Series. Westport, CT: Libraries Unlimited, 2011. ISBN: 978-1-59884-492-4 (print), 978-1-59884-493-1 (e-book).

Catalogers face ever-changing standards, access demand, and outsourcing issues. This compilation provides real-life examples, case studies, model practices, and guidelines for nine topics. Each topic, listed below, includes an introduction, description, conclusion, and references.

Evolving Standards: Making the Jump to RDA in Historical Context

- Impact of Changes in the Library of Congress Cataloging Policy on Working Catalogers
- Making a Multiplicity of Standards: Hybrids Approaches to Traditional and Digital Cataloging
- Training Workshops: How One Trainer Works
- The Janus Effect: On-the-Job Training of Twenty-First-Century Catalogers

- Managing Vendor Cataloging to Maximize Access
- Collaborating with Other Library Departments
- MARC: A New Life through Reusing and Remixing
- Moving Ahead with Metadata: Adding Value through Grant-Funded Projects

240 Miller, Steven J. *Metadata for Digital Collections: A How-to-Do-It Manual.* How-To-Do-It Manuals for Libraries 179. New York: Neal-Schuman, 2011. ISBN: 978-1-55570-746-0.

Miller introduces broad metadata topics such as XML encoding, mapping between different schemes, metadata interoperability and record sharing, OAI harvesting, linked data, the semantic web and the relationship to current digitalization practices. The step-by-step guide on how to design and document a metadata institutional scheme or specific digital collection program includes numerous practical examples to clarify common application issues and challenges.

241 Mugridge, Rebecca, ed. *Cooperative Cataloging: Shared Effort for the Benefit of All.* New York: Routledge, 2011. ISBN: 978-0-41568-973-1.

In this volume experienced cataloging practitioners and managers use case studies, research papers, and opinion pieces to examine the benefits and cost effectiveness of a cooperative cataloging program. Specific programs include the OCLC Enhance program, the Program for Cooperative Cataloging programs (e.g., BIBCO, CONSER, NACO, and SACO), the Library of Congress National Union Catalog of Manuscript Collections (NUCMC), and the ISSN Register. Cooperative cataloging gives managers and administrators a streamlined, rapid method to catalog new materials, reducing patrons' wait time. This book was originally published as a special issue of *Cataloging and Classification Quarterly*.

242 Oliver, Chris. *Introducing RDA: A Guide to the Basics.* ALA Editions Special Reports. Chicago: American Library Association, 2010. ISBN: 978-0-83893-594-1.

This guide helps catalogers make the transition from Anglo-American Cataloguing Rules to the new Resource Description and Access (RDA). Seven chapters cover the definition of RDA, international context, relationship to FRBR/FRAD, and implementation of the new rules and conclude with the chapter "Advantages, Present and Future." Oliver is the cataloguing and authorities coordinator at the McGill University Library and chair of the Canadian Committee on Cataloguing. Charts and diagrams are included.

243 Park, Jung-ran, ed. *Metadata Best Practices and Guidelines: Current Implementation and Future Trends.* New York: Routledge, 2011. ISBN: 978-0-41568-974-8.

Rapidly growing digital repositories and collections in various institutions and organizations have different metadata standards that do not reflect communal needs and equivalent characteristics of available resources. Park provides a common understanding, definitions, and standards for high-quality metadata generation, management, interoperability, and resource sharing among branch libraries and partners that includes the need for systematic examination of documentation practices. This book was also published as a special issue of the *Journal of Library Metadata.*

244 Ramage, Magnus, and David A. Chapman, eds. *Perspectives on Information.* Routledge Studies in Library and Information Science Series 9. New York: Routledge, 2011. ISBN: 978-0-41588-410-5 (print), 978-0-20381-450-5 (e-book).

Contributors look at several academic disciplines such as cybernetics, information and communication technologies, communications theory, semiotics, information systems, library science, linguistics, quantum physics, and public policy to determine information standards and commonalities. Discipline relationships are shown through cybernetics, the information revolution, use of information, and the flow of information for social, policy, and technical gains.

245 Sanchez, Elaine R., ed. *Conversations with Catalogers in the 21st Century.* Westport, CT: Libraries Unlimited, 2011. ISBN: 978-1-59884-702-4 (print), 978-1-59884-703-1 (e-book).

To say that cataloging is in a state of flux is an understatement. In eighteen chapters, practitioners "speak their minds on what is going on in our cataloging world" (p. xii). Part 1 is an overview of AACR2 and RDA cataloging. Part 2, "Visions: New Ideas for Bibliographic Control and Catalogs," covers these topics by looking at systems, identity, formats, and shared catalogs. Part 3 surveys "The Cataloging World in Transition," in which contributors propose various ways of cataloging that reflect evolving new standards and terminology. Part 4 takes a look at professional development issues such as research, education, and recruitment. The book concludes with an examination of librarian skills, education, a chronological bibliography of selected works related to cataloging through 1800, and a selected bibliography of library cataloging history. Original research results based on librarians' views of AACR2, RDA, FRBR, and other cataloging systems or classifications are used to propose new work flows and record structures.

246 Taylor, Arlene G. *Introduction to Cataloging and Classification.* 10th ed. Library and Information Science Series. Westport, CT: Libraries Unlimited, 2006. ISBN: 978-1-59158-230-4.

Taylor offers up-to-date information in this revised edition that focuses on cataloging in the context of bibliographic control and catalogs, development of cataloging codes, electronic formatting, description and access, authority control, subject access, and administrative issues. The textbook also contains an appendix covering arrangement dilemmas and filing rules, glossary of selected terms and abbreviations, selected bibliography, and index.

247 Taylor, Arlene G. *Wynar's Introduction to Cataloging and Classification.* Rev. 9th ed. Library and Information Science Text Series. Westport, CT: Libraries Unlimited, 2004. ISBN: 978-1-59158-213-7.

A classic text updated for the twenty-first century, this is a comprehensive guide to cataloging and classification with special emphasis on online cataloging and related terminology. Topics include analytical materials, access points, various classification systems, subject headings, authority control, processing centers, and catalog management. Taylor includes coverage of the AACR2 2002 revision, MARC 21, the twenty-first edition of the Dewey Decimal classification, current schedule of Library of Congress classifications and subject headings, along with the seventeenth edition of the Sears list of subject headings.

248 Taylor, Arlene G., ed. *Understanding FRBR: What It Is and How It Will Affect Our Retrieval Tools.* Westport, CT: Libraries Unlimited, 2007. ISBN: 978-1-59158-509-1 (print), 978-0-313-363692-7 (e-book).

Contributors describe Functional Requirements for Bibliographic Records (FRBR), the history of this approach, relationships between data records, resources, mapping materials, and collections for librarians, system designers, and information science faculty and students. The focus is on how the FRBR model is used to organize metadata records and improve access to serials, art, music, moving images, maps, and archival materials.

249 Taylor, Arlene G., and Daniel J. Joudrey. *The Organization of Information.* 3rd ed. Library and Information Science Text Series. Westport, CT: Libraries Unlimited, 2008. ISBN: 978-1-59158-586-2.

This classic textbook discusses the theory, principles, standards, and tools for information organization in libraries. It includes information on indexing, abstracting, databases, metadata models, basic retrieval tools, and standards. The appendixes cover an approach to subject analysis, arrangement of physical information resources in libraries, and arrangement of metadata displays. A glossary, selected bibliography, and index conclude the text.

250 Weihs, Jean, and Sheila S. Intner. *Beginning Cataloging.* Westport, CT: Libraries Unlimited, 2009. ISBN: 978-1-59158-687-6.

As the title suggests, this is an introductory text to the subject. The authors examine standardized cataloging through cataloging-in-publication, descriptive cataloging, access points, subject headings, classifications, computer coding, and copy cataloging. Each topic contains an overview, definitions, figures, sample catalog entries, and exercises. This practical guide covers all types of materials, including books, audiovisual materials, pictures, sound recordings, and electronic resources. A glossary of cataloging terms and tools is included.

@ ADDITIONAL RESOURCES

251 Aikawa, Hiroko, Jan DeSirey, Linda Gabel, Susan Hayes, Kathy Nystrom, Mary D. Wilson, and Pat Thomas. *Guidelines on Subject Access to Individual Works of Fiction, Drama, etc.* 2nd ed. Chicago: American Library Association, 2000. ISBN: 978-0-83893-503-3.

252 Baca, Murtha, Patricia Harpring, Eliza Lanzi, Linda McRae, and Ann Baird Whiteside. *Cataloging Cultural Objects: A Guide to Describing Cultural Works and Their Images.* Chicago: American Library Association, 2006. ISBN: 978-0-83893-564-4.

253 Bowman, J. H. *Essential Cataloguing.* London: Facet, 2007. ISBN: 978-1-85604-456-1.

254 Bowman, J. H. *Essential Dewey.* London: Facet, 2004. ISBN: 978-1-85604-519-3.

255 Breeding, Marshall. *Next-Generation Library Catalogs.* Tech Set Series. Chicago: American Library Association, 2010. ISBN: 978-1-

55570-708-8; London: Facet, 2012. ISBN: 978-1-85604-847-7.

256 Broughton, Vanda. *Essential Classification.* London: Facet, 2004. ISBN: 978-1-85604-514-8.

257 Broughton, Vanda. *Essential Library of Congress Subject Headings.* New York: Neal-Schuman, ISBN: 978-1-55570-640-1; London: Facet, ISBN: 978-1-85604-618-3. 2011.

258 Broughton, Vanda. *Essential Thesaurus Construction.* London: Facet, 2006. ISBN: 978-1-85604-565-0.

259 Caplan, Priscilla. *Metadata Fundamentals for All Librarians.* Chicago: American Library Association, 2003. ISBN: 978-0-83890-847-1.

260 Chambers, Sally, ed. *Catalogue 2.0: The Future of the Library Catalogue.* London: Facet, 2012. ISBN: 978-1-85604-716-6.

261 Chowdhury, G. G., and Sudatta Chowdhury. *Organizing Information: From the Shelf to the Web.* London: Facet, 2007. ISBN: 978-1-85604-578-0.

262 *Emerging Issues in Academic Library Cataloging and Technical Services.* New York: Primary Research Group, 2007. ISBN: 978-1-57440-086-1.

263 Fecko, Mary Beth, and Mary Beth Weber. *Cataloging Nonbook Resources: A How-to-Do-It Manual for Librarians.* How-To-Do-It Manuals for Libraries 31. New York: Neal-Schuman, 1993. ISBN: 978-1-55570-124-6.

264 Fritz, Deborah A. *Cataloging with AACR2 and MARC21 for Books, Electronic Resources, Sound Recordings, Video Recordings, and Serials.* 2nd ed. Chicago: American Library Association, 2007. ISBN: 978-0-83890-935-5.

265 Fritz, Deborah A., and Richard J. Fritz. *Marc 21 for Everyone: A Practical Guide.* Chicago: American Library Association, 2003. ISBN: 978-0-83890-842-6.

266 Haynes, David. *Metadata for Information Management and Retrieval.* London: Facet, 2004. ISBN: 978-1-85604-489-9.

267 Hider, Philip. *Information Resource Description: Creating and Managing Metadata.* London: Facet, 2012. ISBN: 978-1-85604-667-1.

268 Hillmann, Diane I., and Elaine L. Westbrooks. *Metadata in Practice.* Chicago: American Library Association, 2004. ISBN: 978-0-83890-882-2.

269 Intner, Sheila S., Joanna F. Fountain, Jean R. Weihs, Deborah A. Fritz, and Julianne Beall, eds. *Cataloging Correctly for Kids: An Introduction to the Tools.* Chicago: American Library Association, 2011. ISBN: 978-0-83893-589-7.

270 Kaplan, Allison G., and Ann Marlow Riedling. *Catalog It! A Guide to Cataloging School Library Materials.* 2nd ed. Westport, CT: Libraries Unlimited, 2006. ISBN: 978-1-58683-197-4 (print), 978-1-58683-307-7 (e-book).

271 Kornegay, Rebecca S., Heidi E. Buchanan, and Hildegard B. Morgan. *Magic Search: Getting the Best Results from Your Catalog and Beyond.* Chicago: American Library Association, 2009. ISBN: 978-0-83890-990-4.

272 Larsgaard, Mary Lynette, and Paige G. Andrew. *RDA and Cartographic Resources.* London: Facet, ISBN: 978-1-85604-772-2; Chicago: American Library Association, ISBN: 978-0-8389-1131-0. 2014.

273 Liu, Jai. *Metadata and Its Applications in the Digital Library: Approaches and Practices.* Westport, CT: Libraries Unlimited, 2007. ISBN: 978-1-59158-306-6.

274 Maxwell, Robert L. *FRBR: A Guide for the Perplexed.* Chicago: American Library Association, 2008. ISBN: 978-0-83890-950-8.

275 Maxwell, Robert L. *Maxwell's Guide to Authority Work.* ALA Editions. Chicago: American Library Association, 2002. ISBN: 978-0-83890-822-8.

276 Maxwell, Robert L. *Maxwell's Handbook for AACR2: Explaining and Illustrating the Anglo-American Cataloguing Rules through the 2003 Update.* Chicago: American Library Association, 2004. ISBN: 978-0-83890-875-4.

277 Maxwell, Robert L. *Maxwell's Handbook for RDA.* Chicago: American Library Association, ISBN: 978-0-8389-1172-3; London: Facet, ISBN: 978-1-85604-832-3. 2013.

278 Miller, David P., and Filiberto Felipe Martinez Arellano, eds. *SALSA de Tópicos/ Subjects in Spanish and Latin American Subject Access.* ALCTS Papers on Library Technical Services and Collections Series. Chicago: American Library Association, 2007. ISBN: 978-0-83898-407-9.

279 Olson, Nancy B., Robert L. Bothmann, and Jessica J. Schomberg. *Cataloging of Audiovisual Materials and Other Special Materials: A Manual Based on AACR2 and MARC 21.* 5th ed. Westport, CT: Libraries Unlimited, 2008. ISBN: 978-1-59158-635-7.

280 Pass, Gregory A. *Descriptive Cataloging of Ancient, Medieval, Renaissance, and Early Modern Manuscripts.* Chicago: Association of College and Research Libraries, American Library Association, 2003. ISBN: 978-0-83898-218-1.

281 *RDA: Resource Description and Access.* Chicago: American Library Association, 2010. ISBN: 978-0-83891-093-1.

282 Reid, Rob. *Children's Jukebox: The Select Subject Guide to Children's Musical Recordings.* Chicago: American Library Association, 2007. ISBN: 978-0-83890-940-9.

283 Scott, Mona L. *Dewey Decimal Classification: A Study Manual and Number Building Guide.* 22nd ed. Westport, CT: Libraries Unlimited, 2005. ISBN: 978-1-59158-210-6.

284 Sleeman, William, and Pamela M. Bluh, eds. *From Catalog to Gateway: Charting a Course for Future Access: Briefings from the ALCTS Catalog Form and Function Committee.* Chicago: American Library Association, 2005. ISBN: 978-0-83898-326-3.

285 Surratt, Brian E., and Anne M. Mitchell. *Cataloging and Organizing Digital Resources: A How-to-Do-It Manual for Librarians.* How-To-Do-It Manuals for Libraries 139. New York: Neal-Schuman, 2005. ISBN: 978-1-55570-521-3.

286 Tarulli, Laurel. *The Library Catalogue as Social Space: Promoting Patron Driven Collections, Online Communities, and Enhanced Reference and Readers' Services.* Westport, CT: Libraries Unlimited, 2012. ISBN: 978-1-59884-629-4 (print), 978-1-59884-630-0 (e-book).

287 Weber, Mary Beth, and Fay Angela Austin. *Describing Electronic, Digital, and Other Media Using AACR2 and RDA: A How-to-Do-It Manual and CD-ROM for Librarians.* How-To-Do-It Manuals for Libraries 168. New York: Neal-Schuman, 2011. ISBN: 978-1-5557-0668-5.

288 Welsh, Anne, and Sue Batley. *Practical Cataloguing: AACR, RDA and MARC21.* London: Facet, 2012. ISBN: 978-1-85604-695-4.

289 Zeng, Marcia Lei, and Jian Qin. *Metadata.* London: Facet, ISBN: 978-1-85604-655-8; Chicago: American Library Association, ISBN: 978-1-55570-635-7. 2008.

📖 PERIODICALS

290 *American Book Publishing Record Monthly.* Amenia, NY: Grey House. Frequency: Monthly. ISSN: 0002-7707.

This journal provides comprehensive up-to-date Library of Congress cataloging records for approximately 10,000 new titles monthly. Entries are arranged by Dewey Decimal classification and indexed by author, title, and subject. These issues are supplements to the yearly editions of *American Book Publishing Record Annual* (see entry 226).

291 *Cataloging and Classification Quarterly.* Philadelphia: Routledge. Frequency: Eight issues per year. ISSN: 0163-9374 (print), 1544-4554 (online). URL: www.tandf.co.uk/journals/WCCQ/.

This journal covers the creation, content, management, use, and usability of bibliographic records. Contributors use principles, functions, and techniques of descriptive cataloging; subject analysis and classification; material formats; and policies, planning, and issues to promote effective and efficient use of bibliographic data. All articles undergo editorial screening and peer review. Topics include the following:

■ Cataloging and preservation
■ Cataloging for digital resources
■ Cataloging for special collections and archives
■ Classification and subject access
■ Descriptive cataloging
■ Cataloging and classification education and training
■ Cataloging internationalization
■ Cataloging and related functions management
■ Maps and other cartographic and spatial materials
■ Online retrieval use and usability issues
■ Use of catalog data by systems outside the OPAC

292 *Journal of Library Metadata.* Philadelphia: Routledge. Frequency: Four issues per year. ISSN: 1938-6389 (print), 1937-5034 (online). URL: www.tandf.co.uk/journals/WJLM/.

This journal is a forum for the latest research, innovations, news, and expert views about all aspects of metadata applications and the role of metadata in information retrieval. Sample subjects include application profiles, best practices, controlled vocabularies, individual metadata schemes, institutional repository metadata, and metadata content standards. All research articles undergo rigorous peer review based on initial editor screening and vetting by two anonymous referees.

293 *Library Resources and Technical Services.* Chicago: Association for Library Collections and Technical Services, American Library Association. Frequency: Four times per year. ISSN: 0024-2527. URL: www.ala.org/ala/mgrps/divs/alcts/resources/lrts/index.cfm.

Library Resources and Technical Services is the official journal of the Association for Library Collections and Technical Services (ALCTS, a subunit of ALA). Peer-reviewed articles focus on collections, scholarly communication, preservation (including digitization), acquisition (including licensing and acquisition economic aspects), continuing resources, and cataloging (including descriptive metadata, authority controls, subject analysis, and classification).

294 *Technical Services Quarterly.* Philadelphia: Routledge. Frequency: Four issues per year. ISSN: 0731-7131 (print), 1555-3337 (online). URL: www.tandf.co.uk/journals/WTSQ/.

This journal provides a forum for both traditional "back office" operations, such as acquisitions, cataloging, and processing of library materials; and newer trends concerning computers, automation, and more recent advances. Subjects include technical services, automation, networking, document delivery, information technology, case studies, cost analysis, staffing, space, organizational behavior, and leadership. Manuscripts undergo editorial screening and peer review by anonymous reviewers.

@ ADDITIONAL RESOURCES

295 *Catalogue and Index.* London: Library Association Cataloging and Indexing Group (CILIP). Frequency: Intermittent (three times per year planned). ISSN: 0008-7629. ESSN: 1544-4554. URL: www.cilip.org.uk/get-involved/special-interest-groups/cataloguing-indexing/Pages/publications.aspx.

296 *Journal of Classification.* New York: Springer (Classification Society of North American). Frequency: Three times per

year. ISSN: 0176-4268 (print), 1432-1343
(online). URL: www.springer.com/statistics/
statistical+theory+and+methods/journal/357/.

297 *Journal of Internet Cataloging.*
Binghamton, NY: Haworth Press. Frequency:
Quarterly. ISSN: 1091-1367. URL: http://
internetcataloging.com.

CENSORSHIP AND INTELLECTUAL FREEDOM

 BOOKS

298 Flinn, Andrew, and Harriet Jones, eds.
Freedom of Information: Open Access, Empty Archives? New York: Routledge, 2009. ISBN: 978-1-85743-420-0.

The Freedom of Information Act (FOIA) requires that access to public records be given within a certain time frame. Contributors to this volume focus on the successes and difficulties of the FOIA and archive studies across the world. This book will interest academic and public librarians who research, procure, catalog, and respond to patron requests concerning public records.

299 *Intellectual Freedom Manual.* 8th ed. Chicago: American Library Association, 2010. ISBN: 978-0-83893-590-3.

Prepared by ALA's Office of Intellectual Freedom, this manual includes an up-to-date interpretation of the Library Bill of Rights and key intellectual freedom guidelines and policies that have changed since the seventh edition was issued in 2005. Topics covered include the latest debates and extension of the USA PATRIOT Act and related measures, the Library Bill of Rights, protecting the freedom to read, the ALA code of ethics, intellectual freedom and the law, and preserving intellectual freedom. A glossary, selected bibliography, and index are included.

300 Jones, Barbara M. *Protecting Intellectual Freedom in Your Academic Library: Scenarios from the Front Lines.* Chicago: American Library Association, 2009. ISBN: 978-0-83893-580-4.

Although Jones tailors this book for academic libraries, the information presented regarding the battleground between intellectual freedom and special-interest groups or individuals who seek to restrict access may apply to any library. The book begins with an introduction to U.S. higher education in the twenty-first century before quickly moving into academic libraries and intellectual freedom. Jones specifically centers the conversation around collection development, Internet access, exhibit spaces, programs, privacy, and confidentiality. The material is enhanced with case studies, sidebars offering sample policies, definitions of key terms, and an analysis of statutes, regulations, and court decisions on intellectual freedom in a library setting. ALA intellectual freedom documents are included in the appendix, and there is an index.

301 LaRue, James. *The New Inquisition: Understanding and Managing Intellectual Freedom Challenges.* Westport, CT: Libraries Unlimited, 2007. ISBN: 978-1-59158-285-4.

This much is a given: At some point, someone is not going to like something in the stacks and will ask that it be removed. Using both his sense of humor and experience as a library director, LaRue shows how library staff can properly respond to complaints that item X, for whatever reason, is offensive. The book opens with a short history of censorship, moves to examples of real-life intellectual freedom challenges, and finishes with suggested responses that are both sensible and practical.

302 Scales, Pat. *Protecting Intellectual Freedom in Your School Library: Scenarios from the Front Lines.* Chicago: American Library Association, 2009. ISBN: 978-0-83893-581-1.

Scales here uses case studies and her experiences as a well-known First Amendment rights spokesperson to write this slim volume to help librarians respond to intellectual freedom challenges within PK–12 schools. Practical advice and a recommended course of action for potential real-life scenarios are supported by useful documents, links to additional documents, ALA resources, court decisions, and appropriate statutes. Helpful features include checklists, selection criteria, Internet access guidelines, acceptable-use policies, and a discussion of privacy issues. The synopsis "Minors' First Amendment Rights to Access Information" by Theresa Chamara and ALA's "Workbook for Selection Policy Writing" are included in the appendixes. The comprehensive index includes subjects, laws, and court cases.

@ ADDITIONAL RESOURCES

303 Becker, Beverley C., Susan M. Stan, Donna R. Pistolis, and the American Library Association Office for Intellectual Freedom. *Hit List for Children 2: Frequently Challenged Books.* Chicago: American Library Association, 2002. ISBN: 978-0-83890-830-3.

304 Doyle, Robert P. *Banned Books: Challenging Our Freedom to Read.* Chicago: American Library Association, 2010. ISBN: 978-0-83898-547-2.

305 Doyle, Robert P. *Banned Books Resource Guide.* Chicago: American Library Association, 2007. ISBN: 978-0-83898-425-3.

306 Garibyan, Masha, Simon McLeish, and John Paschoud. *Access and Identity Management for Libraries: Controlling Access to Online Information.* London: Facet, 2013. ISBN: 978-1-85604-588-9.

307 Lesesne, Teri S., Rosemary Chance, and Chris Crutcher. *Hit List for Young Adults 2: Frequently Challenged Books.* Chicago: American Library Association, 2002. ISBN: 978-0-83890-835-8.

308 Reichman, Henry. *Censorship and Selection: Issues and Answers for Schools.* 3rd ed. Chicago: American Library Association, 2001. ISBN: 978-0-83890-798-6.

309 Scales, Pat. *Teaching Banned Books: 12 Guides for Young Readers.* Chicago: American Library Association, 2001. ISBN: 978-0-83890-807-5.

📓 PERIODICAL

310 *Index on Censorship.* London: Writes and Scholars International. Frequency: Four times per year. ISSN: 0306-4220. URL: www.indexoncensorship.org/subscribe/.

COLLECTION MANAGEMENT

◆ BOOKS

311   Alabaster, Carol. *Developing an Outstanding Core Collection: A Guide for Libraries.* 2nd ed. Chicago: American Library Association, 2010. ISBN: 978-0-83891-040-5.

This edition covers all aspects of developing, selecting materials for, and maintaining an adult core collection in a public library. Alabaster looks beyond the usual best sellers and ready-reference materials to explain how to develop an appropriate core collection that meets community reading habits and needs. The index includes authors, titles, and subjects.

312   Bakers, Sharon L., and Karen L. Wallace. *The Responsive Public Library: How to Develop and Market a Winning Collection.* 2nd ed. Englewood, CO: Libraries Unlimited, 2002. ISBN: 978-1-56308-648-9.

This second edition is a practical guide on identifying library users, making collection choices, creating access, evaluating collections, and marketing services on a low budget. Each chapter includes in-depth strategies, rationale, explanations, tips, tricks, techniques, and figures and ends with a conclusion, notes, and references applicable to chapter material.

313   Bartlett, Wendy K. *Floating Collections: A Collection Development Model for Long-Term Success.* Westport, CT: Libraries Unlimited, 2012. ISBN: 978-1-59884-743-7 (print), 978-1-59884-744-4 (e-book).

Bartlett reviews the pros and cons of implementing a floating collection in which materials "float" freely among libraries in a system rather than being tied to a specific location. Patron requests trigger movement. This guidebook examines core collection, material selection, and weeding a floating collection. Checklists for various stages of floating, along with frequently asked questions, are included.

314 Bishop, Kay. *The Collection Program in Schools.* 4th ed. Library and Information Science Series. Westport, CT: Libraries Unlimited, 2007. ISBN: 978-1-59158-583-1.

Bishop's revised fourth edition updates processes and procedures associated with developing, maintaining, and evaluating collections by location; reflects changes in selection criteria for various formats such as CD-ROMs, video discs, and online databases; and adds information regarding online selection and evaluation tools, remote access, and virtual libraries. Other topics include community analysis, selection, criteria, acquisitions, maintenance and preservation, curriculum, and fiscal issues. The appendixes include agencies, suppliers, resources, and a statement on people's rights.

315 *Books in Print, 2011–2012.* 7 vols. Amenia, NY: Grey House, 2011. ISBN: 978-1-59237-714-5.

A standard resource for half a century, this issue contains more than 400,000 new titles and more than 471,000 new ISBNs for books currently published or distributed in the United States. Different editions and bindings such as hardcover, paperback, spiral binding, and workbooks are listed. There is a title, author, publisher name, and wholesale and distributor list for each reference lookup. The title, author, editor, translator, volumes, edition, pages, language, year of publication, binding, price, ISBN, imprint, and publisher are listed for each entry.

316 Cornog, Martha, and Timothy Perper, eds. *Graphic Novels beyond the Basics: Insights and Issues for Libraries.* Westport, CT: Libraries Unlimited, 2009. ISBN: 978-1-59158-478-0 (print), 978-0-31339-120-0 (e-book).

This guide introducing the world of popular fiction and nonfiction graphic novels is divided into two parts: literature, and the role of graphic novels in the library. Each chapter is devoted to one subject and many are supported with extensive references. The book concludes with appendixes on graphic novels and games, a special topics guide, a bibliography of graphic novels, and an author/title/subject index.

317 Disher, Wayne. *Crash Course in Collection Development.* Crash Course Series. Westport, CT: Libraries Unlimited, 2007. ISBN: 978-1-59158-559-6.

This crash course for librarians covers collection management from beginning to end. Features include collection assessment, policies, budgets, selections, maintenance, preservation, promotion, the publishing industry, and complaints. Disher provides step-by-step instructions for community analysis and collection evaluation. The chapter on statistics for collection developers includes turnover rates, circulation per capita, volumes per capita, material expenditures per capita, and percentage of acquisitions rate. Definitions and examples are provided throughout to support the material being presented.

318 Eaglen, Audrey. *Buying Books: A How-to-Do-It Manual for Librarians.* 2nd. ed. How-To-Do-It Manuals for Libraries 99. New York: Neal-Schuman, 2000. ISBN: 978-1-55570-371-4.

Eaglen explains the U.S. book publishing industry: an overview of its history and how books are manufactured, priced, and distributed. Steps for vendor selection, book ordering, bibliographic tools, automated acquisition systems, and trends are included, along with an annotated bibliography and glossary. Now over a decade old, a third edition is warranted due to changes in the industry, such as the rise of electronic publishing and e-readers.

319 Evans, G. Edward, and Margaret Zarnosky Saponaro. *Collection Management Basics.* 6th ed. Library and Information Science Text Series. Westport, CT: Libraries Unlimited, 2012. ISBN: 978-1-59884-863-2.

Previous editions of this book carried the title *Developing Library and Information Center Collections,* which has been an old standby text since first seeing print in 1979. This totally restructured textbook covers all areas of collection development and management. Topics include needs assessment, policies, procedures, theory and practice for the selection process, legal issues, censorship, intellectual freedom, and new technology. Helpful features include sidebars highlighting real-life experiences of collection management practitioners.

320 Fagan, Bryan D., and Jody Condit Fagan. *Comic Book Collections for Libraries.* Westport, CT: Libraries Unlimited, 2011. ISBN: 978-1-59884-511-2 (print), 978-1-59884-512-9 (e-book).

The authors provide an overview on the structure of comic books, publishers, and genres. Much of the guide focuses on circulation policies and creating, maintaining, cataloging, and promoting a comic book collection. Sample MARC records and circulation reports are provided along with an annotated list of major publishers, writers, artists, and terms. Among the genres included are manga, westerns, crime, and romance. A glossary, core collection list with ISBNs, character and title list for Marvel and DC comics, and recommended reading list complete the guide.

321 Gorman, G. E., ed. *Collection Management: International Yearbook of Library and Information Management 2000–2001.* International Yearbook of Library and Information Management Series. Part 1. London: Facet, 2000. ISBN: 978-1-85604-366-3.

Contributors provide a mixture of research-based, practice-based, and reflective scholarly studies and reports on librarianship development, with international scope. Each article covers exisiting conditions, debates, best practices, possible future developments, and a wide range of collection management subjects. Topics include acquisitions and access, censorship, collection management, digital information, economics, electronic publications, managing government documents, policy issues, storage facilities and services, and weeding.

322 Gregory, Vicki L., and Ardis Hanson. *Selecting and Managing Electronic Resources: A How-to-Do-It Manual for Librarians.* Rev. ed. How-To-Do-It Manuals for Libraries 146. New York: Neal-Schuman, 2005. ISBN: 978-1-55570-548-0.

Gregory discusses the challenges of managing electronic resources, electronic databases, copyrights, and licensing. Chapters cover collection development policies, selection criteria and the selection process, budgeting and acquisitions, organization and access to electronic resources, evaluation and assessment, digital rights, preservation issues, and the future management of electronic resources. Sample worksheets and checklists are included for budgeting, selection criteria, and licensing negotiations.

323 Greiner, Tony, and Bob Cooper. *Analyzing Library Collection Use with Excel.* Chicago: American Library Association, 2007. ISBN: 978-0-83890-933-1.

This hands-on manual shows librarians how to use Microsoft Excel to turn raw data into usable information and statistics. The manual includes Excel basics, downloading information into Excel, cleaning up data, determining the size and age of the library collection, analyzing circulation, correlation and its uses, and summarizing information. Presenting information with color and graphs and management uses of Excel finishes the book. A bibliography and index are included.

324 Halsall, Jane, R. William Edminster, and C. Allen Nichols. *Visual Media for Teens: Creating and Using a Teen-Centered Film Collection.* Libraries Unlimited Professional Guides for Young Adult Librarian Series. Santa Barbara, CA: Libraries Unlimited, 2009. ISBN: 978-1-59158-544-2 (print), 978-0-31339-128-6 (e-book).

Creating a teen film collection, arranging public showings, and supporting programming through film genres generate teen interest in library services. Chapters explore issues of identity, the appeal of heroes, the appeal of strong emotions, education, and the arts. One section is devoted to film reviews and resources, including online video reviews, other online film information services, critical books on film, websites for teen filmmakers, books on filmmaking for teens, and magazines and e-zines.

325 Nisonger, Thomas E. *Evaluation of Library Collections, Access and Electronic Resources: A Literature Guide and Annotated Bibliography.* Library and Information Science Series. Westport, CT: Libraries Unlimited, 2003. ISBN: 978-1-56308-852-0.

This volume covers requirements for collection-centered, client-centered, and combination approaches to collection evaluation. Nisonger covers print and electronic materials for performance measures, standards, serials evaluations, usage, citation analysis, and ranking journals. All types of libraries are included in the evaluation process: public, academic, and special.

326 Nixon, Judith M., Robert S. Freeman, and Suzanne M. Ward, eds. *Patron-Driven Acquisitions: Current Success and Future Directions.* New York: Routledge, 2011. ISBN: 978-0-41561-870-0.

Originally published as a special issue of *Collection Management*, this slender book will appeal to librarians who are concerned that patrons never check out some books selected and purchased. Contributors use case studies from Purdue University, the University of Nebraska–Lincoln, and the University of Illinois to look at printed book as well as e-book demand and subsequent circulation. The conclusion is that it is vital to both collection development and budgets that patrons become involved in material selections.

327 Van Orden, Phyllis. *Selecting Books for the Elementary School Library Media Center: A Complete Guide.* New York: Neal-Schuman, 2000. ISBN: 978-1-55570-368-4.

This is a comprehensive technical guide to elementary school library literature and picture book collections. The first four chapters cover the selection process, general guidelines, criteria and criteria application, purchasing, and process review. Van Orden provides selection measurements for picture books, fiction, genre fiction, folk literature, rhymes and poetry, information books, and reference books. Each chapter includes a list of titles cited, annotated recommended resources, and suggested authors and illustrators. A glossary and index complete the book.

328 Van Orden, Phyllis, and Patricia Pawelak-Kort. *Library Service to Children: A Guide to the History, Planning, Policy, and Research Literature.* Annotated ed. Lanham, MD: Scarecrow Press, 2005. ISBN: 978-0-81085-169-6.

This annotated bibliography includes annual reports, bibliographies, biographies, journal articles, books, brochures, conference proceedings, directories, dissertations, documents, guidelines, master theses, policy documents, position papers, reports, standards, and electronic sources related to public library services to children and children's librarianship. This volume contains 428 works written or published between 1876 and 2003.

329 Van Orden, Phyllis J., and Sunny Strong. *Children's Books: A Practical Guide to Selection.* New York: Neal-Schuman, 2007. ISBN: 978-1-55570-584-8.

Aimed at those new to juvenile collection management, the key word here is "practical," although more experienced hands will no doubt find useful material here. This well-illustrated guide covers selection criteria/tools, genres, diversity, and bang for the buck—that is, worth versus price. Each chapter has a conclusion, references, and recommended materials. Appendixes and indexes cover terms, resources, organizations, and selected policies referred to within the book.

330 Wadham, Tim. *Libros Esenciales: Building, Marketing, and Programming a Core Collection of Spanish Language Children's Materials.* New York: Neal-Schuman, 2006. ISBN: 978-1-55570-575-6.

This is a helpful guide to books, materials, and programs that serve Latino children. Ranging from statistical information on Hispanic populations to an extensive bibliography organized by genre, this book contains planning, marketing, and practical steps to delivering bilingual programs and creating a multicultural collection.

331 Wilkinson, Frances C., and Linda Lewis. *The Complete Guide to Acquisitions Management.* Library and Information Science Series. Westport, CT: Libraries Unlimited, 2003. ISBN: 978-1-56308-890-2.

The authors look at the organization of acquisitions departments, library record systems, the publishing industry, and vendor selection and evaluation. The focus is on acquiring books, media, serials, electronic resources, and out-of-print/antiquarian materials, and there are additional sections on gift and exchange programs, bindery operations, outsourcing acquisitions, and professional ethics. An appendix with web and print resources, comprehensive glossary, and index complete this textbook on acquisition management.

ADDITIONAL RESOURCES

332 Bailey, Steve. *Managing the Crowd: Rethinking Records Management for the Web 2.0 World.* London: Facet, 2008. ISBN: 978-1-85604-641-1.

333 Burgett, James, John M. Haar, and Linda L. Phillips. *Collaborative Collection Development: A Practical Guide for Your Library.* Chicago: American Library Association, 2004. ISBN: 978-0-83890-881-5.

334 Chapman, Liz. *Managing Acquisitions in Library and Information Services.* Rev. ed. London: Facet, 2004. ISBN: 978-1-85604-496-7.

335 Cianciolo, Patricia J. *Informational Picture Books for Children.* Chicago: American Library Association, 2000. ISBN: 978-0-83890-774-0.

336 Clayton, Peter, and G. E. Gorman. *Managing Information Resources in Libraries: Collection Management in Theory and Practice.* London: Facet, 2006. ISBN: 978-1-85604-581-0.

337 Cullingord, Alison. *Special Collections Handbook.* London: Facet, 2011. ISBN: 978-1-85604-757-9.

338 Doll, Carol A., and Pamela Petrick Barron. *Managing and Analyzing Your Collection: A Practical Guide for Small Libraries and School Media Centers.* Chicago: American Library Association, 2002. ISBN: 978-0-83890-821-1.

339 Fieldhouse, Maggie, and Audrey Marshall. *Collection Development in the Digital Age.* London: Facet, 2011. ISBN: 978-1-85604-746-3.

340 Fling, Robert Michael. *Guide to Developing a Library Music Collection.* Chicago: American Library Association, 2008. ISBN: 978-0-83898-482-6.

341 Goldsmith, Francisca. *Graphic Novels Now: Building, Managing, and Marketing a Dynamic Collection.* Chicago: American Library Association, 2005. ISBN: 978-0-83890-904-1.

342 Gregory, Vicki L. *Collection Development and Management for 21st Century Library Collections: An Introduction.* New York: Neal-Schuman, 2011. ISBN: 978-1-55570-651-7.

343 Holden, Jesse. *Acquisitions in the New Information Universe: Core Competencies and Ethical Practices.* London: Facet, ISBN: 978-1-85604-739-5; Chicago: American Library Association, ISBN: 978-1-55570-696-8. 2010.

344 Hughes-Hassell, Sandra, and Jacqueline C. Mancall. *Collection Management for Youth: Responding to the Needs of Learners.* Chicago: American Library Association, 2005. ISBN: 978-0-83890-894-5.

345 Johnson, Peggy. *Fundamentals of Collection Development and Management.* 2nd ed. Chicago: American Library Association, 2009. ISBN: 978-0-83890-972-0.

346 Kaplan, Richard, ed. *Building and Maintaining E-book Collections: A How-to-Do-It Manual.* London: Facet, ISBN: 978-1-85604-837-8; Chicago: American Library Association, ISBN: 978-1-55570-776-7. 2012.

347 Laskowski, Mary S. *Guide to Video Acquisitions in Libraries: Issues and Best Practices.* ALCTS Acquisitions Guides. Chicago: American Library Association, 2011. ISBN: 978-0-83898-575-5.

348 Lee, Stuart D., and Frances Boyle. *Building an Electronic Resource Collection: A Practical Guide.* 2nd ed. London: Facet, 2004. ISBN: 978-1-85604-531-5.

349 Mason-Robinson, Sally. *Developing and Managing Video Collections: A How-to-Do-It Manual for Librarians.* How-To-Do-It Manuals for Libraries 68. New York: Neal-Schuman, 1996. ISBN: 978-1-55570-230-4.

350 Nichols, C. Allen, ed. *Thinking outside the Book: Alternatives for Today's Teen Library Collections.* Libraries Unlimited Professional Guides for Young Adult Librarians Series. Westport, CT: Libraries Unlimited, 2004. ISBN: 978-1-59158-059-1.

351 Patrick, Gay D. *Building the Reference Collection: A How-to-Do-It Manual for School and Public Librarians.* How-to-Do-It Manuals for School and Public Librarians 7. New York: Neal-Schuman, 1992. ISBN: 978-1-55570-105-5.

352 Polanka, Sue, ed. *No Shelf Required Guide to E-book Purchasing.* Chicago: American Library Association, 2012. ISBN: 978-0-83895-836-0.

353 Polanka, Sue, ed. *No Shelf Required 2: Use and Management of Electronic Books.* Chicago: American Library Association, 2012. ISBN: 978-0-83891-145-7.

354 Sargent, Sy. *Managing the How-To Collection and Learner's Advisory Services: A How-to-Do-It Manual for Librarians.* How-To-Do-It Manuals for Libraries 32. New York: Neal-Schuman, 1993. ISBN: 978-1-55570-143-7.

355 Stein, Barbara, Gary Treadway, and Lauralee Ingram. *Finding and Using Educational Videos: A How-to-Do-It Manual.* How-To-Do-It Manuals for Libraries 84. New York: Neal-Schuman, 1998. ISBN: 978-1-5557-0278-6.

356 Welch, Rollie James. *A Core Collection for Young Adults.* 2nd ed. Teens @ The Library Series. New York: Neal-Schuman, 2010. ISBN: 978-1-55570-692-0.

📓 PERIODICALS

357 *Booklist.* Chicago: American Library Association. Frequency: Twenty-two issues per year. ISSN: 0006-7385. URL: www.booklistonline.com.

The premier collection development tool for librarians for over a century, *Booklist* is just that, a list of books along with reviews thereof. It is widely regarded as one of the most reliable sources for unbiased evaluations of reading material, which would explain its longevity. Each issue contains a supplement, *Reference Books Bulletin*, produced by a separate editorial board, which contains reviews of reference material in any format. Subscribers have access to *Booklist Online*, which comprises both a website and a database of material from the print issues. Also included in a subscription is *Book Links* magazine, a quarterly publication intended for teachers, youth librarians, and school library media specialists that contains articles on how to incorporate books in the classroom and on reading advocacy material.

358 *Collection Building.* Westport, CT: Emerald Group. Frequency: Quarterly. ISSN: 0160-4953. URL: www.emeraldinsight.com/products/journals/journals.htm?id=cb.

This magazine focuses on collection development for librarians in academic, public, and specialty libraries. Topics include resource development, technology, resource sharing, and expanding and managing collections; there are bibliographic essays as well. Articles are subject to review by at least two reviewers.

359 *Collection Management.* Philadelphia: Routledge. Frequency: Four issues per year. ISSN: 0146-2679 (print), 1545-2549 (online). URL: www.tandf.co.uk/journals/WCOL.

This journal presents practical, research-based information about building, administering, preserving, assessing, and organizing library collections. *Collection Management* is targeted toward librarians and information specialists working in access services, interlibrary loan, and special collections; library administrators and educators; and archivists, curators, bibliographers, academics, students, and publishers who work with libraries. All articles undergo an initial editorial screening, followed by anonymous double-blind review. Core topics regularly examined include digital collection management, meeting staffing and training challenges, special collections and archive management, data management, risk and financial issues and strategies, consortia and cooperative collections, assessment tools and methods, decision making in the face of access versus ownership, collection development focused on international and area studies, and the latest collection of management tools.

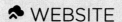 WEBSITE

360 **National Information Standards Organization.** *A Framework of Guidance for Building Good Digital Collections: A NISO Recommended Practice.* 3rd ed. Baltimore, MD: National Information Standards Organization, 2007. URL: www.imls.gov/assets/1/AssetManager/framework3.pdf. ISBN: 978-1-880124-74-1.

NISO developed a framework for building good digital collections to identify best practices and current standards in four areas: collections, digital objects, metadata, and digital projects. Each principle or initiative has a goal, description, general guidelines, and references.

EDUCATION AND PROFESSIONAL DEVELOPMENT

 BOOKS

361 Allan, Barbara. *Developing Library Staff through Work-Based Learning.* Edited by Barbara Moran. Lanham, MD: Scarecrow Press, 2003. ISSN: 978-0-81084-748-4.

Years ago, we had on-the-job training, or OJT for short. It is still with us, but now it is called work-based learning (WBL). Whichever you call it, the benefits are the same: it is a faster and cheaper way to get staff up to speed on the latest and greatest technology, procedures, and so on. Chapters 1 through 5 lay out the rationale for WBL and how to go about implementing such a program at one's facility. The bulk of the volume, however, is an alphabetical listing and discussion of 101 activities that promote, enhance, or enable WBL. A few examples include action learning, benchmarking, computer-based training, delegation, and writing. This book was originally published in 1999 in the United Kingdom under a slightly different title.

362 Allan, Barbara. *Training Skills for Library Staff.* Edited by Barbara Moran. Lanham, MD: Scarecrow Press, 2003. ISBN: 978-0-81084-747-7.

Training, evidently, has come a long way from the workshop with the proverbial "sage on the stage" droning on interminably. According to its introduction, "This book brings together ideas, tools, and techniques from fields such as accelerated learning, neurolinguistic programming (NLP) and brain research. These have been distilled and presented in terms of their relevance to training events in libraries" (p. 3). Part 1, "Background to Training," covers the role and skills of the trainer. Part 2, "The Training Process," contains such chapter titles as "Linking Training with the Needs of the Library," "Designing Effective Training Programs," and "Training Methods." Part 3, "Professional Development for Library Trainers," contains the single chapter "Continuing Professional Development." This book was originally published in the United Kingdom under a slightly different title.

363   Barron, Daniel D., ed. *Benchmarks in Distance Education: The LIS Experience.* Library and Information Science Series. Westport, CT: Libraries Unlimited, 2003. ISBN: 978-1-56308-722-6.

This volume documents the history and growth of distance education, in which the students and teacher are physically separated by distance, and how this has played out for LIS professionals. Twenty-eight case studies from higher education institutions provide experiences, successes, problems, solutions, and benchmarks for LIS curriculum and services.

364   Grealy, Deborah S., and Sylvia D. Hall-Ellis. *From Research to Practice: The Scholarship of Teaching and Learning in LIS Education.* Westport, CT: Libraries Unlimited, 2009. ISBN: 978-1-59158-631-9.

The authors apply seven theories of learning to LIS education. Originally developed by James R. and Adelaide B. Davis in their book *Effective Training Strategies: A Comprehensive Guide to Maximizing Learning in Organizations* (1998, Berrett-Koehler, ISBN: 978-1576750377), the teaching strategies are behavioral, cognitive, inquiry, mental models, group dynamics, virtual reality, and holistic. "Each strategy is deemed most effective in developing exercises to instruct, reinforce, and assess specific types of learning," according to the book's introduction (p. x).

365   Haycock, Ken, and Brooke E. Sheldon, eds. *The Portable MLIS: Insights from the Experts.* Westport, CT: Libraries Unlimited, 2008. ISBN: 978-1-59158-547-3 (print), 978-1-59158-836-8 (e-book).

What does a librarian do? The answer appears by way of the subtitle: specialists in a variety of fields give introductions to their areas of expertise. Separated into three parts— "Foundations, Values, and Context," "Functions and Competencies," and "Moving beyond Boundaries"— this book encompasses knowledge, skills, and abilities for core librarian competencies in areas including management, marketing, organization, information retrieval, reference service, research, reader's advisories, and learning and evaluation. The appendixes include core values of librarianship, a code of ethics, library bill of rights, freedom to read statement, students' bill of information rights, libraries as a cornerstone of the community, sample policies, retention of library usage records, position statements, competencies for information professionals, and professional associations.

366   Lawson, Steve. *Library Camps and Unconferences.* Tech Set Series 8. New York: Neal-Schuman, 2010. ISBN: 978-1-55570-712-5.

This is Lawson's step-by-step process for organizing informal gatherings of librarians to exchange ideas, tips, and knowledge as an alternative to official conferences. Topics include setting a date, location, technological components, planning events, gathering equipment, setting a budget, invitees, activity-day management, troubleshooting, and evaluation.

367   Massis, Bruce E. *The Challenges to Library Learning: Solutions for Librarians.* Routledge Studies in Library and Information Science Series 4. London: Routledge, 2008. ISBN: 978-0-78903-141-9.

Massis confronts problems managers face, including staff shortages, depleted or eliminated training budgets, greater workload, and rapidly changing technology. He presents a plan to inspire librarians to become self-motivated and set goal-orientated initiatives, with an individualized approach to training and professional development. Additional materials include "Design and Implementation of a Training Program for Library Staff," notes, selected bibliography, and index.

368   Massis, Bruce E., and Ruth C. Carter. *The Practical Library Trainer.* New York: Haworth Information Press, 2004. ISBN: 978-0-78902-267-7.

With the ever-quickening pace of change in the information environment, training is more important than ever. Massis quite rightly states that training for library staff "is a serious issue encompassing everything in the library from providing quality customer service to reporting, to recruitment and retention of staff." He goes on to point out that the purpose of the book is to examine "the organization and implementation of the library staff training program and [suggests] the means by which its success and market value may be determined" (p. 2). Ten chapters walk the reader from preparing the library for a staff training program through return on investment, evaluation of the training program, and recruitment and retention of staff, then concludes with a case study of how this program was successfully carried out at the Southeast Florida Library Information Network. Five appendixes present a needs assessment survey, forms, and templates, and an ample bibliography of training materials rounds out this volume.

369 Rehman, Sajjad ur. *Preparing the Information Professional: An Agenda for the Future.* Contributions in Librarianship and Information Science 93. Westport, CT: Greenwood Press, 2000. ISBN: 978-0-31330-673-0.

What is the best way to teach someone how to become a librarian? Though there are lots of ideas, there seems to be little agreement. As Rehman states in his preface, "We find divergent models of information education emerging in different parts of the world. Yet there is more uncertainty and confusion about the requirements for the preparation of the future information professional" (p. ix). The guts of this slim volume concern the identification of specific competencies needed in various institutional settings, such as the public library or academic library. The author also looks at how library science is taught in selected nations around the world. Analysis and recommendations are put forth in chapter 9, "Preparation of Information Professionals: Strategies and Directions."

370 Roy, Loriene, Kelly Jensen, and Alex H. Meyers, eds. *Service Learning: Linking Library Education and Practice.* Chicago: American Library Association, 2009. ISBN: 978-0-83890-981-2.

Contributors from throughout the profession examine how service and internships can enhance LIS students' learning experiences and better prepare them for entry into the profession. Topics include service learning from administrative, faculty, and student perspectives; practicums; experiential learning; virtual worlds; field-based experiences; and community research. A bibliography, author biographies, and index are included.

371 Smallwood, Carol, and Rebecca Tolley-Strokes, eds. *Mentoring in Librarianship: Essays on Working with Adults and Students to Further the Profession.* Jefferson, NC: McFarland, 2012. ISBN: 978-0-78646-378-7.

In this volume divided into four parts, contributors chat about philosophical questions and practical application, mentoring students, and mentoring librarians. Topics include creating mentoring programs, developing criteria and goals, seizing mentoring moments, mentoring across disciplines, mentoring at a distance, and job search mentoring. A list of contributors and index are included.

372 Swigger, Boyd Keith. *The MLS Project: An Assessment after Sixty Years.* Lanham, MD: Scarecrow Press, 2010. ISBN: 978-0-81087-703-0.

There was a time when all it took to become a librarian was a bachelor's degree. That changed in 1951, when accreditation standards were revised upward by the American Library Association Council, which decreed that a master's degree was the new entry-level credential. As the author explains in chapter 1, "An Overview of the MLS Project," "The primary purpose of this book is to recount the reasons ALA enacted the change and to consider its consequences by reviewing relevant data" (p. 3). He goes on to state that a secondary goal is to get a handle on how librarians themselves feel about this situation. For readers who would like to "cut to the chase," there is no need to keep you in suspense any longer: "Data collected from a variety of sources show that the MLS project has had limited success. Changing the level of the accredited degree did not produce anticipated changes in the substance of library education, nor did it produce the anticipated rewards for graduates of library schools" (p. 3). But then again, anyone who has ever worked as a librarian these past six decades already knows this from personal experience.

373 Wheeler, Maurice B., ed. *Unfinished Business: Race, Equity, and Diversity in Library and Information Science Education.* Lanham, MD: Scarecrow Press, 2005. ISBN: 978-0-81085-045-3.

In this examination of segregation, diversity, and other ethnic issues as they relate to library education, thirteen chapters carry such representative titles as "Evolving Issues: Racism, Affirmative Action, and Diversity" and "Minority Student Recruitment in LIS Education: New Profiles for Success."

374 Wood, Aileen. *A Comprehensive Library Staff Training Programme in the Information Age.* Information Professional Series. Oxford: Chandos, 2007. ISBN: 978-1-84334-118-5.

Comprehensive, indeed. Ten chapters plus a conclusion run the gamut from "LIS Competencies and Skills" and "Training Needs Analysis" through learning styles, developing courses, training techniques, and formal education. Leaving no stone unturned, Wood contacted her colleagues around the world "to see what type of material should be included in such a book, and it has consequently been developed from material used to train library and information professionals, such as workshops, courses, seminars and frameworks" (p. xiii). Seven appendixes contain material on professional ethics, examples of forms (staff appraisal, etc.), and passages from the handbook of the Chartered Institute of Library and Information Professionals (Chandos is a British publisher).

ADDITIONAL RESOURCES

375 Agosto, Denise E., and Sandra Hughes-Hassell, eds. *Urban Teens in the Library: Research and Practice.* Chicago: American Library Association, 2010. ISBN: 978-0-83891-015-3.

376 Avery, Elizabeth Fuseler, Terry Dahlin, and Deborah A. Carver, eds. *Staff Development: A Practical Guide.* 3rd ed. Chicago: American Library Association, 2001. ISBN: 978-0-83890-801-3.

377 Bluh, Pamela, and Cindy Hepfer, eds. *Risk and Entrepreneurship in Libraries: Seizing Opportunities for Change.* ALCTS Papers on Library Technical Services and Collections. Chicago: Association for Library Collections and Technical Services, American Library Association, 2009. ISBN: 978-0-83898-516-8.

378 Eynon, Andrew. *CILIP Guidelines for Colleges: Recommendations for Learning Resources.* London: Facet, 2005. ISBN: 978-1-85604-551-3.

379 Reed, Lori, and Paul Signorelli. *Workplace Learning and Leadership: A Handbook for Library and Nonprofit Trainers.* Chicago: American Library Association, 2011. ISBN: 978-0-83891-082-5.

380 Trotta, Marcia. *Staff Development on a Shoestring: A How-to-Do-It Manual for Librarians.* How-To-Do-It Manuals for Libraries 175. New York: Neal-Schuman, 2011. ISBN: 978-1-55570-730-9.

PERIODICAL

381 *Journal of Education for Library and Information Science (JELIS).* Association for Library and Information Science. Frequency: Quarterly. ISSN: 0748-5786. URL: http://jelis.org/about/.

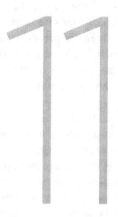
EPISTEMOLOGY AND PHILOSOPHY

ROPERLY, EPISTEMOLOGY, THAT IS, THE STUDY OF THE NATURE OF KNOWLEDGE, falls under the heading of philosophy. However, it seems to me that, if we can truthfully call ourselves "information professionals," then we should know what information is and how it differs from, say, beliefs. Epistemology tries to answer such questions as these: How do we know what we know? What are the differences between data, information, knowledge, and wisdom? How do we distinguish between truth and falsehood? Basically, this is the big picture of the forest, as opposed to the individual trees, such as the factual answers to reference questions we deal with on a daily basis. To put it in other words, being a librarian is more than just what we do. It is also about why we do these things and how we do them. To be truly professional, in my opinion, means to think about these underlying issues, or at least to be aware of them. The resources listed in this chapter help us to come to a deeper understanding of what motivates us and makes us who we are.

◆ BOOKS

382 Audi, Robert. *Epistemology: A Contemporary Introduction to the Theory of Knowledge.* 3rd ed. New York: Routledge, 2011. ISBN: 978-0-415-87922-4.

Long used as a college textbook for philosophy majors, this may also be used by the general reader to get a grasp on this topic. The writing is clear and examples are concrete. One of the more comprehensive surveys of epistemology on the market today, this edition, which has benefited from past comments by readers, covers basic concepts, major theories, and new research. It is an overall excellent introduction to the theory and nature of knowledge.

383 Budd, John M. *Knowledge and Knowing in Library and Information Science: A Philosophical Framework.* Lanham, MD: Scarecrow Press, 2001. ISBN: 0-8108-4041-3.

The topic at hand is the "intellectual heritage" of librarianship, the evolution of thought that has shaped the profession. The author seeks to trace this evolution from the beginnings of modern science in the seventeenth century to the present. There are practical reasons for being aware of what has gone on in the past, Budd asserts: "To be effective, practitioners should be reflexive, should examine and question what we do, how we do it, and why we make the choices we do" (p. 3). This text may be problematic for some, for there is a fairly dense discussion of the ideas of philosophers such as David Hume, John Locke, and Immanuel Kant. Some may be put off by unfamiliar terminology, such as *hermeneutical phenomenology,* but all this is a means to an end, namely, a better understanding of how and why we librarians do what we do to, ultimately, reach our full potential as gatekeepers to the worlds of knowledge and literature.

384   Budd, John M. *Self-Examination: The Present and Future of Librarianship.* Beta Phi Mu Monograph Series. Westport, CT: Libraries Unlimited, 2008. ISBN: 978-1-59158-591-6.

Basically, this is a volume of librarian soul-searching. As the blurb on the back cover asks, "What makes us librarians? What is it we do that is indispensable?" Good questions, even if there are no definite answers. For Budd, "The purpose of this book is to provide opportunities and suggestions for reflection. Within these pages there will be observations, statements by others, opinions, and some serious examination (and certainly not just by me) of librarianship—what it is and what it can be" (p. vii). Heavy stuff, to be sure, but as Socrates famously said, the unexamined life is not worth living. Knowing why we do what we do can make us all better librarians.

ETHICS

BOOKS

385 Besnoy, Amy, ed. *Ethics and Integrity in Libraries.* New York: Routledge, 2009. ISBN: 978-0-78903-756-5.

Staff face daily ethical and integrity challenges when providing services and managing library collections. Contributors highlight dilemmas caused by implementing the USA PATRIOT Act, fair use practices, plagiarism, social networking, licensing, and academic standards. The book concludes with a look at ethical education needs for future librarians. This material was published in the *Journal of Library Administration.*

386 Gorman, Michael. *Our Enduring Values: Librarianship in the 21st Century.* Chicago: American Library Association, 2000. ISBN: 978-0-83890-785-6.

The author, a former ALA president, strongly believes that librarians are stewards and servants carrying out a historic mission to provide information to the masses. This book focuses extensively on eight core values: stewardship, service, intellectual freedom, rationalism, literacy, and learning, equity of access to recorded knowledge and information, privacy, and democracy. The chapters on intellectual freedom and privacy are interesting discussions of how easy it is to cross the line into censorship, who owns what, and the use and abuse of personal information. Basically, this is one man's statement of what librarians stand for and what defines the profession.

387 Preer, Jean L. *Library Ethics.* Westport, CT: Libraries Unlimited, 2008. ISBN: 978-1-59158-636-4 (print), 978-1-59884-854-0 (e-book).

Ethical standards have evolved along with the profession of librarianship. Preer examines ethical choices in service and access, conflicts of interest both philosophical and financial, confidentiality, and professionalism. Besides a library ethics timeline, appendixes contain the ALA Code of Ethics for Librarians, ALA Statement on Professional Ethics, ALA Library Bill of Rights,

American Association of Law Libraries Ethical Principles, Association of College and Research Libraries Code of Ethics for Special Collections Librarians, Medical Library Association Code of Ethics for Health Science Librarianship, Society of American Archivists Code of Ethics for Archivists, and A Librarian's 2.0 Manifesto.

📑 PERIODICALS

388 *Ethics and Behavior.* London: Taylor and Francis. Frequency: Six issues per year. ISSN: 1050-8422 (print), 1532-7019 (online). URL: www .tandf.co.uk/journals/titles/10508422.asp.

389 *Journal of Information Ethics.* Jefferson, NC: McFarland. Frequency: Twice per year. ISSN: 1061-9321. URL: www.mcfarlandbooks .com/?page_id=926.

13

FUNDING AND FINANCE

 BOOKS

390 Gerding, Stephanie K., and Pamela H. MacKellar. *Grants for Libraries: A How-to-Do-It Manual.* How-To-Do-It Manuals for Libraries 144. New York: Neal-Schuman, 2006. ISBN: 978-1-55570-535-0.

The authors of this in-depth planning handbook want to improve the odds of a library receiving a grant. The walkthrough of the grant cycle will help librarians identify goals and objectives, define desired outcomes, select projects, set budgets, write proposals, and evaluate outcomes. A Windows-compatible CD-ROM with sample grant success stories and a toolkit provide many additional resources.

391 Hall-Ellis, Sylvia D., Stacey L. Bowers, Christopher Hudson, Claire Williamson, and Joanne Patrick. *Librarian's Handbook for Seeking, Writing, and Managing Grants.* Westport, CT: Libraries Unlimited, 2011. ISBN: 978-1-59158-870-2 (print), 978-1-59158-872-6 (e-book).

Part 1, on grant development, covers all aspects of applying for a grant, including proposal development, project design, project narrative, project personnel, project evaluation, budget development, and grant appendixes. Part 2 walks through post-submission steps, including resubmissions, implementation, project management, accountability, and project closeout. A glossary of grant terms, bibliography, and index are included.

392 Herring, Mark Youngblood. *Raising Funds with Friends Groups: A How-to-Do-It Manual for Librarians.* How-To-Do-It Manuals for Libraries 128. New York: Neal-Schuman, 2004. ISBN: 978-1-55570-484-1.

Herring covers all the basics for putting together a Friends group: establishing an executive board, marketing the group, developing partnerships, hosting events, and maintaining membership. Topics and illustrations cover using e-mail, blogs, electronic discussion boards, finances, and a Friend's group starter kit. Do's and don'ts and real-life examples and activities highlight many points in the chapters.

393 Kepler, Ann, ed. *The ALA Big Book of Library Grant Money.* 8th ed. Chicago: American Library Association, 2011. ISBN: 978-0-83891-058-0.

This completely updated eighth edition, including hundreds of new entries with grant criteria and application procedures, continues to be the gold standard of books on grants for libraries. The user's guide, nonprofit recipient categories and organization types, and four indexes—grantors by total grant value, grantors by state, named grants, and professional library organization grantors—provide easy access to grant opportunities.

394 Landau, Herbert B. *Winning Library Grants: A Game Plan.* Chicago: American Library Association, 2011. ISBN: 978-0-83891-047-4.

Besides providing basic information and steps for finding and applying for grants, Landau offers several tips and tactics regarding pre- and post-submission marketing. Topics covered include initiating contact with grantors, obtaining solicited competitive grant application packages, pre-proposal research and fact finding, and project planning. Several chapters are devoted to proposal management, writing style, writing a grant proposal section by section, assembly, editing, review, and submission. The appendixes contain sample grantor prospect worksheets and a sample grant final report to a foundation. Resources on writing library grants and an index are included.

395 MacKellar, Pamela H., and Stephanie K. Gerding. *Winning Grants: A How-to-Do-It Manual for Librarians with Multimedia Tutorials and Grant Development Tools.* How-To-Do-It Manuals for Libraries 173. New York: Neal-Schuman, 2010. ISBN: 978-1-55570-700-2.

The authors share all of the steps necessary to create a winning library grant application in part 1, "The Grant Process Cycle." In part 2 they describe several grant-winning processes and tips. The Winning Grant Multimedia Toolkit and accompanying multimedia DVD in part 3 provide reusable checklists, worksheets, templates, and ten instructional videos that cover each step of the grant process cycle.

FYI

FINDING GRANTS

Having a great idea for a new library program is wonderful—finding the funds to get it off the ground, well, not so much. Here is a tool to make locating those elusive dollars a bit easier:

McDonough, Beverley, and Daniel Bazikian, eds. *Annual Register of Grant Support 2012: A Directory of Funding Sources.* 44th ed. Medford, NJ: Information Today, 2011. ISBN: 978-1-57387-417-5.

This annual edition contains the description, type, purpose, duration of grant, amount of funding available, eligibility requirements, and contact information for 2,936 grant support programs in a variety of fields, including librarianship.

ADDITIONAL RESOURCES

396 Barber, Peggy, and Linda D. Crowe. *Getting Your Grant: A How-to-Do-It Manual for Librarians.* How-To-Do-It Manuals for Libraries 28. New York: Neal-Schuman, 1993. ISBN: 978-1-55570-038-6.

397 Clark, Larra, and Denise Davis. *The State of Funding for Library Technology in Today's Economy.* Chicago: American Library Association, 2008. ISBN: 978-0-83895-799-8.

398 Dewey, Barbara I., ed. *Raising Money for Academic and Research Libraries: A How-to-Do-It Manual for Librarians.* How-To-Do-It Manuals for Libraries 18. New York: Neal-Schuman, 1991. ISBN: 978-1-55570-082-9.

399   Ditzler, Pat, and JoAnn Dumas. *A Book Sale How-To Guide: More Money, Less Stress.* Chicago, American Library Association, 2012. ISBN: 978-0-83891-074-0.

400   Dolnick, Sandy. *The Essential Friends of Libraries: Fast Facts, Forms, and Tips (with CD).* Chicago: American Library Association, 2005. ISBN: 978-0-83890-856-3.

401   Harriman, Joy H. P. *Creating Your Library's Business Plan: A How-to-Do-It Manual with Samples on CD-ROM.* London: Facet, ISBN: 978-1-85604-656-5; Chicago: American Library Association, ISBN: 978-1-55570-634-0. 2008.

402   Herring, Mark Youngblood. *Organizing Friends Groups: A How-to-Do-It Manual for Librarians.* How-To-Do-It Manuals for Libraries 29. New York: Neal-Schuman, 1993. ISBN: 978-1-55570-062-1.

403   MacKellar, Pamela H. *Writing Successful Technology Grant Proposals: A LITA Guide.* New York: Neal-Schuman, 2011. ISBN: 978-1-55570-763-7.

404   Pedolsky, Andrea, and Betty J. Turock. *Creating a Financial Plan: A How-to-Do-It Manual for Librarians.* How-To-Do-It Manuals for Libraries 22. New York: Neal-Schuman, 1992. ISBN: 978-1-55570-039-3.

405   Smith, Amy Sherman, and Matthew D. Lehrer. *Legacies for Libraries: A Practical Guide to Planned Giving.* Chicago: American Library Association, 2000. ISBN: 978-0-83890-784-9.

406   Smith, G. Stevenson. *Cost Control for Nonprofits in Crisis.* Chicago: American Library Association, 2011. ISBN: 978-0-83891-098-6.

407   Smith, G. Stevenson. *Managerial Accounting for Libraries and Other Not-for-Profit Organizations.* Chicago: American Library Association, 2002. ISBN: 978-0-83890-568-5.

408   Snyder, Herbert. *Small Change, Big Problems: Detecting and Preventing Financial Misconduct in Your Library.* Chicago: American Library Association, 2006. ISBN: 978-0-83890-921-8.

409   Steele, Victoria, and Stephen D. Elder. *Becoming a Fundraiser: The Principles and Practice of Library Development.* 2nd ed. Chicago: American Library Association, 2000. ISBN: 978-0-83890-783-2.

410   Swan, James, and Bill Katz. *Fundraising for the Small Public Library: A How-to-Do-It Manual for Librarians.* How-To-Do-It Manuals for Libraries 8. New York: Neal-Schuman, 1991. ISBN: 978-1-55570-077-5.

411   Talan, Carole. *Founding and Funding Family Literacy Programs: A How-to-Do-It Manual for Librarians.* How-To-Do-It Manuals for Libraries 92. New York: Neal-Schuman, 1999. ISBN: 978-1-55570-210-6.

📄 PERIODICAL

412   *Bottom Line: Managing Library Finance.* Westport, CT: Emerald Group. Frequency: Four times per year. ISSN: 0888-045X. URL: www.emeraldinsight.com/journals.htm?issn=0888-045X.

Written by library finance professionals, this magazine offers hints and tips for managing library finances. Topics include fund-raising; economics affecting libraries; brief notes about grants, taxes, and levies; Internet connections; business trends; and outsourcing library functions.

☁ WEBSITES

413   Heritage Preservation, National Institute for Conservation. *Capitalize on Collections Care.* Washington, DC: Heritage Preservation, 2009. URL: www.heritagepreservation.org/PDFS/COClo.pdf.

Published in partnership with the Institute of Museum and Library Services, this report outlines fund-raising fundamentals and presents strategies and case studies geared toward generating new contributions, increased support, and new audiences for collection care services.

414   Institute of Museum and Library Services. *Guide to Programs and Opportunities.* Washington, DC: Institute of Museum and Library Services, 2011. URL: www.imls.gov/assets/1/AssetManager/2012_Guide.pdf.

This guide lists concise overviews of the Institute's FY2011–2012 programs and resources available for museums and libraries. Staff contact information for each grant program and helpful tips and tools are listed to help users develop competitive grant applications. Application deadlines and announcements along with a brief overview about the Institute, staff directory, and list of board members are included. The guide is broken down by sections: "Information for Applicants," "Opportunities for Both Libraries and Museums," "Library Opportunities," "Museum Opportunities," "LSTA Grants to States Program," "National Initiatives," and "Planning, Research, and Evaluation."

415   Manjarrez, Carlos A., Lesley Langa, and Kim Miller. *A Catalyst for Change: LSTA Grants to State Program Activities and the Transformation of Library Services to the Public.* (IMLS-2009-RES-01). Washington, DC: Institute of Museum and Library Services, 2009. URL: www.imls.gov/assets/1/AssetManager/CatalystForChange1.pdf.

This report examines the Library Services and Technology Act, how the Grants to State Program works, the inclusion of local context in state plans, implementing state plans, strategies, an overview of state allotments, expenditures and programs, and Grants to State library administrative agencies program data. The human capital development strategies cover education support, lifelong learning, and literacy and reading development. Library service expansion and access strategies cover reference/information services and special services/outreach services. Information infrastructure strategies cover technology infrastructure, enhanced library service infrastructure, and library human resource development.

14

HUMOR

BOOKS

416 Barnes, Bill, and Gene Ambaum. *Reader's Advisory: An Unshelved Collection.* Seattle: Overdue Media, 2009. ISBN: 978-0-97403-536-9.

Unlike the bar in the TV sitcom *Cheers*, everyone here may not know your name; nevertheless, Dewey, his wacky patrons, and dysfunctional coworkers will make you feel right at home at the Mallville Public Library. Something of a paradox? Just wait till you read about "Schrodinger's Catalog."

417 Barnes, Bill, and Gene Ambaum.
Unshelved. Seattle: Overdue Media, 2004. ISBN: 978-0-97403-530-7.

Unshelved is a collection of library-themed daily cartoons. This comic strip, also published as a web comic at www.unshelved.com, centers around teen services librarian Dewey, the zany characters he interacts with (a nudist lawyer, anyone?), and the wacky situations that invariably ensue at the Mallville Public Library.

418 Barnes, Bill, and Gene Ambaum. *Unshelved Volume 2: What Would Dewey Do?* Seattle: Overdue Media, 2004. ISBN: 978-0-97403-531-4

Dewey and his fellow librarians encounter psychic fans, discover identify theft, deal with crashed computer hard drives, and are vexed by nosy FBI agents in this daily comic strip set in a public library. It doesn't help that devious teen patron Merv is once again up to his old tricks.

419 Barnes, Bill, and Gene Ambaum. *Unshelved Volume 3: Library Mascot Cage Match.* Seattle: Overdue Media, 2005. ISBN: 978-0-97403-532-1.

Mallville Public Library fights over a copyright issue in the "Library Mascot Cage Match"; "Empire County Strikes Back" is an inspiring tale of a small, underfunded library's fight against an evil corporate bookmobile.

420 Barnes, Bill, and Gene Ambaum. *Unshelved Volume 4: Book Club.* Seattle: Overdue Media, 2006. ISBN: 978-0-97403-533-8.

Will Dewey be able to upset Merv's plot to reserve every last copy of the Harry Potter series?

What do you do when somebody gives a Ham-of-the-Month-Club membership to the only vegetarian on Mallville's staff? At the Mallville Public Library Book Club, Colleen's blog, which she thinks is a private journal and therefore has committed to its digital pages her deepest and most embarrassing thoughts, is at the top of members' "To Read" list.

421   Barnes, Bill, and Gene Ambaum. *Unshelved Volume 5: Read Responsibly.* Seattle: Overdue Media, 2007. ISBN: 978-0-97403-534-5.

This daily comic strip includes the famous "Pimp My Bookcart" collection and full-page "Unshelved Book Clubs" along with strips featuring the greatest books ever written. Absurd rules, exotic patrons, and some stereotypical staff members touch on the ordinary and extraordinary life of a librarian.

422   Barnes, Bill, and Gene Ambaum. *Unshelved Volume 6: Frequently Asked Questions.* Seattle: Overdue Media, 2008. ISBN: 978-0-97403-535-2.

Once again, Dewey finds himself answering frequently asked questions with his trademark attitude in this daily comic strip set in the Mallville Public Library. Gary Tyrell, a journalist whose beat is graphic novels, referees a plastic coffee-cup-lid contest between Unshelved and Sheldon. Budget shortfalls, silly reference questions, and unruly patrons provide behind-the-scenes vignettes of the everyday work of a librarian.

423   Credaro, Amanda, and Peter Lewis. *Biblia's Guide for Warrior Librarians: Humor for Librarians Who Refuse to Be Classified.* Westport, CT: Libraries Unlimited, 2003. ISBN: 978-1-59158-002-7.

Author Amanda Credaro, better known as "Biblia, the Warrior Librarian," offers readers her Australian brand of off-the-wall humor as it pertains to library work life. Although some of the material is taken from her Warrior Librarian Weekly website (www.warriorlibrarian.com), most of this represents original content. Illustrated by cartoonist Peter Lewis, this collection will appeal to anyone who has ever worked the circulation

desk. Interestingly enough, a serious section presents a glossary of library terms, abbreviations, and a list of professional associations, so the book is helpful as well as humorous.

424   Eberhart, George M. *The Librarian's Book of Lists.* Chicago: American Library Association, 2010. ISBN: 978-0-83891-063-4.

Learn how to say "Where is the library?" in fifty different languages, although readers are left to their own devices regarding pronunciation. Inveterate recorder Eberhart, formerly editor of *College and Research Libraries News* and now editor of *American Libraries Direct* e-newsletter for ALA, has here created a mostly tongue-in-cheek collection of offbeat library-related trivia. A few examples: "15 Favorite Library Postcards," "5 Movies with Librarian Role Models," and "Top 10 Library Music Videos." Although a few of the lists may actually be useful, such as "Top 60 Subject Blogs and News Sources," for the most part these fifty lists are meant to elicit a chuckle or two over a cup of coffee in the staff break room. Eberhart presents a more sober look at library life in *The Whole Library Handbook 4* (see entry 907).

425   Heye, Dennie. *Obnoxious Librarian from Hades.* Raleigh, NC: www.lulu.com, 2008. ISBN: 978-1-40924-412-7.

In his self-published book, Heye exposes the annoyance of incompetent bosses and micromanaging librarians trying to serve oblivious customers. With Dilbertesque humor, this satire stars a librarian with an attitude on a quest to survive boring meetings, exasperating coworkers, clueless managers, and l-users (library users).

426   Lewis, J. Patrick, and Kyle M. Stone. *Please Bury Me in the Library.* Orlando, FL: Gulliver Books/Harcourt. 2005. ISBN: 978-0-15216-387-7.

Lewis creates and Stone illustrates fifteen poems about the magic and mayhem of books and the joy of reading. Youth librarians could use this often silly and humorous collection targeted toward grades 2–5 to generate interest in reading. Some other poem titles (aside from the book title) are "Eating Alphabet Soup," "Reading in the Dark, Are You a Book Person?" and "Ab-so-lu-tas-ti-cal."

427 Low, Kathleen. *Casanova Was a Librarian: A Light-Hearted Look at the Profession.* Jefferson, NC: McFarland, 2007. ISBN: 978-0-78642-981-3.

Low reviews fun facts about librarians in politics, porn, movies, books, history, and comedy. She begins with a statistical review of gender, personality types, education, and salaries and quickly moves into a lighthearted look at health risks, job-related recreation, librarian novelty gifts, bumper stickers, and famous librarians.

428 Parsons, Larry A. *A Funny Thing Happened on the Way to the School Library: A Treasury of Anecdotes, Quotes, and Other Happenings.* Westport, CT: Libraries Unlimited, 1990. ISBN: 978-0-87287-751-1.

FYI

WILL MANLEY AND HIS SIGNATURE BRAND OF HUMOR

No discussion of library humor would be complete without mentioning Will Manley. His wry observations regarding the work life of librarians have their roots in three decades of service in the trenches. Semiretired, his current literary output consists of two magazine columns: "The Manley Arts" appears in *Booklist*, and "Will's World" graces the pages of *American Libraries*. Sadly, all his books are out of print.

For Library Directors Only: Talking about Trustees and for Library Trustees. Illustrations by Richard Lee. Jefferson, NC: McFarland, 1993. ISBN: 978-0-89950-826-9.

The Manley Art of Librarianship. Illustrations by Richard Lee. Jefferson, NC: McFarland, 1993. ISBN: 978-0-89950-866-5.

Snowballs in the Bookdrop: Talking It Over with Your Library's Community. North Haven, CT: Shoe String Press, 1982. ISBN: 978-0-20801-944-8.

The Truth about Catalogers. Illustrations by Richard Lee. Jefferson, NC: McFarland, 1995. ISBN: 978-0-78640-103-1.

The Truth about Reference Librarians. Illustrations by Richard Lee. Jefferson, NC: McFarland, 1996. ISBN: 978-0-78640-220-5.

Uncensored Thoughts: Pot Shots from a Public Librarian. Unseries 4. Illustrations by Richard Lee. Jefferson, NC: McFarland, 1994. ISBN: 978-0-89950-992-1.

Unintellectual Freedoms: Opinions of a Public Librarian. Jefferson, NC: McFarland, 1991. ISBN: 978-0-89950-575-6.

Unprofessional Behavior: Confessions of a Public Librarian. Unseries 2. Illustrations by Gary Handman. Jefferson, NC: McFarland, 1992. ISBN: 978-0-89950-690-6.

Unsolicited Advice: Observations of a Public Librarian. Illustrations by Gary Handman. Jefferson, NC: McFarland, 1992. ISBN: 978-0-89950-745-3.

429 Smith, Jeanette C. *The Laughing Librarian: A History of American Library Humor.* Foreword by Will Manley and Norman D. Stevens. Jefferson, NC: McFarland, 2012. ISBN: 978-0-78646-452-4 (print), 978-0-7864-9056-1 (e-book).

Still think of a librarian as a middle-aged woman in a sweater set with her hair in a bun? That's not the only stereotype held up as a source of merriment in this examination of some two centuries' worth of Yankee library amusement. Other archetypes to be found in these pages include the collector, the organization fanatic, the keeper, and the change agent. Smith uses subtle wit and satire to show that there is more to appreciate than the serious public face professionals display while on the job.

430 Turner, James. *Rex Libris Volume One: I, Librarian.* San Jose, CA: SLG, 2007. ISBN: 978-1-59362-062-2.

Turner bases his graphic novel stories around Rex Libris, head librarian at Middleton Public Library, as he travels the universe looking for overdue books. In this first collection, he must retrieve the overdue *Principia Mathematica* while preventing vandals from burning down the library.

431 Turner, James. *Rex Libris Volume Two: Book of Monsters.* San Jose, CA: SLG, 2009. ISBN: 978-1-59362-153-7.

Turner picks up where he left off in volume 1. Rex Libris travels back in time to the ancient Library of Alexandria, and his two fellow librarians (Circe and Hypatia) must battle a monster unleashed from the pages of books before he will be allowed to return home.

LC SUBJECT HEADINGS

(1) Electronic Information Resource Literacy
(2) Library Orientation
(3) Information Literacy—Study and Teaching
       (Higher)
(4) Information Literacy—Study and Teaching
       (Secondary)
(5) Information resources—Evaluation—Study
       and Teaching (Higher)
(6) Information Retrieval—Study and Teaching
(7) Information Services—User Education
(8) Internet Searching—Study and Teaching

INFORMATION LITERACY AND BIBLIOGRAPHIC INSTRUCTION

 **BOOKS**

432 Barclay, Donald A. *Teaching and Marketing Electronic Information Literacy Programs: A How-to-Do-It Manual for Librarians.* How-To-Do-It Manuals for Libraries 124. New York: Neal-Schuman, 2003. ISBN: 978-1-55570-470-4.

This teach-the-teacher manual is designed for librarians who give public presentations on computer-based information retrieval. Specific topics covered are the definition of electronic information literacy, evaluation of information, effective use of online search tools, and intellectual property protection. The manual is divided into four parts: teaching electronic information literacy; twelve ready-to-go PowerPoint presentations for teaching electronic information literacy; becoming a master electronic information literacy instructor; and managing the successful electronic information literacy program.

433 Bintliff, Barbara, and Duncan Alford, eds. *Teaching Legal Research.* New York: Routledge, 2011. ISBN: 978-0-41558-087-8.

Contributors offer the academic law librarian theoretical and practical guidance on legal research education to teach mandatory, first-year law school curriculum or advanced/specialized legal research. Topics include Hicks's *The Teaching of Legal Bibliography*, complex problem-solving research skills, research philosophy and context, curriculum development, best practices, and professional development. This book is based on a special issue of *Legal Reference Services Quarterly*.

434 Burkhardt, Joanna M., Mary C. MacDonald, and Andree J. Rathemacher. *Creating a Comprehensive Information Literacy Plan: A How-to-Do-It Manual and CD-ROM for Librarians.* How-To-Do-It Manuals for Libraries 150. New York: Neal-Schuman, 2005. ISBN: 978-1-55570-533-6.

This guide to creating, improving, and marketing information literacy plans is for library managers and instructors. Part 1 is the step-by-step instructions for creating a comprehensive plan. Part 2 is a toolkit with an overview, several bibliographies, and standards and guidelines. Part 3 presents six model plans. The accompanying CD-ROM contains sample worksheets, a searchable list of all of the bibliographies, and a hyperlinked list of model plans.

435 Burkhardt, Joanna M., Mary C. MacDonald, and Andree J. Rathemacher. *Teaching Information Literacy: 50 Standards-Based Exercises for College Students.* 2nd ed. Chicago: American Library Association, 2010. ISBN: 978-0-83891-053-5.

The "standards" referred to in the title are the Information Literacy Competency Standards for Higher Education, as promulgated by the Association of College and Research Libraries. These appear in full in an appendix. These established criteria, in turn, form the basis for the assignments sprinkled throughout the text. Either singly or in small groups, students are tasked with "Creating a Research Question" or determining the quality of information. Helpfully, the authors state explicitly which exercise addresses which standards. Eleven chapters progress from "What Is Information" through traditional research tools/methods, culminating in "The Web and Scholarly Research." For this revised edition, authors have put more emphasis on teaching the elements of electronic sources, since this is the continuing trend in information retrieval. This is an excellent guide for those teaching information literacy to either the public or library school students.

436 Callison, Daniel, and Leslie Preddy. *The Blue Book on Information Age Inquiry, Instruction and Literacy.* Westport, CT: Libraries Unlimited, 2006. ISBN: 978-1-59158-325-7.

The authors present a working theoretical model based on key terms to be used in developing and understanding the power of information inquiry in instruction. This revised and updated edition of *Key Words, Concepts and Methods for Information Instruction* (LMS Associates, 2003) includes practical instructional applications for immediate use. The information is divided into three sections: introduction to the concepts of information inquiry, application of inquiry to the student research process, and key words for instruction in information inquiry. The authors use several

case studies and models to illustrate points. Two chapters are devoted to library media specialist instructional roles. Library science topics covered include supporting online learning, virtual library media centers, weeding library collections, and national school library program standards. The appendixes cover information inquiry assessment rubrics and elements, key words in instruction, and information literacy instruction K–12 bibliographic resources and web resources. An index is included.

437 Cook, Douglas, and Ryan Sittler, eds. *Practical Pedagogy for Library Instructors: 17 Innovative Strategies to Improve Student Learning.* Chicago: Association of College and Research Libraries, 2008. ISBN: 978-0-83898-458-1.

This slender volume presents alternatives to the traditional learning model, in which an instructor drones on interminably while a classroom full of students can barely stay awake, much less learn anything. These alternatives, which come from practicing librarians with teaching duties, include such unexpected gambits as incorporating TV game shows, storytelling, props and prizes, and other stratagems into the teaching/learning mix. The key word here is "practical." As stated concisely in the introductory first chapter, "*how* you teach makes a difference in *what your students learn*" (p. 1). The basic premise appears to be that, if we make library instruction enjoyable, future library users will retain more of what is presented to them. Very helpful are the abstracts at the beginning of each chapter, for a quick read on what follows.

438 Deese-Roberts, Susan, and Kathleen Keating. *Library Instruction: A Peer Tutoring Model.* Englewood, CO: Libraries Unlimited, 2000. ISBN: 978-1-56308-652-6.

Students teaching other students is an instructional strategy that has been in use for some time in other academic areas, such as high school writing and math centers. Here, the authors break new ground by suggesting that library students coach their comrades. Although Deese-Roberts and Keating make it clear that this approach is not a substitute for traditional bibliographic instruction by a formally trained librarian, they note that it can serve to alleviate pressure on overextended staff, since "many reference and instruction programs are overwhelmed by increasing demands for assistance and are seeking new solutions" (p. xiii). Eight chapters and three appendixes cover a short history of library instruction, how to establish a library instruction peer tutoring program, and a case study of just such a program instituted at the University of New Mexico General Library. Forms, worksheets, and other reference material are included.

439   Duncan, Donna, Laura Lockhart, and Lisa Ham. *The New iSearch, You Search, We All Learn to Research: A How-to-Do-It Manual for Teaching Research using Web 2.0 Tools and Digital Resources.* How-To-Do-It Manuals for Libraries 180. New York: Neal-Schuman, 2012. ISBN: 978-1-55570-758-3.

Reading this book, one is reminded of Francois Rabelais's dictum that "a child is not a vase to be filled but a fire to be lit." This notion is reinforced by the authors' joint experience, of which they say, "Children learn best when they are given opportunities for exploration and to make decisions about their learning" (p. xiii). The route to this destination follows a five-step path: (1) What do I want to know? (2) Where can I find the answers? (3) How will I record the information that I find? (4) How will I show what I learned? (5) How will I know I did a good job? Well organized and illustrated, this book shows the school media specialist how to help young people take charge of their own learning.

440   Garner, Carolyn. *Teaching Library Media Skills in Grades K–6: A How-to-Do-It Manual for Librarians.* How-To-Do-It Manuals for Libraries 130. New York: Neal-Schuman, 2004. ISBN: 978-1-55570-464-3.

Designed for school library media specialists, this book contains grade-by-grade lessons for teaching library skills. Introductory, reinforcement, and mastery lessons build on one another

as kindergarten and elementary students learn to use the library. The 150 lessons have an objective, procedure plan, desired outcome, and retaining component. Sample lessons include library behavior, using the catalog system, researching material, choosing books, and checking out books. The CD-ROM contains easy-to-use, adaptable lessons in Microsoft Word format.

441   Goodman, Valeda Dent. *Keeping the User in Mind: Instructional Design and the Modern Library.* Oxford: Chandos, 2009. ISBN: 978-1-84334-486-5.

Instructional design is essentially about teaching the teacher how to teach. Within these pages are discussions of learning theory, teaching strategies, curriculum design, and the like, all with a view toward "finding ways to improve how we teach patrons to use library resources" (p. xix). Geared specifically to the academic library, this slim volume is nonetheless of use to public and special librarians as they attempt to help their users help themselves.

442   Harada, Violet H., and Joan M. Yoshina. *Assessing for Learning: Librarians and Teachers as Partners.* 2nd ed. Santa Barbara, CA: Libraries Unlimited, 2010. ISBN: 978-1-59884-470-2 (print), 978-1-59884-471-9 (e-book).

Thoroughly updated, this edition includes new chapters on assessing critical thinking, dispositions, and tech-related learning. Tools for assessment include checklists, rubrics, rating scales, conferences, logs, personal correspondence, graphic organizers (concept maps, webs, K-W-L charts, and matrices), and student portfolios that can be used in library-related instruction. The three chapters on outcome-based approaches for elementary school, middle school, and high school focus specifically on library-related lesson plans, including finding information in a variety of sources, developing criteria to assess student books, asking the right questions, selecting and evaluating resources, evaluating websites, and preparing annotated bibliographies. References and index are included.

443 Hardesty, Larry L., ed. *The Role of the Library in the First College Year.* First-Year Experience Monograph 45. Columbia: National Resource Center for the First-Year Experience and Students in Transition, University of South Carolina, 2007. ISBN: 978-1-88927-154-5.

This monograph focuses on how librarians, faculty, and administrators can help first-year students utilize library resources to enhance their academic experiences. The three sections titled "Foundations," "Initiatives," and "Connections" discuss history, current practices, and the relationship between students with library skills and academic success. The last half of the book, "Campus Case Studies," specifically provides detailed best-practice project descriptions, components, assessments, outcomes, a summary conclusion, relevant notes, and references used to shape student experiences. Sample tables, flowcharts, timelines, a survey instrument, lessons, and scoring rubrics provide hands-on examples to incorporate into academic planning. Case studies average ten pages and incorporate 2006 technology advances. The Association of College and Research Libraries' Information Literacy Competency Standards for Higher Education (appendix A) and Objectives for Information Literacy Instruction: A Model Statement for Academic Librarians (appendix B) provides academic standards. The final section includes a complete list of contributors and their credentials.

444 Hilyer, Lee Andrew. *Presentations for Librarians: A Complete Guide to Creating Effective, Learner-Centred Presentations.* Oxford: Chandos, 2008. ISBN: 978-1-84334-303-5.

This is basically a public-speaking manual for librarians. Having endured innumerable poorly done presentations at conferences, the author decided to remedy the situation himself. He states that his book is "based on the best evidence available about how we learn and process information" (p. xii) and begins with a rather technical opening chapter on "human cognitive architecture," which is fancy language for learning styles. Beyond this theoretical piece is much practical information about the nuts and bolts of speaking before an audience: researching your

topic, writing your script, handouts, and more. Each chapter concludes with a summary. Appendixes include primers on three popular electronic slideshow applications: Microsoft PowerPoint 2007, Apple Keynote Version 3, and OpenOffice Impress Version 2.2.

445 Joyce, Marilyn Z., and Julie I. Tallman. *Making the Writing and Research Connection with the I-Search Process: A How-to-Do-It Manual.* 2nd ed. How-To-Do-It Manuals for Libraries 143. New York: Neal-Schuman, 2006. ISBN: 978-1-55570-534-3.

The authors explain the I-Search writing and research process and provide guidelines for collaboration between teachers and librarians that allows information resources and instructional technologies to be incorporated into multidisciplinary lesson plans. The appendixes include an annotated bibliography, sample papers, time frames, and planning worksheets. An assessment rubric with all figures in the books, additional worksheets, tools, and sample papers are on the companion CD-ROM.

446 Kuhlthau, Carol Collier. *Seeking Meaning: A Process Approach to Library and Information Services.* 2nd ed. Westport, CT: Libraries Unlimited, 2003. ISBN: 978-1-59158-094-2 (print), 978-0-31305-329-0 (e-book).

Kuhlthau's theory of a "seeking meaning" approach to library and information services focuses on the stages—much like the seven stages of grief—that students go through when faced with assignments requiring research. This revised edition includes new studies on the implementation of information search processes (ISP) and the expanded elaboration of the ISP framework. This book has been required reading for LIS graduate classes.

447 Kuhlthau, Carol Collier. *Teaching the Library Research Process.* 2nd ed. Lanham, MD: Scarecrow Press, 2002. ISBN: 978-0-81082-723-3.

This book "provides a comprehensive, sequential program for taking students through the intricacies of gathering information in a library when given a research assignment" (p. iv). Seven chapters, one for each step along the way, cover "Initiating a Research Assignment," "Selecting a Topic," "Exploring Information," "Forming a Focus," "Collecting Information," "Preparing to Present," and "Assessing the Process," helping the library instructor break down the sometimes-daunting task of doing library research into manageable separate tasks and thereby relieving student anxiety. The book is abundantly illustrated with worksheets, activity outlines, flowcharts, and other aids.

448 LaGuardia, Cheryl, and Christine K. Oka. *Becoming A Library Teacher.* New Libraries Series 3. New York: Neal-Schuman, 2000. ISBN: 978-1-55570-378-3.

Who teaches the teacher how to teach? According to the authors, up until fairly recently the answer was no one. They note that "when we were learning how to become library teachers (and it wasn't all that long ago), there was no library instruction manual out there. When we went to library school, there was no formal library instruction courses offered. We had to make up our library teaching as we went along" (p. ix). Such fly-by-the-seat-of-your-pants bibliographic instruction is now a thing of the past, judging by this slender volume. In part 1, "Library Instruction as Performance," chapters cover such topics as "Taming Teaching Terror" (tips on controlling performance anxiety), preparing mentally and physically for teaching, and lots of practical stuff on the presentation itself. Part 2, "Composing Classes," is a bit more theoretical in that these pages discuss the authors' philosophical underpinnings of library instruction, the whys and wherefores of which they speak, and so on. One special feature that is quite appealing is text boxes with a "fist" device pointing at the label "Insider Teaching Tip." These two practice what they preach, and these pearls of pedantic wisdom were hard won. All in all, this is quite a useful book on how to get your ideas across effectively without putting your audience to sleep in the process.

449 Langhorne, Mary Jo, and the Iowa City Community School District, eds. *Developing an Information Literacy Program K–12: A How-to-Do-It Manual and CD-ROM Package.* 2nd ed. How-To-Do-It Manuals for Libraries 135. New York: Neal-Schuman, 2004. ISBN: 978-1-55570-509-1.

"Independent learners are those who have internalized a process of inquiry that includes the ability to locate, evaluate and communicate information. This ability is what defines the information-literate individual" (p. xviii). Well said. The whole of this book, then, is geared toward developing this ability in young people. Furthermore, "it has as its basis the belief that in order to be effective, information seeking strategies must be presented to students in the context of classroom curriculum" (p. xvii). One outstanding feature is several dozen "teaching tools"— worksheets, templates, activity lists—that greatly ease the school media specialist's job of teaching information literacy principles. The book is well illustrated throughout, and the CD-ROM contains many of the forms and templates in the book, so that they may be modified for individual use. The very fact that this book is now in its second edition is an indication of its value.

450 Lederer, Naomi. *Ideas for Librarians Who Teach: With Suggestions for Teachers and Business Presenters.* Lanham, MD: Scarecrow Press, 2005. ISBN: 978-0-81085-212-9.

With over seventeen years of experience teaching everything from orientation-type one-shots to semester-long formal classes in library usage and everything in between, this is someone who knows her stuff. Speaking before groups can be uncomfortable, especially for those with little to no experience, but this volume should go far in making those butterflies line up in formation. Chapters deal with traditional classroom situations, audiovisual aids, use of humor (hint: use sparingly; like spice in food, a little goes a long way), learning styles, handouts, and on and on. Within each chapter, bite-sized nuggets and pearls of pedagogical wisdom are listed point by point—for example, "Walk over and stand next to the student who is disrupting class. Keep an eye on him or her. Most of the time the student does not want all the attention" (p. 179).

451 Lehman, Katherine B., and Lori E. Donovan. *Power Researchers: Transforming Student Library Aides into Action Learners.* Santa Barbara, CA: Libraries Unlimited, 2011. ISBN: 978-1-59884-911-0 (print), 978-1-59884-912-7 (e-book).

This book provides a semester-long program to train high school library aides to become power researchers. Topics include orientation to power researching, shelving Dewey style, effective Internet searching, literature, ethical issues, copyright, steps to information literacy, assessment, and preparing for the twenty-first century. Several examples, tips, fifty original lessons, worksheets, rubrics, generic calendar, bibliography, and index are included.

452 Malone, Debbie, and Carol Videon, eds. *First Year Student Library Instruction Programs.* CLIP Notes 33. Chicago: American Library Association, 2003. ISBN: 978-0-83898-230-3.

This book contains competencies, course syllabi, online tutorials, and exercises gathered from colleges and universities that provide instruction to first-year students. The authors' analysis of survey results from 153 institutions includes works citied and a selected bibliography. Contributors provide information for one-class workshops and credit-bearing courses they used to generate conversations between faculty and librarians on how best to incorporate library skills into the curriculum. The relaxed presentation style allows faculty and librarians to match curriculum requirements to library holdings and integrate results in individual lesson plans.

453 Sittler, Ryan L., and Douglas Cook, eds. *The Library Instruction Cookbook.* Chicago: American Library Association, 2009. ISBN: 978-0-83898-511-3.

Cute concept here: a book on bibliographic instruction geared toward college students but in the guise of a cookbook, complete with "recipes" (the overall plan of attack), "nutrition information" (how lesson was developed, how to proceed, etc.), "cooking time" (time allotted for lesson), and "main ingredients" (bulleted list of items needed). Overall, this is effective in presenting teaching methods concisely, and with a dash of humor to boot. As the editors point out, this book is an attempt to help library instructors avoid the pitfall of the boring lecture. Yes, imparting information is key, but how to do it without your audience falling asleep in their chairs? The answer is hands-on activities and doing something out of the ordinary. This work is highly recommended, especially for librarians with little to no experience in teaching.

454 Smith, Felicia A. *Cybrarian Extraordinaire: Compelling Information Literacy Instruction.* Santa Barbara, CA: Libraries Unlimited, 2011. ISBN: 978-1-59884-605-8.

Lecture bingo. Citation cop. The Pirate Librarian going after "buried treasure" in the stacks. Compelling indeed. These intriguing ideas to get college students fired up about information resources are a testament to the creativity of the author. Billing her angle as "edu-tainment," Smith aims to make library instruction, which is often mandatory for less-than-willing freshmen, fun while still being relevant to these young people's curriculum. Based on her own experiences, she has been quite successful and her routine is taking on a life of its own, resulting in this publication. The book is well illustrated throughout, with bibliography and index.

455 Smith, Susan S. *Web-Based Instruction: A Guide for Libraries.* 3rd ed. Chicago: American Library Association, 2011. ISBN: 978-0-83891-056-6.

Smith shows library instructors how to incorporate web-based instruction into their curricula. Topics covered include setting the stage, library instruction on the web, project frameworks, selecting project development tools, designing the user experience, multimedia, interactivity, evaluation, testing, and assessment. Several charts, graphics, and figures are used to highlight concepts and key points in this easy-to-understand guide. A list of resources, glossary, works cited, and index are included.

456 Suter, Marcia Krautter, and Elizabeth Burns, eds. *Community College Instruction Web Pages.* Chicago: American Library Association, 2004. ISBN: 978-0-83898-312-6.

This is basically a collection of screenshots of library websites focused on pathfinders, subject guides, tips on library research, and so forth. The goal is to "provide some innovative ideas about presenting information and some inspiration for designing exciting and informative library web pages" (p. xii), and the main idea is to show by example generally accepted principles of solid web design, such as lack of clutter, readable fonts, and clear navigation aids.

457 Thomas, Nancy Pickering. *Information Literacy and Information Skills Instruction: Applying Research to Practice in the School Library Media Center.* 2nd ed. Westport, CT: Libraries Unlimited, 2004. ISBN: 978-1-59158-081-2.

In this newer edition, Thomas updates and expands the literature reviews on personal assistance, bibliographic instruction, library development, learning styles, information skills, and technology changes. She incorporates current trends, issues, and applications for the research reviewed along with information processing models, instructional diagnostic models, and information skills instruction assessments into this well-organized review of information literacy. Citations, tables, figures, diagrams, and notes enhance material comprehension. This scholarly work also includes an extensive list of references, author index, and subject index.

458 Veldof, Jerilyn R. *Creating the One-Shot Library Workshop: A Step-by-Step Guide.* Chicago: American Library Association, 2006. ISBN: 978-0-83890-913-3.

Sections on analysis, design, development, implementation, and evaluation provide librarians with step-by-step instruction on how to create one-day library literacy workshops. Each section includes illustrations, summaries, case studies, and reminder lists. "Tips" provide additional definitions or resources to help clarify task activities. The "Are You All Set?" at the end of each section is a summary of the actions needed to complete the section before moving on. The processes are easy to follow and used to maintain consistency, not only for workshop development, but for training others to develop workshops. Following this guide will allow librarians to develop and deliver high-quality instruction targeted to the appropriate setting and participant skill level.

459 Vossler, Joshua J., and Scott Sheidlower. *Humor and Information Literacy: Practical Techniques for Library Instruction.* Santa Barbara, CA: Libraries Unlimited, 2011. ISBN: 978-1-59884-532-7.

Part 1 covers using humor in communication theory, education, library science, psychology, stand-up comedy, and literacy instruction. Part 2 uses various humor devices such as ad-libbing, spontaneous humor, jokes, and more to teach information literacy. These cross-disciplinary literature reviews show how to use humor effectively in an educational setting with a primary focus on library science. The authors end the book with a webliography, references, and index.

460 Webb, Jo, and Chris Powis. *Teaching Information Skills: Theory and Practice.* London: Facet, 2005. ISBN: 978-1-85604-513-1.

In today's information-rich environment, the phrase "information overload" is often bandied about. Part of the solution, at least, resides in the concept of information literacy. In the foreword to this volume, Margaret Watson, president of the Chartered Institute of Library and Information Professionals, states that "this book, written by experienced practitioners, provides a good introduction to the theory underpinning the teaching or facilitation of information skills as well as practical tips an case studies" (p. ix). Ten chapters cover learners and learning styles, motivating learners, finding out what learners need, planning, delivery, assessment, feedback/

evaluation, and building a teaching team. A bibliography and index round out the volume.

461 Weibel, Marguerite Crowley. *Adult Learners Welcome Here: A Handbook for Librarians and Literacy Teachers.* Foreword by Robert Wedgeworth. New York: Neal-Schuman, 2007. ISBN: 978-1-55570-578-7.

In part 1, Weibel looks at what, how, and where literacy is taught from two perspectives: second-language learners, and native speakers with poor reading skills. Part 2 is broken into five different subject areas, each devoted to lesson plans and an annotated bibliography. The subject areas are art and photography, poetry, literature, nonfiction, and print and electronic reference.

462 West, Jessamyn C. *Without a Net: Librarians Bridging the Digital Divide.* Westport, CT: Libraries Unlimited, 2011. ISBN: 978-1-59884-453-5 (print), 978-1-59884-454-2 (e-book).

West puts together tips, guidelines, and techniques that librarians can use to teach those with little to no computer experience how to use e-mail, office software, search engines, and social media. Basic computer terms, elementary computer concepts, and instructions for classroom presentations and training are provided. The appendix includes an edited "Aspects of Computer Literacy" from Phil Agre's *How to Help Someone Use a Computer,* Usability.gov's "Research-Based Web Design and Usability Guidelines," and a selected bibliography.

463 Whitley, Peggy, Susan Williams Goodwin, and Catherine C. Olson. *99 Jumpstarts to Research: Topic Guides for Finding Information on Current Issues.* 2nd ed. Santa Barbara, CA: Libraries Unlimited, 2010. ISBN: 978-1-59884-368-2 (print), 978-1-59884-369-9 (e-book).

This quick reader's guide includes ninety-nine alphabetized jumpstart topics and resources. Each listing contains suggested search terms, topic-related questions, background and sources of statistics, specific Library of Congress and Sears subject headings, specific website URLs,

newspapers and magazines, and private and public resources all related to the topic. Aimed at the high school student, this research guide covers current issues such as airline security, a cashless society, family violence, going green, identify theft, terrorism, universal health care, Wikipedia, and more. A bibliography, subject directory, and index are included.

ADDITIONAL RESOURCES

464 Allan, Barbara. *Blended Learning.* London: Facet, 2007. ISBN: 978-1-85604-614-5.

465 Allan, Barbara. *No-Nonsense Guide to Training in Libraries.* London: Facet, 2013. ISBN: 978-1-85604-828-6.

466 Allan, Barbara. *Supporting Research Students.* London: Facet, 2009. ISBN: 978-1-85604-685-5.

467 Avery, Elizabeth Fuseler, ed. *Assessing Student Learning Outcomes for Information Literacy Instruction in Academic Institutions.* Chicago: American Library Association, 2003. ISBN: 978-0-83898-261-7.

468 Bankhead, Elizabeth, Janet Nichols, and Dawn Vaughn. *Write It! A Guide for Research.* 3rd ed. Westport, CT: Libraries Unlimited, 2009. ISBN: 978-1-59158-818-4.

469 Blanchett, Helen, Chris Powls, and Jo Webb. *A Guide to Teaching Information Literacy: 101 Practical Tips.* London: Facet, 2011. ISBN: 978-1-85604-659-6.

470 Booth, Char. *Reflective Teaching, Effective Learning: Instructional Literacy for Library Educators.* Chicago: American Library Association, 2011. ISBN: 978-0-8389-1052-8.

471 Bowers, Jennifer, Peggy Keeran, Suzanne L. Moulton-Gertig, Michael Levine-Clark, Nonny Schlotzhauer, Esther Gil, Christopher C. Brown, Joseph R. Kraus, and Carrie Forbes. *Research within the Disciplines: Foundations for Reference and Library Instruction.* Lanham, CT: Scarecrow Press, 2007. ISBN: 978-0-81085-688-2.

472   Cook, Douglas, and Natasha Cooper, eds. *Teaching Information Literacy Skills to Social Sciences Students and Practitioners: A Casebook of Applications.* Chicago: American Library Association, 2006. ISBN: 978-0-83898-389-8.

473   Cox, Christopher N., and Elizabeth Blakesley Lindsay, eds. *Information Literacy Instruction Handbook.* Chicago: American Library Association, 2008. ISBN: 978-0-83890-963-8.

474   DeAbreu, Belinha S. *Teaching Media Literacy: A How-to-Do-It Manual and CD-ROM.* How-To-Do-It Manuals for Libraries 156. New York: Neal-Schuman, 2007. ISBN: 978-1-55570-596-1.

475   Eisenberg, Michael, Carrie A. Lowe, and Kathleen L. Spitzer. *Information Literacy: Essential Skills for the Information Age.* 2nd ed. Westport, CT: Libraries Unlimited, 2004. ISBN: 978-1-59158-143-7 (print), 978-0-313-09556-6 (e-book).

476   Ercegovac, Zorana. *Information Literacy: Search Strategies, Tools and Resources for High School Students and College Freshman.* 2nd ed. Columbus, OH: Linworth, 2008. ISBN: 978-1-58683-332-9 (print), 978-1-58683-378-7 (e-book).

477   Furness, Adrienne. *Helping Homeschoolers in the Library.* Chicago: American Library Association, 2008. ISBN: 978-0-83890-955-3.

478   Garrett, Linda J., and JoAnne Moore. *Teaching Library Skills in Middle and High School: A How-to-Do-It Manual.* How-to-Do-It Manuals for School and Public Librarians 11. New York: Neal-Schuman, 1993. ISBN: 978-1-5557-0125-3.

479   Gibson, Craig, ed. *Student Engagement and Information Literacy.* Chicago: Association of College and Research Libraries, American Library Association, 2006. ISBN: 978-0-83898-388-1.

480   Gilton, Donna L. *Lifelong Learning in Public Libraries: Principles, Programs, and People.* Lanham, MD: Scarecrow Press, 2012. ISBN: 978-0-81088-356-7.

481   Godwin, Peter, and Jo Parker, eds. *Information Literacy Beyond Library 2.0.* London: Facet, 2012. ISBN: 978-1-85604-762-3.

482   Godwin, Peter, and Jo Parker, eds. *Information Literacy Meets Library 2.0.* London: Facet, 2008. ISBN: 978-1-85604-637-4.

483   Harker, Christa, and Dorette Putonti. *Library Research with Emergent Readers: Meeting Standards through Collaboration.* Westport, CT: Libraries Unlimited, 2008. ISBN: 978-1-58683-288-9 (print), 978-1-58683-353-4 (e-book).

484   Heath, Marilyn. *MLA Made Easy: Citation Basics for Beginners.* Columbus, OH: Linworth, 2009. ISBN: 978-1-58683-343-5 (print), 978-1-58683-409-8 (e-book).

485   Herring, James E. *Improving Students' Web Use and Information Literacy: A Guide for Teachers and Teacher Libraries.* London: Facet, 2010. ISBN: 978-1-85604-743-2.

486   Intner, Carol F. *Homework Help from the Library: In Person and Online.* Chicago: American Library Association, 2011. ISBN: 978-0-83891-046-7.

487   Kaplowitz, Joan R. *Transforming Information Literacy Instruction Using Learner-Centered Teaching.* New York: Neal-Schuman, 2011. ISBN: 978-1-55570-765-1.

488   Kovacs, Diane. *Seven Steps to Effective Online Teaching Instructional Design and Strategies for Online Teaching and Learning in Libraries.* London: Facet, ISBN: 978-1-85604-833-0; Chicago: American Library Association, ISBN: 978-0-8389-1171-6. 2014.

489   Kuhlthau, Carol C., Leslie K. Maniotes, and Ann K. Caspari. *Guided Inquiry: Learning in the 21st Century.* Westport, CT: Libraries Unlimited, 2007. ISBN: 978-1-59158-435-3 (print), 978-0-313-09615-0 (e-book).

490   LaGuardia, Cheryl, Michael Blake, Lawrence Dowler, Laura Farwell, Caroline M. Kent, and Ed Tallent. *Teaching the New Library: A How-to-Do-It Manual for Planning and*

Designing Instructional Programs. How-To-Do-It Manuals for Libraries 70. New York: Neal-Schuman, 1996. ISBN: 978-1-55570-214-4.

491 Mackey, Thomas P., and Trudi E. Jacobson, eds. *Collaborative Information Literacy Assessments: Strategies for Evaluating Teaching and Learning.* New York: Neal-Schuman, 2010. ISBN: 978-1-55570-693-7.

492 Mackey, Thomas P., and Trudi E. Jacobson, eds. *Teaching Information Literacy Online.* New York: Neal-Schuman, 2011. ISBN: 978-1-55570-735-4.

493 MacMillan, Kathy. *A Box Full of Tales: Easy Ways to Share Library Resources through Story Boxes.* Chicago: American Library Association, 2008. ISBN: 978-0-83890-960-7.

494 MacMillan, Kathy, and Christine Kirker. *Kindergarten Magic: Theme-Based Lessons for Building Literacy and Library Skills.* Chicago: American Library Association, 2011. ISBN: 978-0-83891-069-6.

495 Martin, Allan, and Dan Madigan, eds. *Digital Literacies for Learning.* London: Facet, 2006. ISBN: 978-1-85604-563-6.

496 Melling, Maxine, ed. *Supporting E-Learning: A Guide for Library and Information Managers.* London: Facet, 2005. ISBN: 978-1-85604-535-3.

497 Miller, Pat. *Library Skills.* Stretchy Library Lessons. Madison, WI: Upstart Books, 2003. ISBN: 978-1-57950-083-2.

498 Miller, Pat. *More Library Skills.* Stretchy Library Lessons. Madison, WI: Upstart Books, 2005. ISBN: 978-1-93214-642-4.

499 Miller, Pat. *Research Skills.* Stretchy Library Lessons. Madison, WI: Upstart Books, 2003. ISBN: 978-1-57950-084-9.

500 Neely, Teresa Y. *Information Literacy Assessment: Standards-Based Tools and Assignments.* Chicago: American Library Association, 2008. ISBN: 978-0-83890-914-0.

501 Polette, Nancy. *Stop the Copying with Wild and Wacky Research Projects.* Westport, CT: Libraries Unlimited, 2008. ISBN: 978-1-59158-696-8 (print), 978-0-313-36377-1 (e-book).

502 Ryan, Jenny, and Steph Capra. *Information Literacy Toolkit: Grades Kindergarten–6.* Chicago: American Library Association, 2001. ISBN: 978-0-83893-507-1.

503 Saunders, Laura. *Information Literacy as a Student Learning Outcome: The Perspective of Institutional Accreditation.* Foreword by Peter Hernon. Westport, CT: Libraries Unlimited, 2011. ISBN: 978-1-59884-852-6 (print), 978-1-59884-853-3 (e-book).

504 Secker, Jane, and Emma Coonan, eds. *Rethinking Information Literacy: A Practical Framework for Supporting Learning.* London: Facet, 2012. ISBN: 978-1-85604-822-4.

505 Taylor, Joie. *Information Literacy and the School Library Media Center.* Libraries Unlimited Professional Guides in School Librarianship. Westport, CT: Libraries Unlimited, 2005. ISBN: 978-0-313-32020-0.

506 Valenza, Joyce Kasman. *Power Research Tools: Learning Activities and Posters.* Illustrations by Emily Valenza. Chicago: American Library Association, 2003. ISBN: 978-0-83890-838-9.

507 Valenza, Joyce Kasman. *Power Tools Recharged: 125+ Essential Forms and Presentations for Your School Library Information Program.* Illustrations by Emily Valenza. Chicago: American Library Association, 2004. ISBN: 978-0-83890-880-8.

508 Veccia, Susan H. *Uncovering Our History: Teaching with Primary Sources.* Chicago: American Library Association, 2004. ISBN: 978-0-83890-862-4.

509 Young, Rosemary M., and Stephena Harmony. *Working with Faculty to Design Undergraduate Information Literacy Programs: A How-to-Do-It Manual for Librarians.* How-To-Do-It Manuals for Libraries 90. New York: Neal-Schuman, 2001. ISBN: 978-1-55570-354-7.

INFORMATION TECHNOLOGY

 BOOKS

510   Alcorn, Louise E., and Maryellen Mott Allen. *Wireless Networking: A How-to-Do-It Manual for Librarians.* How-To-Do-It Manuals for Libraries 131. New York: Neal-Schuman, 2006. ISBN: 978-1-55570-478-0.

This manual provides information on standards, transfer rates, equipment costs, site reviews, management issues, and planning and implementation for wireless networking. Security, troubleshooting, and data privacy concerns are discussed. A glossary of terms, bibliography, sample policies, frequently asked questions, and list of manufacturers are included.

511   Austin, Andy, and Christopher Harris. *Drupal in Libraries.* Library Technology Reports. Chicago: American Library Association, 2008. ISBN: 978-0-83895-794-3.

This is a brief overview of content management systems (CMSs) that provide back-end structures for websites, leaving librarians free to focus on content. The author suggests that Drupal is the CMS that provides the best balance of usability and power needed to create a powerful, friendly library website.

512   Barclay, Donald A. *Managing Public-Access Computers: A How-to-Do-It Manual for Librarians.* How-To-Do-It Manuals for Libraries 96. New York: Neal-Schuman, 2000. ISBN: 978-1-55570-361-5.

The public has come to expect free-of-charge computer usage/Internet access at their neighborhood public library, but this service can be a major headache for managers and frontline staff. Barclay begins with a basic introduction to computer concepts before getting into facilities planning, hardware, software, and security management. Other chapters are devoted to printing, staffing issues, and user relations. Especially helpful are the numerous tip sheets and "Focus On" sidebar articles. Among the forms included are checklists for inventory, staff scheduling, usage observation, and user feedback.

513   Berger, Pam, and Sally Trexler. *Choosing Web 2.0 Tools for Learning and Teaching in a*

Digital World. Westport, CT: Libraries Unlimited, 2010. ISBN: 978-1-59158-706-4.

Targeted for school librarians, this book begins with research on student learning behaviors and how to align library practices with American Association of School Librarian (AASL) Standards for the Twenty-First Century Learner and the Stripling Inquiry Process before moving into what are considered the best strategies to use in a digital world. Topics covered include social bookmarking, managing and organizing information, content collaboration, media sharing, social networking, and digital mapping. The appendix Tool Chart is a list of websites along with the relevant chapter. A glossary and index are included.

514 Bilal, Dania. *Automating Media Centers and Small Libraries: A Microcomputer-Based Approach.* 2nd ed. Library and Information Science Text Series. Westport, CT: Libraries Unlimited, 2002. ISBN: 978-1-56308-879-7.

This hands-on guide and textbook for automating a library covers preparation, system architecture, hardware configuration, system selection, preparing the collection for automation, implementing systems, networking, and system migration. Two chapters are devoted to the online public access catalog. This edition contains a bibliography, glossary, and index.

515 Blowers, Helene, and Robin Bryan. *Weaving a Library Web: A Guide to Developing Children's Websites.* Chicago: American Library Association, 2004. ISBN: 978-0-83890-877-8.

Weaving a Library Web is a good practical guide for first planning or redesigning a library website targeted at children. The book contains several sample screenshots, planning tools, recommended structure, and testing tips. Although the book does not cover technical requirements for a website, it does discuss accessibility, privacy, online safety, and models for learning. The black-and-white screenshots are tiny, making it hard to read detail. The overall basic information is still relevant in spite of changing technology.

516 Brandt, D. Scott. *Teaching Technology: A How-to-Do-It Manual for Librarians.* How-To-Do-It Manuals for Libraries 115. New York: Neal-Schuman, 2002. ISBN: 978-1-55570-426-1.

The author describes concepts and techniques for designing technology training programs such as use of the Internet in the library. Step-by-step approaches to program and course design are provided within the context of the library's vision and mission. One section spotlights different approaches for users of all ages and backgrounds those successfully implemented by libraries of different types and sizes. Templates, useful examples, and tips are included.

517 Braun, Linda W. *Teens.Library: Developing Internet Services for Young Adults.* Chicago: American Library Association, 2002. ISBN: 978-0-83890-824-2.

This user-friendly elementary textbook helps librarians incorporate technology and content conducive to teenagers, whose technological literacy often outpaces their understanding of more traditional print products, commonly known as books and magazines. The author centers attention on teen-friendly online services that address forty critical factors for youth growth and development, along with planning advice, site maintenance, and website examples.

518 Brown-Syed, Christopher. *Parents of Invention: The Development of Library Automation Systems in the Late 20th Century.* Westport, CT: Libraries Unlimited, 2011. ISBN: 978-1-59158-792-7 (print), 978-1-59158-791-0 (e-book).

Divided into eight sections, Brown-Syed's book examines the origins of integrated library systems (ILSs), technological and application transformations, and future possibilities. Information on bibliographic databases, utilities, and regional library consortia covers the ILS from conception to commercialization. Case studies, librarian experiences, vendor relationships, and financial requirements illustrate ILS impact on customer perspectives, working conditions, vendors' work, equipment, and library services. Finally, open-source software, mobile access, digital repositories, and technology adoption and convergence set the future for librarians and ILSs.

519   Cohn, John M., Ann. L. Kelsey, and Keith Michael Fiels. *Planning for Integrated Systems and Technologies: A How-to-Do-It Manual for Librarians.* How-To-Do-It Manuals for Librarians 111. New York: Neal-Schuman, 2001. ISBN: 978-1-55570-421-6.

Aimed at small to medium-sized libraries, this book provides staff with steps for installing or replacing an integrated system or multipurpose electronic database. Each chapter contains checklists, photocopy-ready charts, and an annotated list of bibliographic references. Topics include MARC records, cataloging, retrospective conversion, standards, bar coding, and training staff and patrons. The appendix covers how to deal with outside consultants.

520   Collins, Maria D., and Patrick L. Carr, eds. *Managing the Transition from Print to Electronic Journals and Resources: A Guide for Library and Information Professionals.* Routledge Studies in Library and Information Science Series 3. New York: Routledge, 2008. ISBN: 978-0-78903-336-9 (print), 978-0-20388-941-1 (e-book).

Both experienced and novice electronic resource managers will find this discussion of acquisition, access, and standards interesting. Contributor subjects include budgeting, preservation concerns, partnerships, the role of the online catalog, integration and data standards, infrastructure, work flow, and several case studies for managing e-resources.

521   Coombs, Karen A., and Amanda J. Hollister. *Open Source Web Applications for Libraries.* Medford, NJ: Information Today, 2010. ISBN: 978-1-57387-400-7.

Coombs and Hollister explore the use, installation, and configuration of open-source web applications such as WordPress, Drupal, Joomla, and

MediaWiki, along with library-specific application such as SubjectsPlus, Blacklight, VuFind, and Sopac. After a brief overview of open-source web applications, the discussion quickly moves on to blogs, wikis, content management systems, reference and instruction tools, and resource discovery tools. The authors highlight key points with screenshots, program command lines, and numerous figures. A glossary, information about the authors, and index are included.

522   Courtney, Nancy D., ed. *Library 2.0 and Beyond: Innovative Technologies and Tomorrow's User.* Westport, CT: Libraries Unlimited, 2007. ISBN: 978-1-59158-537-4.

Contributors describe Web 2.0 and Library 2.0 and their application to Catalog 2.0 and other new technologies that are affecting library services. Topics discussed include handheld computers, social networking, blogs and wikis, podcasting, gaming, virtual worlds, and digital storytelling. Suggested readings and index are included.

523   Courtney, Nancy, ed. *More Technology for the Rest of Us: A Second Primer on Computing for the Non-IT Librarian.* Westport, CT: Libraries Unlimited, 2010. ISBN: 978-1-59158-939-6 (print), 978-1-59158-941-9 (e-book).

A follow-up to Courtney's 2007 technology guide, these essays provide a basic introduction to information technologies currently affecting libraries and patrons. Each topic provides a brief description and list of references. Topics include web services, digital data preservation, cloud computing, learning management systems, authentication, content management systems, data visualization, free and open-source software, metadata repurposing using XSLT, and communications. A selected bibliography and glossary are provided.

524   Cuddy, Colleen. *Using PDAs in Libraries: A How-to-Do-It Manual.* How-To-Do-It Manuals for Libraries 142. New York: Neal-Schuman, 2005. ISBN: 978-1-55570-543-5.

This is a librarian's guide to personal digital assistants (PDAs): how they work, a comparison of makes and models, their storage capacity, how to provide content, choosing a technology system, and security risks and vulnerabilities. The author discusses how library collections and services may be made accessible to PDAs, whether the patron is in or outside the library. Other topics discussed include how these portable powerhouses fit in with collection development, delivery of materials to patrons, marketing the library's services, and bibliographic instruction.

525 Deyrup, Marta Mestrovic, ed. *Digital Scholarship.* Routledge Studies in Library and Information Science Series 6. New York: Routledge, 2009. ISBN: 978-0-78903-688-9 (print), 978-0-20388-595-6 (e-book).

Contributors actively engaged in building digital collections share their digitization success stories and challenges. They explore how the ability to digitize text and images of historic documents, records, and texts allows for research, comparison, and analysis. The Harvard Project on the Soviet Social System Online, Hemeroteca Digital of the National Library of Spain, and GIS technology as an alternative way of access to historical knowledge are three examples of the impact of global digitization.

526 Gorman, Michael. *Enduring Library: Technology, Tradition, and the Quest for Balance.* Chicago: American Library Association, 2003. ISBN: 978-0-83890-846-4.

Gorman believes that technology should be just another tool in librarians' arsenal of weapons used to respond to patron questions with the most current appropriate information, to catalog the prolific avalanche of information, and to preserve the human record. Focusing on reference and cataloging, he also reviews reading and the web, librarianship, information overload, integrating technology into long- and short-term goals, and the future of libraries.

527 Higgins, Patricia L., ed. *Libraries and Electronic Resources: New Partnerships, New Practices, New Perspectives.* Copublished simultaneously as *Journal of Library Administration* 35, nos. 1/2, 2001. New York: Haworth Information Press, 2001. ISBN: 978-0-78901-729-1.

This volume scrutinizes current trends in e-resource management and the role of libraries in fostering academic electronic publishing. Contributors consider economic issues, e-book publishing standards, digital collections, and global consortia to discuss the changing relationships between librarians, patrons, and publishers created as information technology evolves.

528 Hopkins, Janet. *Assistive Technology: An Introductory Guide for K–12 Library Media Specialists.* Managing the 21st Century Library Media Center. Worthington, OH: Linworth, 2004. ISBN: 978-1-58683-138-7.

Hopkins addresses the emerging role of assistive technology in providing access to information and library services to all students, including those with special needs. Numerous web page references, case studies, "Learn More" boxes, and reference lists are included through the chapters along with diagrams to show software interfaces and technologies. "Linux Operating System and Accessible Free Software," a chapter written by J. P. Schnapper-Casteras, creator and maintainer of the Linux Accessibility Resource Site (LARS), explains system capability and usage. A list of free e-texts and index are included.

529 Howden, Norman. *Buying and Maintaining Personal Computers: A How-to-Do-It Manual for Librarians.* How-To-Do-It Manuals for Libraries 98. New York: Neal-Schuman, 2000. ISBN: 978-1-55570-376-9.

Howden discusses how PC and Mac computer formats have increased prominence in libraries for staff and patrons. He discusses hardware and software issues, security, licenses, warranties, wiring, backup systems, preventive maintenance, and basic information for providing computer access. Although technology has evolved in the ensuing years, this manual provides general review steps, forms, and checklists that can be adapted for current technology plans.

530   Hunter, Gregory S. *Preserving Digital Information: A How-To-Do-It Manual.* How-To-Do-It Manuals for Libraries 93. New York: Neal-Schuman, 2000. ISBN: 978-1-55570-353-0.

As libraries collect ever-larger amounts of information in digital format, the issue of preservation becomes increasingly apparent and important. Although somewhat dated, this book is still a good first step to take in getting a handle on the situation. Topics discussed include guidelines and best practices for handling electronic records research, digital preservation, electronic mail, and web pages during technological change. In chapter 7, Hunter describes ten strategic decisions that are necessary to establish successful preservation systems. This book was the winner of the Society of American Archivists' 2001 Preservation Publication Award.

531   Intner, Sheila S., Susan S. Lazinger, and Jean Weihs. *Metadata and Its Impact on Libraries.* Library and Information Science Text Series. Westport, CT: Libraries Unlimited, 2005. ISBN: 978-1-59158-145-1.

Part 1 covers metadata concepts and definitions (a standard one being "data about data"), including schemas and their relationships to particular communities, libraries and information, monographic materials, and local catalogs and databases. Part 2 covers the impact of metadata on current and future collections and services including digital materials, digital collections, current resources on digital libraries, and future possibilities. This textbooks ends with a list of acronyms, a glossary, answers to exercises contained within the chapters, and index.

532   Jaeger, Paul T., and Gary Burnett. *Information Worlds: Social Context, Technology, and Information Behavior in the Age of the Internet.* Routledge Studies in Library and Information Science Series 8. New York: Routledge, 2010. ISBN: 978-0-41599-778-2 (print), 978-0-20385-163-0 (e-book).

The authors present a theory that information behaviors can serve as a theoretical driver in both library information studies and other disciplines that study information issues. They delve into the fact that how social groups value information can affect the role of information in democracy during periods of technological changes. The chapter on public libraries and the future of information theory will provoke interesting conversations on libraries' and librarians' impact on worldwide information available.

533   Keane, Nancy J., and Terence W. Cavanaugh. *The Tech-Savvy Booktalker: A Guide for 21st Century Educators.* Westport, CT: Libraries Unlimited, 2008. ISBN: 978-1-59158-637-1

Authors share proven ideas for integrating technology into presentations and using booktalks across grades 6–12 curricula. After discussing booktalking concepts and information technology used in libraries, the conversation quickly moves to using text-based, audio, and video presentations in the classroom. How-to-do-it instructions, sample lesson plans, and technology tips provide numerous booktalking techniques. The appendixes address millennial generation students, do's and don'ts of booktalking, file extensions, and booktalks in nonlibrary settings. An index and information about the authors are included.

534   Kochtanek, Thomas R., and Joseph R. Matthews. *Library Information Systems: From Library Automation to Distributed Information Access Solutions.* Library and Information Science Series. Westport, CT: Libraries Unlimited, 2002. ISBN: 978-1-59158-018-8.

The authors provide a useful overview of library systems and the complexities that information technology developments bring to the library. Topics include the history of library systems, their designs, standards, system planning, implementing and managing technology, usability, trends, and digital libraries. This textbook is especially useful to students learning about library automation and information systems.

535   Lee, Sul H., ed. *Bridging the Gap: Connecting Users to Digital Contents.* New York: Routledge, 2009. ISBN: 978-0-78903-787-9.

Patron demand for digital information grew rapidly as the availability of electronic information exploded through digitalization and e-book formats. Contributors look at remote access, digital resource services, preservation of digital resources, digital formats, licensing, and unique collections from librarian, academic, and patron viewpoints. Field leaders explore ways to strip away the myths and misconceptions of digital information to allow library users easy and timely access to information. This book was originally published as a special issue of the *Journal of Library Administration.*

536   Marcum, Deanna B., and Gerald George, eds. *The Data Deluge: Can Libraries Cope with E-science?* Westport, CT: Libraries Unlimited, 2009. ISBN: 978-1-59158-887-0 (print), 978-0-313-39117-0 (e-book).

Admittedly, the term "e-science" is not exactly a household word. Think supercomputers that process astounding amounts of data for the purposes of weather prediction or experiments in particle physics. Here, contributors first focus on an overview of e-science challenges for libraries in the twenty-first century, agenda for action, scholarly communications, and changes in research libraries before moving into western and cloud cyberinfrastructure national and individual perspectives (e.g., Johns Hopkins; University of California, San Diego; and National Agricultural Library). The essays were adapted from papers delivered at the Kanazawa Institute of Technology Annual Library Round Tables held in 2007 and 2008.

537   Marty, Paul F., and Katherine Burton Jones, eds. *Museum Informatics: People, Information, and Technology in Museums.* Routledge Studies in Library and Information Science Series 2. New York: Routledge, 2008. ISBN: 978-0-82472-581-5.

Although the focus here is on museum collections in an electronic era, much of the discussion on access, exhibits, collections, and challenges is applicable to academic and public libraries. The table of contents lists such topics as information resources, information management, information interactions, information behavior, and information collaborations in museums.

538   Miller, Joseph B. *Internet Technologies and Information Services.* Library and Information Science Series. Westport, CT: Libraries Unlimited, 2008. ISBN: 978-1-59158-626-5.

Miller looks at networking, the Internet, hypertext markup language (HTML), web design, programming, and searching as a base of knowledge and skills needed by professionals in the many IT, LIS, business and management information systems, and decision science fields. This book provides a basic working knowledge of Internet technologies, Internet content creation, and the retrieval of Internet information.

539   Miller, William, and Rita M. Pellen, eds. *Adapting to E-books.* New York: Routledge, 2009. ISBN: 978-0-41548-378-0.

This book contains a series of academic discussions about acquiring, cataloging, distributing, and collecting e-books. The articles include statistical information about e-book usage, types of e-books available, surveys of faculty and librarian attitudes toward e-books, and integrating e-books into academic programs. Figures and charts are used throughout to illustrate statistics and survey results.

540   Murphy, Joe, ed. *Mobile Devices and the Library: Handheld Tech, Handheld Reference.* New York: Routledge, 2011. ISBN: 978-0-41568-975-5.

This volume provides timely knowledge of how to use library applications and leverage handheld mobile devices. Beginning with an introduction to handheld devices, contributors describe how text messaging, iPhone Internet access, and e-books changed the way many patrons view library collections and services. Case studies and professional experiences emphasize why front-line librarians, library administrators, system staff, and library professors must pursue new processes and procedures to keep up with patron demands. This book was published as a special issue of *Reference Librarian*.

541 Pandian, M. Paul. *RFID for Libraries: A Practical Guide.* Chandos Information Professional Series. Oxford, Chandos, 2010. ISBN: 978-1-84334-545-9.

Radio frequency identification (RFID) is an electronic tagging technology that uses electromagnetic waves to identify an item at a distance without direct line of sight. Pandian explains RFID and the pros and cons of using it in a library setting. He includes a review of RFID systems available, then provides step-by-step guidelines for implementing RFID. A chapter on technological, social, economic, and digital environmental issues concludes the book. A list of figures and tables, list of abbreviations, references, and index are provided.

542 Polanka, Sue, ed. *No Shelf Required: E-books in Libraries.* Chicago: American Library Association, 2011. ISBN: 978-0-83891-054-2.

Polanka introduces various e-book technologies, e-book readers and e-book history, development, and the impact on library collections. Topics covered are e-books on the Internet, student learning, acquiring e-books, preservation of e-books, e-book standards, and the future of e-book publishing. Three chapters are devoted to e-books in school, public, and academic libraries. A list of contributors and index are included.

543 Rubenstein, Charles P. *Crash Course in Web Design for Libraries.* Crash Course Series. Westport, CT: Libraries Unlimited, 2006. ISBN: 978-1-59158-366-0.

This detailed crash course for librarians covers developing professional-looking websites without having to learn HTML. Rubenstein uses a typical Microsoft Windows environment to cut and paste templates and examples to develop a very basic library web page for the novice user. Basic information is included on how to choose, organize, create, and prepare content using available software programs.

544 Solomon, Laura. *Doing Social Media So It Matters: A Librarian's Guide.* ALA Editions Special Reports. Chicago: American Library Association, 2011. ISBN: 978-0-83891-067-2.

Social media are all the rage these days, with names like Facebook, Twitter, and MySpace being bandied about constantly. Libraries can harness these tools to strengthen relationships with patrons and forge new ones. As the author points out, "Social media can allow your library to create goodwill and direct connections. Not just direct connections within its community, but also connections to a *wider* community." Therefore, opportunities for outreach, branding and a host of other benefits are in store for those institutions that wish to pursue this "new, faster, and more widespread word of mouth" (p. 57). Though slender, this volume contains much practical information on goal setting, strategies for social media success, evaluation of return on investment, and do's and don't's. Illustrations, examples, "Bottom Line" callouts emphasizing key concepts, and a bibliography of further resources make this a welcome guide to these sometimes mystifying new media.

545 Tomaiuolo, Nicholas G. *UContent: The Information Professional's Guide to User-Generated Content.* Medford, NJ: Information Today, 2012. ISBN: 978-1-57387-425-0.

Tomaiuolo examines user-generated content (UContent) and its impact and role in library and information science. The additional duties as both creators and managers of UContent leave librarians and information professionals conflicted. They need to find a balance between information access and intellectual property rights, not to mention handling problems with mining and cataloging the gargantuan volume of information. Topics include blogging, Yahoo! Pipe, and Project Gutenberg. Examples, insights, tips, illustrations, and interviews with industry specialists will help guide librarians through the minefield of public-created content.

546 Tomaiuolo, Nicholas G. *The Web Library: Building a World Class Personal Library with Free Web Resources.* Edited by Barbara Quint. Foreword by Steve Coffman. Medford, NJ: Information Today, 2004. ISBN: 978-0-91096-567-5.

Tomaiuolo bypasses the usual list of popular websites to provide readers with the tools and know-how to search out free information on the Internet. Topics include free articles and indexes, news articles, references, ask-the-expert sites, e-books, images, virtual exhibitions, and software accessories. Search and organization tips and endnotes highlight key points. The companion website (http://web.ccsu.edu/library/tomaiuolon/theweblibrary.htm) contains web links to sites listed by chapter; entries not listed in the book are marked as "new." The companion website was last updated on August 24, 2009. A list of figures and tables, reference websites, and author and editor information are provided.

547 Vage, Lars, and Lars Iselid. *News Search, Blogs and Feeds: A Toolkit.* Chandos Information Professional Series. Oxford, Chandos, 2010. ISBN: 978-1-84334-602-9.

Vage and Iselid provide tools and techniques to monitor free and commercial news search engines and databases. Beginning with a basic introduction to news searching, the authors quickly move on to specifics regarding free news searches, professional news services, news monitoring services, and evaluating news search tools. Next, they look at keeping track of the blogosphere, the power of an XML format known as really simple syndication (RSS), and news discovery via social networking tools. A list of figures, list of abbreviations, further readings, and index are included.

548 Varum, Kenneth J. *Drupal in Libraries.* Edited by Ellyssa Kroski. Tech Set Series 14. Neal-Schuman, 2012. ISBN: 978-1-55570-778-1.

This step-by-step technical guide highlights decisions and tasks needed to develop and launch a library website using Drupal, a free, open-source content management system. They author walks the reader through installing Drupal, adding modules, developing page layout, project management best practices, marketing the website, and measuring impact and success.

549 Webber, Desiree, and Andrew Peters. *Integrated Library Systems: Planning, Selecting, and Implementing.* Westport, CT: Libraries Unlimited, 2010. ISBN: 978-1-59158-897-9 (print), 978-1-59884-734-5 (e-book).

Webber and Peters provide a detailed step-by-step guide to implementing an integrated library system (ILS). Topics include getting started, evaluating ILS software, selecting hardware, adding features, working with sales consultants, project time lines, planning, budgets, RFPs, vendor contracts, implementation, and training. Appendixes provide a list of vendors, features comparison grid, sample long-term public library strategic plan, sample technology plan, and sample RFP. A glossary, selected biography, and index round out the volume.

& ADDITIONAL RESOURCES

550 Ally, Mohamed, and Gill Needham, eds. *M-Libraries 2: A Virtual Library in Everyone's Pocket.* London: Facet, 2010. ISBN: 978-1-85604-696-1.

551 Ally, Mohamed, and Gill Needham, eds. *M-Libraries 3: Transforming Libraries with Mobile Technology.* London: Facet, 2012. ISBN: 978-1-85604-776-0.

552 Ally, Mohamed and Gill Needham, eds. *M-Libraries 4: From Margin to Mainstream— Mobile Technologies Transforming Lives and*

Libraries. London: Facet, 2013. ISBN: 978-1-85604-944-3.

553 **Anglin, Gary J., ed.** *Instructional Technology: Past, Present, and Future.* 3rd ed. Westport, CT: Libraries Unlimited, 2010. ISBN: 978-1-56308-806-3.

554 **Bielskas, Amanda, and Kathleen M. Dreyer.** *IM and SMS Reference Services for Libraries.* Tech Set Series 19. London: Facet, ISBN: 978-1-85604-844-6; Chicago: American Library Association, ISBN: 978-1-55570-782-8. 2012.

555 **Billings, Harold.** *Magic and Hypersystems: Constructing the Information-Sharing Library.* Chicago: American Library Association, 2002. ISBN: 978-0-83890-834-1.

556 **Bisson, Casey.** *Open-Source Software for Libraries.* Library Technology Reports. Chicago: American Library Association, 2007. ISBN: 978-0-83895-787-5.

557 **Bluh, Pamela, and Cindy Hepfer, eds.** *Managing Electronic Resources: Contemporary Problems and Emerging Issues.* ALCTS Papers on Library Technical Services and Collections. Chicago: Association for Library Collections and Technical Services, American Library Association, 2006. ISBN: 978-0-83898-366-9.

558 **Bolan, Kimberly, and Robert Cullin.** *Technology Made Simple: An Improvement Guide for Small and Medium Libraries.* Chicago: American Library Association, 2007. ISBN: 978-0-83890-920-1.

559 **Booth, Char.** *Informing Innovation: Tracking Student Interest in Emerging Library Technologies at Ohio University.* Chicago: Association of College and Research Libraries, American Library Association, 2009. ISBN: 978-0-83898-526-7.

560 **Bradley, Phil.** *Social Media for Creative Libraries: How to Maximise Impact and Reach.* 2nd ed. London: Facet, 2014. ISBN: 978-1-85604-713-5.

561 **Breeding, Marshall.** *Cloud Computing for Libraries.* Tech Set Series 11. London: Facet, ISBN: 978-1-85604-847-7; Chicago: American Library Association, ISBN: 978-1-55570-785-9. 2012.

562 **Breeding, Marshall.** *Opening Up Library Systems through Web Services and SOA: Hype, or Reality?* Library Technology Reports 45, no. 8. Chicago: American Library Association, 2009. ISBN: 978-0-83895-806-3.

563 **Breeding, Marshall.** *Open Source Integrated Library Systems.* Library Technology Reports. Chicago: American Library Association, 2008. ISBN: 978-0-83895-798-1.

564 **Brown, Adrian.** *Archiving Websites: A Practical Guide for Information Management Professionals.* London: Facet, 2006. ISBN: 978-1-85604-553-7.

565 **Brown, Adrian.** *Practical Digital Preservation: A How-to-Guide to Organizations of Any Size.* London: Facet, 2013. ISBN: 978-1-85604-755-5.

566 **Bulow, Anna E., and Jess Ahmon.** *Preparing Collections for Digitization.* London: Facet, 2011. ISBN: 978-1-85604-711-1.

567 **Calhoun, Karen.** *Exploring Digital Libraries: Foundations, Practices, Prospects.* London: Facet, ISBN: 978-1-85604-820-0; Chicago: American Library Association, ISBN: 978-1-55570-985-3. 2014.

568 **Campbell, Nicole, ed.** *Usability Assessment of Library-Related Web Sites: Methods and Case Studies.* Chicago: American Library Association, 2001. ISBN: 978-0-83898-157-3.

569 **Choksy, Carol E. B.** *Creating a Complete Programme for Electronic Records Retention.* London: Facet, ISBN: 978-1-85604-775-3; Chicago: American Library Association, ISBN: 978-1-55570-742-2. 2014.

570 **Chowdhury, G. G. and Schubert Foo, eds.** Digital Libraries and Information Access: Research Perspectives. London: Facet, 2012. ISBN: 978-1-85604-821-7.

571 Chowdhury, G. G. *Introduction to Modern Information Retrieval.* 3rd ed. London: Facet, 2010. ISBN: 978-1-85604-694-7.

572 Chowdhury, G. G., and Sudatta Chowdhury. *Information Users and Usability in the Digital Age.* London: Facet, 2011. ISBN: 978-1-85604-597-1.

573 Chowdhury, G. G., and Sudatta Chowdhury. *Introduction to Digital Libraries.* London: Facet, 2002. ISBN: 978-1-85604-465-3.

574 Clark, Jason. *Building Mobile Library Applications.* Tech Set Series 12. London: Facet, ISBN: 978-1-85604-845-3; Chicago: American Library Association, ISBN: 9781555707835. 2012.

575 Cohen, Steven M. *Keeping Current: Advanced Internet Strategies to Meet Librarian and Patron Needs.* Chicago: American Library Association, 2003. ISBN: 978-0-83890-864-8.

576 Cole, Louise. *Challenges in E-Resource Management: A Practitioner's Guide.* London: Facet, 2014. ISBN: 978-1-85604-814-9.

577 Corrado, Edward M., and Heather Lea Moulalson. *Getting Started with Cloud Computing.* London: Facet, ISBN: 978-1-85604-807-1; Chicago: American Library Association, ISBN: 978-1-55570-749-1. 2011.

578 Cox, Andrew, ed. *Portals: People, Processes and Technology.* London: Facet, 2006. ISBN: 978-1-85604-546-9.

579 Craven, Jenny. *Web Accessibility: Practical Advice for the Library and Information Professional.* London: Facet, ISBN: 978-1-85604-625-1 (print), 978-1-85604-660-2 (e-book); Chicago: American Library Association, ISBN: 978-1-85604-625-1. 2008.

580 *Creating the Digital Art Library.* New York: Primary Research Group, 2005. ISBN: 978-1-57440-074-8.

581 *Creating the Digital Law Library.* New York: Primary Research Group, 2003. ISBN: 978-1-57440-062-5.

582 *Creating the Digital Medical Library.* New York: Primary Research Group, 2003. ISBN: 978-1-57440-061-8.

583 Czarnecki, Kelly Nicole. *Gaming in Libraries.* Tech Set Series 9. London: Facet, ISBN: 978-1-85604-729-6; Chicago: American Library Association, ISBN: 978-1-55570-709-5. 2010.

584 Davidsen, Susanna, and Everyl Yankee. *Web Site Design with the Patron in Mind: A Step-by-Step Guide for Libraries.* Chicago: American Library Association, 2004. ISBN: 978-0-83890-869-3.

585 Deegan, Marilyn, and Simon Tanner. *Digital Futures: Strategies for the Information Age.* London: Facet, 2001. ISBN: 978-1-85604-580-3.

586 Deegan, Marilyn, and Simon Tanner, eds. *Digital Preservation.* Digital Futures Series. London: Facet, 2006. ISBN: 978-1-85604-485-1.

587 De Saulles, Martin. *Information 2.0 New Models of Information Production, Distribution and Consumption.* London: Facet, 2012. ISBN: 978-1-85604-754-8.

588 Dewey, Patrick R. *101 Computer Projects for Libraries.* Chicago: American Library Association, 2000. ISBN: 978-0-83890-772-6.

589 Dodsworth, Eva. *Getting Started with GIS: A LITA Guide.* New York: Neal-Schuman, 2011. ISBN: 978-1-55570-775-0.

590 Fay, Robin, and Michael Sauers. *20 Semantic Web Technologies and Social Searching for Librarians.* Tech Set Series 20. London: Facet, 2012. ISBN: 978-1-85604-842-2.

591 Fleming-May, Rachel A., and Jill Grogg. *The Concept of Electronic Resource Usage and Libraries.* Library Technology Reports. Chicago: American Library Association, 2010. ISBN: 978-0-83895-812-4.

592 Griffiths, Peter. *Managing Your Internet and Intranet Services: The Information and Library Professional's Guide to Strategy.* 2nd ed. London: Facet, 2004. ISBN: 978-1-85604-483-7.

593   Hanson, Cody. *Libraries and the Mobile Web.* Library Technology Reports. Chicago: American Library Association, 2011. ISBN: 978-0-83895-830-8.

594   Harris, Frances Jacobson. *I Found It on the Internet: Coming of Age Online.* 2nd ed. Chicago: American Library Association, 2011. ISBN: 978-0-83891-066-5.

595   Harris, Lesley Ellen. *Licensing Digital Content: A Practical Guide for Librarians.* Chicago: American Library Association, 2009. ISBN: 978-0-83890-992-8.

596   Harvey, Ross. *Digital Curation: A How-to-Do It Guide.* London: Facet, ISBN: 978-1-85604-733-3; Chicago: American Library Association, ISBN: 978-1-55570-694-4. 2010.

597   Hastings, Robin. *Collaboration 2.0.* Library Technology Reports. Chicago: American Library Association, 2009. ISBN: 978-0-83895-802-5.

598   Hastings, Robin N. *Microblogging and Lifestreaming in Libraries.* Tech Set Series 3. London: Facet, ISBN: 978-1-85604-723-4; Chicago: American Library Association, ISBN: 978-1-55570-707-1. 2010.

599   Houghton-Jan, Sarah. *Technology Training in Libraries.* Tech Set Series 6. London: Facet, ISBN: 978-1-85604-726-5; Chicago: American Library Association, ISBN: 978-1-55570-706-4. 2010.

600   Houser, John. *Open Source Public Workstations in Libraries.* Library Technology Reports. Chicago: American Library Association, 2009. ISBN: 978-0-83895-801-8.

601   Howden, Norman. *Local Area Networking for the Small Library: A How-to-Do-It Manual.* 2nd ed. How-To-Do-It Manuals for Libraries 67. New York: Neal-Schuman, 1997. ISBN: 978-1-55570-285-4.

602   Hughes, Lorna M., ed. *Evaluating and Measuring the Value, Use and Impact of Digital Collections.* London: Facet, 2011. ISBN: 978-1-85604-720-3.

603   Imhoff, Kathleen. *Making the Most of New Technology: A How-to-Do-It Manual.* How-To-Do-It Manuals for Libraries 64. New York: Neal-Schuman, 1996. ISBN: 978-1-55570-232-8.

604   Jacobs, Neil, Matthew Davey, and Rachel Bruce. *Digital Infrastructure.* London: Facet, 2014. ISBN: 978-1-85604-856-9.

605   Kahn, Miriam. *Protecting Your Library's Digital Sources: The Essential Guide to Planning and Preservation.* Chicago: American Library Association, 2004. ISBN: 978-0-83890-873-0.

606   King, David L. *Building the Digital Branch: Guidelines for Transforming Your Library Website.* Library Technology Reports. Chicago: American Library Association, 2009. ISBN: 978-0-83895-804-9.

607   Korn, Naomi, and Charles Oppenheim. *The No-Nonsense Guide to Licensing Digital Resources.* London: Facet, 2014. ISBN: 978-1-85604-805-7.

608   Kresh, Diane, ed. *The Whole Digital Library Handbook.* Chicago: American Library Association, 2007. ISBN: 978-0-83890-926-3.

609   Kroski, Ellyssa, ed. *On the Move with the Mobile Web: Libraries and Mobile Technologies.* Library Technology Reports. Chicago: American Library Association, 2008. ISBN: 978-0-83895-795-0.

610   Landis, Cliff. *A Social Networking Primer for Librarians.* Tech Set Series 7. New York: Neal-Schuman, 2010. ISBN: 978-1-55570-704-0.

611   Lascarides, Michael. *Next-Gen Library Redesign.* Tech Set Series 16. London: Facet, ISBN: 978-1-85604-849-1; Chicago: American Library Association, ISBN: 978-1-55570-787-3. 2012.

612   Lazzaro, Joseph J. *Adaptive Technologies for Learning and Work Environments.* 2nd ed. Chicago: American Library Association, 2001. ISBN: 978-0-83890-804-4.

613   Leckie, Gloria J., and John E. Buschman, eds. *Information Technology in Librarianship:*

New Critical Approaches. Westport, CT: Libraries Unlimited, 2008. ISBN: 978-1-59158-629-6.

614   *Library Use of E-books.* 2012 Edition. New York: Primary Research Group, 2012. ISBN: 978-1-57440-184-4.

615   *Library Use of Mega Internet Sites, 2011–12: Google, Facebook, Yahoo!, Twitter, YouTube, Wikipedia, and More.* New York: Primary Research Group, 2012. ISBN: 978-1-57440-177-6.

616   Libutti, Patricia O'Brien, ed. *Digital Resources and Librarians: Case Studies in Innovation, Invention, and Implementation.* Chicago: American Library Association, 2004. ISBN: 978-0-83898-262-4.

617   Lomas, Elizabeth, ed. *Information Management Solutions: Communications and Collaboration in a Web 2.0 World.* London: Facet, 2014. ISBN: 978-1-85604-718-0.

618   Mayo, Diane. *Technology for Results: Developing Service-Based Plans.* PLA Results Series. Chicago: American Library Association, 2005. ISBN: 978-0-83893-550-7.

619   McClure, Charles R., and Paul T. Jaeger. *Public Libraries and Internet Service Roles: Measuring and Maximizing Internet Services.* Chicago: American Library Association, 2009. ISBN: 978-0-83893-576-7.

620   McMenemy, David, and Alan Poulter. *Delivering Digital Services: A Handbook for Public Libraries and Learning Centres.* London: Facet, 2005. ISBN: 978-1-85604-510-0.

621   Miller, Dick R., and Kevin S. Clarke. *Putting XML to Work in the Library: Tools for Improving Access and Management.* Chicago: American Library Association, 2004. ISBN: 978-0-83890-863-1.

622   Morrison, Andrea M., ed. *Managing Electronic Government Information in Libraries: Issues and Practices.* Chicago: American Library Association, 2008. ISBN: 978-0-83890-954-6.

623   Moss, Michael and Barbara Endicott-Popovsky, eds. *Is Digital Different?* How Information Creation, Capture, Preservation and Discovery Are Being Transformed. London: Facet, 2014. ISBN: 978-1-85604-854-5.

624   Murphy, Joe. *Location-Aware Services and QR Codes for Libraries.* Tech Set Series 13. London: Facet, ISBN: 978-1-85604-846-0; Chicago: American Library Association, ISBN: 978-1-55570-784-2. 2012.

625   Ng, Kwong Bor. *Using XML: A How-to-Do-It Manual and CD-ROM for Librarians.* How-To-Do-It Manuals for Libraries 154. New York: Neal-Schuman, 2007. ISBN: 978-1-55570-567-1.

626   Nicholas, David, and Ian Rowlands, eds. *Digital Consumers: Reshaping the Information Professions.* London: Facet, 2008. ISBN: 978-1-85604-651-0.

627   Norlin, Elaina, and CM! Winters. *Usability Testing for Library Web Sites: A Hands-On Guide.* Chicago: American Library Association, 2002. ISBN: 978-0-83893-511-8.

628   Notess, Greg. *Screencasting for Libraries.* Tech Set Series 17. London: Facet, ISBN: 978-1-85604-848-4; Chicago: American Library Association, ISBN: 978-1-55570-786-6. 2012.

629   Pace, Andrew K. *The Ultimate Digital Library: Where the New Information Players Meet.* Chicago: American Library Association, 2003. ISBN: 978-0-83890-844-0.

630   Palmer, Michael. *Making the Most of RFID in Libraries.* London: Facet, 2009. ISBN: 978-1-85604-634-3.

631   Peltier-Davis, Cheryl Ann. *The Cybrarian's Web: The A–Z Guide to 101 Free Web 2.0 Tools and Other Resources.* London: Facet, 2012. ISBN: 978-1-85604-829-3.

632   Peterson, Andrea. *Simplify Web Site Management with Server-Side (includes Cascading Style Sheets and Perl).* Chicago: American Library Association, 2002. ISBN: 978-0-83898-199-3.

633 Pressley, Lauren. *Wikis for Libraries.* Tech Set Series 5. London: Facet, ISBN: 978-1-85604-725-8; Chicago: American Library Association, ISBN: 978-1-55570-710-1. 2010.

634 Price, Kate, and Virginia Havergat. *E-books in Libraries: A Practical Guide.* London: Facet, 2011. ISBN: 978-1-85604-572-8.

635 Ratzan, Lee. *Understanding Information Systems: What They Do and Why We Need Them.* Chicago: American Library Association, 2004. ISBN: 978-0-83890-868-6.

636 Reese, Terry, and Kyle Banerjee. *Building Digital Libraries: A How-to-Do-It Manual.* How-To-Do-It Manuals for Libraries 153. New York: Neal-Schuman, 2007. ISBN: 978-1-55570-617-3.

637 Robinson, Sean. *Library Videos and Webcasts.* Tech Set Series 4. London: Facet, ISBN: 978-1-85604-724-1; Chicago: American Library Association, ISBN: 978-1-55570-705-7. 2010.

638 Rosedale, Jeff, ed. *Managing Electronic Reserves.* Chicago: American Library Association, 2002. ISBN: 978-0-83890-812-9.

639 Schmidt, Aaron, and Amanda Etches. *User Experience (UX) Design for Libraries.* Tech Set Series 18. London: Facet, ISBN: 978-1-85604-843-9; Chicago: American Library Association, ISBN: 978-1-55570-781-1. 2012.

640 Song, Yuwu. *Building Better Web Sites: A How-to-Do-It Manual for Librarians.* How-To-Do-It Manuals for Libraries 123. New York: Neal-Schuman, 2003. ISBN: 978-1-55570-466-7.

641 Steiner, Sarah. *Strategic Planning for Social Media in Libraries.* Tech Set Series 15. London: Facet, ISBN: 978-1-85604-841-5; Chicago: American Library Association, ISBN: 978-1-55570-779-8. 2012.

642 Stielow, Frederick J. *Building Digital Archives, Descriptions, and Displays: A How-to-Do-It Manual for Archivists and Librarians.* How-To-Do-It Manuals for Libraries 116. New York: Neal-Schuman, 2003. ISBN: 978-1-55570-463-6.

643 Theimer, Kate. *Web 2.0 Tools and Strategies for Archives and Local History Collections.* London: Facet, ISBN: 978-1-85604-687-9; Chicago: American Library Association, ISBN: 978-1-55570-679-1. 2010.

644 Trainor, Cindi, and Jason S. Price. *Rethinking Library Linking: Breathing New Life into OpenURL.* Library Technology Reports. Chicago: American Library Association, 2010. ISBN: 978-0-83895-813-1.

645 Vincent, Jane. *Implementing Cost-Effective Assistive Computer Technology: A How-to-Do-It Manual for Librarians.* Foreword by Rhea Rubin. How-To-Do-It Manuals for Libraries 181. New York: Neal-Schuman, 2012. ISBN: 978-1-55570-762-0.

646 Walsh, Andrew. *Using Mobile Technology to Deliver Library Services: A Handbook.* London: Facet, 2012. ISBN: 978-1-85604-809-5.

647 Westman, Stephen R. *Creating Database-Backed Library Web Pages: Using Open Source Tools.* Chicago: American Library Association, 2006. ISBN: 978-0-83890-910-2.

648 White, Martin. *Content Management Handbook.* London: Facet, 2005. ISBN: 978-1-85604-533-9.

649 White, Martin. *Intranet Management Handbook.* London: Facet, 2011. ISBN: 978-1-85604-734-0.

650 White, Martin. *Making Search Work: Implementing Web, Intranet and Enterprise Search.* London: Facet, 2007. ISBN: 978-1-85604-602-2.

651 Whittaker, Beth M., and Lynne M. Thomas. *Special Collections 2.0: New Technologies for Rare Books, Manuscripts, and Archival Collections.* Westport, CT: Libraries Unlimited, 2009. ISBN: 978-1-59158-720-0.

652 Wilson, A. Paula. *Library Web Sites: Creating Online Collections and Services.* Chicago: American Library Association, 2004. ISBN: 978-0-83890-872-3.

653 Younger, Paula, and Peter Morgan, eds.
Using Web 2.0 for Health Information. London:
Facet, 2011. ISBN: 978-1-85604-731-9.

📓 PERIODICALS

654 *Advanced Technology Libraries*
(AT/L). White Plains, NY: Knowledge Industry
Publications. Frequency: Twelve times per
year. ISSN: 0044-636X. URL: www
.advancedtechnologylibraries.com.

Advanced Technology Libraries provides concise
reviews of information technology relevant to
libraries. Topics include integrated library systems; the latest electronic products; online services for public, academic, and special libraries;
major conferences and meetings; current activities of OCLC and RLG; federal legislation relevant
to libraries; intellectual freedom and copyright
issues; and grant awards.

655 *Electronic Library.* Westport, CT: Emerald
Group. Frequency: Six times per year. ISSN:
0264-0473. URL: www.emeraldinsight.com/
products/journals/journals.htm?id=el.

This magazine is devoted to the application and
implication of new technologies, automation,
digitalization, the Internet, user interfaces, and
networks in all type of libraries. Topics include
libraries and the web, digital libraries, software and hardware developments, networking
and automation, integrated systems, user interfaces, e-books and e-journals, e-governance and
e-readiness, and online and distance learning.

**656 *Information Management and Computer
Security.*** Westport, CT: Emerald Group.
Frequency: Five times per year. ISSN: 0968-
5227. URL: www.emeraldinsight.com/products/
journals/journals.htm?id=imcs.

This magazine emphasizes the interaction of
technical and human aspects to advance knowledge concerning the security and assurances of
information and information systems. Topics

include security governance and compliance,
user authentication and biometrics, Internet security and protection, computer ethics and security,
misuse and abuse of computer systems, information security management, and risk assessment
and modeling.

**657 *Information Technology and Libraries
(ITAL).*** Chicago: Library and Information
Technology Association, American Library
Association. Frequency: Four times per year.
ISSN: 0730-9295. URL: www.ala.org/lita/ital/.

This refereed journal covers issues related to all
aspects of libraries and information technology.
Topics may include digital libraries, metadata,
authorization and authentication, electronic
journals, electronic publishing, telecommunica-
tions, distributed systems, networks, computer
security, intellectual property rights, technical
standards, software engineering, and futuristic
forecasting.

658 *Information Technology and People.*
Westport, CT: Emerald Group. Frequency:
Four times per year. ISSN: 0959-3845. URL:
www.emeraldinsight.com/products/journals/
journals.htm?id=itp.

This magazine explores the significance of new
social definitions of institutions, the social environment surrounding production and technology
implementation, and the human scale of social
processes that are both the basis and the outcome of technological change. Case studies, comparative theory, and quantitative research topics
including information technology as a tool, system development, emerging ideas, and impact on
performance are provided.

659 *Internet Research* (previously published
as *Electronic Networks*). Westport, CT: Emerald
Group. Frequency: Five times per year. ISSN:
1066-2243. URL: www.emeraldinsight.com/
products/journals/journals.htm?id=intr.

This refereed international journal describes,
assesses, and fosters understanding of multipurpose computer networks such as the Internet.

Topics include electronic networks in research and education, managerial and organizational issues, standards, network design and operation, and public and private sector roles and responsibilities.

660 *Journal of Electronic Resources Librarianship.* Philadelphia: Routledge. Frequency: Four times per year. ISSN: 1941-126X (print), 1941-1278 (online). URL: www.tandf.co.uk/journals/WACQ/.

This journal is for library administrators, librarians, and other information professionals who manage, purchase, access, teach, and evaluate electronic resources in libraries. All research articles undergo anonymous double-blind review. Articles cover developments in the following areas:

- Collection development and maintenance
- Technical operations, processes, and digitization
- Training, access, and instruction
- Electronic publishing and publications
- Archival issues and preservation
- Institutional repositories
- Open source and open access
- Cost analysis and staffing
- Web design and maintenance

661 *Journal of Web Librarianship.* Philadelphia: Routledge. Frequency: Four times per year. ISSN: 1932-2909 (print), 1932-2917 (online). URL: www.tandf.co.uk/journals/WJWL/.

Articles cover library web page design and redesign, web project management, usability testing of library or library-related sites, cataloging and classification of web information, international issues in web librarianship, library integration with other websites, and future aspects of web librarianship. There are also articles related to user behavior on the web, including search behaviors, social networking site trends, and the connection between the web at large and library web resources. All articles and communications undergo both editorial screening and anonymous, double-blind peer review.

662 *Journal of Systems and Information Technology.* Westport, CT: Emerald Group. Frequency: Four times per year. ISSN: 1328-7265. URL: www.emeraldinsight.com/products/journals/journals.htm?id=jsit.

This journal focuses on information systems, electronic business, and academic research on information technology. Case studies, surveys, experiments, review articles, and theoretical articles address topics such as website development and evaluation, the development of technology policy and technology transfer, the management of information systems, social aspects of information systems, and the influence of politics and culture on systems development and the use of information technology.

663 *Library Hi-Tech.* Westport, CT: Emerald Group. Frequency: Four times per year. ISSN: 0737-8831. URL: www.emeraldinsight.com/products/journals/journals.htm?id=lht.

This periodical focuses on computing and technology for libraries, including a full range of tools employed by libraries and their customers. Topics include integrated library systems, networking, strategic planning, policy implementation, security, automaton systems, resource access initiatives, consortia, electronic publishing, and user perspectives on technology.

664 *Library Hi-Tech News.* Westport, CT: Emerald Group. Frequency: Ten times per year. ISSN: 0741-9058. URL: www.emeraldinsight.com/journals.htm?issn=0741-9058.

This periodical focuses on worldwide developments in library technologies, new products and services, and important issues and activities. Recurring columns offer technology profiles from libraries around the world, conference reviews, news, and a diary of forthcoming events. General topics include new web browsers/search engines, virtual reference/pilots/experiments, blogging, virtual worlds, digital textbooks, technology for library users with disabilities, LibGuides and similar products, cloud computing, and citation managers.

665 *Multimedia Information and Technology (MmIT).* London: Chartered Institute of Library and Information Professionals. Frequency: Quarterly. ISSN: 1499-190X (print), 1466-9358 (online). URL: www.cilip.org.uk/get-involved/special-interest-groups/multimedia/journal/pages/default.aspx.

This quarterly journal contains at least one full-length article, news and technology updates, product reviews, DVD listings, moving images news, and book reviews. Topics include learning systems, new media, assistive technology, multimedia, web searching, and social networking.

666 *New Review of Hypermedia and Multimedia.* Philadelphia: Routledge. Frequency: Three times per year. ISSN: 1361-4568 (print), 1740-7842 (online). URL: www.tandf.co.uk/journals/THAM/.

This journal provides research and information on practical and theoretical developments in hypermedia, hypertext, interactive multimedia, and related technologies. Sample articles examine the integration of images, sound, text, and data to form powerful tools for information retrieval, multimedia links with mass storage, time and synchronization, multimedia authoring tools, navigation and browsing, search systems, and content-based retrieval.

667 *New Review of Information Networking.* Philadelphia: Routledge. Frequency: Two issues per year. ISSN: 1361-4576 (print), 1740-7869 (online). URL: www.tandf.co.uk/journals/RINN/.

Articles focus on the network user's needs and behavior; network roles in teaching, learning, research, and scholarly communication; library and information services networks; development in campus and other information strategies; information publishers' role in the networks; policies for funding and charging for network and information services; and standards and protocols for network applications. All review papers undergo editorial screening and peer review.

668 *OCLC Systems and Services.* Westport, CT: Emerald Group. Frequency: Four issues per year. ISSN: 1065-075X. URL: www.emeraldinsight.com/products/journals/journals.htm?id=oclc.

Digital libraries and digital repositories, relevant standards and techniques, and web-based delivery of digital cultural content are the main focus of this periodical. Feature articles, case studies, news, and views cover digital libraries, digital repositories, digital cultural content services, web metadata standards, web markup languages, digital preservation, imaging and digitalization techniques, and usability studies.

669 *Portal: Libraries and the Academy.* Baltimore, MD: Johns Hopkins University Press. Frequency: Four times per year. ISSN: 1530-7131. URL: http://muse.jhu.edu/journals/portal_libraries_and_the_academy/.

Portal provides regular coverage of technology, publishing, and academic periodical issues. Peer-reviewed articles look at library administration, information technology, and information policies.

670 *Program: Electronic Library and Information Systems.* Westport, CT: Emerald Group. Frequency: Four times per year. ISSN: 0033-0337. URL: www.emeraldinsight.com/products/journals/journals.htm?id=prog.

This refereed journal covers all aspects of the management and use of information technology in libraries and archives and emphasizes practical application of new technologies and techniques. Topics include automation of library and information services, storage and retrieval of all forms of electronic information, database design and management, delivery of information to users, user interface design, knowledge organizational systems as ontologies or terminologies, linked data systems and applications, and metadata specifications and standards for electronic libraries.

@ ADDITIONAL RESOURCES

671 *Computers in Libraries.* Westport, CT: Information Today. Frequency: Monthly. ISSN: 1041-7915. URL: www.infotoday.com/cilmag/.

672 *D-Lib Magazine: The Magazine of Digital Library Research.* Reston, VA: Corporation for National Research Initiatives. Frequency: Six times per year. ISSN: 1082-9873. URL: www.dlib.org.

673 *Database Trends and Applications.* Westport, CT: Information Today. Frequency: Quarterly. ISSN: 1547-9897. URL: www.dbta.com.

674 *Journal of the American Society for Information Science and Technology (JASIST).* New York: John Wiley and Sons. Frequency: Twelve times per year. ISSN: 1532-2882. URL: www.asis.org/jasist.html.

675 *Journal of Database Management.* Hershey, PA: Idea Group Publishing. Frequency: Four times per year. ISSN: 1063-8016. URL: www.igi-global.com/journal/journal-database -management-jdm/1072.

676 *Journal of Digital Information.* Austin: University of Texas Press. Frequency: Intermittent. ISSN: 1368-7506. URL: http:// journals.tdl.org/jodi.

677 *New Review of Information Networking.* London: Taylor and Francis Group. Frequency: Twice per year. ISSN: 1361-4576 (print), 1740-7869 (online). URL: www.tandf.co.uk/journals/ titles/13614576.asp.

♠ WEBSITES

678 "College Students on the Web: Usability Guidelines for Creating Compelling Websites for College Students." Fremont, CA: Nielsen Norman Group, 2010. www.nngroup.com/reports/ students/.

This report contains eighty-six design guidelines based on usability and ethnographic tests of more than 217 websites by university-level undergraduate and graduate students, who varied by age (18–24) and country of origin. The research looks at myths about student use, site credibility, multimedia, promotional content, social media, e-commerce, and web design. A section on websites that students particularly liked and a list of website studies put the information gleaned into proper context.

679 *ITALica.* Chicago: Library and Information Technology Association, American Library Association. Frequency: Ongoing. URL: http:// ital-ica.blogspot.com.

In 2008, the Library and Information Technology Association (LITA, a subunit of ALA) created this blog to allow open discussion among readers, authors, and editors on articles appearing in *Information Technology and Libraries* magazine. *ITALica* is open to all *Information Technology and Libraries* readers and does not require a separate membership.

680 "Teenagers on the Web: 61 Usability Guidelines for Creating Compelling Websites for Teens." Fremont, CA: Nielsen Norman Group, 2010. www.nngroup.com/reports/teens/.

This report contains sixty-one design checklists based on results from one-on-one direct observation usability tests of more than twenty mainstream websites on thirty-eight children, who varied by age (13–17) and mainly resided in the United States. Content was examined for visual, interaction, and promotional design concurrently with navigation and search features. With more than 140 screenshots, the information covers community, entertainment, games, shopping, sports, and search websites.

681 "Usability of Websites for Children: Design Guidelines for Targeting Users Aged 3–12 years." 2nd edition. Fremont, CA: Nielsen Norman Group, 2010. www.nngroup.com/reports/kids.

This updated report contains 130 design guidelines based on usability tests of over fifty websites by ninety children, who varied by age and country of origin. The study addresses similarities and differences in the way kids and adults use, access, and assimilate information through interactivity, audio, animation, and video. A section on user-testing parameters provides insight on how research conducted translated directly to kids' computer usage at libraries. The final section covers online concerns for caretakers and children.

INTERLIBRARY LOAN AND DOCUMENT DELIVERY

 BOOKS

682 Boucher, Virginia, Cherié L. Weible, and Karen L. Janke, eds. *Interlibrary Loan Practices Handbook.* 3rd ed. Chicago: American Library Association, 2011. ISBN: 978-0-83891-081-8.

This handbook covers interlibrary loan basics, borrowing workflow basics, lending workflow basics, U.S. copyright and interlibrary loan practices, management of interlibrary loans, relevant technology, web usage, and the future of interlibrary loans.

683 Hilyer, Lee Andrew. *Interlibrary Loan and Document Delivery in the Larger Academic Library: A Guide for University Research, and Larger Public Libraries.* Annotated ed. Copublished simultaneously as *Journal of Interlibrary Loan, Document Delivery and Information Supply* 13, nos. 1/2, 2002. New York: Haworth Information Press, 2002. ISBN: 978-0-78901-951-6.

This guide provides practical examples, copyright resources, appendixes, and flowcharts of interlibrary loan services, along with an annotated bibliography and list of resources. Particular attention is given to day-to-day operations, workflow, measurement, and evaluation of services from both the librarian and patron point of view.

684 Knox, Emily. *Document Delivery and Interlibrary Loan on a Shoestring.* New York: Neal-Schuman, 2010. ISBN: 978-1-55570-678-4.

This primer has a dual audience; although targeted at small to medium-sized libraries lacking a dedicated department for these services, it is also an excellent training manual for the newer librarian still learning the ropes of getting material from point A to point B. That said, any library facing flat to declining budgets (how many aren't these days?) would profit from this well-illustrated volume, the nine chapters of which detail practical advice for the provision of low-cost services. Opening with an overview of the basics, the author goes on to examine common issues encountered, ILL codes, copyright law, and policies/procedures involved in lending and borrowing. Appendixes contain templates for reproducible forms and examples of time- and money-saving best practices.

✐ ADDITIONAL RESOURCES

685 Kelsey, Paul, ed. *Profiles of Best Practices in Academic Library Interlibrary Loan.* New York: Primary Research Group, 2009. ISBN: 978-1-57440-122-6.

686 Weible, Cherie L. E., and Karen L. E. Janke, eds. *Interlibrary Loan Practices Handbook.* 3rd ed. Chicago: American Library Association, 2011. ISBN: 978-0-83891-081-8.

▤ PERIODICALS

687 *Interlibrary Lending and Document Supply.* Westport, CT: Emerald Group. Frequency: Four times per year. ISSN: 0264-1615. URL: www.emeraldinsight.com/products/journals/journals.htm?id=ilds.

This journal covers a wide range of worldwide activities related to document provision and supply, from traditional to the use of advances technologies. Topics include acquisition, storage and photo duplication of stock, networking, supply of documents between organizations in developed and developing countries, worldwide developments in new technology, and document retrieval.

688 *Journal of Interlibrary Loan, Document Delivery and Electronic Reserve.* Philadelphia: Routledge. Frequency: Five times per year. ISSN: 1072-303X (print), 1540-3572 (online). URL: www.tandf.co.uk/journals/WILD.

This journal has articles on new models and emerging technologies for resource sharing, cooperative training ventures, and shared storage facilities. Attention is given to traditional resource sharing topics of interlibrary loan and electronic reserves, document delivery, cooperative collection development, shared virtual library services and digitization projects, library consortia, networks, cooperatives, and other multilibrary collaborative efforts. All articles undergo editorial screening and peer review.

INTERNATIONAL LIBRARIANSHIP

BOOKS

689 Abdullahi, Ismail, ed. *Global Library and Information Science: A Textbook for Students and Educators.* IFLA Publications 136–137. Munich: K. G. Saur, 2009. ISBN: 978-3-59822-042-5.

The subtitle is a bit of a misnomer, for this volume is not strictly a textbook in the sense of what one would use during a semester-long course in library school. That being said, "global" is certainly an accurate descriptor; seven sections examine the library scene in Africa, Asia, Australia, Europe, Latin America, the Middle East, and North America. Within these broad categories, the contributors cover public libraries, academic libraries, special libraries, school libraries, and LIS education. With globalization and multiculturalism being today's watchwords, the point is well taken that "our increasing technological and economic interconnectedness allows the world's population to share in benefits such as more rapid economic growth, improvements in living standards, reduction of poverty, increased foreign direct investment, and the peaceful resolution of international political and economic tension" (p. 9). This is an excellent overview of how our colleagues in other parts of the world are helping to make the machinery of internationalism work smoothly.

690 Byrne, Alex. *The Politics of Promoting Freedom of Information and Expression in International Librarianship: The IFLA/FAIFE Project.* Libraries and Librarianship: An International Perspective 4. Lanham, MD: Scarecrow Press, 2007. ISBN: 978-0-81086-017-9.

The first sentence of the preface sets the stage: "In August 1997, the Council of the International Federation of Library Associations and Institutions (IFLA) initiated a project to promote and defend the right to information by establishing the Committee on Free Access to Information and Freedom of Expression (FAIFE)" (p. vii). This book is an examination of what has transpired during this initiative's first five years, from inception to IFLA's endorsement of the Glasgow Declaration on Libraries, Information Services and Intellectual Freedom of 2002.

691 Carroll, Frances Laverne, John Frederick Harvey, and Susan Houck, eds. *International Librarianship: Cooperation and Collaboration.* Lanham, MD: Scarecrow Press, 2001. ISBN: 978-0-81083-921-2.

This interesting collection of thirty-two essays presents snapshots of libraries worldwide at the turn of the millennium. As the subtitle alludes, the theme is one of working together for the common good. Typical articles include "Cooperation on an International Scale," "Public Libraries in Nigeria," "Library Education in Japan," and "Assistance for Pakistan Librarianship." Obviously, not all nations can be represented in a volume of this size, but enough are here to remind us that even in so-called developing nations our colleagues are hard at work answering questions, organizing knowledge, and generally acting as gatekeepers to cultural resources. Speaking of the latter, all too often we forget or are unaware of what the rest of the world is up to. One antidote to this problem is the article "International Cultural Exchange through Libraries."

692 Kesselman, Martin Alan, and Irwin Weintraub, eds. *Global Librarianship.* Books in Library and Information Science 67. New York: Marcel Dekker, 2004. ISBN: 978-0-82470-978-5.

As the editors ask, somewhat rhetorically, "Why is it important for libraries and librarians to think globally?" (p. x). Quite simply, they explain, because computerized networks have connected people with information and reading material regardless of physical location, the entire world could be considered a library. They go on to point out that their book "provides a new approach to informing readers about the convergence of old ways and new ideas in libraries around the world and its impact on the future of the profession" (p. x). Examples of the sixteen chapter titles are "Public Libraries in Developed Countries: A Success Story from Scandinavia," "Global Education Information in the Digital Environment," and "International Standards for Global Information."

693 Liu, Yan Quan, and Xiaojun Cheng, eds. *International and Comparative Studies in Information and Library Science: A Focus on the United States and Asian Countries.* Libraries and Librarianship: An International Perspective 3. Lanham, MD: Scarecrow Press, 2008. ISBN: 978-0-81085-915-9.

According to the preface, "The uniqueness of this book is that it is a collection of scholarly publications that compare practices of librarianships between countries. The studies included represent a landscape of themes, and have findings that were collected through empirical methods such as survey and evaluation analyses. Reports from individual countries on the state of the national library systems and introductory level papers are not included in this collection" (p. xii).

694 Patel, Jashu, and Krishan Kumar. *Libraries and Librarianship in India.* Westport, CT: Greenwood, 2001. ISBN: 978-0-31329-423-5.

The authors look at the history of libraries and librarianship in India through an examination of national libraries, academic libraries, public libraries, school libraries, and special libraries from ancient through medieval and modern India to the end of the twentieth century. The complete discussion includes a thorough review of bibliographic control and services, professional organizations, library and information science education, and library automation.

695 Sinder, Janet, ed. *Law Librarians Abroad.* New York: Routledge, Haworth Information Press, 2001. ISBN: 978-0-78901-316-3.

Contributors discuss the ever-growing Law Librarians Abroad, a program in which law librarians spend from a few weeks up to a year or more working in another country, learning its librarianship and culture. Some locations reviewed are Buenos Aires, Athens, London, Dublin, Florence, Korea, East Africa, and Eritrea.

696 **Ward, Patricia Layzell, ed.** *Continuing Professional Education for the Information Society: The Fifth World Conference on Continuing Professional Education for the Library and Information Science Professions.* IFLA Publications 100. Munich: K. G. Saur, 2002. ISBN: 978-3-59821-830-9.

This book represents the proceedings of the Continuing Professional Education Round Table (CPERT) of the International Federation of Library Associations and Institutions. According to the introduction, "Over the seventeen years since the inception of CPERT, the proceedings provide a valuable and ongoing record of trends in the development of continuing professional development programs in the library and information professions" (p. 13). A typical chapter is "Staff Development and Continuing Professional Education: Policy and Practice in Australian Academic and Research Libraries."

697 **Yitai, Gong, and G. E. Gorman.** *Libraries and Information Services in China.* Lanham, MD: Scarecrow Press, 2000. ISBN: 0-8108-3782-X.

Basically, this is a snapshot of Chinese libraries at the beginning of the twenty-first century. Why would westerners want to know about library counterparts in old Cathay? The authors' response is that "it behooves us to have a clear understanding of what this sector of China's infrastructure is able to achieve at present," because "China is likely to assume a more significant international role in librarianship and information management" (p. xi). Eight chapters include a historical overview of Chinese librarianship, a look at "The Present Scenario," and discussions of specific aspects of the profession as they are done in the East, such as collection development, cataloging, and automation/information technology. Especially interesting and helpful is the chapter "Introduction to Selected Libraries in China," a guided tour of some of this nation's more important bibliographic institutions. Five appendixes include a "Chronology of Chinese Library Development," among more esoteric material such as "Standards for the Bibliographic Description of Chinese Materials." For anyone wishing to know how Chinese librarians do their jobs, this is a great introduction to the subject.

@ ADDITIONAL RESOURCES

698 **Farmer, Lesley S. J., Natalia Gendina, and Yuriko Nakamura, eds.** *Youth-Serving Libraries in Japan, Russia, and the United States.* Lanham, MD: Scarecrow Press, 2012. ISBN: 978-0-81088-225-6.

699 *Libraries and Information Services in the UK and Republic of Ireland 2013–2014.* 38th ed. London: Facet, 2012. ISBN: 978-1-85604-801-9.

PERIODICALS

700 *ASLIB Proceedings.* London: Emerald Group. Frequency: Six times per year. ISSN: 0001-253X. URL: www.emeraldinsight.com/journals .htm?issn=0001-253X.

ASLIB is the Association for Information Management in the United Kingdom, and this peer-reviewed journal, its major publication, covers international LIS research and practice. Topics include information management, information organization, librarianship, data protection, information retrieval, digital libraries and repositories, information policy and governance, records management, information architecture, and Internet and web studies.

701 *Bookbird: A Journal of International Children's Literature.* Toronto: University of Toronto Press. Frequency: Quarterly. ISSN: 0006-7377 (print), 1918-6983 (online). URL: http://muse .jhu.edu/journals/bookbird/.

Published by the International Board on Books for Young People, *Bookbird* discusses any topic on international children's literature and publishing of interest to its readers. Regular features include coverage of children's literature studies and children's literature awards around the world.

@ ADDITIONAL RESOURCES

702 African Journal of Library, Archives and Information Science (AJOL). Ibadan, Nigeria: Archilb and Information Services. Frequency: Twice per year. ISSN: 0795-4778. URL: www.ajol .info/index.php/ajlais/.

703 African Research and Documentation. London: African Studies Association of the United Kingdom and the Standing Conference on Library Materials in Africa. Frequency: Three times per year. ISSN: 0305-826X. URL: www2.lse .ac.uk/library/scolma/ardmain.htm.

704 Alexandria: The Journal of the National and International Library and Information Issues. Aldershot, Hampshire: Ashgate. Frequency: Three times per year. ISSN: 0955-7490. URL: www.manchesteruniversitypress.co.uk/ journals/journal.asp?id=19.

705 Australasian Public Libraries and Information Sciences. Blackwood, Australia: Auslib Press. Frequency: Four times per year. ISSN: 1030-5033. URL: www.auslib.com.au/ periodicals.htm.

706 Australian Academic and Research Libraries. Bundoora: Library Association of Australia. Frequency: Four times per year. ISSN: 0004-8623. URL: www.alia.org.au/publishing/ aarl/.

707 Australian Library Journal (AJL). Sydney, Library Association of Australia. Frequency: Four times per year. ISSN: 0004-9670. URL: www.alia .org.au/publishing/alj/.

708 Author. London: Society of Authors. Frequency: Quarterly. ISSN: 0005-0628. URL: www.societyofauthors.net/author/.

709 Brio. London: United Kingdom Branch of the International Association of Music Librarians. Frequency: Twice per year. ISSN: 0007-0173. URL: www.iaml.info/iaml-uk-irl/publications.html.

710 Bulletin of the Association of British Theological and Philosophical Libraries. London: Association of British Theological and Philosophical Libraries. Frequency: Three times per year. ISSN: 0305-781X. URL: www.abtapl.org .uk/pub.html.

711 Chinese Librarianship: An International Electronic Journal. Fort Meyers, FL: Internet Chinese Librarians Club. Frequency: Twice per year. ISSN: 1089-4667. URL: www.white-clouds .com/iclc/cliej/.

712 Feliciter. Ottawa: Canadian Library Association. Frequency: Six times per year. ISSN: 0014-9802. URL: www.cla.ca/AM/ Template.cfm?Section=Feliciter1/.

713 Focus on International Library and Information Work. London: International Library and Information Group. Frequency: Three times per year. ISSN: 0305-8468. URL: www.cilip.org .uk/get-involved/special-interest-groups/interna tional/publications/pages/default.aspx.

714 IAML (International Association of Music Librarians). London: United Kingdom Branch of the International Association of Music Librarians. Frequency: Twice per year. ISSN: 0007-0173. URL: www.iaml.info/iaml-uk-irl/publications.html.

715 IFLA Journal (International Federation of Library Associations and Institutions). Thousand Oaks, CA: Sage. Frequency: Quarterly. ISSN: 0340-0352 (print), 1745-2651 (online). URL: www.ifla.org/publications/ifla-journal/.

716 INCITE. Sydney, Library Association of Australia. Frequency: Eleven issues per year. ISSN: 0158-0876. URL: www.alia.org.au/ publishing/incite/.

717 International Cataloguing and Bibliographic Control. London: International Federation of Library Associations and Institutions. Frequency: Quarterly. ISSN: 1011-8829. URL: www.ifla.org/ publications/international-cataloguing-and -bibliographic-control-icbc/.

718 *International Information and Library Review.* Amsterdam: Elsevier. Frequency: Four times per year. ISSN: 1057-2317. URL: www.journals.elsevier.com/international-information-and-library-review/.

719 *International Journal of Library and Information Science.* Nairobi: Academic Journals. Frequency: Monthly. ISSN: 2141-2537. URL: www.academicjournals.org/IJLIS/index.htm.

720 *International Journal of Web Services Research.* Hershey, PA: Idea Group. Frequency: Four issues per year. ISSN: 1545-7362. URL: www.igi-global.com/journal/international-journal-web-services-research/1079.

721 *International Research: Journal of Library and Information Science (IR).* India: International Research, IRJLIS. Frequency: Twice per year. ISSN: 2249-0213. URL: http://irjlis.com.

722 *Malaysian Journal of Library and Information Science.* Kuala Lumpur: University of Malaysia. Frequency: Annually. ISSN: 1394-6234. URL: http://ejum.fsktm.um.edu.my/VolumeListing.aspx?JournalID=3.

723 *School Libraries in Canada.* Ottawa: Canadian Library Association. Frequency: Four times per year. ISSN: 0227-3780. URL: www.clatoolbox.ca/casl/slic/.

724 *School Libraries Worldwide.* Kalamazoo, MI: International Association of School Librarianship. Frequency: Twice per year. ISSN: 1023-9391. URL: www.iasl-online.org/pubs/slw/.

19

LAW

 BOOKS

725 Agner, Grace. *Digital Rights Management: A Librarian's Guide to Technology and Practise.* Oxford: Chandos, 2008. ISBN: 978-1-84334-125-3.

According to the author, the phrase "digital rights management," or DRM, is often used in a haphazard way. Her definition, for the purposes of this book, is "the *digital* management of rights pertaining to the access and use of *digital* materials" (p. 1). She goes on to state that "at heart, effective DRM involves establishing a framework of policy and practise that supports the rights of the creator/rights owner, the user and the resource. Libraries can address each entity in turn to develop a comprehensive yet manageable digital rights strategy" (p. 2). The individual chapters support these statements with coverage of copyright issues, privacy, and the roles of technology and metadata and a concluding chapter titled "Putting the Pieces Together." Material is well documented, as each chapter concludes with an ample "Notes and References" listing.

726 Almquist, Sharon G., ed. *Distributed Learning and Virtual Librarianship.* Westport, CT: Libraries Unlimited, 2011. ISBN: 978-1-59158-906-8 (print), 978-1-59158-907-5 (e-book).

Contributors explore the gray area between providing library services to off-site students and maintaining copyright standards. Topics covered include terms, guidelines, and issues for distributed and virtual learning; reference assistance support for distant learning; copyright issues; electronic reserves; information delivery; school libraries; and academic libraries. One chapter is a case study of the virtual university and library services at the University of North Texas at Dallas.

727 Chmara, Theresa. *Privacy and Confidentiality Issues: A Guide for Libraries and Their Lawyers.* Chicago: American Library Association, 2009. ISBN: 978-0-83890-970-6.

This is a handy guide to privacy and confidentiality issues, First Amendment and other legal considerations, state statutes, federal laws, and developing privacy policies. Chmara also provides information on privacy and confidentiality for circulation and Internet records, along with a review of minors' First Amendment rights and rights to privacy. An appendix on state privacy and confidentiality statutes and index are provided.

728 Crawford, Walt. *Open Access: What You Need to Know Now.* ALA Editions Special Reports. Chicago: American Library Association, 2011. ISBN: 978-0-83891-106-8.

This special report covers what open access is and is not, the benefits and drawbacks of difference open-access models, and ways to maintain peer review and scholarly publications during skyrocketing expenses and shrinking resources.

729 Crews, Kenneth D. *Copyright Law for Librarians and Educators: Creative Strategies and Practical Solutions.* 2nd ed. Chicago: American Library Association, 2006. ISBN: 978-0-83890-906-5.

Crews covers many aspect of copyrights including rights of ownership, working with fair use, education and library responsibilities, music, digital rights, and unpublished materials. The appendixes present selected provisions from the U.S. Copyright Act, a checklist for fair use, a checklist for the TEACH act, and a model letter for permission requests. A guide to additional reading, cases cited, and index are included.

730 Koegh, Patricia, and Rachel Crowley, Comps. *Copyright Policies in College Libraries.* CLIP Notes 39. Chicago: American Library Association, 2008. ISBN: 978-0-83898-459-8.

Librarians are often forced to walk a tightrope when it comes to copyright issues; patrons clamor for help in copying or sharing material considered to be intellectual property while copyright holders wish to limit such access, which is often deemed an infringement of ownership rights. One answer to this dilemma is to have an up-to-date copyright policy on hand, spelling out what is and is not permissible. But how to write it? Here we have a collection of sixteen actual copyright policies from a variety of academic libraries

to use as examples and guidelines. The book's introduction clearly states, "Neither the work as a whole, nor the example policies that have been included, constitute legal advice" (p. 1). That being said, this is a good place to start when attempting to devise a copyright policy for one's own facility, academic or otherwise.

731 Simpson, Carol Ann. *Copyright Catechism: Practical Answers to Everyday School Dilemmas.* Worthington, OH: Linworth, 2005. ISBN: 978-1-58683-202-5.

Simpson culled material from her "Copyright Questions of the Month" column for *Library Media Connection* to create this FAQ guide for school administrators and librarians. She covers ownership and management of copyright, fair use and public display for print materials and graphic materials, sound recordings, video and film copyrights generally, in-class and public performances, policies, and permission issues. The question-to-answer format features real-world questions from teachers and librarians.

732 Simpson, Carol Ann. *Copyright Catechism II: Practical Answers to Everyday School Dilemmas.* Copyright Series. Santa Barbara, CA: Libraries Unlimited, 2011. ISBN: 978-1-59884-848-9.

Simpson amassed new frequently asked questions and answers from her "Copyright Questions of the Month" column for *Library Media Connection* for this second volume on everyday school copyright issues. Topics include fair use versus license, PowerPoint picture books, podcasting read-alouds, archiving books on CD, systematic copying, public domain songs, and downloading music and videos. The question-to-answer format features real-world questions from teachers and librarians. An index is provided for easy reference/issue lookup.

733 Simpson, Carol. *Copyright for Schools: A Practical Guide.* 5th ed. Copyright Series. Santa Barbara, CA: Linworth, 2010. ISBN: 978-1-58683-393-0.

This fifth edition covers the law, public domain, fair use, print materials in schools, audiovisual material in school, music materials in school (print and recorded), multimedia in schools, distance learning in school, Internet in schools, computer software in schools, school library exemptions, permissions, managing copyright in schools, copyright and administrators, and copyright policies. Extensive appendixes include copyright compliance agreement, do's and don'ts, copyrights for kids, warning notices, sample policy, release form, copyright and plagiarism guideline, bibliography, Internet links, database of copyright actions against schools, questions-and-answers reproducible brochure, and infringement reporting form. Numerous sample logs, record-keeping aids, notices, policies, request letters, forms, and instructional materials are included.

734 Wherry, Timothy L. *Intellectual Property: Everything the Digital-Age Librarian Needs to Know.* Chicago: American Library Association, 2008. ISBN: 978-0-83890-948-5.

A plethora of new high-tech tools, such as Google, YouTube, and the iPod, have given rise to numerous lawsuits over copyrights, trademarks, and patents. Wherry uses examples, trivia, and real-life court cases to provide step-by-step guidance on dealing with patent, copyright, and trademark infringement questions. Appendixes offer intellectual property codes in verse and patent and information on trademark depository libraries. An index provides easy access to topical information.

✐ ADDITIONAL RESOURCES

735 Bell, Alan, and Susan Graham. *Record-keeping, Compliance and the Law.* London: Facet, 2014. ISBN: 978-1-85604-826-2.

736 Butler, Rebecca P. *Copyright for Teachers and Librarians in the 21st Century.* New York: Neal-Schuman, 2011. ISBN: 978-1-55570-738-5.

737 Carson, Bryan M. *Finding the Law: Legal Research for Librarians.* Lanham, CT: Scarecrow Press, 2011. ISBN: 978-0-81088-105-1.

738 Cornelius, Ian. *Information Policies and Strategies.* London: Facet, 2010. ISBN: 978-1-85604-677-0.

739 Cornish, Graham P. *Copyright: Interpreting the Law for Libraries, Archives and Information Services.* 5th ed. London: Facet, 2009. ISBN: 978-1-85604-664-0.

740 Gathegi, John N. *The Digital Librarian's Legal Handbook.* Legal Advisor for Librarians, Educators, and Information Professionals. New York: Neal-Schuman, 2011. ISBN: 978-1-55570-649-4.

741 Hales, Alma, and Bernadette Attwell. *No-Nonsense Guide to Copyright in All Media.* London: Facet, 2014. ISBN: 978-1-85604-764-7.

742 Healey, Paul D. *Professional Liability Issues for Librarians and Information Professionals.* Legal Advisor for Librarians, Educators, and Information Professionals. New York: Neal-Schuman, 2008. ISBN: 978-1-55570-609-8.

743 Heller, James S. *The Librarian's Copyright Companion.* Buffalo, NY: William S. Hein, 2004. ISBN: 978-0-83773-300-5.

744 *Licensing and Copyright Management: Best Practices of College, Special and Research Libraries.* New York: Primary Research Group, 2004. ISBN: 978-1-57440-068-7.

745 Lipinski, Tomas A. *The Librarian's Legal Companion for Licensing Information Resources and Services.* Legal Advisor for Librarians, Educators, and Information Professionals. New York: Neal-Schuman, 2012. ISBN: 978-1-55570-610-4.

746 Minow, Mary, and Tomas A. Lipinski. *The Library's Legal Answer Book.* Chicago: American Library Association, 2003. ISBN: 978-0-83890-828-0.

747 Norman, Sandy. *Practical Copyright for Information Professionals: The CILIP Handbook.* London: Facet, 2004. ISBN: 978-1-85604-490-5.

748 Oppenheim, Charles. *No-Nonsense Guide to Legal Issues in Web 2.0 and Cloud Computing.* London: Facet, 2012. ISBN: 978-1-85604-804-0.

749 Overbeck, Wayne, and Genelle Belmas. *Major Principles of Media Law, 2013 Edition.* Boston, MA: Wadsworth, 2012. ISBN: 978-0-495-90195-2.

750 Padfield, Tim. *Copyright for Archivists and Records Managers.* 4th ed. London: Facet, 2010. ISBN: 978-1-85604-705-0.

751 Pedley, Paul. *Copyright Compliance: Practical Steps to Stay within the Law.* London: Facet, 2008. ISBN: 978-1-85604-640-4.

752 Pedley, Paul. *Essential Law for Information Professionals.* 3rd ed. London: Facet, 2012. ISBN: 978-1-85604-769-2.

753 Peck, Robert S. *Libraries, the First Amendment, and Cyberspace: What You Need to Know.* Chicago: American Library Association, 2000. ISBN: 978-0-83890-773-3.

754 Pedley, Paul. *The E-Copyright Handbook.* London: Facet, 2012. ISBN: 978-1-85604-827-9.

755 Russell, Carrie, and Dwayne K. Buttler. *Complete Copyright: An Everyday Guide for Librarians.* Chicago: American Library Association, 2004. ISBN: 978-0-83893-543-9.

756 Secker, Jane. *Copyright and E-learning: A Guide for Practitioners.* London: Facet, 2010. ISBN: 978-1-85604-665-7.

757 Stead, Alan. *Information Rights in Practice: The Non-legal Professional's Guide.* London: Facet, 2008. ISBN: 978-1-85604-620-6.

758 Stepchyshyn, Vera, and Robert S. Nelson, Comps. *Library Plagiarism Policies.* CLIP Notes 37. Chicago: American Library Association, 2007. ISBN: 978-0-83898-416-1.

📖 PERIODICAL

759 *Legal Reference Services Quarterly.* Philadelphia: Routledge. Frequency: Four times per year. ISSN: 0270-319X (print), 1540-949X (online). URL: www.tandf.co.uk/journals/WLRS.

Typical content includes annotated bibliographies, legal literature overviews, tools of the trade, and other items of legal interest. The target audience is corporate law libraries, judicial libraries, and law school libraries. All articles presented for publication undergo editorial screening and peer review. Special thematic issues covered:

- Federal regulatory research-selected agency knowledge paths
- Law library collection development in the digital age
- Teamwork and collaboration in libraries—tools for theory and practice
- Public services issues with rare and archival law materials
- Teaching legal research and providing access to electronic resources
- Emerging solutions in reference services—implications for libraries in the new millennium
- Law librarians abroad
- The political economy of legal information
- Law publishers symposiums
- Legal bibliography—tradition, transitions, and trends
- Practical approaches to legal research

20

LIBRARIES, GENERAL

 BOOKS

760 Boyer, J. Patrick. *Local Library, Global Passport: The Evolution of a Carnegie Library.* Toronto: Blue Butterfly Books, 2008. ISBN: 978-0-97816-008-1.

Andrew Carnegie discovered a free library that changed his life. Once he had made his fortune, it was time to return the favor by giving new library buildings to several thousand communities in the United States, Canada, the United Kingdom, and other countries. Boyer uses the development of library service in the Canadian town of Bracebridge from 1874 to present to show the impact a Carnegie library had during cultural, economic, and technical change. Sources, notes, and index are provided.

761 Burton, Margaret. *Famous Libraries of the World: Their History, Collections and Administrators.* Owens Press, 2007. ISBN: 978-1-40670-488-4.

This is a reproduction of the 1937 volume published by Grafton and Company in London. Burton describes famous libraries in the British Empire, France, Germany, Greece, Italy, City of the Vatican, Poland, Spain, Portugal, Sweden, U.S.S.R., and the United States. There is a description of each library generally, followed by its history, collections and some key librarians, buildings, catalogues, administration and departments, staff, finance, and bibliography. An index is provided.

762 Eden, Bradford Lee, ed. *More Innovative Redesign and Reorganizations of Technical Services.* Westport, CT: Libraries Unlimited, 2008. ISBN: 978-1-59158-778-1.

This follow-up edition to *Innovative Redesigns and Reorganization of Library Technical Services* (Libraries Unlimited, 2004) includes additional case studies and surveys focusing on providing technical services in libraries. Contributors write about the evolution of technical services at Miami (Ohio) University, Northwestern University Library, Hostos Community College, medical libraries, law libraries, regional libraries, and more. Some of the topics cover Library 2.0, Web 2.0, staffing trends, size restraints, shared responsibilities, reorganization, mission, and environments. Information about the editor and contributors and index are included.

763   Fuller, Sheryl Kindle. *The Shoestring Library.* Westport, CT: Libraries Unlimited, 2010. ISBN: 978-1-58683-520-0 (print), 978-1-58683-521-7 (e-book).

Fuller provides approximately 300 tips and instructions for reusing, repurposing, or recycling materials; making the best use of volunteers; and obtaining free materials. Part 1 on library management covers time management, free education, volunteers, soliciting free items, preparation for emergencies and substitutes, health, contests, diversity projects, and relationships with community organizations. Part 2 covers the physical plant and includes advice from realtors, painting and use of color, ceilings, seating, shelving, desks, library blueprints, lighting, walls, and glass. Materials include photos, icons, and illustrations. A general conclusion and index are included.

764   Griffiths, Jillian R., and Jenny Craven, eds. *Access, Delivery, Performance: The Future of Libraries without Walls: A Festschrift to Celebrate the Work of Professor Peter Brophy.* London: Facet, 2008. ISBN: 978-1-85604-647-3.

For those rusty on their German, *festschrift* is derived from *fest* (celebration) and *schrift* (to write); according to Misters Merriam and Webster, this borrowed term defines "a volume of writings by different authors presented as a tribute or memorial especially to a scholar." That being the case, the contents here are a bit of a grab bag; evidently the themes discussed were professional interests of the now-retired Brophy, who most recently was director of the Centre for Research in Library and Information Management at Manchester Metropolitan University. Four sections, each containing two to three chapters, cover "Libraries, Learning and Distance Learning"; "Widening Access to Information";

"Changing Directions of Information Delivery"; and "Performance, Quality and Leadership." The volume concludes with a selected bibliography of the writings of Brophy.

765   Harland, Pamela Colburn. *The Learning Commons: Seven Simple Steps to Transform Your Library.* Westport, CT: Libraries Unlimited, 2011. ISBN: 978-1-59884-517-4 (print), 978-1-59884-518-1 (e-book).

Each chapter of Harland's book focuses on a way to make the library the resource center for students, researchers, teachers, and other patrons. Checklists, practical examples, and photographs are used to illustrate how to improve facilities. The seven topics covered are user control, flexibility, repetitive questions, joint resources, removing barriers, trusting users, and publicizing services. A library survey for users, in-text citations, a digital portfolio rubric, and a case study of "@ the PRHS library" from the Plymouth Regional High School Library in Plymouth, New Hampshire, are included in the appendixes.

766   Marco, Guy A. *The American Public Library Handbook.* Santa Barbara, CA: Libraries Unlimited, 2012. ISBN: 978-1-59158-910-5 (print), 978-1-59158-911-2 (e-book).

Marco relied on his own experiences, subject matter experts, and extensive research to create this reference handbook that focuses on all aspects of the U.S. public library experience. Topical, biographical, institutional, and bibliographic areas are arranged in an A–Z format. The topical essays are divided into three subdivisions: terminology, historical summary, and current issues. Biographical entries are limited to individuals who died before January 1, 2000, and made significant contributions to public libraries. Institutional entries are limited to one of three categories: libraries serving the 100 largest populations in the United States, libraries awarded momentous recognition in the *Library Journal* or *Hennen's American Public Library Ratings*, and libraries of national or regional historical significance or with current programs of special interest. Each library entry contains the correct name of the library, street address, founding date, population served, circulation in a recent year, holdings in total volumes or items, number of branches, and number of bookmobiles. A prologue on terminology, an index, advisory board information, and contributor information are included.

767 **O'Beirne, Ronan.** *From Lending to Learning: The Development and Extension of Public Libraries.* Chandos Information Professional Series. Oxford: Chandos, 2010. ISBN: 978-1-84334-388-2.

O'Beirne spotlights current trends, policies, functions, and conflicts arising between offering library services that are educationally focused and those focused on leisure time. The author offers practical information on how to set up a learning environment in a public library, followed by discussions of digital citizenship, information and knowledge, and technology in a learning society. A brief discussion of Web 2.0 technologies and social networking sets the tone for future opportunities. A list of figures and tables, list of acronyms, references, and index are provided.

768 **Oswald, Godfrey.** *Library World Records.* 2nd ed. Jefferson, NC: McFarland, 2008. ISBN: 978-0-78643-852-5.

There are more than 380 entries organized into subject headings listed in the table of contents. Topics include national libraries, public and subscription libraries, academic libraries, specialty libraries, archives, books, periodicals, bookstores, and library buildings. An proper name index is included. Although Oswald's pleasurable book contains fun and interesting facts about libraries, librarians, and books, its value as a scholarly reference is extremely limited by the lack of citations or list of consulted sources.

769 **Parks, Stephen, ed.** *The Beinecke Library of Yale University.* New Haven, CT: Beinecke Rare Book and Manuscript Library, 2004. ISBN: 978-0-84573-150-5.

This book celebrates the fortieth anniversary of the Beinecke Library and contains many historic photographs, from its initial dedication to remodeling projects and the present facility. A brief introduction and history of the design, construction, and building's impact, and the Ezra Stoller Dedication Portfolio and humble beginning in the Rare Book Room of the Sterling Library set the stage. Contributors describe library holdings in one of several chapters, which cover both early and modern manuscripts and books and the library's special collections in American literature, German literature, Western Americana, music, and the Osborn Collection of English manuscripts. Readers will gain an understanding of why this library located at Yale University has become a center for students and researchers alike.

770 **Pierce, Charles E., ed.** *The Morgan Library: An American Masterpiece.* New York: Scala, 2006. ISBN: 978-1-85759-217-7.

This lavishly illustrated volume highlights more than 100 items from the J. Pierpont Morgan Library. Beginning with a brief biography of Morgan, the very model of a captain of industry, senior curators trace the history of the library and some of its more colorful librarians. Chapters are arranged by type of art and books and present a general overview of the variety of materials available in the collection. Items highlighted include letters penned by Lord Byron, Thoreau, and Poe; music scores by Bach, Mozart, and Schubert; and sketches by Gainsborough, Rubens, and Carracci, not to mention the beautifully bound books themselves.

771 **Walker, Gregory, Mary Clapinson, and Lesley Forbes, eds.** *The Bodleian Library: A Subject Guide to the Collections.* Cambridge: Cambridge University Press, 2004. ISBN: 978-1-85124-079-1.

The Bodleian Library is the oldest and largest academic library in Great Britain and contains more than 400 special collections. This book describes current holdings in the historical context of four centuries of acquisitions. Each of the twenty-nine chapters in this guide covers the general bibliography of a subject area, its history, unique characteristics, acquisitions philosophy, collection holdings, and selected bibliography. A general descriptive list of the principal special collections and index are provided.

@ ADDITIONAL RESOURCES

772 Brophy, Peter, Jenny Craven, and Margaret Markland, eds. *Libraries without Walls 6.* London: Facet, 2006. ISBN: 978-1-85604-576-6.

773 Brophy, Peter, Jenny Craven, and Margaret Markland, eds. *Libraries without Walls 7.* London: Facet, 2008. ISBN: 978-1-85604-623-7.

774 Brophy, Peter, Shelagh Fisher, and Jenny Craven, eds. *Libraries without Walls 5.* London: Facet, 2004. ISBN: 978-1-85604-511-7.

775 Hage, Christine Lind. *The Public Library Start-Up Guide.* Chicago: American Library Association, 2004. ISBN: 978-0-83890-866-2.

776 Kniffel, Leonard, ed. *Reading with the Stars: A Celebration of Books and Libraries.* American Library Association, 2011. ISBN: 978-1-61608-277-2.

777 Landau, Herbert B. *The Small Public Library Survival Guide: Thriving on Less.* Chicago: American Library Association, 2008. ISBN: 978-0-83893-575-0.

778 McMenemy, David. *Public Library.* London: Facet, 2008. ISBN: 978-1-85604-557-5.

779 Pantry, Sheila, and Peter Griffiths. *Setting Up a Library and Information Service from Scratch.* London: Facet, 2005. ISBN: 978-1-85604-558-2.

📖 PERIODICALS

780 *Libraries and the Cultural Record.* Austin: University of Texas Press. Frequency: Quarterly. ISSN: 0894-8631 (print), 1534-7591 (online). URL: http://sentra.ischool.utexas.edu/~lcr/index.php.

Libraries and the Cultural Record is a peer-reviewed journal devoted to the broad collection history of knowledge that forms the cultural record. Topics include library science and librarianship, archival and records enterprises, preservation/conservation of information, museum studies, information science, and historical perspectives on cultural, social, and intellectual history. *Libraries and the Cultural Record* was formerly known as *Libraries and Culture*, through volume 41, no. 2, Spring 2006.

781 *Library Connect.* New York: Elsevier. Frequency: Monthly. ISSN: 1549-3725. URL: http://libraryconnect.elsevier.com/subscribe/?utm_source=sciencedirect&utm_medium=banner&utm_campaign=libraryconnect/.

Library Connect topics include academic, medical, corporate and government librarianship, advocacy, trends, leadership, and practical advice. Available in print or electronically, this free promotional newsletter highlights Elsevier's products and services.

782 *Library Quarterly.* Chicago: University of Chicago Press. Frequency: Quarterly. ISSN: 0024-2519. URL: www.jstor.org/page/journal/libraryq/about.html.

This scholarly quarterly focuses on historical, sociological, cultural evaluative, statistical, bibliographical, managerial, and educational aspects of libraries and librarianship. Topics include knowledge management, informatics, the Internet, the evolution of library research, preservation, censorship, children's literature, preservation in the age of Google, and information literacy.

783 Library Trends. Baltimore, MD: Johns Hopkins University Press. Frequency: Quarterly. ISSN: 0024-2594. URL: www.ideals.illinois.edu/handle/2142/999/.

Authored by the Graduate School of Library and Information Science at the University of Illinois Library School, this quarterly periodical focuses on current topics of interest to professional librarianship. Articles include practical applications, thorough analyses, and literatures reviews.

784 LIBRES. Curtin, Australia: Curtin University of Technology. Frequency: Twice per year. ISSN: 1058-6768. URL: http://libres.curtin.edu.au/.

Recurring sections in this international peer-refereed electronic journal include research and applications, essays and opinions, reviews, news from other journals, news and announcements, and conferences and meetings. Articles may include any topic of interest to LIS professionals. Recent topics include mobile technologies, exploring archives and their conversion from original to digital, library experiences of Hurricane Katrina, gender and citation in two LIS e-journals, and the public library as a critical institution in South Africa's democracy.

785 Public Libraries Online. Chicago: Public Library Association, American Library Association. URL: www.publiclibrariesonline.org.

This online site is a complement to the printed *Public Libraries* journal published by the Public Library Association (PLA, a subunit of ALA). This website includes expanded content, three full articles from the most recent *Public Libraries*, "Book Talk," "From the Blog," "Newsfeed," "Polls," and "New Product News."

786 Public Library Journal (PLJ). London: Public Libraries Group of the Library Association. Frequency: Archives only. ISSN: 0268-893X. www.cilip.org.uk/get-involved/special-interest-groups/public/journal/Pages/journal.aspx.

The Public Libraries Group of the Library Association announced that it would cease publication of this journal on November 29, 2011, because of funding problems. Volumes 19, Autumn 2004, to Volume 24, no. 4, Winter 2009, are still online to members.

ADDITIONAL RESOURCES

787 Ariadne. Bath: United Kingdom Office for Library and Information Networking. Frequency: Four times per year. ISSN: 1361-3200. URL: www.ariadne.ac.uk/information/#about/.

788 The Information Advisor. Westport, CT: Information Today. Frequency: Ten times per year. ISSN: URL: www.informationadvisor.com.

789 Information Today. Westport, CT: Information Today. Frequency: Eleven issues per year. ISSN: 8755-6286. URL: www.infotoday.com/IT/default.asp.

790 KMWorld. Westport, CT: Information Today. Frequency: Ten issues per year. ISSN: 1099-8284. URL: www.kmworld.com.

791 North Carolina Libraries. Greensboro: State Library of North Carolina. Frequency: Twice per year. ISSN: 0029-2540. URL: www.ncl.ecu.edu/index.php/NCL/.

LIBRARIES, HISTORY OF

 BOOKS

792 Augst, Thomas, and Kenneth Carpenter, eds. *Institutions of Reading: The Social Life of Libraries in the United States.* Studies in Print Culture and the History of the Book. Amherst: University of Massachusetts Press in association with the Library Company of Philadelphia, 2007. ISBN: 978-1-55849-591-3.

This is an anthology of essays that track the development of libraries in the United States from the late eighteenth to the early twenty-first century. The extensive index reflects the wide range of subjects, such as women, ethnic and racial groups, religion, culture, and the digital era, as they relate to the institutions alluded to in the title. Many of the essays were originally presented at the History of Libraries in the United States conference held April 2002 in Philadelphia.

793 Battles, Matthew. *Library: An Unquiet History.* New York: W. W. Norton, 2004. ISBN: 978-0-39332-564-5.

Battle quickly takes readers from ancient times to the present digital age, covering everything from the concept of libraries, book culture, and book burning to an overwhelming thirst for power and knowledge. Chapter titles include "Reading the Library," "Burning Alexandria," "The House of Wisdom," "Battle of the Books," "Books for All," "Knowledge on Fire," and "Lost in the Stacks." Notes on sources and index are provided.

794 Becker, Patti Clayton. *Books and Libraries in American Society during World War II: Weapons in the War of Ideas.* Studies in American Popular History and Culture. New York: Routledge, 2005. ISBN: 978-0-41597-179-9.

Becker examines the difficulties of providing library services to meet both civilian and military needs during World War II. Already faced with distressed collections from an inadequate Depression-era budget, increased demand for military libraries, shortages, rationing, and a shrinking number of wartime library graduates, librarians held book drives, gathered regulations and government publications on emergency topics, rotated collections, and extended interlibrary loans. Extensive notes and bibliography enhance this academic work.

795 Brophy, Peter. *The Library in the Twenty-First Century.* 2nd ed. London: Facet, 2007. ISBN: 978-1-85604-606-0.

Brophy examines libraries in the modern world, including perceptions, physical presence, patrons, resources, and information delivery systems. This is a handy guide to look at how libraries may function in an electronic age and their roles, partnerships, and professional needs. The author provides several diagrams throughout the work, a bibliography, and glossary.

796 Cochrane, Peter, ed. *Remarkable Occurrences: The National Library of Australia's First 100 Years 1901–2001.* Canberra: National Library of Australia, 2001. ISBN: 978-0-64210-730-5.

Cochrane traces the history of unique collections at the National Library of Australia, which includes over 160,000 books, paintings, maps, photographs, sculptures, manuscripts, oral histories, music scores, and early Australian films. One chapter is devoted to its prized possession, Captain Cook's *Endeavor* journal. Others cover famous bookmen E. A. Petherick and J. A. Ferguson and art historian Rex Nan Kivell. Key items in the collections are highlighted by 270 illustrations, mostly color. An index is included.

797 Edwards, Edward. *Free Town Libraries, Their Formation, Management, and History: In Britain, France, Germany, and America.* Cambridge Library Collection—Printing and Publishing History. New York: Cambridge University Press, 2009. ISBN: 978-1-108-00936-2.

This is a reproduction of the 1869 edition published by Trubner in London. Written by the first librarian of the Free Library in Manchester, this volume outlines how free libraries began. Topics include the history, locales, creation, and management of free town libraries in Great Britain, Ireland, Germany, and the United States.

798 Edwards, Edward. *Libraries and Founders of Libraries.* Cambridge Library Collection—Printing and Publishing History. New York: Cambridge University Press, 2009. ISBN: 978-1-108-01052-8.

This reprint of the 1864 edition is a comprehensive history of libraries from classical times to the nineteenth century. The chapter on the ancient libraries of Egypt, Judaea, Greece, and the Roman Empire covers Osymandyar, the Alexandrian Library, the clay tablets of Assyria, the Pergamum library, and more. The "Mediaeval and Modern Libraries" chapter follows the effects of monasticism in the Middle Ages, the revival of learning, the growth of printing, and the foundation of libraries in Paris and at the British Museum. Chapters 3 and 4 cover libraries of monasteries in Great Britain and elsewhere. The next three chapters are devoted to libraries of famous authors, monarchs, and royalty. The final chapters examine early collectors and their collections, state papers, and public records.

799 Faulhaber, Charles B. *Exploring the Bancroft Library: The Centennial Guide to Its History, Spectacular Special Collections, Research Pleasures, Its Amazing Future, and How It All Works.* Contribution by Anthony S. Bliss. Edited by Stephen Vincent. Salt Lake City, UT: Signature Books, 2006. ISBN: 978-1-89366-319-0.

Hubert H. Bancroft founded the Bancroft Library in 1859 to house and organize the documents and artifacts he acquired during his travels from Alaska to Panama. Since the University of California acquired possession in 1906, the collection has been expanded to include the Mark Twain Papers and Project, Tebtunis Papyri rare books and manuscripts, and more. This illustrated book looks at the history of the library, acquisition activities, preservation, and the ability to study original documents.

800 Jordan, Jay, ed. *Weaving Libraries into the Web: OCLC 1998–2008.* New York: Routledge, 2009. ISBN: 978-0-41557-690-1.

Since establishment of OCLC in 1967, its members have wanted to improve access to information while reducing the rate of increasing costs for libraries. This book begins with founding director Frederick Gridley Kilgour's biographical sketch, moves through OCLC's history, and concludes with a chronology. Contributors focus on OCLC's influence on international relationships, professional development, and technological changes. This book was originally published as a special issue of the *Journal of Library Administration*.

801 Lapidge, Michael. *The Anglo-Saxon Library.* New York: Oxford University Press, 2008. ISBN: 978-0-19923-969-6.

Lapidge examines vanished libraries of classical antiquity and Anglo-Saxon England before reconstructing the evidence of inventories, manuscripts, and citations of Anglo-Saxon libraries. More than half of the book is devoted to five appendixes that include six inventories of Latin books from Anglo-Saxon libraries; eighth-century manuscripts from the area of Anglo-Saxon missions in Germany; surviving eighth-century manuscripts from the areas of the Anglo-Saxon missions in Germany; ninth-century manuscripts of Continental origin having preconquest English provenance; and Latin books cited by the principal Anglo-Saxon authors. The book concludes with a catalogue of classical and patristic authors and works composed before 700 and known in Anglo-Saxon England. Surviving inventories, manuscripts, and citations are combined into one alphabetic comprehensive index.

802 Lerner, Frederick Andrew. *The Story of Libraries: From the Invention of Writing to the Computer Age.* 2nd ed. London: Continuum, 2009. ISBN: 978-0-82642-990-2.

Lerner's book tells the history of libraries and librarianship, from ancient times to the present, and examines the critical role libraries have played in the development of world cultures. Topics include libraries of classical antiquity, the Orient, the Islamic world, and the High Middle Ages. Historical context is provided through a review of Gutenberg's legacy, libraries as repositories of knowledge, public access to libraries, the craft of librarianship, and more. A list of illustrations, notes, and bibliography are included.

803 MacLeod, Roy M., ed. *The Library of Alexandria: Centre of Learning in the Ancient World.* New York: I. B. Tauris, 2004. ISBN: 978-1-85043-594-5.

MacLeod explores the Library of Alexandria in history and myth as well as the character of Alexandrian scholarship. He traces the institution from its foundation to its destruction as well as the assimilation of Greek, Roman, Jewish, and Syrian cultures. The story of Alexander the Great and the city named for him is also detailed. A map of Alexandria, notes on contributors, bibliography, and index are included.

804 McCabe, Ronald B. *Civic Librarianship: Renewing the Social Mission of the Public Library.* Lanham, MD: Scarecrow Press, 2001. ISBN: 978-0-81083-905-2.

This book opens with an analysis of the social movements and library history of the past 100 years. The book's premise is that a new approach to the public library as a community resource is needed—one that forces librarians to strengthen their social authority to provide education and context for the community. It follows that the quantity and quality of education, rather than patron demand, should guide material selection. The author makes a strong argument that extreme individualism has damaged social structures in the United States and that it is up to librarians to take charge, use their platform to provide education, and mold the social structure in communities. The viewpoints expressed leave few opportunities for communal brainstorming and multicultural discussion.

805 Murray, Stuart A. P. *The Library: An Illustrated History.* Introduction by Donald G. Davis Jr. Foreword by Nicholas A. Basbanes. New York: Skyhorse, 2009. ISBN: 978-1-60239-706-4.

Printed on heavy glossy paper and offering a myriad of color and black-and-white photographs, this is essentially a valentine to the buildings we know and love. In the well-written introduction by Donald G. Davis Jr., professor emeritus of library history at the University of Texas at Austin, the basic outline of this work is given: "After a chapter on ancient libraries, this survey continues with a balanced treatment of worldwide library development to the middle of the second millennium. Thereafter, following the arrangement of many library historians, the narrative combines a chronological treatment with relevant continental and national concerns. The emphasis is on libraries in the United States, but the rest of the world is hardly slighted. . . . A section with brief sketches of notable and representative libraries (more than fifty, in all) concludes the book" (pp. ix–x). Published in cooperation with ALA, this is a book for book lovers and library aficionados.

806 Polastron, Lucien X. *Books on Fire: The Destruction of Libraries throughout History.* Translated by Jon E. Graham. Rochester, VT: Inner Traditions, 2007. ISBN: 978-1-59477-167-5.

Originally published in French under the title *Livres en feu* (Books on Fire) in 2004, this thoroughly researched and well-written account won the 2004 Société des Gens de Lettres Prize for Nonfiction/History. Disturbing as it is to contemplate, libraries and the knowledge they house have been burned and bombed from the earliest times to the present. Natural disasters too, such as forest fires and earthquakes, have taken their toll, just as surely as man-made warfare. From the destruction of the library at ancient Alexandria to the bombardment of the National Library at Sarajevo, Bosnia, in 1992, it's all here, and it's enough to make a bibliophile weep.

807 Savage, Ernest A. *Old English Libraries: The Making, Collection, and Use of Books during the Middle Ages.* West Valley City, UT: Editorium, 2006. ISBN: 978-1-60096-671-2.

Savage looks at the use of books in early Irish monasteries, English monks and their books, dispersal of monkish libraries, book making, collections in the religious houses, and cathedral and church libraries. He also discusses academic libraries at Oxford and Cambridge and their economies. The book ends with a discussion on the use of books toward the end of the manuscript period, the book trade, the character of the medieval library, and the extent of circulation of books.

808 Sider, David. *The Library of the Villa dei Papiri at Herculaneum.* Los Angeles: J. Paul Getty Museum, 2005. IDBN: 978-0-89236-799-3.

Thousands of papyrus rolls were recovered from Villa dei Papiri in Herculaneum in the 1730s during an excavation to see if any treasures survived the burial of the town from the eruption of Mount Vesuvius in AD 79. Sider walks readers through the discovery, the difficulty of unwinding the damaged rolls, and the deciphering of the text. A brief history of ancient books and private and civic libraries of the ancient world is included. Good-quality photos and illustrations bring the topic to life.

809 Stam, David H., ed. *International Dictionary of Library Histories.* 2 vols. Chicago: Fitzroy Dearborn, 2001. ISBN: 978-1-57958-244-9.

This two-volume set contains entries on more than 200 institutions, many of world renown, of which 122 are in Europe and 59 in the United States. Each entry has a brief directory, statistical information, description, and bibliography. Stam describes the world's most important research libraries and libraries with global or regional collections, hallowed traditions, and significant histories. Volume 1 contains introductory surveys and entries from "Ambrosiana Library" to "National Library of Brazil." Volume 2 continues with profiles from "National Library of Canada" to "Zurich Central Library." The A–Z topical and geographic introductory surveys discuss the history of different types of libraries and include a suggested reading list. There are also lists of advisors, contributors, entries, and abbreviations. The eighty-page index includes organizations and their acronyms, libraries by name and type, countries, continents, persons, and publications.

810 **Too, Yun Lee.** *The Idea of the Library in the Ancient World.* New York: Oxford University Press, 2010. ISBN: 978-0-19957-780-4.

The author looks at the diachronic perspective of libraries, forms of the library, preserving cultural memories, and physicalities in the ancient world. Topics covered include the birth of the library in the ancient world, developing library catalogues, recording cultural memories, collective knowledge, universal history, art collections, and social impact. Too builds the case that a library is more than a building with books, that it is the individual people and individual books that provide power and memory. References, general index, and index locorum are included.

@ ADDITIONAL RESOURCE

811 **Myers, Robin, Michael Harris, and Giles Mandelbrote, eds.** *Libraries and the Book Trade: The Formation of Collections from the Sixteenth to the Twentieth Century.* New Castle, DE: Oak Knoll Press, 2000. ISBN: 978-1-87304-060-7.

22

LIBRARY SCIENCE, GENERAL

 BOOKS

812 Bates, Marcia, and Mary Maack, eds.
The Encyclopedia of Library and Information Sciences. 7 vols. 3rd ed. New York: CRC Press, 2009. ISBN: 978-0-84939-712-7.

Major researchers and practitioners from more than thirty countries contributed hundreds of historical, theoretical, and cultural records from multiple disciplines relevant to LIS. Covered are various disciplines, concepts, theories, models, institutions, collections, systems, literatures, genres, documents, laws, resource management, bibliography, and many other subject areas. This edition contains more than 70 percent new material and is available in print as well as by online subscription or in combination.

813 Evans, G. Edward, Sheila S. Intner, and Jean R. Weihs. *Introduction to Technical Services.* 8th ed. Library and Information Science Text Series. Westport, CT: Libraries Unlimited, 2011. ISBN: 978-1-59158-888-7.

This revised text covers all aspects of library technical services, from acquisition to managing cataloging activities. It is divided into three sections: general background, acquisitions and serials, and cataloging and processing. Each unit contains an overview and thorough explanation of the subject. Topics include staffing, distributors and vendors, electronic serials, subject analysis, and classifications. Each chapter focuses on one topic and contains illustrations, statistics, and review questions.

814 Feather, John, and Paul Sturgers, eds.
International Encyclopedia of Information and Library Science. 2nd ed. New York: Routledge, 2003. ISBN: 978-0-4152-5901-9.

Most articles in this second edition have been revised to reflect LIS developments since the 1997 edition was published. Arranged alphabetically, articles range from one-paragraph descriptions to several pages or more with key subtopics. Many articles list contributors and have short bibliographies. Mainly focused on British librarianship, twelve major topics are covered: communication, economics of information, informatics, information management, information policy, information professions, information society, information systems, information theory, knowledge industries, knowledge management, and organization of knowledge. The book is illustrated with seventeen tables and twenty black-and-white diagrams.

815 Fourie, Denise K., and David R. Dowell. *Libraries in the Information Age: An Introduction and Career Exploration.* 2nd ed. Library and Information Science Text Series. Westport, CT: Libraries Unlimited, 2009. ISBN: 978-1-59158-434-6 (print), 978-0-313-39122-4 (e-book).

HISTORIC INTEREST

FYI

American Reference Books Annual LIS Bibliographies

The most comprehensive—and perhaps only—general bibliographies of library science produced in the past couple of decades are those by the trade publisher Libraries Unlimited. Since 1970, this company has brought out yearly editions of *American Reference Books Annual.* Although encyclopedias, dictionaries, directories, and similar materials are now its stock in trade, there was a time when library literature was reviewed here more or less in its entirety. In what might be called a bibliographic experiment, *ARBA,* as it is more familiarly known, culled the LIS stuff and put it all together in a series of volumes spanning the period 1970–1999. There is a break in the continuity because publication was suspended for several years due to the usual shortages of time and money. Since nothing comparable was found for the more recent literature of our profession, I decided to undertake the task myself. The current work you are holding covers the period 2000 to present, so taken together about four decades of library literature has been reviewed and organized. Because the *ARBA* volumes follow a chronological pattern, I alter the standard citation format a bit, to keep them in yearly order:

ARBA Guide to Library Science Literature, 1970–1983. Edited by Donald G. Davis Jr. and Charles D. Patterson. Littleton, CO: Libraries Unlimited, 1987. ISBN: 0-87287-585-7.

Library Science Annual, 1985, Vol. 1. Edited by Bohdan S. Wynar. Littleton, CO: Libraries Unlimited, 1985. ISBN: 0-87287-495-8.

Library Science Annual, 1986, Vol. 2. Edited by Bohdan S. Wynar. Littleton, CO: Libraries Unlimited, 1986. ISBN: 0-87287-541-5.

Library Science Annual, 1987, Vol. 3. Edited by Bohdan S. Wynar. Littleton, CO: Libraries Unlimited, 1987. ISBN: 0-87287-596-8.

Library and Information Science Annual, 1988, Vol. 4. Edited by Bohdan S. Wynar. Englewood, CO: Libraries Unlimited, 1988. ISBN: 0-87287-683-7.

Library and Information Science Annual, 1989, Vol. 5. Edited by Bohdan S. Wynar. Englewood, CO: Libraries Unlimited, 1989. ISBN: 0-87287-760-4.

Library and Information Science Annual, 1998, Vol. 6. Edited by Bohdan S. Wynar. Englewood, CO: Libraries Unlimited, Inc., ISBN: 1-56308-609-3.

Library and Information Science Annual, 1999, Vol. 7. Edited by Bohdan S. Wynar. Englewood, CO: Libraries Unlimited, 1999. ISBN: 1-56308-785-1.

This revised edition redefines the role of librarians and provides an overview of modern libraries in an ever-changing electronic age. Chapters focus on library history, job opportunities, collections, material preparation, reference services, ethics, the Internet, and job search basics. The appendixes include the Library and Information Studies Education and Human Resource Utilization Statement of Policy, ALA Library Bill of Rights, ALA Code of Ethics, and ALA/AAP Freedom to Read Statement.

816 Henkel, Nancy M. *Ready-Made Book Displays.* Westport, CT: Libraries Unlimited, 2011. ISBN: 978-1-59884-862-5.

Henkel explains the principles behind effective displays and includes fifty-five ready-made reproducible book display handouts, materials, props lists, photographic guides, and a Dewey subject list to help librarians create successful displays. The examples are easily modified to target events, holidays, celebrations, and general book promotion on shelves, in display cases, and at point-of-checkout and other venues.

817 Hunter, Gregory S. *Developing and Maintaining Practical Archives: A How-to-Do-It Manual.* 2nd ed. How-To-Do-It Manuals for Libraries 122. New York: Neal-Schuman, 2003. ISBN: 978-1-55570-467-4.

Hunter describes selection and appraisal, arrangement, description, preservation, security and disaster planning, access, reference, outreach, digital records, and audiovisual material for archives. Charts for organizing information and a cubic-foot table are helpful tools. Numerous anecdotes provide interesting reading. The extensive bibliography includes Canadian and Australian material. The Society of American Archivists' Code of Ethics for Archivists and the Academy of Certified Archivists' Role Delineation Statement for Professional Archivists are included in the appendixes.

818 Levine-Clark, Michael, and Toni M. Carter. *ALA Glossary of Library and Information Science.*

4th ed. Chicago: American Library Association, 2012. ISBN: 978-0-83891-111-2.

This glossary includes specific words, jargon, and phases relevant to librarianship. The vocabulary covers materials, processes, and system definitions written by LIS experts. The fourth edition has been fully updated to include the latest technology and Internet terms related to LIS.

819 Prentice, Ann E. *Public Libraries in the 21st Century.* Library and Information Science Text Series. Westport, CT: Libraries Unlimited, 2010. ISBN: 978-1-59158-854-2 (print), 978-1-59158-855-9 (e-book).

Prentice offers a current overview of what public libraries are today, what librarians need to know, and how to deal with social, political, economic, cultural, and technological influences as library roles change and challenges arise. She also covers leadership, planning, decision making, technology, organizing, and staffing issues.

820 Rubin, Richard E. *Foundations of Library and Information Science.* 2nd ed. New York: Neal-Schuman, 2004. ISBN: 978-1-55570-518-3.

This revised information science textbook for library school students and instructors includes updates on many critical issues and new topics such as digital libraries, information infrastructure, the web, homeland security, the Uniform Computer Information Transaction Act (UCITA), and the revised intellectual freedom policy. Suggested readings are included at the end of each chapter and at the conclusion of the text. Ten chapters, nearly 500 pages, depict significant components of LIS programs. The appendixes cover major LIS periodicals, indexes, encyclopedias, and dictionaries; a summary of major LIS associations and a list of additional associations; accredited LIS master's programs in the United States; the Association for Computing Machinery's Code of Ethics and Professional Conduct; and the Society of Competitive Intelligence Professionals' Code of Ethics. A list of figures, index, and author's information are included.

HISTORIC INTEREST

Encyclopedia of Library and Information Science, 1st ed., 73 volumes

In this writer's opinion, this is the single most comprehensive source of information regarding the library profession: International in scope and spanning clay tablets to computers, this set is, for all intents and purposes, the *Encyclopedia Britannica* of librarianship. Produced by Marcel Dekker, of New York City, the first volume came out in 1968, covering topics from "Abbreviations" to "Associação Brasileira das Escolas de Biblioteconomia e Documentação" (the Brazilian Association of Library Science and Documentation Schools). Knowledge doesn't stop accumulating with the culmination of a publishing project, however, so even after an impressive thirty-three volumes were published the company keep cranking out supplements, until Volume 73 (Indexes to Volumes 48–72) at last saw print in 2003. What is perhaps even more remarkable than the sheer amount of material committed to paper is the fact that a single individual oversaw this operation from beginning to end—executive editor Allen Kent, who had by then attained his eightieth birthday. Granted, even with the updating that occurred in the supplemental volumes, some material is bound to become dated, but much will remain relevant forever, such as biographies of deceased persons or historical overviews. Simply put, it doesn't get any better than this. That, of course, is just one opinion. For a more judicious appraisal, see the article "ELIS in Progress" by reference guru K. F. Kister that appeared in the May 15, 1981, issue of *Library Journal* (vol. 106, no. 10).

@ ADDITIONAL RESOURCES

821 Abell, Angela, and Nigel Oxbrow. *Competing with Knowledge: The Information Professional in the Knowledge Management Age.* London: Facet, 2001. ISBN: 978-1-85604-583-4.

822 Bawden, David, and Lyn Robinson. *Introduction to Information Science.* London: Facet, 2012. ISBN: 978-1-85604-810-1.

823 Chowdhury, G. G., Paul F. Barton, David McMenemy, and Alan Poulter. *Librarianship: An Introduction.* London: Facet, 2007. ISBN: 978-1-85604-617-6.

824 Ford, Nigel. *Introduction to Information Behaviour.* London: Facet, 2014. ISBN: 978-1-85604-850-7.

825 Gilchrist, Alan, ed. *Information Science in Transition.* London: Facet, 2009. ISBN: 978-1-85604-693-0.

826 Ruthven, Ian, and Diane Kelly, eds. *Interactive Information Seeking, Behaviour and Retrieval.* London: Facet, 2011. ISBN: 978-1-85604-707-4.

827 Totterdell, Anne. *An Introduction to Library and Information Work.* 3rd ed. London: Facet, 2005. ISBN: 978-1-85604-557-5.

▤ PERIODICALS

828 American Libraries. Chicago: American Library Association. Frequency: Ten issues per year. ISSN: 0002-9769. URL: http://americanlibrariesmagazine.org.

This official publication of the ALA is a major membership benefit, with news, how-to articles, regular columns (Joseph Janes with think pieces, Will Manley with his signature brand of humor), association business, job postings, and more. All areas of interest to librarians are covered.

829 Canadian Journal of Information and Library Science. Toronto: Canadian Association for Information Science. Frequency: Quarterly. ISSN: 1195-096X. URL: www.cais-acsi.ca/journal/journal.htm.

This journal provides reviews of LIS books, web resources, reports, and other major publications.

830 Journal of Access Services: Service Innovations for 21st Century Libraries. Philadelphia: Routledge. Frequency: Four issues per year. ISSN: 1536-7967 (print), 1536-7975 (online). URL: www.tandf.co.uk/journals/WJAS/.

According to the "Aims and Scope" portion of this journal's website, *access services* are defined as "the broad field and collective term of all the services that provide, facilitate, and manage the access of the clientele to the information resources acquired or made available by the libraries or archives with the aim of allowing for easy and convenient retrieval of needed information, utilization of information resources to the fullest extent, and greatest availability of resources to each of the clientele." Emphasis is on best practices and new developments in this area. All articles undergo editorial screening and peer review by anonymous reviewers.

831 Journal of Documentation. Westport, CT: Emerald Group. Frequency: Six times per year. ISSN: 0022-0418. URL: www.emeraldinsight.com/products/journals/journals.htm?id=jd.

This journal disseminates scholarly articles, research reports, and critical reviews in information science. Topics include information science, librarianship, and related disciplines; information and knowledge management; information and knowledge organization; information seeking and retrieval; and human behaviors, information, and digital literacy.

832 Journal of Knowledge Management. Westport, CT: Emerald Group. Frequency: Six times per year. ISSN: 1367-3270. URL: www.emeraldinsight.com/products/journals/journals.htm?id=jkm.

This peer-reviewed journal focuses on the exchange of the latest academic research and practical information on all aspects of managing knowledge in organizations. Topics include developing an appropriate culture and communication strategy, integrating learning and knowledge infrastructure, knowledge management and the learning organization, information organization and retrieval technologies, and using information technology.

833 Journal of Library and Information Services in Distance Learning. Philadelphia: Routledge. Frequency: Four issues per year. ISSN: 1533-290X (print), 1533-2918 (online). URL: www.tandf.co.uk/journals/WLIS/.

Articles address delivery of library services in distance learning education. Original research, theoretical papers, substantive articles, essays, book and literature reviews, and research reports cover collection development strategies, faculty/librarian partnerships or collaborations, cutting-edge instruction and reference techniques, document delivery, remote access, and evaluations. Manuscripts undergo editorial screening and peer review by anonymous reviewers.

834 Library Journal. New York: Reed Business Information. Frequency: Twenty issues per year. ISSN: 0363-0277. URL: www.libraryjournal.com.

Established in 1876, the year ALA was founded, this is the leading general-interest publication for the profession. Besides library-related news and feature articles, each issue contains a generous helping of reviews for books, e-books, audiobooks, DVDs, and databases, totaling about 8,000 reviews annually. Opinion pieces, regular columns, and interviews with library movers and shakers round out each bimonthly issue. Each year sees two special theme issues: Star (top-rated) Libraries, and the Year in Architecture, which highlights the latest and greatest in library design. This journal should be required reading for anyone who considers him- or herself an info pro. By the way, a free online archive allows access to articles back to 2002.

835 Library Review. Westport, CT: Emerald Group. Frequency: Nine times per year. ISSN: 0024-2535. URL: www.emeraldinsight.com/products/journals/journals.htm?id=lr.

This magazine links communications between researchers, educators, and library professionals in academic, public, corporate, and specialty libraries. Topics in these double-blind reviewed articles include developing information services, hybrid and digital libraries, information literacy and e-learning, metadata and distributed searching, library collaboration and resource sharing, library history, information strategies and knowledge management, and national and international policy.

836 New World Library. Westport, CT: Emerald Group. Frequency: Six issues per year. ISSN: 0307-4803. URL: www.emeraldinsight.com/products/journals/journals.htm?id=nlw.

This journal provides an international appraisal of current library trends and emerging patterns. Topics include demographic trends, developments in the educational environment, impacts of electronic publishing, new information technologies, service of future libraries, role of the library in its marketing of knowledge, and news and views on the modern library and what's to come.

837 Public Library Quarterly. Philadelphia: Routledge. Frequency: Four times per year. ISSN:

0161-6846 (print), 1541-1540 (online). URL: www.tandf.co.uk/journals/WPLQ/.

Directors and operating officers tell how they accomplished change to fulfill their service missions in the twenty-first century. Typical topics:

- Best practices and models to improve service
- Management case studies, with results and failures
- Library mythologies that retard individual and institutional development
- How to plan results and accomplish desired outcomes
- Marketing and fund-raising tools that work
- Budget and financial analysis tools and tips
- How new technology works in practice
- Innovative, high-quality programs for children

838 VINE: The Journal of Information and Knowledge Management Systems. Westport, CT: Emerald Group. Frequency: Four times per year. ISSN: 0305-5728. URL: www.emeraldinsight.com/products/journals/journals.htm?id=vine.

The title is a reminder of humble origins; in 1971 this publication started out as a "very informal newsletter." Topical themed issues with well-researched, timely, unbiased articles and practical overviews recognize the reality and need of organizations to operate interdependently where collaboration and knowledge information are critical for achieving competitive advantage. Topics include the roles of library science in knowledge valuation, international knowledge management, protecting knowledge/knowledge assets, development, and key initiatives in information service systems.

ADDITIONAL RESOURCES

839 Annals of Library and Information Studies (ALIS). New Delhi: Indian National Scientific Documentation Centre. Frequency: Quarterly. ISSN: 0972-5423. URL: www.niscair.res.in/sciencecommunication/researchjournals/rejour/annals/annals0.asp.

840 *CILIP Update.* London: Chartered Institute Library and Information Professionals. Frequency: Twelve issues per year. ISSN: 2046-0406. URL: www.cilip.org.uk/publications/update-magazine/subscribe/pages/default.aspx.

841 *CILIP Update Blog.* London: Chartered Institute Library and Information Professionals. URL: http://communities.cilip.org.uk/blogs/update/default.aspx.

842 *Evidence Based Library and Information Practice.* Edmonton: University of Alberta, Learning Services. Frequency: Quarterly. ISSN: 1715-720X. URL: http://ejournals.library.ualberta.ca/index.php/EBLIP.

843 *Harvard Library Bulletin.* Cambridge, MA: Harvard University Library. Frequency: Four times per year. ISSN: 0017-8136. URL: http://hcl.harvard.edu/libraries/houghton/departments.cfm#bulletin.

844 *Journal of Information Science.* Thousand Oaks, CA: Sage. Frequency: Six times per year. ISSN: 0165-5515. URL: http://jis.sagepub.com.

845 *Journal of Librarianship and Information Science (JOLIS).* Thousand Oaks, CA: Sage. Frequency: Four times per year. ISSN: 0961-0006. URL: http://lis.sagepub.com.

846 *Library Collections,* Acquisitions, and Technical Services. Amsterdam: Elsevier. Frequency: Four issues per year. ISSN: 1464-9055. URL: www.journals.elsevier.com/library-collections-acquisitions-and-technical-services/.

847 *Unabashed Librarian.* New York: Unabashed Librarian. Frequency: Four times per year. ISSN: 0049-514X. URL: www.unabashedlibrarian.com.

⬈ DATABASES

848 Library, Information Science and Technology Abstracts (LISTA). URL: www.ebscohost.com/public/library-information-science-technology-abstracts-lista.

EBSCO makes LISTA available free of charge to any library. This database indexes more than 500 core journals, more than fifty priority journals, and 125 selective journals, plus books, research reports, and proceedings. Topics include librarianship, classification, cataloging, bibliometrics, online information retrieval, and information management.

849 Library Literature and Information Science Full Text. URL: www.ebscohost.com/academic/library-literature-information-science-full-text.

More than 150 journals covering all aspects of LIS are represented here, such as automation, cataloging, education, and reference. Full-text articles are available, as the title denotes, as are PDF images of illustrative material such as charts, diagrams, and photographs. The scope of this subscription database is 1997 to the present.

LIBRARY SCIENCE, HISTORY OF

 **BOOKS**

850 Baker, David, and Wendy Evans, eds.
*Libraries and Society: Role, Responsibility and
Future in an Age of Change.* Oxford: Chandos,
2011. ISBN: 978-1-84334-131-4.

Contributors look at the devaluing of books and
the change in librarian expectations as patrons
increasingly are able to access information electronically in the digital age. Contributors define
social responsibility, usage, research, education,
and access in terms of a fluid information marketplace rather than via the traditional picture
of librarians as keepers of books and magazines.
The authors' thesis is that a librarian is now an
educator rather than just the provider of educational materials.

851 Bobinski, George. *Libraries and Librarianship:
Sixty Years of Challenge and Change, 1945–2005.*
Lanham, MD: Scarecrow Press, 2007. ISBN: 978-
0-81085-899-2.

Having spent forty-seven years in the library profession, the author has witnessed many of the
developments discussed in this book. In ten chapters, Bobinski records the evolution (some might
reasonably say revolution) of the profession by
looking at "Types of Libraries" and "Library
Cooperation: Systems, Consortia, and Networks,"
in addition to library associations, the role of gender and ethnic groups, the education of librarians
to be, and prominent players in the field. Interesting and well written, this is a good synopsis of
what has gone on in librarianship during the past
six decades. A chronology for this period and bibliography are included.

852 D'Angelo, Ed. *Barbarians at the Gates of
the Public Library: How Postmodern Consumer
Capitalism Threatens Democracy, Civil Education
and the Public Good.* Preface by Kathleen de la
Peña McCook. Duluth, MN: Library Juice Press,
LLC, 2006. ISBN: 978-0-97786-171-2.

This slim volume offers technical economic
and abstract philosophical concepts to describe
the evolution of libraries from a primarily

educational facility to a major emphasis on providing alternative forms of entertainment, (movies, video games, food, and drinks). The historical context relies heavily on the economic perspective. D'Angelo explains how the political climate, consumer interest, and pandering to the lowest common denominator are desecrating the professional librarian and contributing to a lack of critical thinking by the general public.

853 Feather, John. *Information Society: A Study of Continuity and Change.* 6th ed. London: Facet, 2013. ISBN: 978-1-85604-818-7.

Feather discusses historical dimensions, mass media and new technology, the political aspect, and the information profession in relation to the information society, both myth and reality. Topics covered include significant changes since 2008 in technologies and systems that affect the traditional boundaries of librarianship. Notes on further reading and index are provided.

854 Wilhite, Jeffrey M. *A Chronology of Librarianship: 1960–2000.* Lanham, MD: Scarecrow Press, 2009. ISBN: 978-0-8108-5255-6.

According to the preface, this volume is meant to be a continuation of *A Chronology of Librarianship* by Josephine Metcalfe Smith, likewise published by Scarecrow Press, in 1968. The scope of that work was "the beginning of the Christian era to 1959" (p. v). A major improvement by Wilhite is the addition of subject headings (fifteen altogether) that subdivide material listed under each year. Every item is followed by a parenthetical citation listing the original source; a bibliography at the back of the book gives full details regarding those sources for those who wish to read the original article or study the website for themselves. Five years in the making, this appears to be a fairly complete and well-documented record of personalities, events, technological advances, and all things library related.

MARKETING, PUBLIC RELATIONS, AND ADVOCACY

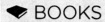 **BOOKS**

855 Alman, Susan Webreck. *Crash Course in Marketing for Libraries.* Crash Course Series. Westport, CT: Libraries Unlimited, 2007. ISBN: 978-1-59158-430-8.

Brief and to the point, this is an easy-to-read guide for developing and implementing a library marketing plan with an additional section on fund-raising activities. Over half of the book is devoted to samples of marketing plans, posters, annual reports, and newsletters. Other sections include a marketing bibliography and a synopsis of the John Cotton Dana Library Public Relations Award winners between 2002 and 2007, along with website addresses.

856 Barber, Peggy, and Linda Wallace. *Building a Buzz: Libraries and Word-of-Mouth Marketing.* Chicago: American Library Association, 2010. ISBN: 978-0-83891-011-5.

This slim volume is packed with sample communication plans, surveys, workshop agendas, and marketing scripts for word-of-mouth marketing (WOMM), used to generate positive advertising. The case studies explain how to implement WOMM, goals, audience, message, strategies, budget, tools, impacts, and lessons learned. The "Power Pack" chapter includes definitions, checklists, communication plan surveys, agendas, related marketing resources, and scenarios to consider. A synopsis of the Buzz Grant Project conducted by the DuPage Library System and Northern Suburban Library System in Illinois illustrates the use of a grant to provide training, planning support, and information resources to implement WOMM.

857 Blake, Barbara Radke, Robert Sidney Martin, and Yunfei Du. *Successful Community Outreach: A How-to-Do-It Manual for Librarians.* How-To-Do-It Manuals for Libraries 157. New York: Neal-Schuman, 2011. ISBN: 978-1-55570-772-9.

This guide is specifically designed to help librarians develop, plan, and implement community outreach programs. Step-by-step instructions are broken into three areas: identifying the environment, gathering supports and partners, and developing and implementing the outreach plan. Sample vision and mission statements, goals, demographic examples, marketing tips, and library roles are used to highlight key concepts. The companion CD-ROM includes several ready-to-go outreach plans and sample worksheets.

858 Doucett, Elisabeth. *Creating Your Library Brand: Communicating Your Relevance and Value to Your Patrons.* Chicago: American Library Association, 2008. ISBN: 978-0-83890-962-1.

With the rise of the Internet and mega-bookstores, libraries have been facing increased competition in the past couple of decades. This manual aims to show how a library can set itself apart from the for-profit purveyors of information and entertainment. It opens with a sample project plan that shows the overall branding process. Each stand-alone chapter includes step-by-step instructions, frequently asked questions, suggestions for success, pitfalls to avoid, tips, and exercises. Main topics include developing a logo, taglines, visuals, working with consultants, and evaluating results.

859 Edelman, Hendrik, and Robert P. Holley, eds. *Marketing to Libraries for the New Millennium: Librarians, Vendors, and Publishers Review the Landmark Third Industry-Wide Survey of the Library Marketing Practices and Trends.* Lanham, MD: Scarecrow Press, 2002. ISBN: 978-0-81084-271-7.

This compilation discusses striking a balance between maintaining print collections and incorporating the ever-more digitized elements in today's society. The book contains an interesting discussion of the library marketplace. The questionnaire and results from the 1999 Third Industry-Wide Survey of Library Marketing Practices and Trends provide a snapshot in time and include comments that are still relevant today.

860 Gould, Mark R., ed. *The Library PR Handbook: High-Impact Communications.* Chicago: American Library Association, 2009. ISBN: 978-0-83891-002-3.

This instructional manual covers how to increase public awareness, develop support, increase attendance, and communicate through a variety of resources. Packed with how-to-do-it examples, case studies, illustrations, and tips, each chapter provides readers with practical ideas. Partnerships to provide game days, cooking demonstrations, podcasts, and social media are some of the approaches used to attract attention and bring new patrons to the library.

861 Halsey, Richard S. *Lobbying for Public and School Libraries: A History and Political Playbook.* Lanham, MD: Scarecrow Press, 2003. ISBN: 978-0-81084-783-5.

From grassroots organizations and Friends of the Library groups to local, state, and national politicians, perception and advocacy go hand in hand to increase credibility and clout with library boards, local officials, and legislators. This book focuses primarily on lobbying governmental organizations, using the same tactics employed by the private sector, in order to enhance library reputation and funding sources. Sixteen grassroots lobbying tactics fit into one of four categories: participation in legislative alerts, direct personal interaction with legislators, mobilization of public support, and coalition building.

862 Imhoff, Kathleen R., and Ruthie Maslin. *Library Contests: A How-to-Do-It Manual.* How-To-Do-It Manuals for Libraries 152. New York: Neal-Schuman, 2007. ISBN: 978-1-55570-559-6.

This manual provides librarians with step-by-step instructions through all the stages of planning, promoting, budgeting, and running a contest. Each of the nine steps has its own chapter that contains a detailed description, overview, steps, tips, and conclusion. A tenth chapter offers four model contests to implement or modify to fit local areas of interest.

863 Karp, Rashelle S., ed. *Powerful Public Relations: A How-To Guide for Libraries.* Chicago: American Library Association, 2002. ISBN: 978-0-83890-818-1.

This how-to-do-it guide has practical, applicable, and effective tips, tricks, and techniques for news releases, photo releases, public service announcements, publications, exhibits, kiosks, special events, desktop publishing, and web-based activities. Notes, sources of additional information, and a selected annotated bibliography provide references for further reading on marketing, business, communication, and advertising. This volume has been updated and expanded since it was originally published as "Part-Time Public Relations with Full-Time Results" (*Library Journal*, March 1, 1996).

864 Kranich, Nancy, ed. *Libraries and Democracy: The Cornerstones of Liberty.* Chicago: American Library Association, 2001. ISBN: 978-0-83890-808-2.

This collection of articles focuses on the impact library services have in a democratic society. Contributors range from field professionals to activists to information scholars. Each article presents a basic premise, supporting arguments, conclusion, and notes. Topics include technology, information access, and advocacy, along with the role of the Library of Congress.

865 Lindsay, Anita Rothwell, comp. *Marketing and Public Relations Practices in College Libraries.* CLIP Notes 34. Chicago: Association of College and Research Libraries, American Library Association, 2004. ISBN: 978-0-83898-295-2.

Comprising a literature review, survey results, and sample documents, this book consists primarily of documents to be used to handle public relations and marketing library services. Arranged by topic, each marketing and public relations document chapter includes submissions from at least three libraries that can be modified to fit individual needs.

866 Mathews, Brian. *Marketing Today's Academic Library: A Bold New Approach to Communicating with Students.* Chicago: American Library Association, 2009. ISBN: 978-0-83890-984-3.

Mathews wants the campus library to become a place that college students make part of their daily routine. Moving away from traditional marketing strategies, he stresses the importance of targeted services, that is, those that are centered around students' schedules, grade levels, disciplines, peers, and community, including providing a safe place for homesick freshmen and a resource for job-hunting seniors. Numerous examples of building relationships, developing brand strategies, designing messages, and measuring results are gathered within each topic area.

867 Petruzzelli, Barbara Whitney, ed. *Real-Life Marketing and Promotion Strategies in College Libraries: Connecting with Campus and Community.* Copublished simultaneously as *College and Undergraduate Libraries* 12, no. 1, 2005. Binghamton, NY: Haworth Information Press, 2005. ISBN: 978-0-78903-158-7.

This book offers several practical approaches to marketing and promotional techniques that are effective and affordable for college libraries. Although the illustrations, charts, surveys, Quick Bib, references, and appendixes provide clarification and quick guides, some of the black-and-white illustrations are of poor quality.

868 Pfeil, Angela B. *Going Places with Youth Outreach: Smart Marketing Strategies for Your Library.* Chicago: American Library Association, 2005. ISBN: 978-0-83890-900-3.

Pfeil provides a comprehensive marketing plan for libraries to promote youth services through public presentations, community partnerships, and program evaluations. This step-by-step volume contains sample letters and forms and gives many success stories to imitate. Appendixes offer sample programs, marketing information, and additional reading suggestions. A general bibliography and a detailed, accurate index are included.

869 Siess, Judith A. *Visible Librarian: Asserting Your Value with Marketing and Advocacy.* Chicago: American Library Association, 2003. ISBN: 978-0-83890-848-8.

Customer service, marketing, publicity, public relations, and advocacy are discussed through basic elements, implementation guides, and case studies of librarians becoming more visible to their supporters, stakeholders, and patrons. Tips and case studies focus on customer needs, marketing, and accessing resources needed to maintain the library. The techniques used to counter concern about librarians and libraries fading into the background are especially relevant during these economically trying times of staff reductions, limited hours, and library closings.

870 Smallwood, Carol, Vera Gubnitskaia, and Kerol Harrod, eds. *Marketing Your Library: Tips and Tools That Work.* Jefferson, NC: McFarland, 2012. ISBN: 978-0-78646-543-9.

Practical how-to case studies provide approaches to improve branding, organize campaigns, develop community outreach, improve marketing, engage social media, and plan events. Contributors maintain that public, school, academic, and special libraries must focus on self-preservation and use marketing to increase library use and public perception of worth. A list of contributors and index are included.

871 Wolfe, Lisa A. *Library Public Relations, Promotions, and Communications: A How-to-Do-It Manual.* 2nd ed. How-To-Do-It Manuals for Libraries 126. New York: Neal-Schuman, 2005. ISBN: 978-1-55570-471-1.

This updated edition of real-world advice includes planning, evaluation, strategies, and methods for public relations and communications. The numerous figures and successful public relations examples found throughout the two sections—"Planning and Evaluation" and "Strategies and Methodologies"—are simple, concise, and easy to adapt. The sample public relations, school library, and academic plans included in the appendix provide the basis for any librarian looking to promote a library.

872 Woodward, Jeannette. *Creating the Customer-Driven Library: Building on the Bookstore Model.* Chicago: American Library Association, 2005. ISBN: 978-0-83890-888-4.

For-profit bookstores offer amenities and physical comforts to encourage patron browsing and promote loyalty. This book focuses on how to use bookstore ambience, color choice, displays, e-services, refreshments, and signage to support library patronage and obtain greater customer satisfaction. This thirteen-step guide to reviving a "Library on a Zero Budget"—using inexpensive supplies and a lot of hard work for a quick makeover—is a must read.

✒ ADDITIONAL RESOURCES

873 Blake, Barbara Radke, and Barbara Stein Martin. *Creating Newsletters, Brochures, and Pamphlets: A How-to-Do-It Manual.* How-to-Do-It Manuals for School and Public Librarians 2. New York: Neal-Schuman, 1992. ISBN: 978-1-55570-107-9.

874 Byrd, Susannah Mississippi. *¡Bienvenidos! = ¡Welcome! A Handy Resource Guide for Marketing Your Library to Latinos.* Chicago: American Library Association, 2005. ISBN: 978-0-83890-902-7.

875 de Sáez, Eileen Elliott. *Marketing Concepts for Libraries and Information Services.* 3rd ed. London: Facet, 2014. ISBN 978-1-85604-870-5.

876 Dowd, Nancy, Mary Evangeliste, and Jonathan Silberman. *Bite-Sized Marketing: Realistic Solutions for the Overworked Librarian.* Chicago: American Library Association, 2010. ISBN: 978-0-83891-000-9.

877 Ellis, Mike. *Managing and Growing a Cultural Heritage Web Presence: A Strategic Guide.* London: Facet, 2011. ISBN: 978-1-85604-710-4.

878 Fisher, Patricia H., Marseille M. Pride, and Ellen G. Miller. *Blueprint for Your Library Marketing Plan: A Guide to Help You Survive and Thrive.* Chicago: American Library Association, 2006. ISBN: 978-0-83890-909-6.

879 Grant, Maria J., Barbara Sen, and Hannah Spring, eds. *Research, Evaluation and Audit: Key Steps in Demonstrating Your Value.* London: Facet, 2013. ISBN: 978-1-85604-741-8.

880 Hall, Richard B. *Winning Library Referenda Campaigns: A How-to-Do-It Manual.* How-To-Do-It Manuals for Libraries 50. New York: Neal-Schuman, 1995. ISBN: 978-1-55570-224-3.

881 James, Russell D., and Peter J. Wosh, eds. *Public Relations and Marketing for Archives.* New York: Neal-Schuman, 2011. ISBN: 978-1-55570-733-0.

882 Kendrick, Terry. *Developing Strategic Marketing Plans That Really Work: A Toolkit for Public Libraries.* London: Facet, 2006. ISBN: 978-1-85604-548-3.

883 *Libraries Prosper with Passion, Purpose, and Persuasion! A PLA Toolkit for Success.* Chicago: Public Library Association, 2007. ISBN: 978-0-83898-430-7.

884 McCook, Kathleen de la Peña. *A Place at the Table: Participating in Community Building.* Chicago: American Library Association, 2000. ISBN: 978-0-83890-788-7.

885 Nichols, Mary Anne. *Merchandising Library Materials to Young Adults.* Libraries Unlimited Professional Guides for Young Adult Librarians. Santa Barbara, CA: Libraries Unlimited, 2002. ISBN: 978-1-41773-296-8.

886 Potter, Ned. *Library Marketing Toolkit.* London: Facet, 2012. ISBN: 978-1-85604-806-4.

887 Reed, Sally Gardner. *Making the Case for Your Library: A How-to-Do-It Manual.* How-To-Do-It Manuals for Libraries 104. New York: Neal-Schuman, 2001. ISBN: 978-1-55570-399-8.

888 Smallwood, Carol, ed. *Librarians as Community Partners: An Outreach Handbook.* Chicago: American Library Association, 2010. ISBN: 978-0-83891-006-1.

889 Streatfield, David, and Sharon Markless. *Evaluating the Impact of Your Library.* 2nd ed. London: Facet, 2012. ISBN: 978-1-85604-812-5.

890 Wallace, Linda K. *Libraries, Mission and Marketing: Writing Mission Statements That Work.* Chicago: American Library Association, 2004. ISBN: 978-0-83890-867-9.

891 Walters, Suzanne. *Marketing: A How-to-Do-It Manual.* How-To-Do-It Manuals for Libraries 20. New York: Neal-Schuman, 1992. ISBN: 978-1-55570-095-9.

📖 PERIODICAL

892 *MLS—Marketing Library Services.* Westport, CT: Information Today. Frequency: Six times per year. ISSN: 0896-3908. URL: www.infotoday.com/mls/default.shtml.

MISCELLANEOUS

 BOOKS

893   Augst, Thomas, and Wayne A. Wiegand, eds. *Libraries as Agencies of Culture: Print Culture History in Modern America.* Madison: University of Wisconsin Press, 2003. ISBN: 978-0-29918-304-2.

Originally published as a special issue of the journal *American Studies* (Vol. 42, no. 3, Fall 2001), this monograph examines a library's cultural roles. In each article, a contributor describes how a library system originated, what impact it had as a provider of cultural materials, and its historic effect on area culture.

894   Avrin, Leila. *Scribes, Script, and Books: The Book Arts from Antiquity to the Renaissance.* Chicago: American Library Association, 2010. ISBN: 978-0-83891-038-2.

This reprint of the 1991 edition provides a history of the book before printing presses. The book is considered an academic reference for pre-codex formats.

895   Bailey, Charles W., Jr. *Digital Curation and Preservation Bibliography 2010.* Houston, TX: Digital Scholarship, 2011. ISBN: 978-1-46091-332-1.

The author presents more than 500 English-language articles, books, and technical reports covering digital curation and preservation, copyright issues, digital formats, metadata, models, policies, research studies, and repository concerns. The appendixes contain related bibliographies and information about the author.

896   Baker, Nicholson. *Double Fold: Libraries and the Assault on Paper.* New York: Vintage, 2002. ISBN: 978-0-37572-621-7.

Baker is not happy that librarians are using alternative media, digitization, and other high-tech methods to maintain book, periodical, and newspaper collections. He contends that many items lose substance, not to mention color, when transferred to microfilm. The copies are hard to read and pages are sometimes missed. An argument is made that microfilm itself is not a durable material for archiving. Although it is fair to say that some documents have not fared well in the past and mistakes have occurred, there are still issues of physical space and funding (or, more accurately, a lack thereof) to address. This volume offers questions but does not supply any solutions at a time when funding and space are at a premium.

897 Balloffet, Nelly, and Jenny Hille. *Preservation and Conservation for Libraries and Archives.* Chicago: American Library Association, 2004. ISBN: 978-0-83891-005-4.

Preservation refers to overall safekeeping of collections, *conservation* to hands-on care, repair, and treatment of materials. This guide contains step-by-step instructions on how to repair books and documents in an easily set up conservation area. Packed full of photographs and line drawings, the book covers basic information the beginner conservator needs to know about the techniques, equipment, and materials of preservation.

898 Bertot, John Carlo, Paul T. Jaeger, and Charles R. McClure, eds. *Public Libraries and the Internet: Roles, Perspectives, and Implications.* Westport, CT: Libraries Unlimited, 2011. ISBN: 978-1-59158-776-7 (print), 978-1-59158-777-4 (e-book).

Contributors examine the impact of the Internet and network expansion in U.S. public libraries from five perspectives: overview, contexts and connections, populations, institutions and support, and moving forward. Articles track how libraries have changed since 1994 as a result of the Internet explosion onto the national scene and suggest future opportunities in a networked environment.

899 Bogart, Dave, ed. *Library and Book Trade Almanac.* 56th ed. Contributions by Julia C. Blixrud. Medford, NJ: Information Today, 2011. ISBN: 978-1-57387-412-0.

For many years, this title went by the name *The Bowker Annual of Library and Book Trade Information.* Basically a grab bag of miscellaneous facts and figures, hence "almanac" in the title,

the book's typical contents are statistics on book prices, numbers of books published, library expenditures, average salaries, new legislation, funding programs, calendar of events, and directory of organizations.

900 Brown, Mary E., and Rebecca Power. *Exhibits in Libraries: A Practical Guide.* Jefferson, NC: McFarland, 2006. ISBN: 978-0-78642-352-1.

The authors use visual, hands-on, and traveling exhibits to stimulate interest in subject material and the host library. Much of the book centers on creating exhibits. Many examples of exhibits, development and design, and fabrication are included to stimulate ideas. A general step-by-step beginning-to-end process takes into consideration safety, funding, public relations, security, and more. Illustrations, photographs, and templates are useful tools for exhibit planners. A three-course syllabus, along with a self-study guide, chapter notes, and bibliography, allows further discussions through either a workshop or course on exhibits.

901 Buschman, John E. *Dismantling the Public Sphere: Situating and Sustaining Librarianship in the Age of New Public Philosophy.* Contributions in Librarianship and Information Science. Westport, CT: Libraries Unlimited, 2003. ISBN: 978-0-31332-199-3.

The author uses the critical analytical framework developed by the German sociologist and philosopher Jürgen Habermas, with concepts of *communicative rationality* and the *public sphere* with emphasis on German politics, as the basis for the discussion. This material highlights an ongoing debate between library as public service and library as economic necessity. The selected bibliography includes critical and historical perspectives along with references for library management and the future of technologies.

902 Buschman, John E., and Gloria J. Leckie, eds. *The Library as Place: History, Community, and Culture.* Westport, CT: Libraries Unlimited, 2007. ISBN: 978-1-59158-382-0.

The editors gather fourteen specially written articles concerning the library as a physical entity, along with the social, cultural, and symbolic influences that buildings naturally entail. Section 1, "The Library's Place in the Past," takes a look at how brick-and-stone edifices reinforced our Victorian forebears' sense of social order and rectitude (think athenaeums and Carnegie libraries). Section 2, "Libraries as Places of Community," discusses the "town square" aspect of libraries as gathering places for social interaction among the local populace. The title of section 3, "Research Libraries as Places of Learning and Scholarship," is self-explanatory. Section 4, "Libraries, Place and Culture," perhaps the most abstract part of this volume, covers symbolism and meaning, with one chapter even considering an imaginary place, the library in the television show *Buffy the Vampire Slayer*.

903 Carr, David. *Open Conversations: Public Learning in Libraries and Museums.* Westport, CT: Libraries Unlimited, 2011. ISBN: 978-1-59158-771-2 (print), 978-1-59158-770-5 (e-book).

Carr challenges librarians to become instruments of personal, social, and cultural change. He discusses libraries and museums as places to open conversation, provide provocative tests, and embrace the unknown as a basis for human thinking in a democratic society, rather than just as repositories of information or places for research. The author bases this work on lectures, previously published writings, and newly conducted research.

904 Dewey, Barbara I., and Loretta Parham, eds. *Achieving Diversity: A How-to-Do-It Manual for Librarians.* How-To-Do-It Manuals for Libraries 140. New York: Neal-Schuman, 2006. ISBN: 978-1-5557-0554-1.

The editors gather more than thirty articles on higher education diversity presented by public and academic librarians at a National Diversity in Libraries Conference. The first three sections are "How to Create a Successful Diversity Plan," "How to Recruit and Retain a Diverse Work Force," and "How to Improve Diversity through

Services, Collections, and Collaborations." Sample documents, including strategic plans, questionnaires, and brochures, make up the fourth and final section.

905 Dilevko, Juris, and Lisa Gottlieb. *The Evolution of Library and Museum Partnerships: Historical Antecedents, Contemporary Manifestations, and Future Directions.* Libraries Unlimited Library Management Collection. Westport, CT: Libraries Unlimited, 2004. ISBN: 978-1-59158-064-5.

This is an academic review of the role that museum artifacts and library collections play during the proliferation of electronic resources, commercialization, and social media. The authors propose a combination of education and entertainment, called *edutainment*, to provide interactive experiences for patrons and sustain their value for the future. Each chapter's notes contain a list of source documentation. An extensive bibliography and index provide supplemental references.

906 Eastwood, Terry, and Heather MacNeil, eds. *Currents of Archival Thinking.* Westport, CT: Libraries Unlimited, 2009. ISBN: 978-1-59158-656-2 (print), 978-0-313-39121-7 (e-book).

Contributors examine the foundations, functions, models, and metaphors in the theory and practice of archival studies. Each essay looks at historical and contemporary frameworks. Topics include life cycle, description debates, provenance, preservation, and the nature of archives.

907 Eberhart, George M., ed. *The Whole Library Handbook 4: Current Data, Professional Advice, and Curiosa about Libraries and Library Services.* Chicago: American Library Association, 2006. ISBN: 978-0-83890-915-7.

This compendium of library lore follows along the same lines as the three earlier editions, which Eberhart also edited. Ten chapters cover "Libraries," "People," "The Profession," "Materials," "Operations," "The Underserved," "Promotion," "Technology," "Issues," and "Librariana." The bulk of the book consists of excerpts from books, magazines, and websites, with the source citation listed at the end so readers may consult the original longer article. This and previous editions have been highly praised for breadth and depth of material. The fifth edition was published in 2013, again by ALA.

908 Edwards, Julie Biando, and Edwards, Stephan P., eds. *Beyond Article 19: Libraries and Social and Cultural Rights.* Duluth, MN: Library Juice Press, 2010. ISBN: 978-1-93611-719-2.

This monograph focuses on Article 27 of the United Nations Universal Declaration of Human Rights. Librarians and academics examine the relationship between libraries' accessibility to collections and cultural rights recognized internationally. A common theme throughout the essays is the balance between author rights and the right of access to information. The articles of the Declaration of Human Rights are included at the end of the book.

909 Gorman, Michael. *Our Own Selves: More Meditations for Librarians.* Chicago: American Library Association, 2005. ISBN: 978-0-83890-896-9.

The author presents 100 new meditations covering reading and books, places books are found, library people, freedom of information, library services, historical development, technological changes, and practicalities. Each essay centers around a library-related theme. This collection is a follow-up to Gorman's *Our Singular Strengths* (ALA, 1997).

910 Haven, Kendall. *Story Proof: The Science behind the Startling Power of Story.* Westport, CT: Libraries Unlimited, 2007. ISBN: 978-1-59158-546-6 (print), 978-0-313-09587-0 (e-book).

Haven gathers anecdotal experiences and research studies regarding the importance of story, story reading, and storytelling as these factors relate to brain development in children and adults; he builds a case for creating a common definition of story that includes neural, psychological, and brain development. In part 1, "Story

Smarts," he examines what a story is, how stories affect the brain, and what constitutes memories. In part 2 he examines research conducted within the previous ten years; the value of anecdotal evidence; how to use stories to improve literacy, writing, and memory; and the critical role school and public libraries play in providing a print-rich environment. A bibliography and index are included.

911 Kalfatovic, Martin R. *Creating a Winning Online Exhibition: A Guide for Libraries, Archives, and Museums.* Chicago: American Library Association, 2002. ISBN: 978-0-83890-817-4.

Kalfatovic, digital projects librarian and head of the New Media Office at the Smithsonian Institution Libraries, designed this guide for beginners to be able to create online exhibitions based around a theme with narrative explanations, as opposed to just online digital collections. The information on creating the idea, writing a proposal, staffing, technology, and design is applicable to basic website development. He cites several samples of online exhibitions and other informational websites.

912 Kollen, Christine, Wangyal Shawa, and Mary L. Larsgaard. *Cartographic Citations: A Style Guide.* 2nd ed. Chicago: American Library Association, 2010. ISBN: 978-0-83898-556-4.

The authors review and update every entry from the 1992 edition. They also expand the electronic spatial data section and include numerous new entries for real-time online maps, interactive online maps, and GIS data. Cartographic items covered include stand-alone maps, maps printed in periodicals and books, cross sections, facsimiles, relief models, globes, and aerial photographs.

913 Lavender, Kenneth, and Scott Stockton. *Book Repair: A How-to-Do-It Manual.* 2nd ed. How-To-Do-It Manuals for Libraries 178. New York: Neal-Schuman, 2011. ISBN: 978-1-55570-747-7.

Libraries must make the most of limited resources in times of shrinking budgets and rising acquisition prices. Commonplace repairs such as cleaning, mending, hinge and spine repairs, and strengthening paperbacks are part of the daily routine. The book provides illustrated steps on all aspects of basic book repair and conservation. Wet and water-damaged books, mold- and mildew-infected volumes, and torn book linings and spines are just a few of the topics covered in new illustrated sections, along with affordable repair tools, acid-free paper, and other book repair supplies.

914   Leckie, Gloria J., Lisa M. Given, and John E. Buschman, eds. *Critical Theory for Library and Information Science: Exploring the Social from across the Disciplines.* Library and Information Science Text Series. Westport, CT: Libraries Unlimited, 2010. ISBN: 978-1-59158-938-9 (print), 978-1-59158-940-2 (e-book).

Rather than attempt to define what critical theory is, which admittedly is a tough nut to crack for anyone who is not a philosopher, it might be more productive to describe what it does. In the words of the introduction, "Critical theory expands the boundaries of what we know and how we think, and thus opens up new possibilities and avenues for LIS research" (p. xii). Fair enough. Things get dicey when scanning the table of contents, however. Typical chapter headings read "Transformative Library Pedagogy and Community-Based Libraries: A Freirean Perspective" and "Chantal Mouffe's Theory of Agonistic Pluralism and Its Relevance for Library and Information Science Research." At its best, this is a work that examines the sociological and philosophical underpinnings of our profession; at its worst, it amounts to 300 some pages worth of LIS-themed psychobabble.

915   Lee, Marta K. *Mentoring in the Library: Building for the Future.* Chicago: American Library Association, 2011. ISBN: 978-0-83893-593-4.

Lee discusses mentoring and its impacts on the overall health of a library or library system. Topics include an introduction to mentoring, internships, library school assignments, potential librarians, developing a new librarian in the workplace, promotions, volunteers, electronic

mentoring, and other kinds of mentoring in the library field. The appendixes include a request for internship form, sample request for enrollment in a practicum, school of information studies proposal form, video viewing information for the AFR manual form, and promotion review timetable. A bibliography and index are included.

916   Lewis, Alison, ed. *Questioning Library Neutrality: Essays from Progressive Librarian.* Duluth, MN: Library Juice Press, 2008. ISBN: 978-0-97786-177-4.

This collection of academic essays is on the practicality of librarians being neutral in the distribution of information at a time when shrinking resources limit collection selection while access to electronic materials through the Internet is growing rapidly. The authors question whether making collection selection is a negation of neutrality by the very act of selecting. The final argument concludes that librarians have a moral responsibility to shape and define information access and that to remain neutral would contribute to society's downward spiral.

917   Lynch, Sherry, Shirley Amore, and Jerrie Bethel, eds. *The Librarian's Guide to Partnerships.* Handbook Series. Fort Atkinson, WI: Highsmith Press, 1999. ISBN: 978-1-57950-002-3.

Editor Lynch uses her Broward County (Florida) Library experience as the basis for exploring cooperative agreements with a variety of entities. She shows how joining forces with other libraries, art organizations, youth services, businesses, and special-needs communities can leverage benefits for both. Attention is also paid to the role technology can play in fostering such collaboration. Many of the examples are miniature case studies for library delivery of services by alternative models.

918   Maxwell, Nancy Kalikow. *Sacred Stacks: The Higher Purpose of Libraries and Librarianship.* Chicago: American Library Association, 2006. ISBN: 978-0-83890-917-1.

In this mixture of history, analysis, and anecdotal reflection, Maxwell compares libraries to churches and librarians to ministers in her premise of libraries as a sacred trust and communal gathering place.

919 Miller, Kathryn. *Public Libraries Going Green.* ALA Public Library Handbooks. Chicago: American Library Association, 2010. ISBN: 978-0-83891-018-4.

Miller provides basic information on how libraries can become environmental leaders through shared use and reuse of resources. Tips and topics include the library green role, the library as a green place, green services at the library, and the library as a green teacher. Lists of environmental fiction and nonfiction for different ages, other related resources, and index are included.

920 Miller, William, and Rita M. Pellen, eds. *Libraries within Their Institutions: Creative Collaborations.* Copublished simultaneously as *Resource Sharing an Information Networks* 17, nos. 1/2, 2004. New York: Haworth Information Press, 2004. ISBN: 978-0-78902-720-7.

This book provides firsthand accounts of partnerships between libraries, faculty members, city governments, information technology departments, and research institutes used to develop lifelong libraries users. The academic library's main focus is campus-wide service integration, digital thesis preservation, collection management, and external partnerships.

921 Ott, Bill. *The Back Page.* Foreword by Joyce Saricks. Chicago: American Library Association, 2009. ISBN: 978-0-83890-997-3.

Longtime columnist Ott compiles a collection of humorous anecdotes, stories, quizzes, and commentary on the various facets of the book business, taken from "The Back Page," which is literally the last page of *Booklist.* Topics cover books and authors, genre fiction, life at *Booklist,* life beyond books, and quizzes. The index includes authors, books, periodicals, and films mentioned in the book.

922 Pijers, Guus. *Information Overload: A System for Better Managing Everyday Data.* Microsoft Executive Leadership Series. Hoboken, NJ: John Wiley and Son, 2010. ISBN: 978-0-47062-574-3.

Pijers looks at information principles and information in practice. After a brief discussion of the history, meaning, characteristics, attributes, definition, and value of information, he moves the discussion to the overwhelming amount of information available, how the human brain absorbs information, and how information affects behavior before looking at the practicalities of information usage. Case studies, checklists, best practices, and tips explain how to use information management practices geared to avoid information overload at home, at work, or in social settings. References and index are included.

923 Shorley, Deborah, and Michael Jubb, eds. *Future of Scholarly Communication.* London: Facet, ISBN: 978-1-85604-817-0; Chicago: American Library Association, ISBN: 978-1-85604-817-0. 2013.

Contributors look at the changing roles of journal editors, publishers, and social media used for scholarly communication. Several essays are devoted to the role of research libraries and how evolving technologies, changes in the social science research process, the data deluge, government policies, and research funders affect trends and drive change. The book is split into three sections, on technological context, changing research behavior, and the roles and responsibilities of interested players.

924 Siess, Judith A., and Jonathan Lorig, eds. *Out Front with Stephen Abram: A Guide for Information Leaders.* Chicago: American Library Association, 2009. ISBN: 978-0-83890-932-4.

Siess and Lorig compile Stephen Abram's writings on the library profession: public, school, special, and corporate libraries; vendors; and technology. As vice president for innovation at SirsiDynix, a leading library automation firm, and past president of the Canadian Library Association, Abram has been recognized by many as a leading library visionary. The book is divided into four sections, on advocacy, technology, communities and generations, and the future. An extensive bibliography, recommended reading list, and index are included.

925 Squires, Tasha. *Library Partnerships: Making Connections between School and Public Libraries.* Foreword by Gail Bush. Medford, NJ: Information Today, 2009. ISBN: 978-1-57387-362-8.

The main topic is the communication and steps needed to create partnerships between public libraries and K–12 public schools. Throughout the book, sidebar conversations highlight opportunities for success or sticking points that could lead to failure. Joint programs such as author visits, contests, booktalks, blogs, story readings, and resource sharing (e.g., grant proposal, volunteers, interlibrary loans) could benefit both partners and increase public visibility. Squires examines seasonal activities, after-school programs, joint ventures, field trips, and funding sources in the context of partnerships, technology, and resource sharing. Step-by-step examples, tricks of the trade, communication techniques, and problem-solving skills are included in the articles and sidebars. An extensive index acts as a quick to-do program list.

926 Ziarnik, Natalie Reif. *School and Public Libraries: Developing the Natural Alliance.* Chicago: American Library Association, 2003. ISBN: 978-0-83890-841-9.

This brief introduction to promoting collaboration between school and public libraries is geared toward joint grant proposals, field trips, shared resources, and combined program activities. "A Day in the Life" chapter shows a typical day in the life of elementary school, public, and university librarians. Each sample program includes possible partners, age levels, descriptions, planning tips, expected outcomes, and suggested resources.

ADDITIONAL RESOURCES

927 Banks, Paul N., and Roberta Pilette. *Preservation: Issues and Planning.* Chicago: American Library Association, 2000. ISBN: 978-0-83890-776-4.

928 Bastian, Jeannette A., and Ben Alexander, eds. *Community Archives: The Shaping of Memory.* Principles and Practice in Records Management and Archives. New York: Neal-Schuman, 2010. ISBN: 978-1-85604-639-8.

929 Bleiweis, Maxine. *Helping Business: The Library's Role in Community Economic Development: A How-to-Do-It Manual.* How-To-Do-It Manuals for Libraries 73. New York: Neal-Schuman, 1997. ISBN: 978-1-5557-0231-1.

930 Cleveland, Donald B. *Cartooning for the Librarian: A How-to-Do-It Manual.* How-to-Do-It Manuals for School and Public Librarians 8. New York: Neal-Schuman, 1992. ISBN: 978-1-55570-102-4.

931 Crockett, Margaret, and Janet Foster. *The No-Nonsense Guide to Archives and Recordkeeping.* London: Facet, ISBN: 978-1-85604-855-2; Chicago: American Library Association, ISBN: 978-1-85604-817-0. 2013.

932 Czarnecki, Kelly Nicole. *Gaming in Libraries.* Tech Set Series. New York: Neal-Schuman, ISBN: 978-1-55570-709-5; Chicago: American Library Association, ISBN: 978-1-55570-709-5. 2010.

933 Dearstyne, Bruce W., ed. *Leading and Managing Archives and Records Programmes: Strategies for Success.* London: Facet, ISBN: 978-1-85604-654-1; Chicago: American Library Association, ISBN: 978-1-55570-615-9. 2008.

934 Desouza, Kevin C., and Scott Paquette. *Knowledge Management: An Introduction.* London: Facet, ISBN: 978-1-85604-735-7; Chicago: American Library Association, ISBN: 978-1-55570-720-0. 2011.

935 **East, Kathy.** *Inviting Children's Authors and Illustrators: A How-to-Do-It Manual for School and Public Librarians.* How-To-Do-It Manuals for Libraries 49. New York: Neal-Schuman, 1995. ISBN: 978-1-5557-0182-6.

936 **Elmborg, James K., and Sheril Hook, eds.** *Centers for Learning: Writing Centers and Libraries in Collaboration.* ACRL Publications in Librarianship. Chicago: American Library Association, 2005. ISBN: 978-0-83898-335-5.

937 **Forde, Helen and Jonathan Rhys-Lewis.** *Preserving Archives.* 2nd. ed. London: Facet, ISBN: 978-1-85604-823-1; Chicago: American Library Association, ISBN: 978-1-85604-823-1. 2013.

938 **Foster, Allen, and Pauline Rafferty, eds.** *Innovations in Information Retrieval: Perspectives for Theory and Practice.* London: Facet, ISBN: 978-1-85604-697-8; Chicago: American Library Association, ISBN: 978-1-85604-697-8. 2011.

939 **Franks, P.** *Records and Information Management.* London: Facet, ISBN: 978-1-85604-836-1; Chicago: American Library Association, ISBN: 978-1-55570-910-5. 2013.

940 **Gilchrist, Alan, and Barry Mahon, eds.** *Information Architecture: Designing Information Environments for Purpose.* London: Facet, ISBN: 978-1-85604-487-5; Chicago: American Library Association, ISBN: 978-1-55570-493-3. 2003.

941 **Goodrich, Jeanne, and Paula M. Singer.** *Human Resources for Results: The Right Person for the Right Job.* Chicago: American Library Association, 2007. ISBN: 978-0-83893-570-5.

942 **Gorman, G. E., and Sydney J. Shep, eds.** *Preservation Management for Libraries, Museums and Archives.* London: Facet, ISBN: 978-1-85604-574-2; Chicago: American Library Association, ISBN: 978-1-85604-574-2. 2006.

943 **Grindley, Neil, and William Kilbride, eds.** *The Good Digital Preservation Guide.* London: Facet, ISBN: 978-1-85604-753-1; Chicago: American Library Association, ISBN: 978-1-85604-753-1. 2015.

944 **Gunnels, Claire B., Susan E. Green, and Patricia M. Butler.** *Joint Libraries: Models That Work.* Chicago: American Library Association, 2012. ISBN: 978-0-83891-138-9.

945 **Hernon, Peter, and John R. Whitman.** *Delivering Satisfaction and Service Quality: A Customer-Based Approach for Libraries.* Chicago: American Library Association, 2001. ISBN: 978-0-83890-789-4.

946 **Higginbotham, Barbra B., and Judith W. Wild.** *The Preservation Program Blueprint.* Frontiers of Access to Library Materials 6. Chicago: American Library Association, 2001. ISBN: 978-0-83890-802-0.

947 **Hill, Jennie, ed.** *The Future of Archives and Recordkeeping: A Reader.* London: Facet, 2010. ISBN: 978-1-85604-666-4.

948 **Himmel, Ethel E., and William J. Wilson, comps.** *The Functions and Roles of State Library Agencies.* Edited by GraceAnne A. DeCandido. Chicago: American Library Association, 2000. ISBN: 978-0-83898-105-4.

949 **Hughes-Hassell, Sandra, and Anne Wheelock, eds.** *The Information-Powered School.* Chicago: American Library Association, 2001. ISBN: 978-0-83893-514-9.

950 **Hull, Barbara.** *Understanding Librarians: Communication Is the Issue.* New York: Neal-Schuman, 2011. ISBN: 978-1-84334-615-9.

951 **Kahn, Miriam B.** *The Library Security and Safety Guide to Prevention, Planning, and Response.* Chicago: American Library Association, 2008. ISBN: 978-0-83890-949-2.

952 **Kuharets, Olga R. ed.** *Venture into Cultures: A Resource Book of Multicultural Materials and Programs.* 2nd. ed. Chicago: American Library Association, 2001. ISBN: 978-0-83893-513-2.

953 **Larson, Jeanette, and Association for Library Service to Children.** *El Día de los Niños/ El Día de los Libros: Building a Culture of Literacy in Your Community through Día.* Celebrating

Culture in Your Library. Chicago: American Library Association, 2011. ISBN: 978-0-83893-599-6.

954   Law, Merry, ed. *Guide to International Subscription Agencies and Book Distributors.* Amsterdam: Worldvu, 2003. ISBN: 978-0-97169-491-0.

955   Levine, Jenny. *Gaming and Libraries: Learning Lessons from the Intersections.* Library Technology Reports. Chicago: American Library Association, 2009. ISBN: 978-0-83895-803-2.

956   *Library Use of Video and Audio.* New York: Primary Research Group, 2012. ISBN: 978-1-57440-181-3.

957   Macevičiūtė, Elena, and T. D. Wilson, eds. *Introducing Information Management: An Information Research Reader.* London: Facet, 2005. ISBN: 978-1-85604-561-2.

958   Mason, Florence M., and Chris Dobson. *Information Brokering: A How-to-Do-It Manual.* How-To-Do-It Manuals for Libraries 86. New York: Neal-Schuman, 1998. ISBN: 978-1-55570-342-4.

959   Mayer, Brian, and Christopher Harris. *Libraries Got Game: Aligned Learning through Modern Board Games.* Chicago: American Library Association, 2010. ISBN: 978-0-83891-009-2.

960   Melling, Maxine, and Margaret Weaver, eds. *Collaboration in Libraries and Learning Environments.* London: Facet, ISBN: 978-1-85604-858-3; Chicago: American Library Association, ISBN: 978-1-85604-858-3. 2012.

961   Millar, Laura A. *Archives: Principles and Practices.* New York: Neal-Schuman, 2011. ISBN: 978-1-55570-726-2.

962   Neiburger, Eli. *Gamers—in the Library?! The Why, What, and How of Videogame Tournaments for All Ages.* Chicago: American Library Association, 2007. ISBN: 978-0-83890-944-7.

963   O'Connor, Brian C., Jodi Kerans, and Richard L. Anderson. *Doing Things with Information: Beyond Indexing and Abstracting.*

Westport, CT: Libraries Unlimited, 2008. ISBN: 978-1-59158-577-0.

964   Ray, Louise, ed. *Management Skills for Archivists and Records Managers.* London: Facet, ISBN: 978-1-85604-584-1; Chicago: American Library Association, ISBN: 978-1-85604-584-1. 2014.

965   Ross, Catherine Sheldrick, and Patricia Dewdney. *Communicating Professionally: A How-to-Do-It Manual for Library Applications.* 2nd ed. How-To-Do-It Manuals for Libraries 58. New York: Neal-Schuman, 1998. ISBN: 978-1-55570-340-2.

966   Rubin, Rhea Joyce. *Defusing the Angry Patron: A How-to-Do-It Manual for Librarians.* 2nd ed. How-To-Do-It Manuals for Libraries 177. New York: Neal-Schuman, 2011. ISBN: 978-1-55570-731-6.

967   Wallace, Danny P. *Knowledge Management: Historical and Cross-Disciplinary Themes.* Libraries Unlimited Knowledge Management Series. Westport, CT: Libraries Unlimited, 2007. ISBN: 978-1-59158-502-2.

968   Weiss, Luise, Elizabeth Malafi, and Sophia Serlis-McPhillips. *Small Business and the Public Library: Strategies for a Successful Partnership.* Chicago: American Library Association, 2011. ISBN: 978-0-83890-993-5.

969   Whatley, Patricia, and Caroline Brown, eds. *Archives and Recordkeeping: Theory into Practice.* London: Facet, 2013. ISBN: 978-1-85604-825-5.

970   Willis, Mark R. *Dealing with Difficult People in the Library.* 2nd ed. Chicago: American Library Association, 2011. ISBN: 978-0-83890-760-3.

971   Woodward, Hazel, and Lorraine Estelle, eds. *Digital Information: Order or Anarchy.* London: Facet, ISBN: 978-1-85604-680-0; Chicago: American Library Association, ISBN: 978-1-85604-680-0. 2009.

📖 PERIODICALS

972 *Book History.* University Park: Pennsylvania State University Press. Frequency: Annual. ISSN: 1098-7371 (print), 1529-1499 (online). URL: www.psupress.org/books/titles/0-271-02151-9.html.

Book History is the official publication of the Society for the History of Authorship, Reading and Publishing. Topics include research on the social, economic, and cultural history of authorship; editing; publishing; printing; the book arts; the book trade; periodicals; newspapers; ephemera; copyright; censorship; literary agents; and libraries.

973 *The Information Society.* Philadelphia: Routledge. Frequency: Five issues per year. ISSN: 0197-2243 (print), 1087-6537 (online). URL: www.tandf.co.uk/journals/UTIS/.

This multidisciplinary journal reviews international data flow, regulatory issues, information industries, and public and private organizational performance information. Topics include virtual communities, digital libraries, e-commerce, information infrastructure, and "electronic democracy." All research articles undergo editorial screening and peer review.

974 *Library and Archival Security.* Philadelphia: Routledge. Frequency: Two issues per year. ISSN: 0196-0075 (print), 1540-9511 (online). URL: www.tandf.co.uk/journals/WLAS/.

These articles provide information on all aspects of security in libraries, archives, and other information centers, including physical security, data and communications security, disaster preparedness and recovery, and studies of related social/legal/ethical issues. Topics may include patron privacy, theft detection and prevention, inventory methods, security systems and equipment, safety in libraries, legal and societal issues, digital collections, the Internet, electronic records, networks, and communications security. All research articles undergo rigorous peer review, based on initial editor screening and refereeing by at least two anonymous referees.

975 *Logos.* New York: John Wiley and Sons. Frequency: Four times per year. ISSN: 0957-9656 (print), 1878-4712 (online). URL: www.brill.nl/logos/.

Logos serves as a forum for communication between professionals in the book publishing and bookselling industries, librarians, authors, and those in allied professions. Representative topics cover history, personal experiences, critical analysis, and futuristic trends. This journal would interest those who write, edit, manufacture, publish, disseminate, preserve, or read books, journals, and electronic media.

976 *RBM: A Journal of Rare Books, Manuscripts, and Cultural Heritage.* Chicago: Association of College and Research Libraries, American Library Association. Frequency: Two issues per year. ISSN: 1529-6407. URL: http://rbm.acrl.org/site/misc/about.xhtml.

RBM covers issues pertaining to special collections libraries and cultural heritage institutions. Topics include fundraising, emerging technologies, strategic partnerships, special collections, cultural heritage, exhibition preparation, historical articles, legal and ethical issues, and trends.

🔗 ADDITIONAL RESOURCES

977 *American Archivist. Chicago: Society of American Archivist.* Frequency: Semiannual. ISSN: 0360-9081. URL: www2.archivists.org/american-archivist/.

978 *Archifacts.* Wellington, New Zealand: Archives and Records Association of New Zealand. Frequency: Twice per year. ISSN: 0303-7940. URL: www.aranz.org.nz/Site/publications/archifacts/default.aspx.

979 *Archival Science.* Dordrecht, the Netherlands: Kluwer Academic. ISSN: 1389-0166.

Frequency: Four times per year. URL: www
.springer.com/computer/

980 *Achivaria.* Ottawa: Association of Canadian
Archivists. Frequency: Twice annually. ISSN: 0318-
6954. URL: http://journals.sfu.ca/archivar/index
.php/archivaria.

981 Archives and Manuscripts. Brisbane:
Library Association of Australia, Australian
Society of Archivists. Frequency: Twice annually.
ISSN: 0157-6895. URL: http://69.73.133.147/
asa-journal-archives-and-manuscripts/.

982 *Indexer.* London: Society of Indexers.
Frequency: Four times per year. ISSN: 0019-4131
(print), 1756-0632 (online). URL: www.theindexer
.org.

983 *Journal of Archival Organization (JAO).*
London: Taylor and Francis Group. Frequency:
Four issues per year. ISSN: 1533-2748 (print),
1533-2576 (online). URL: www.tandf.co.uk/
journals/WJAO/.

984 *Journal of the Society of Archivists.*
London: Taylor and Francis Group. Frequency:
Twice per year. ISSN: 0037-9816 (Print), 1465-
3907 (online). URL: www.tandf.co.uk/journals/
CJSA/.

985 *Sidelights: The Newsletter of the Society.*
London: Society of Indexers. Frequency:
Quarterly. ISSN: 1363-9854. URL: www.indexers
.org.uk/index.php?id=228.

❧ WEBSITES

986 Feinberg, Sandra, and Diantha D. Schull.
*Family Place Libraries: Transforming Public
Libraries to Serve Very Young Children and
Their Families.* www.familyplacelibraries.org/
documents/FamilyPlaceLibraries-Transforming
PublicLibrariestoServeVeryYoungChildrenand
Their Families.pdg.

This article is on the transition to a family-
centered library that offers specially designed

workshops, space, collections, and resource
access to serve very young children, parents, and
caregivers. Specially trained staffs emphasize literacy and are actively involved with educators,
social workers, and health and human services
professionals to build strong coalitions. A sidebar describes funding available from the Rauch
Foundation for the early development of Family
Place programs.

987 Gasaway, Lolly N. *When Work Passes into
the Public Domain.* 2003. www.unc.edu/-unclng/
public-d.htm.

Gasaway provides a quick reference chart to
guide librarians in deciding if a work completed
in the United States is in the public domain. The
chart includes "Date of Work," "Protected From,"
and "Term" columns.

988 Sonnenberg, Nina. *Family Place Libraries:
From One Long Island Library to the Nation.*
www.familyplacelibraries.org/documents/
Portrait_FamilyPlace.pdf.

At 6,000 square feet, the Middle County Public
Library in Centereach, New York, was remod-
eled to become an early childhood mecca that
includes a twelve-foot book barge, Lego table,
puppet theater, and stuffed lion pit. This article describes the transition to a family-centered
library that offers parent/child workshops, a specially designed area for young children, multimedia collections, resource access that emphasizes
literacy, and outreach to new and underserved
populations.

PATRON SERVICES

BOOKS

CHILDREN

989 Bird, Elizabeth. *Children's Literature Gems: Choosing and Using Them in Your Library Career.* Chicago: American Library Association, 2009. ISBN: 978-0-83890-995-9.

This slim volume provides a brief overview of children's literature and an annotated list of "100 Children's Books That Belong in Every Library." Other lists cover baby books, overlooked picture books and novels, read-aloud picture books, and middle-grade titles that bear a look by first-year librarians and library school students. Best known for her children's library blog, "Fuse #8" on the *School Library Journal* website, Bird here provides concise advice on standards and quality in literature, finding collection materials, how to make the most of the collection materials, and presenting children's programs. The chapter "Your Own Time" presents an interesting outlook on what being a children's librarian can mean outside of work and what activities contribute to one's professional development.

990 Diamant-Cohen, Betsy. *Crash Course in Library Services to Preschool Children.* Crash Course Series. Westport, CT: Libraries Unlimited, 2010. ISBN: 978-1-59884-688-1.

This book covers programming, collection management, policies and procedures, child development, caregivers, atmosphere, community partnerships, events, computer use, and other aspects of library services for preschoolers. Along with practical tips scattered throughout the book, the author includes a reading list of professional materials and a short list of suggested picture books for storytelling.

991 Diamant-Cohen, Betsy, ed. *Children's Services: Partnerships for Success.* Chicago: American Library Association, 2010. ISBN: 978-0-83891-044-3.

Articles describe children's programming connections between libraries and other community organizations that are used to secure funding and remain relevant to the community. The contributors show how partnerships with law enforcement, academic institutions, museums, cultural institutions, businesses, and community organizations can be created with little to no expense. Success stories, how-to-do-it steps, and sample forms provide several ideas about how to create joint ventures. Background information about each author is at the conclusion of each article.

992   Ernst, Linda L. *Lapsit Services for the Very Young II: A How-to-Do-It Manual.* How-To-Do-It Manuals for Libraries 106. New York: Neal-Schuman, 2000. ISBN: 978-1-55570-391-2.

Part 1 focuses on early childhood development, basic biology, child development, and library service areas (e.g., in-house, outreach, resources). Part 2 provides program building blocks with more than 125 annotated entries concerning books used in programs and services aimed at children ages 12–24 months. The book is illustrated with nursery rhymes, fingerplays, and songs. The appendixes provide bibliographies, acronyms, and agencies along with sample handouts.

993   Fasick, Adele M. *From Boardbook to Facebook: Children's Services in an Interactive Age.* Santa Barbara, CA: Libraries Unlimited, 2011. ISBN: 978-1-59884-468-9 (print), 978-1-59884-469-6 (e-book).

Fasick looks at how to apply new technologies to children's collections, programming, and services. Section 1 covers changes in children's lives by age category: birth to 4, 5–9, and 9–18. Section 2 addresses such topics as illiteracy, visual and media literacy, and developing reliable sources and information on providing children's library services. The third section describes changing library departments to blend physical and electronic media. The final section explores ways to manage children's services, market programs, and maintain professional contacts while making change happen as needed. References, further readings, and index are included.

994   Fasick, Adele M., and Leslie E. Holt. *Managing Children's Services in the Public Library.* 3rd ed. Westport, CT: Libraries Unlimited, 2008. ISBN: 978-1-59158-412-4.

In this update to reflect changes in children's services, library services, and communities, the authors consider changes in demographics, economics, social patterns, and technology. Each updated chapter has new information, examples, and ideas that provide policy guidance, reflect practical advice, and suggest additional readings. Topics include planning children's services in the context of a community, recruiting and retaining staff, communicating with colleagues, annual reports, budgeting, security, collection development, electronic resources, intellectual freedom, outreach, and professional development.

995   Peck, Penny. *Crash Course in Children's Services.* Crash Course Series. Westport, CT: Libraries Unlimited, 2006. ISBN: 978-1-59158-352-3.

This concise guide to children's services is directed at librarians just starting their professional careers. Seven major areas covered are reference, homework help, reader's advisory, book selection, storytime, programming, and issues in children's library services. Ongoing issues include latchkey kids, behavior, Internet access, and computer usage. Numerous illustrations, tables, and figures accompany this quick and easy-to-read text.

996   Steele, Anitra T., and Association for Library Service to Children. *Bare Bones Children's Services: Tips for Public Library Generalists.* Chicago: American Library Association, 2001. ISBN: 978-0-83890-791-7.

Steele acknowledges that many libraries do not have formally trained children's librarians to oversee juvenile collections and services. This guide describes the basic differences between serving adults and children. Chapters have practical tips on storytimes, collection development, booktalks, displays, tours, outreach, and bibliographic instruction. There is one chapter devoted to issues and challenges. Appendixes include "Competencies for Librarians Serving Children in Public Libraries," "Statement of Commitment to Excellence in Library Service," and bibliographies of children's books and professional publications.

997 Sullivan, Michael. *Connecting Boys with Books: What Libraries Can Do.* Chicago: American Library Association, 2003. ISBN: 978-0-83890-849-5.

Focusing on boys between the ages of 8 and 12 years old, Sullivan examines the way boys are introduced to the library, male role models at the library, and cultural expectations relevant to boys reading books. Some suggestions offered are providing chess sets, other board games, and storytelling classes that fit with boys' learning styles and mental capabilities. The author addresses the gap between boys and girls in reading, writing, and library use and provides lists of books and authors by genre that will appeal to boys.

998 Sullivan, Michael. *Connecting Boys with Books 2: Closing the Reading Gap.* Chicago: American Library Association, 2009. ISBN: 978-0-83890-979-9.

Building on his initial volume regarding this topic (see previous entry), Sullivan addresses the gap between boys' and girls' use of library services and materials. He discusses the necessity of providing boy-friendly formats, boy's literature, and programming for boys. He recognizes that much progress has been made in the years since the original title was published but believes much remains to be done. He introduces a concept he calls "Literary Lunch," in which male role models read aloud to boys during their lunch period, along with several other programming ideas designed to increase boys' interest in reading.

999 Sullivan, Michael. *Fundamentals of Children's Services.* ALA Fundamentals Series. Chicago: American Library Association, 2005. ISBN: 978-0-83890-907-2.

This general overview textbook is suited to new librarians and students studying the library profession. The basics for children's service in the context of the library's mission, collections, services, programming, management, administration, and leadership are covered. Inserts scattered throughout include roles, principles, and issues faced by the novice librarian. The appendixes address competencies for librarians serving children, a library bill of rights, and the ALA Code of Ethics.

1000 Walter, Virginia A. *Children and Libraries: Getting It Right.* Chicago: American Library Association, 2001. ISBN: 978-0-83890-795-5.

The author reviews traditional public library services provided to children but also discusses current services, changing clientele, emerging trends, and future library access. Walter's "10 Steps to Getting It Right" and "Five Laws of Librarianship" acknowledge the challenges of dealing with a juvenile audience. This is a thought-provoking philosophical discussion of providing services in the twenty-first century. A lengthy list of references is included in the appendix.

DISABLED/HANDICAPPED

1001 Alter, Rachel, Linda Walling, Lynn Akin, Susan Beck, and Kathleen Garland. *Guidelines for Library Services for People with Mental Illnesses.* Chicago: American Library Association, Association of Specialized and Cooperative Library Agencies, 2007. ISBN: 978-0-8389-8410-9.

This 40-page book describes library service needs for the mentally disabled. One chapter provides guidelines for everyday responses to access, interactions, and settings for people with mental illnesses. A short history of mental health treatment systems, features of a disability, glossary, and references are included.

1002   Green, Ravonne A., and Vera Blair. *Keep It Simple: A Guide to Assistive Technologies.* Westport, CT: Libraries Unlimited, 2011. ISBN: 978-1-59158-866-5 (print), 978-1-59158-867-2 (e-book).

The authors focus on Microsoft Office applications and other low-cost technologies to incorporate common assistive aids into the library's infrastructure. Section 1 provides background information for assistive technology in a library. Section 2 describes types of equipment needed to provide services to patrons with print, mobility, hearing, and speech disabilities. The third section looks at providing accessible buildings and learning spaces. The remaining two sections cover staff training and how to market library services to individuals with disabilities.

1003   Mates, Barbara T. *Assistive Technologies in the Library.* Contributions by William R. Reed IV. Chicago: American Library Association, 2011. ISBN: 978-0-83891-070-2.

This practical guidebook shows librarians how to come to informed decisions about making services and collections accessible to people with various disabilities. Mates examines technology, equipment, and collection management from a user's perspective. Lists of vendors, disability resources, and possible funding sources are helpfully included. Illustrations and equipment details enable libraries to evaluate their assistive technology needs.

1004   *Revised Standards and Guideline of Service for the Library of Congress Network of Libraries for the Blind and Physically Handicapped.* Rev. ed. Chicago: American Library Association, Association of Specialized and Cooperative Library Agencies, 2005. ISBN: 978-0-83898-328-7.

History, standards, and structures are used to review and analyze the Library of Congress network of libraries to determine when to improve and where standards are being met or exceeded for the blind and handicapped areas. The book provides standards, guidelines, criteria, agreements, policies, a glossary, and the Pratt-Smoot Act and major amendments.

1005   Roberts, Ann, and Richard J. Smith. *Crash Course in Library Services to People with Disabilities.* Crash Course Series. Westport, CT: Libraries Unlimited, 2010. ISBN: 978-1-59158-767-5.

This crash course helps librarians quickly identify different types of mental and physical disabilities and remove obstacles to providing them with library services. Topics include library accessibility policies, leadership roles, assistive technology and total access, library services to help baby boomers and older adults, and library services to persons with mental and learning disabilities. A list of national library services, state and regional libraries that provide services to people with disabilities, three library policies for rules of conduct, references, and index complete the book.

1006   Rubin, Rhea Joyce. *Planning for Library Services to People with Disabilities.* ASCLA Changing Horizons Series 5. Chicago: American Library Association, 2001. ISBN: 978-0-83898-168-9.

This brief but well-written guide addresses how to gather information, identify issues, determine goals and objectives, determine resources, and compile a service delivery plan for serving people with disabilities. Appendixes include two bibliographies, directory of state offices on disabilities, Internet resources, statistics, terminology, and tip sheets.

GENERAL PATRONS

1007   Curtis, Donnelyn, ed. *Attracting, Educating, and Serving Remote Users through the Web: A How-to-Do-It Manual for Librarians.* How-To-Do-It Manuals for Libraries 114. New York: Neal-Schuman, 2002. ISBN: 978-1-55570-436-0.

This examination of online services describes the librarian's role in providing reference services, library instruction, document delivery, and licensed resources to remote users. A section on fund-raising and public relations in the electronic environment concludes the book. The author walks readers through identifying patron needs, attracting users, making electronic access user friendly, and providing electronic collections.

1008 Dilger-Hill, Jeannie, and Eric MacCreaigh, eds. *On the Road with Outreach: Mobile Library Services.* Westport, CT: Libraries Unlimited, 2009. ISBN: 978-1-59158-678-4.

This step-by-step guide is for librarians contemplating either starting or expanding outreach services. Contributors begin by discussing outreach management through self-evaluation, community needs identification, staffing, and mobile library collections. Next is an overview of service delivery, including staff qualifications, types of vehicles, technology, location, schedules, and marketing. Sections are devoted to services for children, seniors, the homebound, and incarcerated patrons. The section covering outreach vehicle design, specifications, maintenance, and communications includes detailed step-by-step design, sample maintenance checklists, glossary, and vendor contact lists. All sections include an introduction, service areas, sample forms, designs, conclusion, and references. Appendixes include 2008 Association of Bookmobile and Outreach Services Guidelines, sample bookmobile specifications, and bookmobile preconstruction questionnaire. Suggested readings and index are also provided.

1009 Evans, G. Edward, and Thomas L. Carter. *Introduction to Library Public Services.* 7th ed. Westport, CT: Libraries Unlimited, 2011. ISBN: 978-1-59158-596-1 (print), 978-1-59884-815-1 (e-book).

Evans and Carter completely revise and update this edition to reflect recent economic, industry, and technological developments. They cover all aspects of running a public library, including staffing, customer service, reference service, interlibrary loans, archives and special collections, programming, and security. Each chapter focuses on one topic and contains role, purpose,

points to ponder, forms, review questions, and suggested readings.

1010 Feinberg, Sandra, Kathleen Deerr, Barbara Jordan, Marcellina Byrne, and Lisa Kropp. *The Family-Centered Library Handbook.* New York: Neal-Schuman, 2007. ISBN: 978-1-55570-541-1.

Feinberg is the founder and a coordinator of the Family Place Libraries (FPL) initiative started in 1996 at the Middle Country Public Library in Centereach, New York. Serving as the project's training manual, this volume seeks to take children's services at the public library to the next level, that of a go-to place for early childhood literacy. After starting with a description of the program, the authors and FPL coordinators share how they used family-centered interaction to build community visibility by using library resources to support parents and caregivers. Chapter 14, "Culturally Diverse Families," and chapter 15, "Teen Parent Families," are just two specific user outreach examples that show the value of partnerships. Space considerations, programming, collections, and tips focus on the library as a central resource for early childhood literacy. A helpful tool to assess staff competencies is also included.

1011 Hill, Chrystie. *Inside, Outside, and Online: Building Your Library Community.* Chicago: American Library Association, 2009. ISBN: 978-0-83890-987-4.

This volume is a guide for librarians to build a vibrant community involved in library and family activities by providing networking, sharing, and connection across the community between patrons and staff. Activities to increase patronage and circulation include senior exercise classes, homework helpers, bilingual programs, chat rooms, job-hunting assistance, storytime, and wireless public access.

1012 Jerrard, Jane. *Crisis in Employment: A Librarian's Guide to Helping Job Seekers.* Foreword by Denise Davis. ALA Editions Special Reports. Chicago: American Library Association,

Office for Research and Statistics, 2009. ISBN: 978-0-83891-013-9.

Library computers and Internet connections are used by patrons to access job ads, prepare resumes, and file for unemployment benefits. Jerrard looks at resources and alternative methods for providing employment information. Mobile computer labs, volunteers, partnerships, training modules for information literacy, a key word resume list, and special events (job fairs, networking meetings, support groups) are some of the creative ways libraries respond to employment needs. A "Key Resources and Sample Documents" appendix provides additional job search materials.

1013   Matthews, Joseph R. *The Customer-Focused Library: Re-inventing the Public Library from the Outside-In.* Westport, CT: Libraries Unlimited, 2009. ISBN: 978-1-59158-875-7 (print), 978-1-59158-876-4 (e-book).

Matthews looks at traditional library thinking, constraints, library as a place, collections, services, information technology, staffing, and implementing change. Each chapter includes topic introduction, notes, and conclusion. The primary focus is looking at library services and facilities from the patron's perspective, rather than the usual constraints placed by location, budget, staffing, and traditional library services.

INCARCERATED

1014   Clark, Sheila, and Erica MacCreaigh. *Library Services to the Incarcerated: Applying the Public Library Model in Correctional Facility Libraries.* Westport, CT: Libraries Unlimited, 2006. ISBN: 978-1-59158-290-8.

This practical approach shows how the public library role can be applied in a correctional setting in terms of facilities, equipment, collection development, library services, and programming. The authors look closely at the librarian's role personally and professionally when dealing with offenders in an enclosed system. Numerous

examples and anecdotes highlight interactions between offenders and staff. A glossary of terms, core collection suggestions, job descriptions, performance measures, suggested readings, and index are included.

1015   Vogel, Brenda. *The Prison Library Primer: A Program for the Twenty-First Century.* Lanham, MD: Scarecrow Press, 2009. ISBN: 978-0-81085-403-1.

For all intents and purposes, this is a revised and expanded edition of the author's previous prison library guidebook, *Down for the Count: A Prison Library Handbook* (Scarecrow Press, 1995). Vogel begins with a brief history of outreach to prisoners before getting into specifics on services, space, equipment, collections, and patrons in a correctional environment. Chapters on digital and Internet access, contraband, networking, jailhouse lawyers, and boundary violations along with a list of frequently asked questions quickly highlight the differences between correctional and public settings. Recommended readings, online resources, and sources for additional information and advocacy are included. Appendixes cover information skills training curriculum, library assistance to state institutions, Colorado Department of Corrections offender reading material and library services regulations, and criteria for evaluating corrections libraries from the Illinois Department of Corrections. An index and author information are included.

SENIOR CITIZENS

1016   Honnold, RoseMary, and Saralyn A. Mesaros. *Serving Seniors: A How-to-Do-It Manual for Librarians.* How-To-Do-It Manuals for Libraries 127. New York: Neal-Schuman, 2004. ISBN: 978-1-55570-482-7.

In the first half of this book, the authors describe how to bring seniors into the library through collection development, discussion groups, programs, Internet lessons, partnerships, and volunteerism. The second half discusses ways to bring library services and materials to seniors who are homebound or in residential facilities. Appendixes include a questionnaire, contributors list, collegial wisdom, electronic resources, booklists, and ESL and international resources.

1017 Rothstein, Pauline, and Diantha Dow Schull, eds. *Boomers and Beyond: Reconsidering the Role of Libraries.* Chicago: American Library Association, 2010. ISBN: 978-0-83891-014-6

It's no secret that the overall population of the United States is getting older. As of this writing, the baby boomer generation—the proverbial "pig in a python"—is now reaching retirement age. With ever-improving health care and social services, men and women are living well into their eighties and nineties. According to the introduction, this new reality will "challenge librarians and others to explore the implications of extended adulthood on professional practice" (p. vii). As a response to that challenge, this book is designed to help librarians meet the needs of senior citizens (in some cases very senior). Part 1, "Older Adults: Essential Concepts and Recent Discoveries," gives the reader a news flash, so to speak, from the field of gerontology, which is the science of aging. Part 2, "Institutional Opportunities," deals with how the library profession might best respond to the unique requirements of older adults. In part 3, "Librarians' Perspectives," a trio of experienced information professionals give their personal takes on what's in store as they gaze into their crystal balls and share their visions. Ultimately, "as a resource for institutional and service planning, *Boomers and Beyond* will prompt readers to rethink the entire spectrum of services for older individuals" (p. viii).

SEXUAL ORIENTATION

1018 Greenblatt, Ellen, ed. *Serving LGBTIQ Library and Archives Users: Essays on Outreach, Service, Collections and Access.* Jefferson, NC: McFarland, 2011. ISBN: 978-0-78644-894-4.

Essays gathered from academic and practicing librarians are sorted into seven sections that cover new communities, context, archives, collection development, bibliographic access, censorship, and professionalism as related to lesbian, gay, bisexual, transgender, intersex, and other community users. Several personal accounts of individuals' experiences illustrate the importance of library services, barriers, and censorship faced by both users and providers. The selective glossary, notes, and references provide context and venues for the material presented.

1019 Martin, Hillias J., Jr., and James R. Murdock. *Serving Lesbian, Gay, Bisexual, Transgender, and Questioning Teens: A How-to-Do-It Manual for Librarians.* How-To-Do-It Manuals for Libraries 151. New York: Neal-Schuman, 2007. ISBN: 978-1-55570-566-4.

Identifying LGBTQ teens and creating awareness of their library service needs is examined in light of community sentiment and possible prejudice. According to the authors, libraries should establish ground rules for a safe place, match appropriate collection materials to the targeted population, and integrate LGBTQ themes into programs and services. The sections on materials and programs provide excellent examples to follow in order to incorporate these concepts into a library collection or service plan.

SPANISH SPEAKERS

1020 Alire, Camila, and Jacqueline Ayala. *Serving Latino Communities: A How-to-Do-It Manual for Librarians.* 2nd ed. How-To-Do-It Manuals for Libraries 158. New York: Neal-Schuman, 2007. ISBN: 978-1-55570-606-7.

This guide to providing library services to Latinos includes identifying demographics, community needs, programs, partnerships, marketing, workforce skills, and funding. Supporting documents include such items as national Latino holidays, sample marketing materials, forms, and Spanish words and phrases for library use. A resource directory, bibliography, and index round out the volume.

1021   Avila, Salvador. *Crash Course in Serving Spanish-Speakers.* Crash Course Series. Westport, CT: Libraries Unlimited, 2008. ISBN: 978-1-59158-713-2.

This is an entry-level introduction to providing library services to the Spanish-speaking population. The material focuses on how librarians should approach Spanish-speaking community patrons from a cultural point of view to provide relevant services. The translation of Library of Congress headings from English to Spanish provided in appendix D is a useful tool.

1022   Ayala, John L., and Salvador Guerena, eds. *Pathways to Progress: Issues and Advances in Latino Librarianship.* Latinos and Libraries Series. Westport, CT: Libraries Unlimited, 2011. ISBN: 978-1-59158-644-9.

Contributors to this anthology are Latino librarian practitioners from across the United States. Articles examine special collections; library leadership; public, academic, and special library services; and other issues as they pertain to Latino/Hispanic patrons in an English-speaking culture. This work emphasizes progress made on many fronts as well as challenges yet to be met.

1023   Baumann, Susana G. *¡Hola, Amigos! A Plan for Latino Outreach.* Latinos and Libraries Series. Santa Barbara, CA: Libraries Unlimited, 2011. ISBN: 978-1-59158-474-2.

As the introduction plainly states, "The purpose of this book is to present a plan template to help libraries come up with goals, strategies, and tactics to develop or improve outreach services to Latinos" (p. xxv). By now, we have all been made aware of the statistics showing that the Latino/Hispanic demographic segment is one of the fasting growing within the United States. Ten chapters provide step-by-step instructions on planning, promotion, understanding the cultural background of Latino patrons, and evaluating one's efforts. Numerous worksheets are time-savers for collecting data and making decisions. There is also a generous bibliography for further research.

STUDENTS

1024   Goodson, Carol F. *Providing Library Services for Distance Education Students: A How-to-Do-It Manual.* How-To-Do-It Manuals for Libraries 108. New York: Neal-Schuman, 2001. ISBN: 978-1-55570-409-4.

Goodson compiles ideas, examples, documents, forms, policies, handbooks, bibliographies, and web sources for planning delivery of services to academic library users regardless of location and program. Part 1 describes the links between distance education and library services. Part 2 covers the nuts and bolts of creating and implementing a strategic plan for supporting distance learners. Part 3 examines what other libraries, universities, and support programs have done. Part 4 addresses finding the best resources—whether they be from other institutions, case studies, research, or accreditation activities.

TEENS/YOUNG ADULTS

1025   Agosto, Denise E., and June Abbas, eds. *Teens, Libraries, and Social Networking: What Librarians Need to Know.* Libraries Unlimited Professional Guides for Young Adult Librarians Series. Westport, CT: Libraries Unlimited, 2011. ISBN: 978-1-59884-575-4 (print), 978-1-59884-576-1 (e-book).

Organized around ten major topics, such as social networking access, data security, and privacy issues, this book is designed for librarians to help young people use social networking tools to engage more effectively with library services. Facebook, MySpace, Ning, Twitter, and RSS are examined, along with fandom and virtual worlds. Case studies and examples highlight forums and best practices for using library web pages, blogs, video book reviews, online book clubs, and book-sharing networks to engage youth and expand youth services.

1026 Dresang, Eliza T., Melissa Gross, and Leslie Edmonds Holt. *Dynamic Youth Services through Outcome-Based Planning and Evaluation.* Chicago: American Library Association, 2006. ISBN: 978-0-83890-918-8.

This is a brief overview of Project CATE, an outcome-based planning and evaluation model used for providing library services and programs through four phases: gathering information, determining outcomes, developing programs and services, and conducting evaluations. The authors propose using patron-centered outcomes to improve communication between staff and patrons, plan programs, and maximize user benefits.

1027 Farrelly, Michael Garrett. *Make Room for Teens! Reflections on Developing Teen Spaces in Libraries.* Libraries Unlimited Professional Guides for Young Adult Librarian Series. Santa Barbara, CA: Libraries Unlimited, 2011. ISBN: 978-1-59158-566-4 (print), 978-1-59884-910-3 (e-book).

Farrelly describes the unique challenges faced in providing space and services to teens or young adults. He examines locations, budgets, furniture and decor, computers, collections, perceptions, technology, and stereotypes and provides tools, tips, and guidelines for dealing with a diverse population. Bibliographical references and index are included.

1028 Gorman, Michele, and Tricia Suellentrop. *Connecting Young Adults and Libraries: A How-to-Do-It Manual.* 4th ed. A How-To-Do-It Manuals for Libraries 167. New York: Neal-Schuman, 2009. ISBN: 978-1-55570-665-4.

This latest incarnation of a resource for young adult librarians covers trends in teen services and addresses customer service, information literacy, collection development, outreach, programming, social networking, and technology. Chapters are well organized with topic background, suggestions on how to improve services, useful ideas and tips, information sources, and works cited. Throughout the manual there are "links" in the margins that point to additional resources found in the accompanying CD. Sample policies, surveys, planning charts, calendars, and other basic forms are included on the CD.

1029 Higgins, Susan E. *Youth Services and Public Libraries.* Oxford: Chandos, 2007. ISBN: 978-1-84334-156-7.

These discussions of the principles of library service, practice, and professionalism include more history and management overview than hands-on practical information for meeting youth or young adult services expectations. Higgins emphasizes that respectful interchanges have greater positive effects on youths' and young adults' confidence than simply providing competent answers to questions.

1030 Miller, Donna P. *Crash Course in Teen Services.* Crash Course Series. Westport, CT: Libraries Unlimited, 2007. ISBN: 978-1-59158-565-7 (print), 978-0-313-09642-6 (e-book).

This crash course for librarians covers the world of teens today: reality check, teen collections, reader's advisory, programming, and creating a teen-friendly library. The book concludes with a look at professional resources, professional growth, and public relations and marketing. This book includes web resources, bibliography, and index.

1031 Tuccillo, Diane P. *Teen-Centered Library Service: Putting Youth Participation into Practice.* Libraries Unlimited Professional Guides for Young Adult Librarians Series. Santa Barbara, CA: Libraries Unlimited, 2009. ISBN: 978-1-59158-765-1.

Tuccillo focuses on how to get teens involved through collection development, teen advisory boards, volunteers, library aides, programming, community outreach, and partnerships. Success stories, forms, fliers, brochures, tips, and examples brighten up the book. A selected bibliography, appendix of organizations that foster youth participation, and index are included.

@ ADDITIONAL RESOURCES

1032 Anderson, Sheila B. *Extreme Teens: Library Services to Nontraditional Young Adults.* Libraries Unlimited Professional Guides for Young Adult Librarians Series. Westport, CT: Libraries Unlimited, 2005. ISBN: 978-1-59158-170-3.

1033 Anderson, Sheila B., ed. *Serving Young Teens and 'Tweens.* Libraries Unlimited Professional Guides for Young Adult Librarians Series. Westport, CT: Libraries Unlimited, 2006. ISBN: 978-1-59158-259-5.

1034 Avila, Salvador. *Serving Latino Teens.* Libraries Unlimited Professional Guides for Young Adult Librarians Series. Westport, CT: Libraries Unlimited, 2012. ISBN: 978-1-59884-609-6.

1035 Bailey, Donald Russell, and Barbara Gunter Tierney. *Transforming Library Service through Information Commons: Case Studies for the Digital Age.* Chicago: American Library Association, 2008. ISBN: 978-0-83890-958-4.

1036 Braun, Linda W., Hillias J. Martin, and Connie Urquhart. *Risky Business: Taking and Managing Risks in Library Services for Teens.* Chicago: American Library Association, 2010. ISBN: 978-0-83893-596-5.

1037 Brehm-Heeger, Paula. *Serving Urban Teens.* Libraries Unlimited Professional Guides for Young Adult Librarians Series. Westport, CT: Libraries Unlimited, 2008. ISBN: 978-1-59158-377-6.

1038 Briggs, Diane. *Preschool Favorites: 35 Storytimes Kids Love.* Illustrations by Thomas Briggs. Chicago: American Library Association, 2007. ISBN: 978-0-83890-938-6.

1039 Carman, L. Kay, and Carol S. Reich, eds. *Reaching Out to Religious Youth: A Guide to Services, Programs, and Collections.* Libraries Unlimited Professional Guides for Young Adult Librarians Series. Westport, CT: Libraries Unlimited, 2004. ISBN: 978-0-31332-041-5.

1040 Cerny, Rosanne, Penny Markey, and Amanda Williams. *Outstanding Library Service to Children: Putting the Core Competencies to Work.* Chicago: American Library Association, 2009. ISBN: 978-0-83890-922-5.

1041 Chelton, Mary K., ed. *Excellence in Library Services to Young Adults: The Nation's Top Programs.* 2nd ed. Chicago: American Library Association, Young Adult Library Services, 2000. ISBN: 978-0-83893-474-6.

1042 Christopher, Connie. *Empowering Your Library: A Guide to Improving Service, Productivity, and Participation.* Chicago: American Library Association, 2003. ISBN: 978-0-83890-858-7.

1043 Deines-Jones, Courtney, and Connie Van Fleet. *Preparing Staff to Serve Patrons with Disabilities: A How-to-Do-It Manual.* How-To-Do-It Manuals for Libraries 57. New York: Neal-Schuman, 1996. ISBN: 978-1-55570-234-2.

1044 Devine, Jane, and Francine Egger-Sider. *Going beyond Google Again.* London: Facet, ISBN: 978-1-85604-838-5; Chicago: American Library Association, ISBN: 978-1-55570-633-3. 2012.

1045 Durrance, Joan C. *Meeting Community Needs with Job and Career Services: A How-to-Do-It Manual for Librarians.* How-To-Do-It Manuals for Libraries 42. New York: Neal-Schuman, 1994. ISBN: 978-1-55570-177-2.

1046 Durrance, Joan C., Karen E. Fisher, and Marian B. Hinton. *How Libraries and Librarians Help: A Guide to Identifying User-Centered Outcomes.* Chicago: American Library Association, 2005. ISBN: 978-0-83890-892-1.

1047 Edwards, Margaret A. *The Fair Garden and the Swarm of Beasts: The Library and the Young Adult.* Foreword by Betty Carter. Chicago: American Library Association, 2002. ISBN: 978-0-83893-533-0.

1048 Farmer, Lesley S. J. *Digital Inclusion, Teens, and Your Library: Exploring the Issues and*

Acting on Them. Libraries Unlimited Professional Guides for Young Adult Librarians Series. Westport, CT: Libraries Unlimited, 2005. ISBN: 978-1-59158-128-4.

1049   Feinberg, Sandra, and Sari Feldman. *Serving Families of Children with Special Needs: A How-to-Do-It Manual.* How-To-Do-It Manuals for Libraries 65. New York: Neal-Schuman, 1996. ISBN: 978-1-55570-227-4.

1050   Feinberg, Sandra, Barbara Jordan, Kathleen Deerr, and Michelle Langa. *Including Families of Children with Special Needs: A How-to-Do-It Manual for Librarians.* How-To-Do-It Manuals for Libraries 88. New York: Neal-Schuman, 1999. ISBN: 978-1-55570-339-4.

1051   Flowers, Sarah. *Young Adults Deserve the Best: YALSA's Competencies in Action.* Chicago: American Library Association, 2011. ISBN: 978-0-83893-587-3.

1052   Holt, Leslie Edmonds, and Glen E. Holt. *Public Library Services for the Poor: Doing All We Can.* Chicago: American Library Association, 2010. ISBN: 978-0-83891-050-4.

1053   Jones, Patrick, and Linda L. Waddle. *New Directions for Library Service to Young Adults.* Chicago: American Library Association, 2002. ISBN: 978-0-83890-827-3.

1054   Jurewicz, Lynn, and Todd Cutler. *High Tech, High Touch: Library Customer Service through Technology.* Chicago: American Library Association, 2003. ISBN: 978-0-83890-860-0.

1055   Klor, Ellin, and Sarah Lapin. *Serving Teen Parents: From Literacy to Life Skills.* Foreword by Maryann Mori. Libraries Unlimited Professional Guides for Young Adult Librarians Series. Westport, CT: Libraries Unlimited, 2011. ISBN: 978-1-59884-693-5.

1056   Lerch, Maureen T., and Janet Welch. *Serving Homeschooled Teens and Their Parents.* Libraries Unlimited Professional Guides for Young Adult Librarians Series. Westport, CT: Libraries Unlimited, 2004. ISBN: 978-0-31332-052-1.

1057   Lupa, Robyn M., ed. *More Than MySpace: Teens, Librarians, and Social Networking.* Libraries Unlimited Professional Guides for Young Adult Librarians Series. Westport, CT: Libraries Unlimited, 2009. ISBN: 978-1-59158-760-6.

1058   Mates, Barbara T. *5-Star Programming and Services for Your 55+ Library Customers.* Chicago: American Library Association, 2003. ISBN: 978-0-83890-843-3.

1059   Mediavilla, Cindy. *Creating the Full-Service Homework Center in Your Library.* Chicago: American Library Association, 2001. ISBN: 978-0-83890-800-6.

1060   Melling, Maxine, and Joyce Little, eds. *Building a Successful Customer-Service Culture.* London: Facet, ISBN: 978-1-85604-449-3; Chicago: American Library Association, ISBN: 978-1-85604-449-3. 2002.

1061   Mikkelson, Sheila, ed. *Serving Older Teens.* Libraries Unlimited Professional Guides for Young Adult Librarians Series. Westport, CT: Libraries Unlimited, 2004. ISBN: 978-0-31331-762-0.

1062   O'Dell, Katie. *Library Materials and Services for Teen Girls.* Libraries Unlimited Professional Guides for Young Adult Librarians Series. Westport, CT: Libraries Unlimited, 2002. ISBN: 978-0-31331-554-1.

1063   Olson, Christi A., and Paula M. Singer. *Winning with Library Leadership: Enhancing Services through Connection, Contribution, and Collaboration.* Chicago: American Library Association, 2004. ISBN: 978-0-83890-885-3.

1064   Pantry, Sheila, and Peter Griffiths. *How to Give Your Users the LIS Services They Want.* London: Facet, ISBN: 978-1-85604-672-5; Chicago: American Library Association, ISBN: 978-1-85604-672-5. 2009.

1065   Pierce, Jennifer Burek. *Sex, Brains, and Video Games: A Librarian's Guide to Teens in the Twenty-First Century.* Chicago: American Library Association, 2008. ISBN: 978-0-83890-951-5.

1066   Rankin, Carolynn, and Avril Brock. *Delivering the Best Start: A Guide to Early Years Libraries.* London: Facet, ISBN: 978-1-85604-610-7; Chicago: American Library Association, ISBN: 978-1-85604-610-7. 2008.

1067   Rankin, Carolynn, and Avril Brock, eds. *Library Services for Children and Young Adults.* London: Facet, ISBN: 978-1-85604-712-8; Chicago: American Library Association, ISBN: 978-1-85604-712-8. 2012.

1068   Smith, Kitty. *Serving the Difficult Customer: A How-to-Do-It Manual for Library Staff.* How-To-Do-It Manuals for Libraries 39. New York: Neal-Schuman, 1994. ISBN: 978-1-55570-161-1.

1069   Trotta, Marcia. *Managing Library Outreach Programs: A How-to-Do-It Manual for Librarians.* How-To-Do-It Manuals for Libraries 33. New York: Neal-Schuman, 1993. ISBN: 978-1-55570-121-5.

1070   Vaillancourt, Renée J. *Bare Bones Young Adult Services: Tips for Public Library Generalists.* Chicago: American Library Association, Young Adult and Library Services Association, 2000. ISBN: 978-0-83893-497-5.

1071   Walling, Linda L. *Library Services to the Sandwich Generation and Serial Caregivers.* Chicago: American Library Association, 2001. ISBN: 978-0-83898-139-9.

1072   Walter, Virginia A. *Twenty-First-Century Kids, Twenty-First-Century Librarians.* Chicago: American Library Association, 2010. ISBN: 978-0-83891-007-8.

1073   Walter, Virginia A., and Elaine E. Meyers. *Teens and Libraries: Getting It Right.* Chicago: American Library Association, 2003. ISBN: 978-0-83890-857-0.

1074   Walters, Suzanne. *Customer Service: A How-to-Do-It Manual for Librarians.* How-To-Do-It Manuals for Libraries 41. New York: Neal-Schuman, 1994. ISBN: 978-1-55570-137-6.

1075   Webb, Jo, Pat Gannon-Leary, and Moira Bent. *Providing Effective Library Services for Research.* London: Facet, ISBN: 978-1-85604-589-6; Chicago: American Library Association, ISBN: 978-1-85604-589-6. 2007.

1076   Webster, Kelly, ed. *Library Services to Indigenous Populations: Viewpoints and Resources.* Contributions by Bonnie Biggs and David Ongley. Chicago: American Library Association, 2005. ISBN: 978-0-83898-316-4.

1077   Welch, Rollie James. *The Guy-Friendly YA Library: Serving Male Teens.* Libraries Unlimited Professional Guides for Young Adult Librarians Series. Westport, CT: Libraries Unlimited, 2007. ISBN: 978-1-59158-270-0.

1078   Wright, Keith C., and Judith F. Davie. *Serving the Disabled: A How-to-Do-It Manual for Librarians.* How-To-Do-It Manuals for Libraries 13. New York: Neal-Schuman, 1991. ISBN: 978-1-55570-085-0.

☁ WEBSITES

1079   Becker, Samantha, Michael D. Crandall, Karen E. Fisher, Rebecca Blakewood, Bo Kinney, and Cadi Russell-Sauve. *Opportunity for All: How Library Policies and Practices Impact Public Internet Access.* IMLS-2011-RES-01. Washington, DC: Institute of Museum and Library Services, 2011. URL: www.imls.gov/assets/1/AssetManager/OppForAll2.pdf.

This study examines the impact of free access to computers and the Internet in U.S. public libraries. The analysis looks at coalitions and strategies for digital inclusion, public access services in four communities, factors that affect the character of public access services, and recommendations on how to sustain and improve public access services. A list of references is included.

1080   Becker, Samantha, Michael D. Crandall, Karen E. Fisher, Bo Kinney, Carol Landry, and Anita Rocha. *Opportunity for All: How the American Public Benefits from Internet Access at U.S. Libraries.* IMLS-2010-RES-01. Washington, DC: Institute of Museum and Library Services, 2010. URL: www.imls.gov/assets/1/AssetManager/OpportunityForAll.pdf.

This study looks at who uses public computers and Internet services in public libraries. The report begins with an executive summary, introduction, background, and purpose and methods. It continues to consideration of public library visits, accessing online library resources, public library Internet users, and uses of public library Internet connections and concludes with recommendations, future research, references, further reading, and appendixes. The appendixes covering theoretical frameworks, research methods, tables, a telephone survey instrument, and a web survey instrument are accessible through hyerlinks.

1081   Family Place Libraries. www.familyplace libraries.org.

This website was created through a partnership between Libraries for the Future and the Middle County Public Library in Selden, New York, to expand the role of public libraries as community centers and key players in lifelong learning. The web menu contains a definition of a the Family Place Library, locations, membership, training and events, news, and resources that link readers to specific areas of interest.

1082   University of Washington. *Universal Access: Making Library Resources Accessible to People with Disabilities.* www.washington.edu/doit/UA/PRESENT/libres.html.

The website covers legal issues, access issues, library staff, library services, adaptive technology for computers, electronic resources, and helpful communication hints. A series of questions helps guide making a library universally accessible.

27

PHILANTHROPY

 BOOK

1083 Roberts, Ann. *Crash Course in Library Gift Programs: The Reluctant Curator's Guide to Caring for Archives, Books, and Artifacts in a Library Setting.* Crash Course Series. Westport, CT: Libraries Unlimited, 2007. ISBN: 978-1-59158-530-5 (print), 978-0-31309-452-1 (e-book).

This crash course for librarians covers how to accept or reject gifts such as artifacts, letters, historical documents, pictures, and postcards from donors. Recognizing ramifications of the to-keep-or-not-to-keep decision is particularly helpful for maintaining good customer relations. Maintenance, cataloging, restoration, and item circulation are other themes discussed throughout the book.

POPULAR CULTURE

BOOKS

1084 Crawford, Walt. *The Liblog Landscape 2007–2008: A Lateral Look.* CreateSpace, 2008. ISBN: 978-1-44047-384-5.

This self-published analysis of more than 600 web logs maintained by librarians, as opposed to official library blogs, contains a detailed breakdown of each with twenty-seven measurements along with a discussion of how these blogs have evolved over a year's time. The book is illustrated with tables and charts.

1085 Johnson, Marilyn. *This Book Is Overdue! How Librarians and Cybrarians Can Save Us All.* New York: Harper Perennial, 2011. ISBN: 978-0-06143-161-6.

Forget the stereotypical quiet, shy ladies in sweater sets who wear their hair in a dignified bun; that is the image of librarians of yesteryear. Get ready to embrace the boxing archivist, a blue-haired radical who helps street protestors get around, not to mention the tattooed, party-hardy children's librarian. In a modern day when librarians have been transformed into cybrarians, there is more than a little adventure involved with information specialist and library services. This topical, often humorous, examination of modern libraries with a bit of librarian hero worship ends with librarians at the forefront leading society into the emerging hypertext universe.

1086 Kneale, Ruth. *You Don't Look Like a Librarian: Shattering Stereotypes and Creating Positive New Images in the Internet Age.* Medford, NJ: Information Today, 2009. ISBN: 978-1-57387-366-6.

Kneale examines stereotypes, librarians in pop culture, today's perceptions, and thoughts on the future. Pop culture topics include books, comics, movies, music, television, advertising, toys and tees, and other stuff. The appendixes contain results from "You Don't Look Like a Librarian" surveys conducted in 2001 and 2008. References, a list of websites, and other resources are included.

1087 Lefebvre, Madeleine, ed. *The Romance of Libraries.* Foreword by Michael Gorman. Lanham, MD: Scarecrow Press, 2005. ISBN: 978-0-81085-352-2.

People can fall in love anywhere. For these folks, that includes you know where. Lefebvre compiles happy, sad, and bittersweet but true stories of cupid roaming the stacks in this delightful anthology. These tales are told in the words of the librarians and patrons themselves and are organized loosely by context, such as the bookmobile or reading room.

1088 Manguel, Alberto. *The Library at Night.* New Haven, CT: Yale University Press, 2006. ISBN: 978-0-300-13914-3.

Manguel is in love with books and libraries, and his *The Library at Night* eloquently expresses that love through words and essays. He explores the library as myth, order, space, power, shadow, shape, chance, workshop, mind, island, survival, oblivion, imagination, identity, and home. He recounts books on a shelf, brick and digital libraries, personal collections, book bans, and oral histories. Acknowledgments, notes, and index complete the book.

PROGRAMMING

BOOKS

1089   Bauer, Caroline Feller. *Leading Kids to Books through Crafts.* Illustrated by Richard Laurent. Mighty Easy Motivators Series. Chicago: American Library Association, 2000. ISBN: 0-8389-0769-5.

Bauer introduces children to reading through news stories and poems with related activities that allow them to create a story-related craft to take home. Each of the fifteen themes have stories, poems, craft supply lists, instructions, and a list of related books. Each theme includes one or more read-aloud sections. The second half of the book includes an additional nine general themes for items such as door hangers, read pins, hug-a-book vest, and paper fortune cookies.

1090   Benton, Gail, and Trisha Waichulaitis. *Low-Cost High-Interest Programming: Seasonal Events for Preschoolers.* New York: Neal-Schuman, 2004. ISBN: 1-55570-502-2.

The authors provide four easy-to-prepare seasonal programs targeted at preschoolers. "Teddy Bear Picnic," "Winterfest," "Spring Fling," and "Halloween Boo" are based on original stories and each includes a description, activities, and suggested alternative stories that follow the same general theme. The authors include numerous figures in a coloring book format for each story. A Windows-compatible CD-ROM with eight audio stories is provided.

1091   Benton, Gail, and Trisha Waichulaitis. *Ready-to-Go Storytimes: Fingerplays, Scripts, Patterns, Music, and More.* New York: Neal-Schuman, 2003. ISBN: 1-55570-449-2.

This book is a beginner's guide for preparing 20-minute storytimes for children age 18 months through 5 years. Gathered into six themes, each chapter includes a welcome song, read-aloud story, and activities such as fingerplays, songs, coloring projects, and games. The accompanying CD has fourteen songs; each one matches one of the themes. Some props require craft-making skills or lots of time to construct, so plan ahead and allow plenty of time.

1092   Bromann, Jennifer. *More Storytime Action! 2000+ More Ideas for Making 500+ Picture Books Interactive.* New York: Neal-Schuman, 2009. ISBN: 978-1-55570-675-3.

Picking up where Bromann's last volume left off (see next entry), this book begins with an overview of how to select materials, prepare props, and conduct an interactive storytime for children. After illustrating twenty theme-based plans for storytime, Bromann selects 520 picture stories and provides a single-sentence summary of the story along with a child-friendly activity and list of materials needed for the activity. Two highlights are the sections on Japanese storytelling and using volunteers. Theme and title indexes are included.

1093   Bromann, Jennifer. *Storytime Action! 2,000+ Ideas for Making 500 Picture Books Interactive.* New York: Neal-Schuman, 2003. ISBN: 978-155570-459-9.

Stories can be more than just one person performing a recitation while others listen. Here is an alphabetical listing by author of 500 books that Bromann shows can be easily made interactive. Each entry includes a plot summary, one or more activities related to the theme of the story, and publication information. "Barnyard Banter" has children making animal noises, and "Yellow Ball" involves—you guessed it—a yellow ball passed from kiddy to kiddy. "Fox Tale Soup" provides an opportunity to combine reading and cooking as children add pictures or felt cutouts of vegetables to put into the pot. Clever and fun, this book includes a list of topics and index.

1094   Diamant-Cohen, Betsy, and Selma K. Levi. *Booktalking Bonanza: Ten Ready-to-Use Multimedia Sessions for the Busy Librarian.* Chicago: American Library Association, 2008. ISBN: 978-0-83890-965-2.

Although each of the 30-minute multimedia booktalk scripts are for children in the upper elementary grades, additional theme-related material at the end of each chapter allows the presentation to be modified for different audiences ranging from younger children to adults. Topics include lightning, immigration, wishes, lies, dreams, body parts, art, mummies, names, cats, and dogs. One chapter focuses on using science experiments, music, crafts, video, film, role-playing, and more to enhance presentations.

1095   Haven, Kendall, and MaryGay Ducey. *Crash Course in Storytelling.* Crash Course Series. Westport, CT: Libraries Unlimited, 2006. ISBN: 978-1-59158-399-8 (print), 978-0-3133-7491-3 (e-book).

This crash course for librarians covers the various levels of storytelling, the impact on listeners, presentations, choosing material, preparation and delivery, props, and troubleshooting. The appendixes cover the structure of stories, the value of storytelling, copyrights, and definitions of traditional tales. The bibliography is divided into references, storytelling advice, research guides, traditional tales collections, family and personal stories, participation stories, story enhancements, and webliography (see also entry 1109, *Crash Course in Storytime Fundamentals*).

1096   John, Lauren Zina. *Running Book Discussion Groups: A How-to-Do-It Manual.* How-To-Do-It Manuals for Libraries 147. New York: Neal-Schuman, 2006. ISBN: 978-1-55570-542-8.

John provides steps, checklists, examples, and resources on how to launch and run a successful book discussion group. Ten book discussions with sample publicity material and resources can easily be adapted for time, audience, and topic. "Resources for Book Discussion Groups" includes an annotated bibliography, online tools for choosing and evaluating books, professional support, and partnership strategies.

1097   Keane, Nancy J. *Booktalks and Beyond: Thematic Learning Activities for Grades K–6.* Fort Atkinson, WI: Upstart Books, 2001. ISBN: 978-1-57950-062-7.

A booktalk assumes that you are recommending the book, because the book is the source of the discussion or promotion. Each of the fifteen subject area chapters has a short description of the subject followed by an annotated bibliography divided into grades K–3 and grades 4–6 that concludes with suggested activities to incorporate into lesson plans. The content is geared toward novice elementary teachers but is applicable to school media specialists as well.

1098 Lowe, Joy L., and Kathryn I. Matthew.
Puppet Magic. New York: Neal-Schuman, 2007. ISBN: 978-1-55570-599-2.

Tips for creating puppets and step-by-step guidance on how to incorporate puppets into any library program are given. The material in *Puppet Magic* is most useful for library students, beginning librarians, and anyone else looking to turn favorite stories or poems into puppet presentations. Sample annotations of nursery rhymes, poems, stories, folktales, fables, and songs are included throughout the book. Additional resources include a guide to puppet retailers and puppet material distributors. The index matches puppets to specific book titles. The authors also list additional titles and tools for the novice puppeteer.

1099 Ludwig, Sarah. *Starting from Scratch: Building a Teen Library Program.* Libraries Unlimited Professional Guides for Young Adult Librarians Series. Westport, CT: Libraries Unlimited, 2011. ISBN: 978-1-59884-607-2 (print), 978-1-59884-608-9 (e-book).

Ludwig covers all aspects of teen programs, including policies, space, collections, teen advisory boards, outreach, budgets, and professional development. Many of the topics and suggested steps are easily applied to other types of library programming. Anecdotal examples, new technologies, social networking, and gaming activities are used to highlight tasks and responsibilities that come with serving teen patrons.

1100 Marino, Jane. *Babies in the Library!* Lanham, MD: Scarecrow Press, 2003. ISBN: 978-0-81084-576-3.

This slim volume tells you everything you need to know to hold baby laptimes in your library, aimed specifically at pre-walkers and walkers up to 30 months old. Suggested movements and gestures to keep the children's attention accompany the numerous rhymes and songs. The resource section lists rhyme and story collections, age-appropriate books, programming books, and professional resources.

1101 McElmeel, Sharron L. *ABCs of an Author/Illustrator Visit.* 2nd ed. Professional Growth Series. Worthington, OH: Linworth, 2001. ISBN: 978-1-58683-034-2.

This step-by-step guide to organizing actual visits or "virtual" celebrations gives many examples of how to gain community support and enhanced literacy. Reproducible forms include those for planning, budget, sample newsletters, floor plans, book orders, and autograph forms. Alternative promotional opportunities discussed are communication networks, U.S. mail, Internet venues, and bookstore, museum, and community center visits.

1102 Niebuhr, Gary Warren. *Read 'em Their Writes: A Handbook for Mystery and Crime Fiction Book Discussions.* Westport, CT: Libraries Unlimited, 2006. ISBN: 978-1-59158-303-5.

Niebuhr provides 100 classic and contemporary crime and mystery books, their themes, inside tips, background material, and sample questions for book club discussion. An additional fifty mystery and crime books are listed to consider for discussion.

1103 Pavon, Ana-Elba, and Diana Borrego. *25 Latino Craft Projects: Celebrating Culture in Your Library.* Chicago: American Library Association, 2003. ISBN: 978-0-83890-833-4.

The authors gathered detailed instructions, background material, and patterns for twenty-five craft projects related to Latino holidays. Inspired mostly by Mexican folk traditions, the projects require inexpensive and easy-to-find materials.

Grouped by topic, each chapter contains suggested books and additional activities for children and families. Sample celebrations include Cinco de Mayo, Hispanic Heritage month, Day of the Dead, and Christmas.

1104   Peck, Penny. *Crash Course in Storytime Fundamentals.* Crash Course Series. Westport, CT: Libraries Unlimited, 2008. ISBN: 978-1-59158-715-6 (print), 978-1-59884-505-1 (e-book).

This crash course for librarians covers storytime basics for babies, toddlers, preschoolers, and families using music, song, puppets, props, and fingerplay. Other topics include bilingual storytime, special issues, and using volunteers. Themed preschool storytime outlines, bibliography, and index are provided (see also entry 1100, *Crash Course in Storytelling*).

1105   Peters, Thomas A. *Library Programs Online: Possibilities and Practicalities of Web Conferencing.* Westport, CT: Libraries Unlimited, 2009. ISBN: 978-1-59158-349-3 (print), 978-0-313-39124-8 (e-book).

Peters's guide is specifically for libraries and library-related organizations to develop online programs for customers. The introduction to web conferencing and online programs is described in the context of library services. Topics such as basic web conferencing systems, training, orientation, support, and promotions, along with event timing, recording, archiving, podcasting, and evaluating, round out the steps to implementing an online program. The chapters on key issues and future possibilities help librarians avoid pitfalls. Additional references and resources are provided.

1106   Reid, Rob. *Something Funny Happened at the Library: How to Create Humorous Programs for Children and Young Adults.* Chicago: American Library Association, 2003. ISBN: 978-0-83890-836-5.

Reid divides the book into two main sections, hosting a humorous program and program content suggestions. The material is divided by genre

and age level (preschoolers to primary-grade children, intermediate school–age children, and middle school and high school students). The annotated bibliography, which comprises the majority of the book, contains materials published prior to 2003 that may not be readily found in current library collections. Sample programs give the reader ideas on how to plan, market, and deliver short programs.

1107   Reid, Rob. *Something Musical Happened at the Library: Adding Song and Dance to Children's Story Programs.* Chicago: American Library Association, 2007. ISBN: 978-0-83890-942-3.

Reid discusses eight ready-to-use lesson plans and simple ways to incorporate music into storytimes and other library programs with minimal planning and expense. The resources section lists individual artists and websites where librarians can purchase recorded materials for musical programs. An ample annotated bibliography is included.

1108   Robertson, Deborah A., and ALA Public Programs Office. *Cultural Programming for Libraries: Linking Libraries, Communities, and Culture.* Chicago: American Library Association, 2005. ISBN: 978-0-83893-551-4.

Here we have the how-to basics for organizing public library cultural events and programming to meet the changing needs and interests of communities. From planning to funding and promoting, Robertson looks at all steps, common problems, and how to develop solutions. Sample programs, advertisements, planning worksheets, case studies, and "five star" programs provide practical examples for novice planners to modify.

1109   Soltan, Rita. *Reading Raps: A Book Club Guide for Librarians, Kids, and Families.* Westport, CT: Libraries Unlimited, 2006. ISBN: 978-1-59158-234-2.

Soltan focused this well-organized book on book discussion basics and provides the nature and specific challenges for mother/daughter, father/son, family, and traditional reading circles. Each suggested reading includes reading level, genre, themes, awards, plot summary, main characterization, books with similar issues or themes, author-related sources, and discussion questions. Roughly 100 books for third- to eighth-graders are considered.

1110   Struckmeyer, Amanda Moss, and Svetha Hetzler. *DIY Programming and Book Displays: How to Stretch Your Programming without Stretching Your Budget and Staff.* Santa Barbara, CA: Libraries Unlimited, 2010. ISBN: 978-1-59884-472-6 (print), 978-1-59884-473-3 (e-book).

A few caveats: the programming mentioned in the title is geared entirely toward children, and advice about book displays is pretty much limited to lists of suggested titles. Those concerns aside, this book will help children's librarians deal with reluctant readers and other little folks with short attention spans. The basic idea is "set it and forget it"; with some basic materials, such as color crayons and photocopied activity sheets, and a small space of their own, the young'uns can do their own thing quietly while staff attend to more pressing matters. Twelve thematic chapters, one for each month of the year, list featured activity, materials needed, preparation/setup, and a "Tips and Flourishes" section for the ambitious who want to get seriously creative. Representative activities are "What's your pirate name?" and "I scream, you scream, we all scream for ice cream." There are lots of templates for easy photocopying.

1111   Vardell, Sylvia M. *Poetry Aloud Here! Sharing Poetry with Children in the Library.* Chicago: American Library Association, 2006. ISBN: 978-0-83890-916-4.

Vardell explains why poetry is important, which poets to select, and how to promote and present poetry to children ages 5 to 12. She provides criteria for selecting poetry that is age appropriate and is also within physical reach of the intended audience. Each chapter begins and ends with a poem, has at least one poet profile, and includes multiple "Practitioner Perspective" sidebars that highlight actual experiences promoting poetry.

The appendixes recommends noteworthy poets who write for young children and offers a bibliography of children's poetry books. A list of references and index finish off the book.

1112   Yousha, Ladona. *Teddy Bear Storytimes: Ready-to-Go Flannel and Magnetic Storyboard Programs That Captivate Children.* New York: Neal-Schuman, 2009. ISBN: 978-1-55570-677-7.

The youngest member of a bear family, appropriately named "Teddy Bear," features in these original tales. Complete with easy cut-out patterns, performance tips, storytelling guides, suggested activities, and recommended books to supplement themes presented, each chapter covers a single theme. Themes include how Teddy Bear learns to be a good sport, how to interact with friends, and what to expect on vacation and holidays. A companion CD-ROM provides easy access to character and scenery patterns to share and print for use and distribution.

✐ ADDITIONAL RESOURCES

1113   Alessio, Amy J., and Kimberly A. Patton. *A Year of Programs for Teens.* Chicago: American Library Association, 2007. ISBN: 978-0-83890-903-4.

1114   Alessio, Amy J., and Kimberly A. Patton. *A Year of Programs for Teens 2.* Chicago: American Library Association, 2011. ISBN: 978-0-83891-051-1.

1115   Alexander, Linda B., and Nahyun Kwon, eds. *Multicultural Programs for Tweens and Teens.* Chicago: American Library Association, 2010. ISBN: 978-0-83893-582-8.

1116   Bauman, Stephanie G., ed. *Storytimes for Children.* Westport, CT: Libraries Unlimited, 2010. ISBN: 978-1-59884-565-5 (print), 978-1-59884-566-2 (e-book).

1117   Braun, Linda W. *Technically Involved: Technology-Based Youth Participation Activities for Your Library.* Chicago: American Library Association, 2003. ISBN: 978-0-83890-861-7.

1118 **Brown, Barbara Jane.** *Programming for Librarians: A How-to-Do-It Manual.* How-To-Do-It Manuals for Libraries 26. New York: Neal-Schuman, 1992. ISBN: 978-1-55570-112-3.

1119 **Cali, Charlene C.** *Library Mania: Games and Activities for Your Library.* Madison, WI: Upstart Books, 2009. ISBN: 978-1-60213-043-2.

1120 **Carlson, Ann D., and Mary Carlson.** *Flannelboard Stories for Infants and Toddlers.* Chicago: American Library Association, 2005. ISBN: 978-0-83890-911-9.

1121 **Cole, Sonja.** *Booktalking Around the World: Great Global Reads for Ages 9–14.* Westport, CT: Libraries Unlimited, 2010. ISBN: 978-1-59884-613-3 (print), 978-1-59884-614-0 (e-book).

1122 **Coleman, Tina, and Peggie Llanes.** *The Hipster Librarian's Guide to Teen Craft Projects.* Chicago: American Library Association, 2009. ISBN: 978-0-83890-971-3.

1123 **Colston, Valerie.** *Teens Go Green! Tips, Techniques, Tools, and Themes for YA Programming.* Libraries Unlimited Professional Guides for Young Adult Librarians Series. Westport, CT: Libraries Unlimited, 2011. ISBN: 978-1-59158-929-7.

1124 **Edwards, Kirsten.** *Teen Library Events: A Month-by-Month Guide.* Libraries Unlimited Professional Guides for Young Adult Librarians Series. Westport, CT: Libraries Unlimited, 2001. ISBN: 978-0-31331-482-7.

1125 **Faurot, Kimberly K.** *Books in Bloom: Creative Patterns and Props That Bring Stories to Life.* Chicago: American Library Association, 2003. ISBN: 978-0-83890-852-5.

1126 **Feinberg, Sandra, and Kathleen Deerr.** *Running a Parent/Child Workshop: A How-to-Do-It Manual for Librarians.* How-To-Do-It Manuals for Libraries 46. New York: Neal-Schuman, 1995. ISBN: 978-1-55570-189-5.

1127 **Folini, Melissa Rossetti.** *Story Times Good Enough to Eat! Thematic Programs with Edible Story Crafts.* Santa Barbara, CA: Libraries Unlimited, 2011. ISBN: 978-1-59158-898-6 (print), 978-1-59158-899-3 (e-book).

1128 **Fox, Kathleen.** *Fun-Brarian: Games, Activities, and Ideas to Liven Up Your Library.* Madison, WI: Upstart Books, 2007. ISBN: 978-1-93214-686-8.

1129 **Freeman, Judy.** *Once Upon a Time: Using Storytelling, Creative Drama, and Reader's Theater with Children in Grades PreK–6.* Westport, CT: Libraries Unlimited, 2007. ISBN: 978-1-59158-663-0 (print), 978-0-313-09568-9 (e-book).

1130 **Frey, Yvonne Amar.** *One-Person Puppetry: Streamlined and Simplified with 38 Folktale Scripts.* Chicago: American Library Association, 2005. ISBN: 978-0-83890-889-1.

1131 **Ghoting, Saroj N., and Pamela Martin-Díaz.** *Art and Craft Activities for Early Literacy @ Your Fingertips.* Chicago: American Library Association, 2010. ISBN: 978-0-83891-028-3.

1132 **Ghoting, Saroj N., and Pamela Martin-Díaz.** *Early-Literacy-Enhanced Storytimes @ Your Fingertips.* Chicago: American Library Association, 2010. ISBN: 978-0-83891-026-9.

1133 **Ghoting, Saroj N., and Pamela Martin-Díaz.** *Early Literacy Storytimes @ Your Library: Partnering with Caregivers for Success.* Chicago: American Library Association, 2006. ISBN: 978-0-83890-899-0.

1134 **Ghoting, Saroj N., and Pamela Martin-Díaz.** *Songs and Movement Activities for Early Literacy @ Your Fingertips.* Chicago: American Library Association, 2010. ISBN: 978-0-83891-029-0.

1135 **Greene, Ellin, and Janice M. Del Negro.** *Storytelling: Art and Technique.* 4th ed. Santa Barbara, CA: Libraries Unlimited, 2010. ISBN: 978-1-59158-600-5.

1136 **Hardesty, Constance.** *The Teen Centered Writing Club: Bringing Teens and Words Together.* Libraries Unlimited Professional Guides for Young Adult Librarians Series. Westport, CT: Libraries Unlimited, 2008. ISBN: 978-1-59158-548-0.

1137 **Helmrich, Erin, and Elizabeth Schneider.** *Create, Relate, and Pop @ the Library: Services and Programs for Teens and Tweens.* New York: Neal-Schuman, 2011. ISBN: 978-1-55570-722-4.

1138 **Hostmeyer, Phyllis, and Marilyn Adele Kinsella.** *Storytelling and QAR Strategies.* Santa Barbara, CA: Libraries Unlimited, 2011. ISBN: 978-1-59884-494-8 (print), 978-1-59884-495-5 (e-book).

1139 **Karle, Elizabeth M.** *Hosting a Library Mystery: A Programming Guide.* Chicago: American Library Association, 2009. ISBN: 978-0-83890-986-7.

1140 **Kunzel, Bonnie, and Hardesty, Constance.** *Teen-Centered Book Club: Readers into Leaders.* Libraries Unlimited Professional Guides for Young Adult Librarians Series. Westport, CT: Libraries Unlimited, 2006. ISBN: 978-1-59158-193-2.

1141 **Lear, Brett W.** *Adult Programs in the Library.* ALA Programming Guides. Chicago: American Library Association, 2002. ISBN: 978-0-83890-810-5.

1142 **Littlejohn, Carol.** *Book Clubbing! Successful Book Clubs for Young People.* Westport, CT: Libraries Unlimited, 2011. ISBN: 978-1-58683-414-2 (print), 978-1-58683-415-9 (e-book).

1143 **MacDonald, Margaret Read, and Roxane Murphy.** *Twenty Tellable Tales: Audience Participation Folktales for the Beginning Storyteller.* Illustrations by Roxane Murphy. Chicago: American Library Association, 2005. ISBN: 978-0-83890-893-8.

1144 **MacMillan, Kathy, and Christine Kirker.** *Storytime Magic: 400 Fingerplays, Flannelboards, and Other Activities.* Chicago: American Library Association, 2009. ISBN: 978-0-83890-977-5.

1145 **Mahood, Kristine.** *Booktalking with Teens.* Libraries Unlimited Professional Guides for Young Adult Librarians Series. Westport, CT: Libraries Unlimited, 2010. ISBN: 978-1-59158-714-9.

1146 **Nespeca, Sue McCleaf.** *Library Programming for Families with Young Children: A How-to-Do-It Manual.* How-To-Do-It Manuals for Libraries 45. New York: Neal-Schuman, 1994. ISBN: 978-1-55570-181-9.

1147 **Nespeca, Sue McCleaf, and Joan B. Reeve.** *Picture Books Plus: 100 Extension Activities in Art, Drama, Music, Math, and Science.* Chicago: American Library Association, 2003. ISBN: 978-0-83890-840-2.

1148 **Nichols, Judy.** *Storytimes for Two-Year-Olds.* Illustrations by Lori D. Sears. Chicago: American Library Association, 2007. ISBN: 978-0-83890-925-6.

1149 **Ott, Valerie.** *Teen Programs with Punch: A Month-by-Month Guide.* Libraries Unlimited Professional Guides for Young Adult Librarians Series. Westport, CT: Libraries Unlimited, 2000. ISBN: 978-1-59158-293-9.

1150 **Polette, Nancy.** *Fairy Tale Fun.* New York: Neal-Schuman, 2011. ISBN: 978-1-55570-773-6.

1151 **Polette, Nancy.** *The Library Film Party: Activities with Children's Classic Films.* Illustrations by Paul Dillon. Westport, CT: Libraries Unlimited, 2011. ISBN: 978-1-59884-820-5 (print), 978-1-59884-821-2 (e-book).

1152 **Reid, Rob.** *Cool Story Programs for the School-Age Crowd.* Chicago: American Library Association, 2004. ISBN: 978-0-83890-887-7.

1153 **Reid, Rob.** *More Family Storytimes: Twenty-Four Creative Programs for All Ages.* Chicago: American Library Association, 2009. ISBN: 978-0-83890-973-7.

1154 **Reid, Rob.** *Reid's Read-Alouds: Selections for Children and Teens.* Chicago: American Library Association, 2009. ISBN: 978-0-83890-980-5.

1155 **Reid, Rob.** *Reid's Read-Alouds 2: Modern Day Classics from C. S. Lewis to Lemony Snicket.* Chicago: American Library Association, 2011. ISBN: 978-0-83891-072-6.

1156   **Rubin, Rhea Joyce.** *Intergenerational Programming: A How-to-Do-It Manual for Librarians.* How-To-Do-It Manuals for Libraries 36. New York: Neal-Schuman, 1993. ISBN: 978-1-55570-157-4.

1157   **Rubin, Rhea Joyce, and Peggy O'Donnell.** *Humanities Programming: A How-to-Do-It Manual.* How-To-Do-It Manuals for Libraries 72. New York: Neal-Schuman, 1997. ISBN: 978-1-55570-083-6.

1158   **Schall, Lucy.** *Value-Packed Booktalks: Genre Talks and More for Teen Readers.* Westport, CT: Libraries Unlimited, 2011. ISBN: 978-1-59884-735-2 (print), 978-1-59884-736-9 (e-book).

1159   **Strauss, Kevin.** *Story Solutions: Using Tales to Build Character and Teach Bully Prevention, Drug Prevention, and Conflict Resolution.* Westport, CT: Libraries Unlimited, 2011. ISBN: 978-1-59158-764-4.

1160   **Taylor-DiLeva, Kim.** *Once Upon a Sign: Using American Sign Language to Engage, Entertain, and Teach All Children.* Westport, CT: Libraries Unlimited, 2011. ISBN: 978-1-59884-476-4 (print), 978-1-59884-477-1 (e-book).

1161   **Wadham, Tim.** *Programming with Latino Children's Materials: A How-to-Do-It Manual for Librarians.* How-To-Do-It Manuals for Libraries 89. New York: Neal-Schuman, 1999. ISBN: 978-1-55570-352-3.

1162   **Wetzel, Jennifer A.** *Liven Up Your Library: Creative and Inexpensive Programming Ideas.* Madison, WI: Upstart Books, 2009. ISBN: 978-1-60213-047-0.

📖 PERIODICAL

1163   ***Local Studies Librarian.*** London: Chartered Institute Library and Information Professionals. Frequency: Frequency: Annually (print), twice a year (online). ISSN: 0263-0273. URL: www.cilip .org.uk/get-involved/special-interest-groups/ local-studies/publications/journal/pages/ default.aspx.

This annual journal from the Local Studies Group of the Chartered Institute of Library and Information Professionals covers local studies, connecting with new audiences, case studies, awards, committee news and activities, and more.

⌂ **LC SUBJECT HEADINGS**

(1) Librarians—Quotations, maxims, etc.
(2) Libraries—Quotations, maxims, etc.
(3) Library Science—Quotations, maxims, etc.

QUOTATIONS

 BOOK

 WEBSITES

1164 Eckstrand, Tatyana, comp. *The Librarian's Book of Quotes.* Chicago: American Library Association, 2009. ISBN: 978-0-83890-988-1.

"A truly great library contains something in it to offend everyone," according to Jo Godwin (p. 5). That sentiment certainly seems to be borne out by the fact that just about every major work of literature has had calls for its removal from library shelves, but that's another chapter (chapter 8, to be specific). Eckstrand compiles almost 300 choice selections from librarians, writers, thinkers, and other individuals about libraries and the people who work there. A biographical dictionary helps to shed some light on the originators of these bons mots, and a section on sources provides citations of where these passages first saw print.

1165 *Library Quotes.* Chicago: American Library Association. URL: www.libraryquotes.org.

A handy and ease-to-use website, *Library Quotes* is a searchable database comprising quotations about libraries, reading, books, literacy, and more. Searches may be performed by entering a keyword in a search box, then selecting either "name," "quote," or "source" from a drop-down menu. Alternatively, one may retrieve random quotes by selecting a category, say, "Historical Figures," and then sifting through the words of wisdom of such personages as Abraham Lincoln and Ralph Waldo Emerson. Although sources of each quote are given, too often they are of a secondary nature, as from a Friends of the Library newsletter, rather than the original sources, such as a speech or letter. As of this writing, 241 quotes are freely available. ALA president Roberta Stevens, the Association of Library Trustees, Advocates, Friends and Foundations, and the Office for Library Advocacy make this site possible.

1166 *Wikiquotes.* "Libraries." URL: http://en.wikiquote.org/wiki/Libraries.

Straightforward listings of library quotations are divided into four sections: quotes with source cited, quotes with no source cited, quotes by unidentified author, and, curiously, quotes from *Hoyt's New Cyclopedia of Practical Quotations* from 1922.

LC SUBJECT HEADINGS

(1) Middle School Students—Books and Reading
(2) Preteens—Books and Reading
(3) Public Libraries—United States—Book Lists
(4) Readers' Advisory Services—United States
(5) Teenagers—Books and Reading

READERS' ADVISORY

BOOKS

1167 Adamson, Lynda G. *Literature Links to American History, K-6: Resources to Enhance and Entice.* Children's and Young Adult Literature Reference Series. Westport, CT: Libraries Unlimited, 2010. ISBN: 978-1-59158-468-1.

This volume contains approximately 3,100 annotated entries for books, CDs, and DVDs covering American history from before 1600 through the twentieth century, for children in kindergarten through grade 6. Each annotated entry contains a short subject overview, bibliographic information, and listing of applicable prizes. Author/illustrator, title, and subject/grade level indexes conclude the book.

1168 Adamson, Lynda G. *Literature Links to American History, 7-12: Resources to Enhance and Entice.* Children's and Young Adult Literature Reference Series. Westport, CT: Libraries Unlimited, 2010. ISBN: 978-1-59158-469-8.

This volume contains approximately 3,100 annotated entries for books, CDs, and DVDs covering American history from before 1600 through the twentieth century for grades 7 through 12. Each annotated entry contains a short subject overview, bibliographic information, and listing of applicable prizes. Author/illustrator, title, and subject/grade level indexes conclude the book.

1169 Adamson, Lynda G. *Literature Links to World History, K-12: Resources to Enhance and Entice.* Children's and Young Adult Literature Reference Series. Westport, CT: Libraries Unlimited, 2010. ISBN: 978-1-59158-470-4.

This volume contains approximately 2,700 annotated entries for books, CDs, and DVDs covering world history for kindergarten through grade 12. Arranged by time period and geographic area, each entry contains an overview of the historic event or person concerned; and bibliographic information for historical fiction and fantasy, history, biography, and collective biography. Author/illustrator, title, and subject/grade level indexes conclude the book.

1170 Alpert, Abby, and Barry Trott. *Read On . . . Graphic Novels: Reading Lists for Every Taste.* Read On Series. Westport, CT: Libraries Unlimited, 2012. ISBN: 978-1-59158-825-2.

Alpert compiles an annotated list of more than 500 graphic novels under seventy themes. Organized by character, story, setting, language, and mood, these selections cover several fiction and nonfiction genres including mystery, science fiction, superheroes, manga, memoirs, travelogues, history, and textbooks.

1171 Barr, Catherine. *Best Books for High School Readers: Grades 9–12. Supplement to the Second Edition.* Children's and Young Adult Literature Reference Series. Westport, CT: Libraries Unlimited, 2012. ISBN: 978-1-59884-785-7.

This supplemental volume contains approximately 2,500 annotated entries for fiction and nonfiction titles published from 2008 through 2010 for children in grades 9–12 arranged alphabetically by major subject. Each annotated entry contains a plot summary, reading level, review citations, and bibliographic information. Author, title, and subject/grade-level indexes conclude the book.

1172 Barr, Catherine. *Best Books for Middle School and Junior High Readers: Grades 6–9. Supplement to the Second Edition.* Children's and Young Adult Literature Reference Series. Westport, CT: Libraries Unlimited, 2012. ISBN: 978-1-59884-783-3.

This supplemental volume contains approximately 2,800 annotated entries for fiction and nonfiction titles published from 2008 through 2010 for children in grades 6–9 arranged alphabetically by major subject. Each annotated entry contains a plot summary, reading level, review citations, and bibliographic information. Author, title, and subject/grade-level indexes conclude the book.

1173 Barr, Catherine. *Best New Media, K–12: A Guide to Movies, Subscription Web Sites, and Educational Software and Games.* Westport, CT: Libraries Unlimited, 2008. ISBN: 978-1-59158-467-4.

This volume contains approximately 2,000 annotated fiction and nonfiction entries for titles arranged alphabetically by grade followed by a reference section that lists subscription databases for the period 2001–2007. Each annotated entry contains a plot summary, grade level, review citations, and bibliographic information. Title and subject indexes conclude the book.

1174 Barr, Catherine, and John T. Gillespie. *Best Books for Children: Preschool through Grade 6.* Children's and Young Adult Literature Reference Series. 9th ed. Westport, CT: Libraries Unlimited, 2010. ISBN: 978-1-59158-575-6.

This volume contains approximately 25,000 annotated entries for fiction and nonfiction titles in print at the end of 2008 published for children pre-K through grade 6 arranged alphabetically by major subject. Each annotated entry contains plot summaries, reading level, review citations, and bibliographic information. Author, title, and subject/grade-level indexes conclude the book.

1175 Barr, Catherine, and John T. Gillespie. *Best Books for High School Readers: Grades 9–12.* Children's and Young Adult Literature Reference Series. 2nd ed. Westport, CT: Libraries Unlimited, 2009. ISBN: 978-1-59158-576-3.

This volume contains approximately 13,000 annotated fiction and nonfiction entries for titles published from 2004 through 2008 for children in grades 9–12 arranged alphabetically by major subject. Each annotated entry contains a plot summary, reading level, review citations, and bibliographic information. Author, title, and subject/grade-level indexes conclude the book.

1176 Barr, Catherine, and John T. Gillespie. *Best Books for Middle School and Junior High Readers: Grades 6–9.* Children's and Young Adult Literature Reference Series. 2nd ed. Westport, CT: Libraries Unlimited, 2009. ISBN: 978-1-59158-573-2.

This volume contains approximately 15,000 annotated entries for fiction and nonfiction titles arranged alphabetically by major subject published from 2004 through 2008. Each entry contains a plot summary, reading level, review citations, and bibliographic information. Author, title, and subject/grade-level indexes conclude the book.

1177 Buker, Derek M. *The Science Fiction and Fantasy Readers' Advisory: The Librarian's Guide to Cyborgs, Aliens, and Sorcerers.* ALA Readers' Advisory Series. Chicago: American Library Association, 2002. ISBN: 978-0-83890-831-0.

This humorous guide to science fiction and fantasy literature is for librarians unfamiliar with the two genres. Author-suggested readings and short annotated lists of recommended titles emphasize the wide scope and subgenres. Part 1 is devoted to science fiction and covers aliens, androids, superheroes, space operas, and otherworldly phenomena. Part 2 concerns epic fantasy, fairy tales, historical settings, sword and sorcery, talking beasties, and the like. The appendixes have lists of Hugo Award, Nebula Award, Mythopeic, and World Fantasy winners.

1178 Chance, Rosemary. *Young Adult Literature in Action: A Librarian's Guide.* Library and Information Science Text Series. Westport, CT: Libraries Unlimited, 2008. ISBN: 978-1-59158-558-9 (print), 978-1-59158-926-6 (e-book).

Chance combines literature with activities to provide an overview of how to present genre-driven material in the classroom. She begins with an introduction to young adults and the literature that interests them. Quick reads, realistic fiction, fantasy fiction, informational books, cultural diversity, and the freedom to read are other topics covered. An index, professional references, and reference list of young adult books are also provided.

1179 Cords, Sarah Statz. *The Inside Scoop: A Guide to Nonfiction Investigative Writing and Exposés.* Real Stories Series. Westport, CT:

Libraries Unlimited, 2009. ISBN: 978-1-59158-650-0.

Cords reviews and provides descriptive annotations for more than 500 current and classic volumes of reportage. Themes include in-depth reporting, exposés, immersion journalism, character profiles, political reporting, and business reporting. Each chapter contains a definition, audience appeal, chapter organization, subgenres, read-alikes, further readings, and references. The appendixes include investigative writing book awards, documentary films, Internet resources, and magazines offering investigative writing and authors. Author/title and subject indexes are included.

1180 Drew, Bernard A. *The 100 Most Popular African American Authors: Biographical Sketches and Bibliographies.* Popular Authors Series. Revised ed. Westport, CT: Libraries Unlimited, 2006. ISBN: 978-1-59158-322-6.

Drew provides biographical background, written works, contributed works, and further information on 100 popular African American authors. The entries are alphabetical by author. Title and author indexes are included for easy lookup.

1181 Drew, Bernard A. *The 100 Most Popular Contemporary Mystery Authors: Biographical Sketches and Bibliographies.* Popular Authors Series. Westport, CT: Libraries Unlimited, 2011. ISBN: 978-1-59884-445-0 (print), 978-1-59884-446-7 (e-book).

Drew provides biographical background, written works, contributed works, and further information on 100 popular contemporary mystery authors. The entries are alphabetical by author. Title and author indexes are included for easy lookup.

1182 Drew, Bernard A. *The 100 Most Popular Genre Authors: Biographical Sketches and Bibliographies.* Popular Authors Series. Revised ed. Westport, CT: Libraries Unlimited, 2005. ISBN: 978-1-59158-126-0.

Drew provides biographical background, written works, contributed works, and further information on 100 popular genre authors. The entries are alphabetical by author. Title and author indexes are included for easy lookup.

1183 Drew, Bernard A. *The 100 Most Popular Nonfiction Authors: Biographical Sketches and Bibliographies.* Popular Authors Series. Revised ed. Westport, CT: Libraries Unlimited, 2007. ISBN: 978-1-59158-487-2.

Drew provides biographical background, written works, contributed works, and further information on 100 popular nonfiction authors. The entries are alphabetical by author. Title and author indexes are included for easy lookup.

1184 Drew, Bernard A. *The 100 Most Popular Thriller and Suspense Authors: Biographical Sketches and Bibliographies.* Popular Authors Series. Westport, CT: Libraries Unlimited, 2009. ISBN: 978-1-59158-699-9.

Drew provides biographical background, written works, contributed works, and further information on 100 popular contemporary thriller and suspense authors. The entries are alphabetical by author. Title and author indexes are included for easy lookup.

1185 Drew, Bernard A. *The 100 Most Popular Young Adult Authors: Biographical Sketches and Bibliographies.* Popular Authors Series. Revised ed. Westport, CT: Libraries Unlimited, 2002. ISBN: 978-1-56308-920-6.

Drew provides biographical background, written works, contributed works, and further information on 100 popular young adult authors. The entries are alphabetical by author. Title and author indexes are included for easy lookup.

1186 Fichtelberg, Susan. *Encountering Enchantment: A Guide to Speculative Fiction for Teens.* Edited by Diana Tixier Herald. Genreflecting Advisory Series. Westport, CT: Libraries Unlimited, 2006. ISBN: 978-1-59158-316-5.

This standard reference and readers' advisory guide includes 1,400 bibliographic entries of fantasy, science fiction, and horror titles sorted into middle school (grades 6–7), junior high (grades 7–9), and senior high (grades 10–12) categories. Some graphic novels, audiovisual materials, programming ideas, and author websites are included. Author, title, subject, and award-winning-book indexes are provided.

1187 Fichtelberg, Susan, and Bridget Dealy Volz. *Primary Genreflecting: A Guide to Picture Books and Easy Readers.* Genreflecting Advisory Series. Westport, CT: Libraries Unlimited, 2010. ISBN: 978-1-56308-907-7.

This standard reference and readers' advisory guide includes 2,500 entries of picture books and easy readers sorted into twelve chapters for students in grades PreK–3. Each entry contains bibliographic information and suggested grade level. Author, title, specialty story, and subject indexes are included.

1188 Fonseca, Anthony J., and June Michele Pulliam. *Hooked on Horror III: A Guide to Reading Interests in Horror Fiction.* 3rd ed. Westport, CT: Libraries Unlimited, 2009. ISBN: 978-1-59158-540-4.

This expanded third edition, a standard reference and readers' advisory guide, includes more than 500 new annotated horror genre titles published between 2003 and 2008, sorted into thirteen subgenres. Each chapter contains author picks and read-alike listings. The guide begins with an introduction to horror fiction, a brief history of the genre, and its current trends before moving into the bibliographic entries with related films. Resources, major awards, and publishers and publishers' series provide additional references. The appendixes include cross-genre horror fiction, a core list for collection development, and true ghost stories. Author, title, subject, and short story indexes are included.

1189 Fraser, Elizabeth. *Reality Rules! A Guide to Teen Nonfiction Reading Interests.* Westport,

CT: Libraries Unlimited, 2008. ISBN: 978-1-59158-563-3.

This guide includes nonfiction genres, life stories, and subject interest books for teen recreational reading. Themes include true adventure, memoirs, history, science, math, sports, and the arts. The appendixes give nonfiction readers' advisory resources for young adult librarians and a bibliography. Author/title and subject indexes are included.

1190 Freeman, Judy. *Books Kids Will Sit Still For 3: A Read-Aloud Guide.* Children's and Young Adult Literature Reference Series. Westport, CT: Libraries Unlimited, 2006. ISBN: 978-1-59158-163-5.

Freeman's annotated bibliography of 1,700 titles published since 1995 includes picture books, fiction, poetry, folklore, biography, and nonfiction books, indexed by author/illustrator, title, and subject for students in grades K–6.

1191 Freeman, Judy. *The Winners! Handbook: A Closer Look at Judy Freeman's Top-Rated Children's Books of 2010.* Westport, CT: Libraries Unlimited, 2011. ISBN: 978-1-59884-977-6 (print), 978-1-59884-982-0 (e-book).

Freeman lists her choices of the 100 best kids books of 2010, many of them winners of major literary awards. Each annotated entry has a list of related titles, subject designations, lessons, and activities to use in class curriculum or library programming. Author/title and subject indexes are included.

1192 Gannon, Michael B. *Blood, Bedlam, Bullets, and Badguys: A Reader's Guide to Adventure/ Suspense Fiction.* Genreflecting Advisory Series. Westport, CT: Libraries Unlimited, 2004. ISBN: 978-1-56308-732-5.

This standard reference and readers' advisory guide includes 3,000 mostly annotated entries of adventures and suspense books published between 1941 and 2003. The appendixes contain lists of film and television movie versions and authors for core collection lists. A glossary and author/title and subject indexes are included.

1193 Gillespie, John T. *The Family in Literature for Young Readers: A Resource Guide for Use with Grades 4 to 9.* Children's and Young Adult Literature Reference Series. Westport, CT: Libraries Unlimited, 2011. ISBN: 978-1-59158-915-0 (print), 978-1-59158-916-7 (e-book).

Part 1 introduces a brief history of the family, including roles, family in literature, and criteria for evaluating fiction and family stories. Part 2 contains a detailed analysis of more than forty books, including plot, principal characters, themes, subject, and selected passages for discussion. Part 3 is a bibliography of family stories still in print at the end of 2010. The book concludes with an index of authors of family literature and an index to part 2 entries.

1194 Gillespie, John T. *Introducing Historical Fiction for Young Readers (Grades 4–8).* Children's and Young Adult Literature Reference Series. Westport, CT: Libraries Unlimited, 2008. ISBN: 978-1-59158-621-0 (print), 978-1-59884-913-4 (e-book).

Gillespie lists the eighty best English-language historical fiction books, set in Europe, Asia and Oceania, Africa, Latin America, and Canada and the United States for grades 4–8 published between 1992 and 2007. Each annotated title contains historical background, lengthy synopsis, selected passages for discussion, theme, bibliographic information, and information about the author. The book concludes with author, title, and subject indexes.

1195 Haynes, Elizabeth. *Crime Writers: A Research Guide.* Author Research Series. Westport, CT: Libraries Unlimited, 2011. ISBN: 978-1-59158-914-3 (print), 978-1-59158-919-8 (e-book).

Haynes provides writing styles, biographical background, written works, contributed works, awards, websites, online resources, and further information on fifty popular crime fiction authors. An overview of the genre and subgenres, time line, and comprehensive bibliography provide a guide for readers' advisors, book clubs, and genre readers.

1196 Heaphy, Maura. *The 100 Most Popular Science Fiction Authors: Biographical Sketches and Bibliographies.* Popular Authors Series. Westport, CT: Libraries Unlimited, 2009. ISBN: 978-1-59158-746-0.

Heaphy provides biographical background, written works, contributed works, and further information on 100 popular contemporary science fiction authors. The entries are alphabetical by author. Title and author indexes are included for easy lookup.

1197 Heaphy, Maura. *Science Fiction Writers: A Research Guide.* Author Research Series. Westport, CT: Libraries Unlimited, 2008. ISBN: 978-1-59158-515-2.

Heaphy provides writing styles, biographical background, written works, contributed works, awards, websites, online resources, and further information on 100 science fiction authors. An overview of the genre and subgenres, time line, and comprehensive bibliography provide a guide for readers' advisors, book clubs, and genre readers.

1198 Herald, Diana Tixier. *Fluent in Fantasy: The Next Generation.* Genreflecting Advisory Series. Englewood, CO: Libraries Unlimited, 2007. ISBN: 978-1-59158-198-7.

This standard reference and readers' advisory guide includes more than 2,000 epic, heroic, fairy tale, time travel, and other fantasy books. The appendixes cover award-winning and humorous fantasy. Author/title and subject indexes are provided.

1199 Herald, Diana Tixier. *Genreflecting: A Guide to Reading Interests in Genre Fiction.* Edited by Wayne A. Wiegand. 6th ed. Genreflecting Advisory Series. Englewood, CO:

Libraries Unlimited, 2005. ISBN: 978-1-59158-286-1.

This standard reference and readers' advisory guide includes more than 5,000 historical fiction, western, crime, adventure, romance, science fiction, fantasy, horror, Christian fiction, and emerging genre titles. Genreflecting is a process of examining and analyzing the pattern and characteristics of literacy genres to identify titles with similar appeal to readers to make reading suggestions to patrons.

1200 Herald, Diana Tixier. *Teen Genreflecting 3: A Guide to Reading Interests.* Genreflecting Advisory Series. 3rd ed. Greenwood Village, CO: Libraries Unlimited, 2010. ISBN: 978-1-59158-729-3.

This revised standard reference and readers' advisory guide includes more than 1,300 popular titles for teens published between 2003 and 2010. Organized by subgenre and theme, each annotated entry includes a concise subject list and read-alikes books. Practical tips and information on teen readers' advisory, genres, publishing trends, and building a collection are included.

1201 Herald, Diana Tixier, and Bonnie Kunzel. *Strictly Science Fiction: A Guide to Reading Interests.* Genreflecting Advisory Series. Greenwood Village, CO: Libraries Unlimited, 2002. ISBN: 978-1-56308-893-3.

This standard reference and readers' advisory guide includes more than 900 bibliographic entries for science fiction titles. This is mainly geared for adults, but there is a section on books written for young adults and children. A chapter on resources for teachers, librarians, and readers is included along with award-winning titles, best authors, best works, author/title, subject, and character indexes.

1202 Hollands, Neil. *Fellowship in a Ring: A Guide for Science Fiction and Fantasy Book Groups.* Westport, CT: Libraries Unlimited, 2009. ISBN: 978-1-59158-703-3 (print), 978-0-31339-119-4 (e-book).

This guide includes fifty fantasy and science fiction titles and guides for forty popular speculative fiction themes. Entries include bibliographic information, author background, plot summary, discussion questions, references, and read-alikes. The appendixes contain a chronology of science fiction/fantasy history and resources for further study. Author and title/series indexes are included.

1203 Hollands, Neil. *Read On . . . Fantasy Fiction: Reading Lists for Every Taste.* Read On Series. Westport, CT: Libraries Unlimited, 2007. ISBN: 978-1-59158-330-1.

Hollands organizes more than 800 titles into 100 reading lists. Entries include details about story, character, setting, mood, and language in this standard reference and readers' advisory guide on fantasy fiction. Sections are included for World Fantasy Awards for Best Novel, Locus Awards for Fantasy Novel, Mythopoeic Award winners, Hugo Award winners, and Nebula Award winners.

1204 Honig, Megan. *Urban Grit: A Guide to Street Lit.* Westport, CT: Libraries Unlimited, 2010. ISBN: 978-1-59158-857-3.

This guide offers more than 400 works of urban fiction, ghetto lit, hip-hop lit, and gangsta lit—all of which are commonly known as "street lit." Each of the eleven chapters is organized by popular subgenres to assist identifying read-alikes. Themes include players and hustlers, coming of age, drama, love stories, erotica, thrillers, hard times, prison, family, friendship, poetry, memoir, and nonfiction. Appendixes include core collection lists for adults, young adults in public libraries, and young adults in school libraries as well as a list of street lit publishers and imprints. Author, title, and keyword/subject indexes and glossary are included.

1205 Hopper, Brad. *Read On . . . Historical Fiction: Reading Lists for Every Taste.* Read On Series. Westport, CT: Libraries Unlimited, 2006. ISBN: 978-1-59158-239-7.

Hopper presents an annotated list of hundreds of popular historical fiction books organized by character, story, setting, language, and mood. Subjects include flights of fantasy, politics, Machiavellian men and women, lost worlds of privilege, hard times, and alternative lifestyles.

1206 Johnson, Sarah L. *Historical Fiction: A Guide to the Genre.* Genreflecting Advisory Series. Westport, CT: Libraries Unlimited, 2005. ISBN: 978-1-59158-129-1.

This standard reference and readers' advisory guide includes more than 3,800 historical fiction, mystery, western, alternative history, adventure, and other genre titles set in times prior to the mid-1990s. The appendixes cover award-winning historical novels and reading lists by plot pattern or theme.

1207 Johnson, Sarah L. *Historical Fiction II: A Guide to the Genre.* Genreflecting Advisory Series. Westport, CT: Libraries Unlimited, 2009. ISBN: 978-1-59158-624-1.

This standard reference and readers' advisory guide includes more than 2,700 English-language historical fiction, mystery, western, alternative history, adventure, and other genre titles published between mid-2004 and mid-2008. The author classifies titles by subgenres, grouping read-alikes together.

1208 Kallio, Jamie. *Read On . . . Speculative Fiction for Teens: Reading Lists for Every Taste.* Read On Series. Westport, CT: Libraries Unlimited, 2012. ISBN: 978-1-59884-653-9.

Here we have more than 350 speculative fiction books for teens organized by character, story, setting, language, and mood. Themes include fantasy, science fiction, and paranormal.

1209 Lima, Carolyn W., and Rebecca L. Thomas. *A to Zoo: Subject Access to Children's Picture Books.* Children's and Young Adult Literature Reference Series. 8th ed. Westport, CT: Libraries Unlimited, 2010. ISBN: 978-1-59884-406-1.

This work focuses on children's books published during the decade 2000–2009, bringing the subject index to over 12,000 titles for kids preschool through grade 2. Classic and other popular picture books of the past are included. The authors provide long lists of children's picture books that can be helpful in identifying books for programs and displays, organized into five areas—subject heading, subject guide, bibliographic guide, title index, and illustrator index. Unless users know the author, illustrator, or title, they may have to use the indexes and flip back and forth to locate books on a particular topic. Entries are not annotated. Full bibliographic information is included.

1210 Martínez, Sara E., ed. *Latino Literature: A Guide to Reading Interests.* Genreflecting Advisory Series. Westport, CT: Libraries Unlimited, 2009. ISBN: 978-1-59158-292-2.

This standard reference and readers' advisory guide includes more than 750 Latino titles published between 1995 and 2008. Each entry has complete bibliographic information, plot summary, subject list, brief quote, and list of read-alike books. This edition includes a glossary and a publishers, resources, and awards appendix. Author/translator/title and subject indexes are included.

1211 McElmeel, Sharon L. *100 Most Popular Authors and Illustrators: Biographical Sketches and Bibliographies.* Revised ed. Popular Authors Series. Westport, CT: Libraries Unlimited, 2000. ISBN: 978-1-56308-647-2.

McElmeel provides biographical background, written works, contributed works, and further information on 100 popular children's authors and illustrators. The entries are alphabetical by author. Title and author indexes are included for easy lookup.

1212 McElmeel, Sharon L. *Children's Authors and Illustrators Too Good to Miss: Biographical Sketches and Bibliographies.* Revised ed. Popular Authors Series. Westport, CT: Libraries Unlimited, 2004. ISBN: 978-1-59158-027-0.

McElmeel provides biographical background, written works, contributed works, and further information on forty-five popular children's authors and illustrators for grades K–6. The entries are alphabetical by author. Title and author indexes are included for easy lookup.

1213 Meloni, Christine. *Teen Chick Lit: A Guide to Reading Interests.* Genreflecting Advisory Series. Westport, CT: Libraries Unlimited, 2009. ISBN: 978-1-59158-756-9.

This standard reference and readers' advisory guide includes more than 500 contemporary teen chick books in six popular major subgenres: traditional, gossip, international relations, magical maidens, spies and mystery solvers, and lad lit. Each annotated entry has bibliographic information, age recommendation, book awards, media connection, and keywords. Author/title and subject indexes are included for easy lookup.

1214 Moyer, Jessica E., ed. *Integrated Advisory Service: Breaking through the Book Boundary to Better Serve Library Users.* Westport, CT: Libraries Unlimited, 2010. ISBN: 978-1-59158-718-7.

Contributors review similarities among fiction, nonfiction, graphic novels, television shows, video games, and movies to find a connection to crime stories, fantasy, historical fiction, horror, popular science, romance, science fiction, street literature, teens, women's lives, and relationships genres. Each genre chapter includes an introduction, integrated advisory, characters, plots, theme, means for making connections, conclusion, and resources. Contributors and editor biographical information is provided along with an author/title index.

1215 Naidoo, Jamie Campbell. *Rainbow Family Collections: Selecting and Using Children's Books with Lesbian, Gay, Bisexual, Transgender, and Queer Content.* Children's and Young Adult Literature Reference Series. Westport, CT: Libraries Unlimited, 2012. ISBN: 978-1-59884-960-8.

This volume contains approximately 200 annotated entries for children's picture books and chapter books from around the world covering lesbian, gay, bisexual, transgender, and queer content for children from infancy to age 12. Each annotated entry contains a short subject overview and cites professional reviews, genre, grade level, bibliographic information, and list of applicable prizes.

1216 Niebuhr, Gary Warren. *Caught Up in Crime: A Reader's Guide to Crime Fiction and Nonfiction.* Genreflecting Advisory Series. Westport, CT: Libraries Unlimited, 2009. ISBN: 978-1-59158-428-5.

This standard reference and readers' advisory guide includes more than 600 annotated crime titles arranged by similar crimes within three broad categories: "Professional Criminals," "Caught Up in a Crime," and "Criminal Detectives." Each entry includes a plot summary and special character descriptions. An author index with biographical notes and title and subject indexes are provided.

1217 Niebuhr, Gary Warren. *Make Mine a Mystery: A Reader's Guide to Mystery and Detective Fiction.* Genreflecting Advisory Series. Westport, CT: Libraries Unlimited, 2003. ISBN: 978-1-56308-784-4.

This standard reference and readers' advisory guide include more than 2,500 annotated mystery titles arranged in amateur, public, and private detective sections. Niebuhr begins this guide with an introduction to mystery fiction, its history, collection, development, and preservation. Author, title, character, subject, and location indexes conclude the book.

1218 Niebuhr, Gary Warren. *Make Mine a Mystery II: A Reader's Guide to Mystery and Detective Fiction.* Genreflecting Advisory Series. Westport, CT: Libraries Unlimited, 2011. ISBN: 978-1-59884-589-1.

This follow-up guide to the first *Make Mine a Mystery* includes 700 new popular, recently published mystery titles. As with the first book, entries are arranged in amateur, public, and private detective sections.

1219 O'Connor, Maureen. *Life Stories: A Guide to Reading Interests in Memoirs, Autobiographies, and Diaries.* Real Stories Series. Westport, CT: Libraries Unlimited, 2011. ISBN: 978-1-59158-527-5.

This readers' advisory guide includes travel and adventures, celebrities, creative life, working life, place and time, life away from home, life with others, the inner life, the political life, changing lives in history, life on the dark side of history, life at war, and surviving life. Each chapter includes a description, audience appeal, chapter organization, classics, subgenre topics, read-alikes, and works cited. The appendixes contain a list of classics, controversial titles, awards, and resources. Author/title and subject indexes end the book.

1220 Pearl, Nancy. *Now Read This II: A Guide to Mainstream Fiction, 1990–2001.* 2nd ed. Genreflecting Advisory Series. Westport, CT: Libraries Unlimited, 2010. ISBN: 978-1-56308-867-4 (print), 978-0-313-00907-5 (e-book).

This second edition is a standard reference and readers' advisory guide to approximately 500 titles on popular and contemporary mainstream fiction published between 1990 and 2001. The guide is divided into four categories: setting, story, characters, and language. Entries are arranged alphabetically by author and include title, publisher, date, pagination, brief plot summary, and suggested readings. Author/title and subject indexes are provided.

1221 Pearl, Nancy, and Joyce G. Saricks. *Now Read This: A Guide to Mainstream Fiction, 1978–1998.* Adapted by Martha Knappe and Chris Higashi. Genreflecting Advisory Series. Westport, CT: Libraries Unlimited, 2010. ISBN: 978-1-56308-659-5 (print), 978-0-313-09001-1 (e-book).

This standard reference and readers' advisory guide includes more than 1,000 mainstream fiction titles arranged by character, setting, language, and story. Annotated entries include a plot summary, suggested book discussion groups, and suggested readings for similar stories. Author/title and subject indexes are provided.

1222 Pearl, Nancy, and Sarah Statz Cords. *Now Read This III: A Guide to Mainstream Fiction.* Genreflecting Advisory Series. Westport, CT: Libraries Unlimited, 2010. ISBN: 978-1-59158-570-1.

This third title in the *Now Read This* group of books is a standard reference and readers' advisory guide to approximately 500 titles on popular and contemporary mainstream fiction. The appendixes contain "Bridges to Genre Fiction," book awards, resources, and "How to Create a Dynamic Book Club." Author/title and subject indexes are provided.

1223 Peck, Penny. *Readers' Advisory for Children and 'Tweens.* Westport, CT: Libraries Unlimited, 2010. ISBN: 978-1-59884-387-3 (print), 978-1-59884-388-0 (e-book).

Peck defines readers' advisory and examines attendant issues before moving on to age-defined chapters with book lists for birth to age 5, 5–6, 6–8, and 'tweens ages 9–12. The last chapters are divided by type of literature (e.g., multicultural, nonfiction, folklore, poetry, and graphic novels). A chapter on promoting books to children and 'tweens, suggested readings, and index conclude the book.

1224 Pulliam, June M., and Anthony J. Fonseca. *Read On . . . Horror Fiction.* Read On Series. Westport, CT: Libraries Unlimited, 2006. ISBN: 978-1-59158-176-5.

The authors categorize over 350 popular horror fiction titles by story, mood and atmosphere, setting, character, and language. Each entry has bibliographic information and plot summaries that can be used to create reading lists. Appendixes include information on horror on films, series titles, and genre blends.

1225 Rabey, Melissa. *Historical Fiction for Teens: A Genre Guide.* Genreflecting Advisory Series. Westport, CT: Libraries Unlimited, 2010. ISBN: 978-1-59158-813-9.

This standard reference and readers' advisory guide includes 300 annotated titles arranged by subgenre and theme for teen historical fiction published between 1975 and 2010. An appendix with brief thematic book lists is included.

1226 Reisner, Rosalind. *Jewish American Literature: A Guide to Reading Interests.* Genreflecting Advisory Series. Westport, CT: Libraries Unlimited, 2004. ISBN: 978-1-56308-984-8.

This standard reference and readers' advisory guide includes more than 700 annotated entries for Jewish American fiction and nonfiction works, including mysteries, thrillers, historical fiction, science fiction, fantasy, romance, works on the Holocaust, and biography/autobiography genres. Organized by subgenre and theme, each chapter contains books that appeal to young adult readers grades 9 and up.

1227 Reisner, Rosalind. *Read On . . . Life Stories: Reading Lists for Every Taste.* Read On Series. Westport, CT: Libraries Unlimited, 2009. ISBN: 978-1-59158-766-8.

Reisner compiles an annotated list of nearly 450 books on real-life stories organized by character, story, setting, language, and mood. Topics cover celebrities, memoirs, sports, scientists, outdoor adventures, diaries, love lost and found, spiritual journeys, and more.

1228 Roche, Rick. *Read On . . . Biography: Reading Lists for Every Taste.* Read On Series. Westport, CT: Libraries Unlimited, 2009. ISBN: 978-1-59884-701-7.

Roche compiles an annotated list of nearly 450 biographies organized by character, story, setting, language, and mood. Topics cover life stories from various time periods, locations, occupations, and more.

1229 Roche, Rick. *Real Lives Revealed: A Guide to Reading Interests in Biography.* Real Stories Series. Westport, CT: Libraries Unlimited, 2009. ISBN: 978-1-59158-664-7.

The author reviews and provides descriptive annotations for over 600 biographies. Themes include adventure, true crime, war, inspirational, investigative, coming of age, cultural, celebrity, historical, political, science, and sports biographies. Each chapter contains a definition, genre appeal, chapter organization, subgenres, read-alikes, and further readings. The appendixes include biography awards, top biographers, and biography series. Author/title, subject, and chronological indexes are included.

1230 Saricks, Joyce G. *Read On . . . Audiobooks: Reading Lists for Every Taste.* Read On Series. Westport, CT: Libraries Unlimited, 2011. ISBN: 978-1-59158-804-7 (print), 978-1-59158-807-8 (e-book).

Saricks compiles an annotated list of over 300 audiobook titles organized by language/voice, mood, story, characters, and setting, which serves as a tool for collection development and listeners' advisory. Topics cover a variety of subjects such as romantic comedy, classic thrillers, virtuoso performances, full cast readings, and gothic tales.

1231 Sheehan, Sarah E. *Romance Authors: A Research Guide.* Author Research Series. Westport, CT: Libraries Unlimited, 2010. ISBN: 978-1-59884-386-6.

Sheehan provides writing styles, biographical background, written works, contributed works, awards, websites, online resources, and further information on romance authors. An overview of the genre and subgenres, time line, and comprehensive bibliography provide a guide for readers' advisors, book clubs, and genre readers.

1232 Smith, Sharron, and Maureen O'Connor. *Canadian Fiction: A Guide to Reading Interests.* Foreword by Catherine Sheldrick Ross. Genreflecting Advisory Series. Westport, CT: Libraries Unlimited, 2005. ISBN: 978-1-59158-166-6.

This standard reference and readers' advisory guide includes 500 annotated entries for contemporary Canadian fiction books. Organized by language, character, setting, and story, each annotated entry includes bibliographic information. The appendixes include resources and websites and information on literary awards and Canadian publishers and publishing. References are provided along with author/title and subject indexes.

1233 Stevens, Jen, and Dorothea Salo. *Fantasy Authors: A Research Guide.* Author Research Series. Westport, CT: Libraries Unlimited, 2008. ISBN: 978-1-59158-497-1.

Sheehan provides writing styles, biographical background, written works, contributed works, awards, websites, online resources, and further information about fantasy authors. An overview of the genre and subgenres, time line, and comprehensive bibliography provide a guide for readers' advisors, book clubs, and genre readers.

1234 Torres-Roman, Steven A. *Read On . . . Science Fiction: Reading Lists for Every Taste.* Read On Series. Westport, CT: Libraries Unlimited, 2010. ISBN: 978-1-59158-769-9.

Torres-Roman compiles an annotated list for a broad spectrum of science fiction books, organized by story, character, setting, mood, and language. Subjects include mad scientists, alternative universes, space invaders, designer genes, empires, and telepaths. A list of interesting and important anthologies and an index of authors, titles, and series are provided for easy reference.

1235 Trott, John Barry. *Read On . . . Crime Fiction: Reading Lists for Every Taste.* Read On Series. Westport, CT: Libraries Unlimited, 2007. ISBN: 978-1-59158-373-8.

Trott compiles an annotated list of mystery and crime fiction, organized by story, character, setting, mood, and language. Topic categories include "Reading the Bones," "Dynamic Duos," "Bright Lights," "Dead Bodies," and "Love You to Death."

1236 Vardell, Sylvia M. *Children's Literature in Action: A Librarian's Guide.* Libraries Unlimited Library and Information Science Series. Westport, CT: Libraries Unlimited, 2008. ISBN: 978-1-59158-657-9 (print), 978-1-59158-837-5 (e-book).

Vardell provides a textbook introduction to children and their literature through an examination of picture books, traditional tales, poetry for children, contemporary realistic fiction, historical fiction, fantasy, and informational books. Each chapter contains author comments, activities, special topics and activities, selected awards, historical connections, items for discussion, suggested assignments, and recommended resources.

1237 Vnuk, Rebecca. *Read On . . . Women's Fiction: Reading Lists for Every Taste.* Read On Series. Westport, CT: Libraries Unlimited, 2009. ISBN: 978-1-59158-634-0.

Vnuk compiles an annotated list of popular women's fiction titles organized by story, character, setting, mood, and language. There are categories on dating, working women, mothers, romance, and more.

1238 Vnuk, Rebecca. *Women's Fiction Authors: A Research Guide.* Author Research Series. Westport, CT: Libraries Unlimited, 2009. ISBN: 978-1-59158-642-5.

Vnuk provides writing styles, biographical background, written works, contributed works, awards, websites, online resources, and further information on women's fiction authors. An overview of the genre and subgenres, time line, and comprehensive bibliography provide a guide for readers' advisors, book clubs, and genre readers.

1239 Wadham, Rachel L. *This Is My Life: A Guide to Realistic Fiction for Teens.* Genreflecting Advisory Series. Westport, CT: Libraries Unlimited, 2010. ISBN: 978-1-59158-942-6.

This standard reference and readers' advisory guide includes titles with contemporary, realistic problems and issues fiction for young adults. Although emphasis is on books published since 2000, some classics and older benchmark titles are included.

1240 Webber, Carlisle K. *Gay, Lesbian, Bisexual, Transgender and Questioning Teen Literature: A Guide to Reading Interests.* Genreflecting Advisory Series. Westport, CT: Libraries Unlimited, 2010. ISBN: 978-1-59158-506-0.

This standard reference and readers' advisory guide includes 300 annotated contemporary gay, lesbian, bisexual, transgender, and questioning teen books for students in grades 6–12. A guide to GLBTQ collection development, appendix with websites and professional resources, and author/title, subject, and keyword indexes conclude the book.

1241 Wesson, Lindsey Patrick. *Green Reads: Best Environmental Resources for Youth, K–12.* Children's and Young Adult Literature Reference Series. Westport, CT: Libraries Unlimited, 2009. ISBN: 978-1-59158-834-4 (print), 978-1-59158-835-1 (e-book).

This volume contains approximately 450 annotated entries for books, CDs, and DVDs covering environmental issues for grades K–12 published from 2004 to 2008. Each annotated entry contains a short subject overview, grade level, bibliographic information, and list of applicable prizes, organized into five areas: global warming, pollution, the earth's resources, recycling, and conservation. Icons highlight resources that are good to read aloud, contain many facts, or provide practical tips. Symbols, series, author, title, subject, and grade-level indexes conclude the book.

1242 Zbaracki, Matthew D. *Best Books for Boys: A Resource for Educators.* Introduction by Jon Scieszka. Children's and Young Adult Literature Reference Series. Westport, CT: Libraries Unlimited, 2008. ISBN: 978-1-59158-599-2.

This volume contains approximately 500 annotated entries for fiction and nonfiction titles arranged alphabetically by genre, published for children in grades 3–10. Each entry contains plot summary, reading level, review citations, and bibliographic information. Author, title, and subject indexes conclude the book.

1243 Zellers, Jessica. *Women's Nonfiction: A Guide to Reading Interests.* Real Stories Series. Westport, CT: Libraries Unlimited, 2009. ISBN: 978-1-59158-658-6.

Zellers reviews and provides annotations for over 600 popular titles about women and women's experiences. Themes include life stories, personal growth, health, wellness and beauty, women's history, adventure and travel, feminism and activism, women at work, and women and society. Each chapter contains a definition, audience appeal, chapter organization, subgenres, suggested readings, and read-alikes. The appendixes include biography awards, top biographers, and biography series. Author/title, subject, and chronological indexes are included.

𝓮 ADDITIONAL RESOURCES

1244 Barron, Neil, ed. *Anatomy of Wonder: A Critical Guide to Science Fiction.* 5th ed. Westport, CT: Libraries Unlimited, 2004. ISBN: 978-1-59158-171-0.

1245 Barstow, Barbara, Leslie A. Molnar, and Judith Riggle. *Beyond Picture Books: Subject Access to Best Books for Beginning Readers.* *3rd ed.* Children's and Young Adult Literature Reference Series. Westport, CT: Libraries Unlimited, 2007. ISBN: 978-1-59158-545-9.

1246 Bartel, Julie, and Pam Spencer Holley. *Annotated Books Lists for Every Teen Reader: The Best from the Experts at YALSA-BK.* New York: Neal-Schuman, 2010. ISBN: 978-1-55570-658-6.

1247 Baxter, Kathleen A., and Marcia Agness Kochel. *Gotcha Again for Guys!* Westport, CT: Libraries Unlimited, 2010. ISBN: 978-1-59884-376-7 (print), 978-1-59884-377-4 (e-book).

1248 Bomhold, Catharine R., and Terri E. Elder. *Twice Upon a Time: A Guide to Fractured, Altered, and Retold Folk and Fairy Tales.* Children's and Young Adult Literature Reference Series. Westport, CT: Libraries Unlimited, 2008. ISBN: 978-1-59158-390-5.

1249 Booth, Heather. *Serving Teens through Readers' Advisory.* Chicago: American Library Association, 2007. ISBN: 978-0-83890-930-0.

1250 Bosman, Ellen, and John P. Bradford. *Gay, Lesbian, Bisexual, and Transgendered Literature: A Genre Guide.* Edited by Robert B. Ridinger. Westport, CT: Libraries Unlimited, 2008. ISBN: 978-1-59158-194-9.

1251 Bouricius, Ann. *The Romance Readers' Advisory: The Librarian's Guide to Love in the Stacks.* Chicago: American Library Association, 2000. ISBN: 978-0-83890-779-5.

1252 Burgin, Robert. *Nonfiction Reader's Advisory.* Westport, CT: Libraries Unlimited, 2004. ISBN: 978-1-59158-115-4.

1253 Carstensen, Angela, ed. *Outstanding Books for the College Bound: Titles and Programs for a New Generation.* A YALSA Publication. Chicago: American Library Association, 2011. ISBN: 978-0-83898-570-0.

1254 Cart, Michael. *Young Adult Literature: From Romance to Realism.* Chicago: American Library Association, 2010. ISBN: 978-0-83891-045-0.

1255 Charles, John, Joanna Morrison, and Candace Clark. *The Mystery Readers' Advisory: The Librarian's Clues to Murder and Mayhem.* ALA Readers' Advisory Series. Chicago: American Library Association, 2002. ISBN: 978-0-83890-811-2.

1256 Cords, Sarah Statz. *The Real Story: A Guide to Nonfiction Reading Interests.* Edited by Robert Burgin. Westport, CT: Libraries Unlimited, 2006. ISBN: 978-1-59158-283-0.

1257 Dawson, Alma, and Connie J. Van Fleet. *African American Literature: A Guide to Reading Interests.* Westport, CT: Libraries Unlimited, 2004. ISBN: 978-1-56308-931-2.

1258 Day, Betty H., and William A. Wortman, eds. *Literature in English: A Guide for Librarians in the Digital Age.* ACRL Publication in Librarianship. Chicago: American Library Association, 2000. ISBN: 978-0-83898-081-1.

1259 Drew, Bernard A. *The 100 Most Popular Young Adult Authors.* Revised first ed. Popular Authors Series. Westport, CT: Libraries Unlimited, 1997. ISBN: 978-1-56308-615-1.

1260 East, Kathy A., and Rebecca L. Thomas. *Across Cultures: A Guide to Multicultural Literature for Children.* Children's and Young Adult Literature Reference Series. Westport, CT: Libraries Unlimited, 2006. ISBN: 978-1-59158-336-3.

1261 Farrelly, Michael Garrett. *Make Room for Teens! Reflections on Developing Teen Spaces in Libraries.* Westport, CT: Libraries Unlimited, 2011. ISBN: 978-1-59158-566-4 (print), 978-1-59884-910-3 (e-book).

1262 Ford, Deborah B. *Scary, Gross, and Enlightening Books for Boys Grades 3–12.* Westport, CT: Libraries Unlimited, 2009. ISBN: 978-1-58683-344-2 (print), 978-1-58683-406-7 (e-book).

1263 Frolund, Tina. *Genrefied Classics: A Guide to Reading Interests in Classic Literature.* Westport, CT: Libraries Unlimited, 2007. ISBN: 978-1-59158-172-7.

1264 Goldsmith, Francisca. *The Readers' Advisory Guide to Graphic Novels.* Chicago: American Library Association, 2010. ISBN: 978-0-83891-008-5.

1265 Herald, Nathan. *Graphic Novels for Young Readers: A Genre Guide for Ages 4–14.* Westport, CT: Libraries Unlimited, 2011. ISBN: 978-1-59884-395-8.

1266 Holley, Pam Spencer, ed. *Quick and Popular Reads for Teens.* Chicago: American Library Association, 2009. ISBN: 978-0-83893-577-4.

1267 Hooper, Brad. *The Short Story Readers' Advisory: A Guide to the Best.* ALA Readers' Advisory Series. Chicago: American Library Association, 2000. ISBN: 978-0-83890-782-5.

1268 Husband, Janet, and Jonathan F. Husband. *Sequels: An Annotated Guide to Novels in Series.* 4th ed. Chicago: American Library Association, 2009. ISBN: 978-0-83890-967-6.

1269 Kalen, Elizabeth. *Mostly Manga: A Genre Guide to Popular Manga, Manhwa, Manhua, and Anime.* Genreflecting Advisory Series. Westport, CT: Libraries Unlimited, 2012. ISBN: 978-1-59884-938-7.

1270 Koelling, Holly, ed. *Best Books for Young Adults.* 3rd ed. Foreword by Betty Carter. Chicago: American Library Association, 2009. ISBN: 978-0-83893-569-9.

1271 Lynn, Ruth. *Fantasy Literature for Children and Young Adults: A Comprehensive Guide.* Children's and Young Adult Literature Reference Series. 5th ed. Westport, CT: Libraries Unlimited, 2005. ISBN: 978-1-59158-050-8.

1272 Maatta, Stephanie L. *A Few Good Books: Using Contemporary Readers' Advisory Strategies to Connect Readers with Books.* New York: Neal-Schuman, 2010. ISBN: 978-1-55570-669-2.

1273 Mathews, Patricia O. B. *Fang-tastic Fiction: Twenty-First-Century Paranormal Reads.* Chicago: American Library Association, 2011. ISBN: 978-0-83891-073-3.

1274 McDaniel, Deanna J. *Gentle Reads: Great Books to Warm Hearts and Lift Spirits, Grades 5–9.* Children's and Young Adult Literature Reference Series. Westport, CT: Libraries Unlimited, 2008. ISBN: 978-1-59158-491-9.

1275 Morris, Vanessa Irvin. *The Readers' Advisory Guide to Street Literature.* Foreword by Teri Woods. ALA Readers' Advisory Series. Chicago: American Library Association, 2011. ISBN: 978-0-83891-110-5.

1276 Mort, John. *Christian Fiction: A Guide to the Genre.* Greenwood Village, CO: Libraries Unlimited, 2002. ISBN: 978-1-56308-871-1.

1277 Mort, John. *Read the High Country: Guide to Western Books and Films.* Genreflecting Advisory Series. Westport, CT: Libraries Unlimited, 2006. ISBN: 978-1-59158-134-5.

1278 Moyer, Jessica E., ed. *Integrated Advisory Service: Breaking through the Book Boundary to Better Serve Library Users.* Westport, CT: Libraries Unlimited, 2010. ISBN: 978-1-59158-718-7.

1279 Moyer, Jessica E. *Research-Based Readers' Advisory.* ALA Readers' Advisory Series. Chicago: American Library Association, 2008. ISBN: 978-0-83890-959-1.

1280 Moyer, Jessica E., and Kaite Mediatore Stover, eds. *The Readers' Advisory Handbook.* ALA Readers' Advisory Series. Chicago: American Library Association, 2010. ISBN: 978-0-83891-042-9.

1281 Naidoo, Jamie Campbell, ed. *Celebrating Cuentos: Promoting Latino Children's Literature and Literacy in Classrooms and Libraries.* Children's and Young Adult Literature Reference Series. Westport, CT: Libraries Unlimited, 2010. ISBN: 978-1-59158-904-4 (print), 978-1-59158-905-1 (e-book).

1282 *The Newbery and Caldecott Awards: A Guide to the Medal and Honor Books, 2010 Edition.* Chicago: American Library Association, Association for Library Service to Children, 2010. ISBN: 978-0-83893-595-8.

1283 Pawuk, Michael. *Graphic Novels: A Genre Guide to Comic Books, Manga, and More.* Genreflecting Advisory Series. Westport, CT: Libraries Unlimited, 2007. ISBN: 978-1-59158-132-1.

1284 Saricks, Joyce G. *The Readers' Advisory Guide to Genre Fiction.* 2nd ed. ALA Readers' Advisory Series. Chicago: American Library Association, 2009. ISBN: 978-0-83890-989-8.

1285 Saricks, Joyce G. *Readers' Advisory Service in the Public Library.* 3rd ed. Chicago: American Library Association, 2005. ISBN: 978-0-83890-897-6.

1286 Shearer, Kenneth D., and Robert Burgin, eds. *The Readers' Advisor's Companion.* Englewood, CO: Libraries Unlimited, 2001. ISBN: 978-1-56308-880-3.

1287 Spratford, Becky Siegel, and Tammy Hennigh Clausen. *The Horror Readers' Advisory: The Librarian's Guide to Vampires, Killer Tomatoes, and Haunted Houses.* ALA Readers' Advisory Series. Chicago: American Library Association, 2004. ISBN: 978-0-83890-871-6.

1288 Sullivan, Michael. *Serving Boys through Readers' Advisory.* ALA Readers' Advisory Series. Chicago: American Library Association, 2010. ISBN: 978-0-83891-022-1.

1289 Thomas, Rebecca L., and Catherine Barr. *Popular Series: Fiction for K–6 Readers: A Reading and Selection Guide.* 2nd ed. Children's and Young Adult Literature Reference Series. Westport, CT: Libraries Unlimited, 2008. ISBN: 978-1-59158-659-3.

1290 Thomas, Rebecca L., and Catherine Barr. *Popular Series: Fiction for Middle School and Teen Readers: A Reading and Selection Guide.* 2nd ed. Children's and Young Adult Literature Reference Series. Westport, CT: Libraries Unlimited, 2008. ISBN: 978-1-59158-660-9.

1291 Thompson, Sally A., Compiler. *60 Years of Notable Children's Books.* Chicago: American Library Association, 2003. ISBN: 978-0-83898-265-5.

1292 **Volz, Bridget D., Cheryl P. Scheer, and Lynda B. Welborn.** *Junior Genreflecting: A Guide to Good Reads and Series Fiction for Children.* Genreflecting Advisory Series. Englewood, CO: Libraries Unlimited, 2000. ISBN: 978-1-56308-556-7.

1293 **Waddle, Linda, ed.** *More Outstanding Books for the College Bound.* Chicago: American Library Association, 2006. ISBN: 978-0-83893-553-8.

1294 **Walter, Virginia A., and Catherine Barr, eds.** *War and Peace: A Guide to Literature and New Media, Grades 4–8.* 2nd ed. Children's and Young Adult Literature Reference Series. Westport, CT: Libraries Unlimited, 2006. ISBN: 978-1-59158-271-7.

1295 **Wyatt, Neal.** *The Readers' Advisory Guide to Nonfiction.* Chicago: American Library Association, 2007. ISBN: 978-0-83890-936-2.

READING ADVOCACY, INSTRUCTION, AND PROMOTION

◆ BOOKS

1296   Diamant-Cohen, Betsy, and Saroj Nadkarni Ghoting. *The Early Literacy Kit: A Handbook and Tips Card.* Chicago: American Library Association, 2010. ISBN: 978-0-83890-999-7.

The authors provide readiness skills needed for children from birth to age 5, with discussions of background information, school readiness domains, and why and how to reach parents and caregivers. Besides the handbook with a resources section, this kit includes 105 reusable tip cards with coordinated activities covering approaches to learning, cognition and general knowledge, language and literacy, mathematical and scientific thinking, physical development, social/emotional development, and the arts. Tips directed at specific developmental activity areas have instructions for the selected activity.

1297   Herb, Steven, and Sara Willoughby-Herb. *Connecting Fathers, Children, and Reading: A How-to-Do-It Manual.* How-To-Do-It Manuals for

Libraries 105. New York: Neal-Schuman, 2002. ISBN: 978-1-55570-390-5.

This book focuses on the ways libraries can support fathers' positive influence on the language and literacy development of young children. Case studies, anecdotes, and sidebars highlight practical advice on book selection, programming, and outreach to fathers and children. The authors cover storytelling, writing, various types of conversation, and collaborations of the library, father, and child. The book concludes with an extensive bibliography of children's books about fathers and fathering, resources, websites for parents and librarians, and index.

1298   Johnson, Debra Wilcox. *Let Data Be Your Guide: A Planning Handbook for and by Library Adult Literacy Programs.* Champaign, IL: Illinois Literacy Resource Development Center, 2000. ISBN: 978-1-88509-557-2.

This thin guide contains objectives, priorities, questionnaires, suggested focus group members, and a step-by-step model for planning an adult literacy program. The Public Library Association

Planning Model developed in the 1980s included in appendix A provides a basic planning outline that can be used for any library program.

1299 Krashen, Stephen D. *The Power of Reading: Insights from the Research.* 2nd ed. Westport, CT: Libraries Unlimited, 2004. ISBN: 978-1-59158-169-7 (print), 978-0-313-05335-1 (e-book).

Broken into three sections (the research, the cure, and other issues and conclusions), this updated second edition continues Krashen's case for free voluntary reading. Research covers reading programs, direct instruction, and reading and cognitive development. The cure section looks at access at home, at school, and in the libraries, along with the experience that comes from such light reading as comic books, teen romances, and magazines. The section on other issues and conclusions looks at the limits of reading, writing styles, the effects of television, and second-language readers. References, researcher, and subject indexes are included.

1300 Soltan, Rita. *Solving the Reading Riddle: The Librarian's Guide to Reading Instruction.* Santa Barbara, CA: Libraries Unlimited, 2010. ISBN: 978-1-59158-844-3 (print), 978-1-59158-843-6 (e-book).

Soltan explains reading instruction theories and shows how librarians can effectively integrate such theory into children's services by being reading advocates, family reading coaches, partners with educators, and collection developers. An annotated list of teaching and reading instruction references, glossary of reading instruction terms, and index are included.

@ ADDITIONAL RESOURCES

1301 Anderson, Dee. *Reading Is Funny! Motivating Kids to Read with Riddles.* Chicago: American Library Association, 2009. ISBN: 978-0-83890-957-7.

1302 Balkin, Alfred. *Tune Up to Literacy: Original Songs and Activities for Kids.* Chicago: American Library Association, 2009. ISBN: 978-0-83890-998-0.

1303 Bernadoewski, Carianne, and Patricia Liotta Kolencik. *Research-Based Reading Strategies in the Library for Adolescent Learners.* Westport, CT: Libraries Unlimited, 2009. ISBN: 978-1-58683-347-3 (print), 978-1-58683-404-3 (e-book).

1304 Canavan, Diane D., and LaVonne Hayes Sanborn. *Using Children's Books in Reading/ Language Arts Programs: A How-to-Do-It Manual for Library Applications.* How-to-Do-It Manuals for School and Public Librarians 3. New York: Neal-Schuman, 1992. ISBN: 978-1-55570-101-7.

1305 Court, Joy, ed. *Read to Succeed: Strategies to Engage Children and Young People in Reading for Pleasure.* London: Facet, 2011. ISBN: 978-1-85604-747-0.

1306 Davis, Robin Works. *Promoting Reading with Reading Programs: A How-to-Do-It Manual.* How-to-Do-It Manuals for School and Public Librarians 9. New York: Neal-Schuman, 1992. ISBN: 978-1-55570-115-4.

1307 DeCandido, GraceAnne A., ed. *Literacy and Libraries: Learning from Case Studies.* Chicago: American Library Association, 2001. ISBN: 978-0-83893-516-3.

1308 Fink, Megan, ed. *Teen Read Week and Teen Tech Week: Tips and Resources for YALSA's Initiatives.* Chicago: American Library Association, 2011. ISBN: 978-0-83898-559-5.

1309 Flore, Carole D. *Running Summer Library Reading Programs: A How-to-Do-It Manual.* How-To-Do-It Manuals for Libraries 81. New York: Neal-Schuman, 1998. ISBN: 978-1-55570-312-7.

1310 Ghoting, Saroj N., and Pamela Martin-Díaz. *Early Literacy Reading Program @ Your Fingertips.* Chicago: American Library Association, 2010. ISBN: 978-0-83891-027-6.

1311   Gooch, C. Kay, and Charlotte Massey. *Camp Summer Read: How to Create Your Own Summer Reading Camp.* Westport, CT: Libraries Unlimited, 2011. ISBN: 978-1-59884-447-4 (print), 978-1-59884-448-1 (e-book).

1312   Grimes, Sharon. *Reading Is Our Business: How Libraries Can Foster Reading Comprehension.* Chicago: American Library Association, 2006. ISBN: 978-0-83890-912-6.

1313   Hornby, Susan, and Bob Glass, eds. *Reader Development in Practice: Bringing Literature to Readers.* London: Facet, 2008. ISBN: 978-1-85604-624-4.

1314   Kan, Katharine L. *Sizzling Summer Reading Programs for Young Adults.* 2nd ed. Chicago: American Library Association, 2006. ISBN: 978-0-83893-563-7.

1315   Knell, Suzanne, and Janet Scogins. *Adult Literacy Assessment Tool Kit.* Chicago: American Library Association, 2000. ISBN: 978-0-83893-502-6.

1316   Knowles, Elizabeth, and Martha Smith. *Reading Rules! Motivating Teens to Read.* Englewood, CO: Libraries Unlimited, 2001. ISBN: 978-1-56308-883-4.

1317   Koelling, Holly. *Classic Connections: Turning Teens on to Great Literature.* Libraries Unlimited Professional Guides for Young Adult Librarians Series. Westport, CT: Libraries Unlimited, 2009. ISBN: 978-1-59158-072-0.

1318   Krashen, Stephen D. *Free Voluntary Reading.* Westport, CT: Libraries Unlimited, 2011. ISBN: 978-1-59884-844-1 (print), 978-1-59884-845-8 (e-book).

1319   Mahood, Kristine. *A Passion for Print: Promoting Reading and Books to Teens.* Libraries Unlimited Professional Guides for Young Adult Librarians Series. Westport, CT: Libraries Unlimited, 2006. ISBN: 978-1-59158-146-8.

1320   Moreillon, Judi. *Collaborative Strategies for Teaching Reading Comprehension: Maximizing Your Impact.* Chicago: American Library Association, 2009. ISBN: 978-0-83890-929-4.

1321   Preddy, Leslie B. *Social Readers: Promoting Reading in the 21st Century.* Westport, CT: Libraries Unlimited, 2010. ISBN: 978-1-59158-869-6 (print), 978-1-59158-871-9 (e-book).

1322   Ross, Catherine Sheldrick, Lynne (E. F.) McKechnie, and Paulette M. Rothbauer. *Reading Matters: What the Research Reveals about Reading, Libraries, and Community.* Westport, CT: Libraries Unlimited, 2006. ISBN: 978-1-59158-066-9.

1323   Symons, Ann K., and Charles Harmon. *Protecting the Right to Read: A How-to-Do-It Manual for School and Public Librarians.* How-To-Do-It Manuals for Libraries 60. New York: Neal-Schuman, 1995. ISBN: 978-1-55570-216-8.

1324   Warlick, David F. *Redefining Literacy 2.0.* 2nd ed. Columbus, OH: Linworth, 2009. ISBN: 978-1-58683-333-6 (print), 978-1-58683-241-4 (e-book).

1325   Yesner, Bernice L., and M. Mary Murray. *Developing Literature-Based Reading Programs: A How-to-Do-It Manual.* How-to-Do-It Manuals for School and Public Librarians 13. New York: Neal-Schuman, 1993. ISBN: 978-1-55570-122-2.

REFERENCE WORK

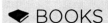 BOOKS

1326 ALA Guide to Sociology and Psychology Reference. Chicago: American Library Association, 2010. ISBN: 978-0-83891-025-2.

This is an authoritative annotated bibliography of psychology and sociology reference books, databases, and the like that serves both as a guide to the current literature and as a collection management tool. The table of contents is quite detailed, breaking down each major subject into headings and subheadings. For example, under part one ("Sociology"), chapter 3 ("Social Conditions and Social Welfare") has subsections "Aging and the Elderly," "Alcoholism and Drug Abuse," "Childhood and Adolescence," and so on. Annotations are well written and concise. Helpfully, each citation lists both Dewey Decimal and LC call numbers, so that readers can find similar materials on their local library shelves.

1327 Bell, Suzanne S. *Librarian's Guide to Online Searching.* 2nd ed. Westport, CT: Libraries Unlimited, 2009. ISBN: 978-1-59158-763-7 (print), 978-1-59158-824-5 (e-book).

This second edition of Bell's online searching guide features database structure, a searcher's toolkit, and social science, numeric, bibliographic, humanities, and science and medicine databases. The focus on people, choosing the right resource, evaluating databases, and teaching others how to navigate various databases will help librarians improve not only their own search skills but those of their patrons as well.

1328 Bopp, Richard E., and Linda C. Smith, eds. *Reference and Information Services: An Introduction.* 4th ed. Santa Barbara, CA: Libraries Unlimited, 2011. ISBN: 978-1-59158-374-5.

Widely used as a textbook in library school classrooms, this volume's popularity among LIS instructors is indicative of its value. Indeed, these well-written and solidly researched chapters, as a whole, rival Katz's classic work, *Introduction to Reference Work* (see entry 1340). Part 1, "Concepts and Processes," covers the history of reference work, ethical concerns, the reference

FYI

AMERICAN REFERENCE BOOKS ANNUAL (ARBA)

Beginning in 1970, and continuing each year since then, Libraries Unlimited has produced these bibliographies of reference works. Since the advent of the Internet, reference-based websites have been included. Each volume surveys the reference literature of the previous year; for example, the volume for 2012 contains reviews of works published in 2011. A small army of librarian-writers contribute reviews. Because these folks are practitioners themselves, they know what to look for in an encyclopedia or dictionary and are generally well versed in what separates a high-quality piece of work from a poorly executed one. Particularly handy is the subject index, which follows Library of Congress subject headings. These annual volumes are one of the best ways to keep current on what is being churned out by reference book publishers, not only for LIS subjects but for just about any subject imaginable.

interview, bibliographic control, and other bedrock information. Part 2, "Information Sources and Their Use," begins with a chapter on the selection and evaluation of reference sources and from there goes on to examine various types and formats: directories, encyclopedias, biographical sources, and so forth. As would be expected, there is an increased emphasis on Internet searching and electronic databases. This is a solid choice for those new to library science who desire a firm foundation for what librarians do and why.

1329 Brumley, Rebecca. *The Reference Librarian's Policies, Forms, Guidelines and Procedures Handbook with CD-ROM.* New York: Neal-Schuman, 2006. ISBN: 978-1-55570-569-5.

No one wants to have to reinvent the wheel, and with this book the reader can simply copy somebody else's wheel. As stated in the preface, "This guide places the work and wisdom of over 180 libraries at your fingertips. Culling a healthy mix from both public and academic libraries, it contains more than 475 of the best real-world policies and forms in use today" (p. xiii). Eight chapters cover such broad areas as selection and evaluation of the reference collection, circulation and interlibrary loan, virtual reference, and children's reference services. The table of contents is extremely detailed, breaking these subjects down into categories and subcategories and finally into individual policies. Included are a list of participating institutions, a list of policies available online, and a CD-ROM in MS Word format of the policies printed in the book.

1330 Dowell, David R. *Crash Course in Genealogy.* Crash Course Series. Westport, CT: Libraries Unlimited, 2011. ISBN: 978-1-59884-939-4 (print), 978-1-59884-940-0 (e-book).

Aimed at librarians helping patrons with genealogical research, this crash course covers colonial, nineteenth-century, and twentieth-century research. Chapters cover researching people of color, researching in another country, field trips, and incorporating DNA research. Dowell uses several examples from his own experiences as a guide. Census record illustrations, glossary of genealogical terms, and index help readers understand the overall research process.

1331 Ford, Charlotte. *Crash Course in Reference.* Crash Course Series. Westport, CT: Libraries Unlimited, 2008: ISBN: 978-1-59158-463-6.

With the ongoing trend of having paraprofessionals fill roles traditionally held by full-fledged librarians, there is an accompanying need for these folks to know at least the rudiments of effective reference work. That is where this book comes in. Although not a substitute for a master's degree in library science, which the author fully admits, this work nonetheless will be of great benefit to those who are "eager to understand more about librarianship and wish to master the skills it takes to provide excellent library service." To that end, typical chapter headings include "Building and Maintaining a Reference Collection," "Searching Print and Electronic Sources," and "Finding Books: Library Catalogs and Bibliographies." Essentially, this is a book of basics that help answer patrons' questions and requests for information. Each chapter has a three-part conclusion: "In Sum" provides a concise wrap-up of the chapter, "Review" is a short list of questions to practice the principles learned, and "Notes" is a bibliography of sources cited within the text.

1332 Frost, William J., ed. *The Reference Collection: From the Shelf to the Web.* Binghampton, NY: Haworth Information Press, 2005. Copublished simultaneously as *Reference Librarian* 44, nos. 91/92. ISBN: 978-0-78902-840-2.

The title refers to the ongoing migration of reference works from print to digital format. Frost points out in his introduction: "While we reference librarians still refer to print sources, we find ourselves spending an increasing amount of time referring clients to electronic sources and an increasing amount of our materials budget is being transferred as well from books to electronic reference materials. Library schools now offer classes on collection development for electronic materials" (p. 1). Sixteen chapters cover evolution of reference collections, electronic versus print reference sources in public library collections, and reference websites for specific subjects (science, medicine, business, etc.). By Internet years a bit dated, this is still a useful work.

1333 Hirko, Buff, and Mary Bucher Ross. *Virtual Reference Training: The Complete Guide to Providing Anytime Anywhere Answers.* Chicago:

American Library Association, 2004. ISBN: 978-0-83890-876-1.

Rather than focus on the nuts and bolts of getting a virtual reference service up and running, this slender volume assumes that is already the case. What may be lacking is adequate training for those librarians in the hot seat who, lacking visual and aural clues of a face-to-face reference interview, may not understand how best to get patrons what they want. Chapter 3, "Core Competencies: Knowledge, Skills, and Aptitudes Needed for Virtual Reference," is especially valuable; there, fourteen points, such as "keyboarding proficiency," "online communication skills," and "effective reference performance," are each defined and explained. Other chapters cover learning activities, online behaviors, and follow-up. Also quite useful are the nine appendixes that contain sample virtual reference transcripts, policies, and procedures; support materials; and trainer notes and tips. The volume concludes with a glossary and bibliography for further reading.

1334 Hysell, Shannon Graff, ed. *Recommended Reference Books for Small and Medium-Sized Libraries and Media Centers.* 2011 ed., Vol. 31. Santa Barbara, CA: Libraries Unlimited, 2011. ISBN: 978-1-59884-915-8.

Academic, public, and school librarians and other professionals contributed over 500 critical book, digital resource, and website reviews for material published in 2009–2010. The book is organized into general reference works, social sciences, humanities, and science and technology sections.

1335 Katz, William A., ed. *Introduction to Reference Work.* 2 vols. 8th ed. New York: McGraw-Hill, 2002. ISBN: 978-0-07244-107-9 (Vol. 1), 978-0-07244-143-7 (Vol. 2).

Having been in print for over three decades (the first edition of this work came out in 1969), this is an old standby in its field, and for good reason. Solidly written and covering the waterfront, these two volumes together provide an excellent overview of what reference librarianship is all about. Volume 1, *Basic Information Services,* concerns itself with the "what" of our profession, with the bulk of this first half mapping out the tools of our trade, such as bibliographies, indexing and abstracting services, encyclopedias, and government documents. Volume 2 covers the "why" and "how" aspects of reference librarianship. Carrying the title *Reference Services and Reference Processes*, these pages cover the finer points of the reference interview, effective online search strategies, reference service policies and evaluation, and the like.

Librarians of long standing will immediately recognize the name of Katz, sadly now deceased. He was one of the biggest of the profession's big guns, having published prolifically over the years in this field. Not only that, but as a professor of LIS at SUNY he taught this material as well, so the man knows whereof he speaks. Taken together, these two volumes are the equivalent of a semester's worth of Reference Work 101 and therefore a must-read for the aspiring reference librarian.

1336 Kern, M. Kathleen. *Virtual Reference Best Practices: Tailoring Services to Your Library.* Chicago: American Library Association, 2009. ISBN: 978-0-83890-975-1.

The introduction states that what works for one institution would be inappropriate for another. Although "Suggested Practices" might have been a better choice of words to appear on the cover, the fact remains that what is presented here are guidelines that have had their baptism of fire in the digital trenches. Fourteen chapters walk the reader through the various steps in the journey, from analyzing needs of the library community, to rallying support, to selecting software, to training and marketing your institution's new virtual reference service. Special features include "Library Field Reports," which are real-world examples of some of the possibilities in this still developing service, and "Research You Can Use," "one-page synopses of significant research in the area of virtual reference with an emphasis on how the research is of practical importance to librarians" (p. viii).

1337 Kovacs, Diane K. *The Virtual Reference Handbook: Interview and Information Delivery Techniques for the Chat and E-mail Environments.* New York: Neal-Schuman, 2007. ISBN: 978-1-55570-598-5.

This is a slim yet informative primer on the intricacies of answering reference questions online. Four quite detailed chapters contain lists of competencies covering technical skills (file transfer options, chat software, etc.), communication skills (being professional under pressure, virtual reference interview), and just plain old Internet savvy, such as being aware of the possibilities and limitations of search engines. Learning activities are sprinkled throughout text, giving readers a chance to apply knowledge gained. Especially helpful are transcripts of eight e-mail conversations between the author and experienced virtual reference librarians that help clarify some of the fuzzier concepts, such as use of emoticons to replace the missing body language, tone of voice, and other cues that inform face-to-face reference interviews.

1338 Lankes, R. David, Scott Nicholson, Marie L. Radford, Joanne Silverstein, Lynn Westbrook, and Philip Nast, eds. *Virtual Reference Service: From Competencies to Assessment.* Virtual Reference Desk Series. New York: Neal-Schuman, 2008. ISBN: 978-1-55570-528-2.

These nine chapters were originally papers presented at the 7th Annual Virtual Reference Desk Conference held in San Francisco in 2005. The content covers establishing a virtual reference service, how to deal with likely problems (rude patrons, inappropriate questions), virtual reference training, and staff buy-in for such a program. Charts and diagrams provide good illustrations.

1339 Lipow, Anne Grodzins. *The Virtual Reference Librarian's Handbook.* New York: Neal-Schuman, in association with Library Solutions Press, 2003. ISBN: 1-55570-445-X.

Meant to be "a practical guide for librarians and administrators who are somewhere along the path to providing virtual reference service" (p. xvii), this handbook lays out a step-by-step plan, from conception to implementation to evaluation. Special features abound: Five appendixes include such helpful material as "Chat Communication Tips" and "Virtual Reference Desk Service Policies, Scripted Messages, and Tales from the Trenches." There are also exercises, checklists, lined white space along margins for jotting down notes/ideas, and a CD with forms, surveys, and other elements that can be customized by the user. This is a great introduction to the subject for those just getting onboard.

1340 Mabry, Celia Hales, ed. *Cooperative Reference: Social Interaction in the Workplace.* New York: Haworth Information Press, 2003. Copublished simultaneously as *Reference Librarian* 40, nos. 83/84, 2004. ISBN: 978-0-78902-370-4.

Organized in much the same manner as Mabry's *Doing the Work of Reference* (see next entry), this volume examines cooperation, collaboration, and just plain old getting along with one another—patrons, fellow librarians, faculty members. Friction can occur anywhere and any time, especially when people have differing but still valid ideas on how something should get done. This book posits that working together to achieve a common purpose is to groups what oil is to a machine. Topics covered include interpersonal skills, clear communication, team building, and the like. Each chapter begins with a summary and is written by a working reference librarian.

1341 Mabry, Celia Hales, ed. *Doing the Work of Reference: Practical Tips for Excelling as a Reference Librarian.* New York: Haworth Information Press, 2001. Copublished simultaneously as *Reference Librarian* 34, no. 72, and 35, no. 73, 2001. ISBN: 978-0-78901-323-1.

The key word here is "practical." Working reference librarians report from "the trenches" on orientation programs for the new hire, customer service, professional development, bibliographic instruction, and a host of other issues relevant to our everyday work lives. Helpfully, each article is preceded by a summary that nicely encapsulates the gist of the piece in question. This is a very "hands on" guide to reference librarianship.

1342 Meola, Marc, and Sam Stormont. *Starting and Operating Live Virtual Reference Services: A How-to-Do-It Manual for Librarians.* How-To-Do-It Manuals for Libraries 118. New York: Neal-Schuman, 2002. ISBN: 978-1-55570-444-5.

Temple University's six key steps to starting and operating a virtual "real-time" chat reference service are preparation and planning, selecting software, staffing pattern decisions, training, marketing, and evaluating effectiveness. The focus in this book is on five different live virtual reference models that can be adapted for use according to library size, technical ability, and financial availability.

1343 Miller, William, and Rita M. Pellen, eds. *Improving Internet Reference Services to Distance Learners.* Binghampton, NY: Haworth Information Press, 2004. Copublished simultaneously as *Internet Reference Services Quarterly* 9, nos. 1/2. ISBN: 978-0-78902-718-4.

As often as not these days, college students are completing coursework outside the classroom. Online classes, also known as "distance learning," bring their own challenges, not to mention opportunities, regarding the provision of reference services, both of which are examined here at some length. Typical chapter titles include "Librarian Participation in the Online Classroom," "Beyond Instruction: Integrating Library Service in Support of Information Literacy," and "Got Distance Services? Marketing Remote Library Services to Distance Learners." This is a generally excellent overview of reference service as it relates to what has become known as the "university without walls."

1344 Morgan, Pamela J. *Training Paraprofessionals for Reference Service: A How-to-Do-It Manual for Librarians.* 2nd ed. How-To-Do-It Manuals for Libraries 164. New York: Neal-Schuman, 2009. ISBN: 978-1-55570-643-2.

This book include tips and strategies for basic and advanced skills for using both print and electronic resources, performance evaluation, and supplemental training for paraprofessionals assigned to answer reference questions on a daily basis. Chapters discuss statistics, medical and health information, government information, international information, and corporate information.

1345   Murphy, Sarah Anne. *The Librarian as Information Consultant: Transforming Reference for the Information Age.* Chicago: American Library Association, 2011. ISBN: 978-0-83891-086-3.

For years, librarians had a monopoly when it came to answering questions, but with so many competitors providing information (the quality or lack thereof notwithstanding), we no longer have that market cornered. For us to remain relevant to our various constituencies, Murphy argues, we have to rebrand ourselves, to use the current corporate lingo: "Reference librarians must embrace their role as library and information consultants, by first recognizing their traditional advisory role for matching consumers' information needs with the resources available to satisfy those needs, and then adapting the business model and practices of consultants working outside of the library and information science profession. In an information environment crowded with distractions and competitors for library consumers' attention, librarians must reposition themselves to maintain their effectiveness, visibility, and value to the clients they serve" (p. ix). That thesis is debatable (I submit that providing the best customer service possible is what keeps our patrons' coming back, regardless of what we call ourselves), there is nonetheless much food for thought here about running the library as if it were a business, in terms of customer relations management, marketing, consumer demand, and so on.

FYI

HISTORIC INTEREST

Early American Reference

Murfin, Marjorie E., and Lubomyr R. Wynar. *Reference Service: An Annotated Bibliographic Guide.* Littleton, CO: Libraries Unlimited, 1977. ISBN: 978-0-87287-132-8.

Covering the period 1876 to 1975, this sourcebook provides over 1,200 citations to early American reference literature. Although the individual works themselves, as detailed in the annotations, are primarily of use to those tracing the development of reference services, some subjects are timeless. Chapter 2, for example, "Theory and Philosophy of Reference Work," discusses books and articles that spell out our bedrock principles and what we as reference librarians stand for. Here and now, in the Age of Google, reference service has become much diminished in some respects, but this volume makes clear that, until quite recently, this aspect of our work was a cornerstone of the profession.

1346   Radford, Marie L., and R. David Lankes, eds. *Reference Renaissance: Current and Future Trends.* New York: Neal-Schuman, 2010. ISBN: 978-1-55570-680-7.

There is a fairly heated debate going on right now as to whether reference service is headed for extinction or experiencing a rebirth of relevance. The title of this book obviously assumes the latter scenario. These chapters were originally presented as papers at the Reference Renaissance Conference held in Denver in 2008. The editors contend that this book "demonstrates an exploration of the rapid growth and changing nature of reference, as an escalating array of information technologies blend with traditional reference service to create vibrant hybrids" (p. xv). Part 1 is "The State of Reference Services:

An Overview," which tells readers where we are right now. Part 2, "What Research Tells Us about Reference," looks at where we are going, such as the rise of virtual reference and other technological marvels. Part 3, "Reference in Action: Reports from the Field," reveals how some of the aforementioned newfangled tools are actually working and, for better or worse, affecting the delivery of reference service. Part 4, "Staff Development and Training," offers suggestions on how we can improve our service to our patrons by improving ourselves.

1347   Ross, Catherine Sheldrick, Kirsti Nilsen, and Marie L. Radford. *Conducting the Reference Interview: A How-to-Do-It Manual for Librarians.* 2nd ed. How-To-Do-It Manuals for Libraries 166. New York: Neal-Schuman, 2009. ISBN: 978-1-55570-655-5.

As we all learned in library school, the whole point of the reference interview is to get at the heart of the matter—to ascertain what the patron really wants to know. A question such as "Do you have any books on dogs?" may really mean "I just got myself a puppy and I'd like to know how to housebreak him." What we may not have learned in library school is that the give-and-take of the reference interview is both an art and a science. Theory and practice receive equal attention within these pages, the material of each chapter building on the foundation of what appears before it. The authors take the reader from "Why Bother with a Reference Interview?" (chapter 1), through necessary skill sets, touching on special situations (e.g., patrons with learning disabilities), the virtual reference interview, and finally "Establishing Policy and Training for the Reference Interview" (chapter 8). Special features include numerous sidebars with titles such as "Did You Know" (interesting research findings and facts) and "A Quick Tip" (helpful hints), exercises for putting principles into practice, and case studies. All in all, this is an excellent guide to helping us help our patrons with their information needs.

1348   Sauers, Michael P. *Searching 2.0.* New York: Neal-Schuman, 2009. ISBN: 978-1-55570-607-4.

This substantial book deals with finding information on the "new" Internet. In the past, websites were passively viewed; these days the web is interactive. Sites such as Wikipedia, for example, can be edited by anyone, and so the information contained in its articles is constantly evolving, we hope for the better. In these eleven chapters, all of which contain exercises to practice what has been learned, the author takes a look at this fast-changing electronic landscape (many of the tools he discusses did not exist a mere ten years ago). Topics covered include the "Big 3" search engines (Google, Microsoft Live, and Yahoo!), and tips and tricks for finding specific media formats, such as print, videos, and maps, are provided. This book is well illustrated with screenshots, diagrams, and photos, and a companion website contains links to resources mentioned in text.

1349   Sauers, Michael P. *Using the Internet as a Reference Tool: A How-to-Do-It Manual for Librarians.* How-To-Do-It Manuals for Libraries 109. New York: Neal-Schuman, 2001. ISBN: 978-1-55570-417-9.

A decade is a long time in Internet years, so this volume is already dated, but I include it here because of its overall excellence. Chapters on "Assessing the Impact of the Internet on Reference Services," "Evaluating Internet-Based Reference Resources," "Creating an Effective Ready Reference Strategy," "Comparing Search Engines and Directories," "Creating a Complex Reference Strategy," and "Exploring Larger Issues of Internet Reference" are concise. Appendixes offer "Ready Reference Meta Pages" (a list of librarian-created websites, such as "The Internet Public Library") and "Online Vertical Files" (a digital version of the old pamphlet and newspaper clippings libraries used to maintain, containing odd but useful bits of information). The book is well illustrated with computer screenshots.

1350 Slavens, Thomas P. *Reference Interviews, Questions, and Materials.* 3rd ed. Lanham, MD: Scarecrow Press, 2003. ISBN: 978-0-81084-741-5.

The reason for this book's existence, and it is a perfectly valid one, is the old saying "Tell me and I forget, show me and I remember, make me do and I understand." Essentially, this is a list of reference exercises to be completed by first-year students in library school. Each of the ten chapters focuses on a major category of print reference, such as encyclopedias, yearbooks, and statistical sources (although the copyright of this paperback edition is 2003, the hardcover version on which it is based is dated 1994, when the Internet was in its infancy, so online reference is absent here). Within each chapter are three subdivisions. The first offers short reference interviews (three to five questions/responses each) that were recorded verbatim; this is the real deal, giving newcomers actual examples of how patrons phrase their questions. Each interview concludes with "Where would you check?" or something similar. The second section consists of a long list of reference questions, such as this one from the chapter on handbooks: "What is the origin of April Fool's Day?" No answers are provided here (readers are required to write the publisher for such). The third section is a list of standard reference works which, at one time at least, were staples of the reference collection. This is great stuff for getting one's feet wet in print reference and not a bad way for old pros to brush up on skills that may be getting rusty.

1351 Zabel, Diane, ed. *Reference Reborn: Breathing New Life into Public Services Librarianship.* Preface by Linda C. Smith. Santa Barbara, CA: Libraries Unlimited, 2011. ISBN: 978-1-59158-828-3 (print), 978-1-59158-829-0 (e-book).

This collection of twenty-five essays looks at the myriad ways reference work is evolving, hence the "reborn" of the title. Topics include service models, new roles of reference librarians, the ever-changing technological landscape, collection development, staffing issues, and the education/training of reference librarians. Each essay concludes with a list of references cited.

✒ ADDITIONAL RESOURCES

1352 *ALA Guide to Economics and Business Reference.* Chicago: American Library Association, 2011. ISBN: 978-0-83891-024-5.

1353 *ALA Guide to Medical and Health Sciences Reference.* Chicago: American Library Association, 2011. ISBN: 978-0-83891-023-8.

1354 Anderson, Charles R., and Peter Sprenkle. *Reference Librarianship: Notes from the Trenches.* Binghamton, NY: Haworth Information Press, 2006. ISBN: 978-0-78902-947-8.

1355 Bobick, James E., and G. Lynn Berard. *Science and Technology Resources: A Guide for Information Professionals and Researchers.* Library and Information Science Text Series. Westport, CT: Libraries Unlimited, 2011. ISBN: 978-1-59158-793-4 (print), 978-1-59158-801-6 (e-book).

1356 Bradley, Phil. *Expert Internet Searching [formerly The Advanced Searcher's Handbook].* 4th ed. London: Facet, ISBN: 978-1-85604-605-3; Chicago: American Library Association, ISBN: 978-1-85604-605-3. 2013.

1357 Cassell, Kay Ann. *Developing Reference Collections and Services in an Electronic Age: A How-to-Do-It Manual for Librarians.* How-To-Do-It Manuals for Libraries 95. New York: Neal-Schuman, 1999. ISBN: 978-1-55570-363-9.

1358 Cassell, Kay Ann, and Ulma Hiremath. *Reference and Information Services in the 21st Century.* 3rd ed. London: Facet, ISBN: 978-1-85604-839-2; Chicago: American Library Association, ISBN: 978-1-55570-859-7. 2012.

1359 Coffman, Steve, P. M. Fiander, Kay Henshall, and Bernie Sloan. *Going Live: Starting and Running a Virtual Reference Service.* Chicago: American Library Association, 2003. ISBN: 978-0-83890-850-1.

1360 **Connor, Elizabeth, ed.** *An Introduction to Reference Services in Academic Libraries.* Haworth Series in Introductory Information Science Textbooks. Binghamton, NY: Haworth Information Press, 2006. ISBN: 978-0-78902-957-7.

1361 **Cooke, Alison.** *A Guide to Finding Quality Information on the Internet.* 2nd ed. London: Facet, ISBN: 978-1-85604-379-3; Chicago: American Library Association, ISBN: 978-1-85604-379-3. 2001.

1362 **Crawford, Gregory A.** *The Medical Library Association Guide to Finding Out about Complementary and Alternative Medicine.* Medical Library Association Guides. New York: Neal-Schuman, 2010. ISBN: 978-1-55570-727-9.

1363 **Duckett, Bob, Peter Walker, and Christinea Donnelly.** *Know It All, Find It Fast: An A–Z Source Guide to the Enquiry Desk.* 3rd ed. London: Facet, ISBN: 978-1-85604-652-7; Chicago: American Library Association, ISBN: 978-1-85604-534-6. 2008.

1364 **Forte, Eric, Cassandra Hartnett, and Andrea Sevetson.** *Fundamentals of Government Information: Mining, Finding, Evaluating, and Using Government Resources.* Contributions by Susan Edwards. New York: Neal-Schuman, 2011. ISBN: 978-1-55570-737-8.

1365 **Harper, Meghan.** *Reference Sources and Services for Youth.* New York: Neal-Schuman, 2011. ISBN: 978-1-55570-641-8.

1366 **Healey, Paul D.** *Legal Reference for Librarians: How and Where to Find the Answers.* Chicago: American Library Association, 2011. ISBN: 978-0-83891-117-4.

1367 **Janes, Joseph.** *Introduction to Reference Work in the Digital Age.* New York: Neal-Schuman, 2003. ISBN: 978-1-55570-429-2.

1368 **Katz, Bill, ed.** *Digital Reference Services.* Binghamton, NY: Haworth Information Press, 2003. ISBN: 978-0-78902-319-3.

1369 **Katz, William A.** *New Technologies and Reference Services.* Binghamton, NY: Haworth Information Press, 2000. Copublished simultaneously as *Reference Librarian* 38 nos. 79/80, 2002. ISBN: 978-0-78901-180-0.

1370 **Kelly, Melody S.** *Using Government Documents: A How-to-Do-It Manual for School Librarians.* How-to-Do-It Manuals for School and Public Librarians 5. New York: Neal-Schuman, 1992. ISBN: 978-1-55570-106-2.

1371 **Knoer, Susan.** *The Reference Interview Today.* Santa Barbara, CA: Libraries Unlimited, 2011. ISBN: 978-1-59884-822-9.

1372 **Kovacs, Diane K.** *Virtual Reference Handbook: Interview and Information Delivery Techniques for the Chat and E-mail Environments.* London: Facet, 2007. ISBN: 978-1-85604-626-8.

1373 **Lankes, R. David, Eileen G. Abels, Marilyn Domas White, and Saira N. Haque, eds.** *The Virtual Reference Desk: Creating a Reference Future.* New York: Neal-Schuman, 2006. ISBN: 978-1-55570-555-8.

1374 **Lankes, R. David, Scott Nicholson, Marie L. Radford, Joanne Silverstein, Lynn Westbrook, and Philip Nast, eds.** *Virtual Reference Service: From Competencies to Assessment.* London: Facet, 2008. *ISBN: 978-1-85604-638-1.*

1375 **Lanning, Scott, and John Bryner.** *Essential Reference Services for Today's School Media Specialists.* 2nd ed. Westport, CT: Libraries Unlimited, 2009. ISBN: 978-1-59158-883-2 (print), 978-0-313-39118-7 (e-book).

1376 **Lester, Ray, ed.** *The New Walford Guide to Reference Resources, Vol. 1: Science, Technology and Medicine.* London: Facet, 2005. ISBN: 978-1-85604-495-0.

1377 **Lester, Ray, Peter Clinch, Heather Dawson, Helen Edwards, and Susan Tarrant, eds.** *The New Walford Guide to Reference Resources, Vol. 2: Social Sciences.* London: Facet, 2007. ISBN: 978-1-85604-498-1.

1378 **Marmor, Max, and Alex Ross.** *Guide to the Literature of Art History 2.* Chicago: American Library Association, 2005. ISBN: 978-0-83890-878-5.

1379 **Moss, Rita W., and David G. Ernsthausen.** *Strauss's Handbook of Business Information: A Guide for Librarians, Students, and Researchers.* 3rd ed. Westport, CT: Libraries Unlimited, 2012. ISBN: 978-1-59884-807-6.

1380 **O'Gorman, Jack, ed.** *Reference Sources for Small and Medium-Sized Libraries.* 7th ed. Chicago: American Library Association, 2008. ISBN: 978-0-83890-943-0.

1381 **Owen, Tim Buckley.** *Successful Enquiry Answering Every Time (formerly Success at the Enquiry Desk).* 6th ed. London: Facet, 2012. ISBN: 978-1-85604-811-8.

1382 **Perez, Alice J., ed.** *Reference Collection Development: A Manual.* Chicago: American Library Association, 2004. ISBN: 978-0-83898-277-8.

1383 **Radford, Marie L., ed.** *Leading the Reference Renaissance: Today's Ideas for Tomorrow's Cutting-Edge Services.* New York: Neal-Schuman, 2011. ISBN: 978-1-55570-771-2.

1384 **Riedling, Ann Marlow.** *Reference Skills for the School Library Media Specialist: Tools and Tops.* 2nd ed. Westport, CT: Libraries Unlimited, 2005. ISBN: 978-1-58683-190-5.

1385 **Robinson, Lyn.** *Understanding Healthcare Information.* London: Facet, ISBN: 978-1-85604-662-6; Chicago: American Library Association, ISBN: 978-1-85604-662-6. 2010.

1386 **Ross, Celia.** *Making Sense of Business Reference: A Guide for Librarians and Research Professionals.* Chicago: American Library Association, 2011. ISBN: 978-0-83891-084-9.

1387 **Scheeren, William O.** *The Hidden Web: A Sourcebook.* Westport, CT: Libraries Unlimited, 2012. ISBN: 978-1-59884-627-0 (print), 978-1-59884-628-7 (e-book).

1388 **Singer, Carol A.** *Fundamentals of Managing Reference Collections.* ALA Fundamental Series. Chicago: American Library Association, 2012. ISBN: 978-0-83891-153-2.

1389 **Steiner, Sarah K., and M. Leslie Madden, eds.** *The Desk and Beyond: Next Generation Reference Services.* Chicago: Association of College and Research Libraries, 2008. ISBN: 978-0-83890-964-5.

1390 **Swan, James.** *The Librarian's Guide to Genealogical Services and Research.* New York: Neal-Schuman, 2004. ISBN: 978-1-55570-491-9.

1391 **Sweetland, James H., Frances N. Cheney, and Wiley J. Williams.** *Fundamental Reference Sources.* 3rd ed. Chicago: American Library Association, 2001. ISBN: 978-0-83890-780-1.

1392 **Thompson, Laurie L., Esther Carrigan, Mori Lou Higa, and Rijia Tobia, eds.** *The Medical Library Association's Master Guide to Authoritative Information Resources in the Health Sciences.* Medical Library Association Guides. New York: Neal-Schuman, 2011. ISBN: 978-1-55570-719-4.

1393 **Tucker, Virginia, and Marc Lampson.** *Finding the Answers to Legal Questions: A How-to-Do-It Manual.* How-To-Do-It Manuals for Libraries 174. New York: Neal-Schuman, 2011. ISBN: 978-1-55570-718-7.

1394 **Whitlatch, Jo Bell.** *Evaluating Reference Services: A Practical Guide.* Chicago: American Library Association, 2000. ISBN: 978-0-83890-787-0.

📖 PERIODICALS

1395 *Internet Reference Service Quarterly.* Philadelphia: Routledge. Frequency: Four times per year. ISSN: 1087-5301 (print), 1540-4749 (online). URL: www.tandf.co.uk/journals/WIRS/.

The goal of this quarterly is to update librarians on Internet reference and librarianship developments. All research articles undergo initial editor screening and then anonymous double-blind review. The journal aims to keep readers up-to-date with information on topics such as these:

- Course management systems
- Social media platforms
- Statistical packages and analyzers
- Web tutorials
- Library website innovations
- Digital or chat reference
- Internet and copyright law
- Link resolvers
- Discovery platform technologies
- Management of electronic resources
- iPods and carry-along collections on hand-held devices
- Instruction and distance education

1396   Online Information Review. Westport, CT: Emerald Group. Frequency: Six issues per year. ISSN: 1468-4527. URL: www.emeraldinsight.com/journals.htm?issn=1468-4527.

This referred journal addresses issues related to online sources, systems and services, and a broad field of online information in academic, corporate, scientific, and commercial contexts. Topics include getting the best out of search engines, key developments in the field of metadata, changing roles of the information professional, and web use and content.

1397   The Reference Librarian. Philadelphia: Routledge. Frequency: Four issues per year. ISSN: 0276-3877 (print), 541-1117 (online). URL: www.tandf.co.uk/journals/WREF/.

Under the heading of "Aims and Scope" of this publication's official website, it is stated that this quarterly aspires to be "a standard resource for everyone interested in the practice of reference work, from library and information science students to practicing reference librarians and full-time researchers. It enables readers to keep up with the changing face of reference, presenting new ideas for consideration," and features articles "about all aspects of the reference process, some research-based and some applied. Current trends and traditional questions are equally welcome. Many articles concern new electronic tools and resources, best practices in instruction and reference service, analysis of marketing of

services, and effectiveness studies." Articles are peer reviewed. According to a recent edition of *Magazines for Libraries* (Cheryl LaGuardia, ed.), this title is "recommended reading for all reference librarians."

1398   Reference Reviews. Westport, CT: Emerald Group. Frequency: Eight times per year. ISSN: 0950-4125. URL: www.emeraldinsight.com/products/journals/journals.htm?id=rr.

This magazine provides a comprehensive and unbiased appraisal of current literature and concise analyses of the latest and more significant reference materials available. Reference material review fields covered include philosophy and religion, social sciences, business, management, languages and literature, science and technology, arts, leisure and sports, geography, biography, history, and area studies. Reviews include title, author, year of publication, and quality indicators showing the significance for research and practice, originality, and readability.

1399   Reference Services Review (RSR). Westport, CT: Emerald Group. Frequency: Four times per year. ISSN: 0090-7324. URL: www.emeraldinsight.com/products/journals/journals.htm?id=rsr.

This refereed journal covers the enrichment of reference knowledge and the advancement of reference and library user services worldwide. Topics include current and best practices, service design and delivery, reference and service user services providers, service forecasting, management and assessment, existing and emerging technologies, and professional competencies for reference and user services librarians.

1400   RUSQ (Reference and User Services Quarterly). Chicago: American Library Association. Frequency: four issues per year. Print ISSN: 1094-9054. URL: www.rusq.org.

Founded in 1960 under the simpler title *RQ (Reference Quarterly)*, this official publication of the Reference and User Services Association

(RUSA, a subunit of ALA) is generally regarded as a must-read for reference folks and a must-have for library serial collections. According to the editorial policy posted on the official website, "The purpose of *Reference and User Services Quarterly* is to disseminate information of interest to reference librarians, information specialists, and other professionals involved in user-oriented library services. The scope of the journal includes all aspects of library service to adults, and reference service and collection development at every level and for all types of libraries. The journal follows a policy of double-blind refereeing of articles in advance of publication." In practical terms, feature articles tend toward the theoretical/abstract variety, that is to say, heavy on studies, surveys, and literature reviews. A case in point: "Perception and Use of PowerPoint at Library Instruction Conferences" (September 8, 2009 issue). Several columns provide good practical information in the areas of technology, management, and reader's advisory, among others, but for my money, the most valuable is the "Sources" column, which collects reviews/evaluations of recently published reference books and "professional materials," that is, books of interest to the library community. A charge applies to an annual subscription (the journal is a perk for RUSA members), much of the content from the print version is freely available online at the official website listed above.

ADDITIONAL RESOURCES

1401 *CyberSkeptic's Guide to Internet Research.* Westport, CT: Information Today. Frequency: Monthly. ISSN:. URL: www.cyberskeptic.com.

1402 *ONLINE Magazine.* Westport, CT: Information Today. Frequency: Six times per year. ISSN: 0146-5422. URL: www.infotoday.com/online/default.shtml.

1403 *Searcher.* Westport, CT: Information Today. Frequency: Ten times per year. ISSN: 1070-4795. URL: www.infotoday.com/searcher/default.asp.

WEBSITE

1404 *RUSQBlog.* Chicago: Reference and User Services Association, American Library Association. URL: http://rusa.ala.org/blog/.

The official blog of the Reference and User Services Association (RUSA, a subunit of ALA), this site includes the latest news from RUSQ; tips to help with patrons; discussion on current issues, resources, archives; and links to other RUSQ sites and services.

(1) Information Science—Research—Methodology
(2) Library Science—Research—Methodology

34

RESEARCH

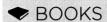 BOOKS

1405 Connaway, Lynn Silipigni, and Ronald R. Powell. *Basic Research Methods for Librarians.* 5th ed. Library and Information Science Text Series. Westport, CT: Libraries Unlimited, 2010. ISBN: 978-1-59158-863-4 (print), 978-1-59158-868-9 (e-book).

The authors cover research and librarianship: developing the research study, selecting the research method, survey research and sampling, data collection techniques, experimental research, qualitative research methods, historical research, analysis of data, and writing the research proposal and report in detail. Targeted specifically at research methodologies used by librarians, this textbook includes author and subject indexes along with a reference section.

1406 Hernon, Peter, Robert E. Dugan, and Danuta A. Nitecki. *Engaging in Evaluation and Assessment Research.* Westport, CT: Libraries Unlimited, 2011. ISBN: 978-1-59884-573-0 (print), 978-1-59884-574-7 (e-book).

The authors review current issues affecting library operations and their ability to serve patrons efficiently and effectively while remaining accountable for the results. Evaluation and assessment methods are applied to planning, decision making, and accountability. Tables and figures illustrate keys points. Readers can apply the supplemental readings and learning tools in the appendix to real-life situations and communications.

1407 Radford, Marie L., and Pamela S. Nelson, eds. *Academic Library Research: Perspectives and Current Trends.* ACRL Publications in Librarianship. Chicago: American Library Association, 2009. ISBN: 978-0-83890-983-6.

Contributors combine research, cases studies, user surveys, and theoretical scholarship to describe how advances in technology, networked systems, and the Internet have affected academic libraries. Part 1 covers perceptions and trends in reference service, information literacy, collection management, organization, and leadership. Part 2 consists of two chapters on recently developed usability testing and measurements using LibQUAL+.

1408 Wildemuth, Barbara M. *Applications of Social Research Methods to Questions in Information and Library Science.* Westport, CT: Libraries Unlimited, 2009. ISBN: 978-1-59158-503-9 (print), 978-1-59884-966-0 (e-book).

Wildemuth introduces research methods, their strengths and weaknesses, examples, and case studies. Topics covered include questions asked, research design and sampling, methods for data collection, and methods for data analysis. Different types of research designs (e.g., case studies, naturalistic research, longitudinal studies, Delphi studies) and experimental design and sampling methods (e.g., interviews, surveys, transaction log analysis, participant observation) are presented in combination. An index of the authors of examples discussed and subject index are provided.

@ ADDITIONAL RESOURCES

1409 Dobreva, Milena, Andy O'Dwyer, and Pierluigi Feliciati, eds. *User Studies for Digital Library Development.* London: Facet, ISBN: 978-1-85604-765-4; Chicago: American Library Association, ISBN: 978-1-85604-765-4. 2012.

1410 Gorman, G. E., and Peter Clayton. *Qualitative Research for the Information Professional: A Practical Handbook.* 2nd ed. London: Facet, ISBN: 978-1-85604-472-1; Chicago: American Library Association, ISBN: 978-1-85604-472-1. 2004.

1411 Moore, Nick. *How to Do Research: A Practical Guide to Designing and Managing Research Projects.* 3rd ed. London: Facet, ISBN: 978-1-85604-594-0; Chicago: American Library Association, ISBN: 978-1-85604-358-8. 2006.

1412 Pickard, Alison Jane. *Research Methods in Information.* 2nd ed. London: Facet, ISBN: 978-1-85604-813-2; Chicago: American Library Association, ISBN: 978-1-55570-936-5. 2013.

1413 Pryor, Graham. *Managing Research Data.* London: Facet, ISBN: 978-1-85604-756-2; Chicago: American Library Association, ISBN: 978-1-85604-756-2. 2012.

1414 Ward, David. *Getting the Most Out of Web-Based Surveys.* Chicago: American Library Association, 2000. ISBN: 978-0-83898-108-5.

1415 Wilson, T. D., and Elena Maceviciute, eds. *Theory in Information Behaviour Research.* London: Facet, 2012. ISBN: 978-1-85604-852-1.

🔖 PERIODICALS

1416 *Library and Information Research (LIR) (formerly Library and Information Research News).* London: Chartered Institute Library and Information Professionals. Frequency: Four times per year. ISSN: 0141-6561. URL: www.lirg.org.uk/lir/lir2.htm.

1417 *Library and Information Science Research.* Amsterdam: Elsevier. Frequency: Four times per year. ISSN: 0740-8188. URL: www.journals.elsevier.com/library-and-information-science-research/.

SERIALS

 BOOKS

1418 Black, Steve. *Serials in Libraries: Issues and Practices.* Westport, CT: Libraries Unlimited, 2006. ISBN: 978-1-59158-258-8.

This book "is designed to introduce library students and librarians with little experience in serials management to the principal themes and challenges of selecting, acquiring, receiving, and maintaining serials in libraries. Best practices will be introduced in areas where they exist. In areas where best practice is currently in flux, available choices will be described" (p. xiii). Black does an admirable job of delineating the current challenges and potential solutions to working with serial publications and has "sought to accurately and economically introduce the scope of issues facing serials librarians in a readable style that is neither too academic nor too informal" (p. xiii). The text is relatively jargon free and yet sufficiently detailed to allow the novice serials librarian to do the job properly. Nine chapters cover such topics as "Remote Access Serials," "Budgeting, Selection, and Deselection," "Serials Workflow in Libraries," and "Bibliographic Control of Serials." There is a short glossary of serials-related terms.

1419 Curtis, Donnelyn, and Virginia M. Scheschy. *E-journals: A How-to-Do-It Manual for Building, Managing, and Supporting Electronic Journal Collections.* How-To-Do-It Manuals for Libraries 134. New York: Neal-Schuman, 2004. ISBN: 978-1-55570-465-0.

The University of Nevada–Reno librarians revisit e-journals (see next entry), this time targeting library students and new librarians with little or no knowledge of digital publications. The authors look at the pros and cons of changing from print to electronic resources. Shifting library resources and trafficking in intellectual property are still relevant issues as more electronic formats become available and publishers put more focus on electronic resources.

1420 Curtis, Donnelyn, Virginia M. Scheschy, and Adolfo R. Tarango. *Developing and Managing Electronic Journal Collections: A*

How-to-Do-It Manual for Librarians. How-To-Do-It Manuals for Libraries 102. New York: Neal-Schuman, 2000. ISBN: 978-1-55570-383-7.

Developed by University of Nevada–Reno librarians, this manual provides a comprehensive overview of e-journal collection management. Topics include an introduction to e-journals, selection, ordering, licensing, technical issues, cataloging, and user services. Two sample collection policies, sample forms, charts, sample catalog records, and checklists, along with easy-to-follow instructions, make e-journals easier to manage.

1421 Genereux, Cecilia, and Paul D. Moeller, eds. *Notes for Serials Cataloging.* 3rd ed. Westport, CT: Libraries Unlimited, 2009. ISBN: 978-1-59158-653-1.

This in-depth look at serials cataloging is arranged in MARC tag order and by topical subdivision to allow periodical professionals to describe complex characteristics and relationships clearly and concisely. This latest edition addresses the huge influx of electronic journals and online subscriptions. Extremely detailed notes cover all aspects of serial catalog entries. Sources, works consulted and cited, and index are provided.

1422 Jones, Wayne, ed. *E-journals Access and Management.* Routledge Studies in Library and Information Science Series 5. New York: Routledge, 2009. ISBN: 978-0-78903-385-7.

E-journals have changed library services and collections, creating a range of issues such as budget impact, accessibility, copyright, and web access. Contributors offer various strategies to deal with the massive proliferation of e-journals and e-journal access requests. Topics include copyright, open-access journals, digital preservation, research, knowledge base maintenance, electronic systems, and collaborations. Practical information is presented using case studies, electronic resource management tips, and bibliographic resources.

1423 LaGuardia, Cheryl, ed. *Magazines for Libraries.* Created by Bill Katz. 20th ed. Ann Arbor, MI: ProQuest , 2011. ISBN: 978-1-60030-633-4.

Essentially, this is an annotated bibliography of magazine titles deemed suitable for libraries. Approximately 5,000 titles are broken down into about 170 categories, ranging from "General Interest" to quite specialized fields such as "Accounting and Taxation" and "Paleontology." Each such section begins with several paragraphs of introductory material on the topic at hand, followed by the listings themselves. Entries present basic factual information—publisher, ISSN, frequency and price, and so forth—followed by an analysis of the content of the title that focuses on scope, purpose, editorial slant, and intended audience.

1424 Lawson, Karen G., ed. *Serial Collection Management in Recessionary Times.* New York: Routledge, 2011. ISBN: 978-0-415-58961-1.

Previously published as a special issue of *Serials Librarian*, these contributions examine global technological and economic challenges in libraries and higher education as they relate to the periodicals collection. Key topics include maximizing resources, using database management programs to support purchase decisions, shared digital access, and assessment of vendor viability.

1425 Millard, Scott. *Introduction to Serials Work for Library Technicians.* Binghamton, NY: Haworth Press, 2004. ISBN: 978-0-78902-154-0.

This primer covers everything serial related: journals, magazines, newspapers, monograph series, and more. Twelve concisely written chapters take a beginning-to-end approach, starting with "Introduction to Serials Work" and then, in succession, examining each step of the process, such as acquisitions, ordering, receipt/check-in of serials, cataloging, processing, binding, and renewals. There is no preface or introduction, but the back cover blurb states that "the complete glossary, bibliography, numerous definitions, figures and tables, as well as the real-life examples throughout this manual, will help you navigate the challenges of record keeping, claiming, and cataloging serials in any library."

1426 Nicola, Irma. *Serials Binding: A Simple and Complete Guidebook to Processes.* Routledge Studies in Library and Information Science Series 7. New York: Routledge, 2009. ISBN: 978-0-78902-504-3 (print), 978-0-20386-439-5 (e-book).

Nicola presents step-by-step information for faculty and staff to begin a journal-binding project at their school library. This guide includes how to select serials for binding, manual binding procedures, and how to obtain funding for the projects. A photo essay illustrates how the automated binding process works. The author reviews user statistics, vendors, and inventory along with disaster planning and preparedness. The workflow concept-to-completion chapter is especially useful to the novice binder.

1427 *Ulrich's Periodicals Directory, 2012.* 50th ed. 4 vols. Ann Arbor, MI: ProQuest, 2012. ISBN: 978-1-60030-632-7.

In print since 1932, this is the ultimate compendium of serial publications. International in scope, this work covers the waterfront, offering basic bibliographic information on popular magazines, scholarly journals, newspapers, and so on, published in a variety of languages; roughly 220,000 entries are classified under 903 separate subject headings. Contents include ISSNs, serials available online, producer listings, online service listings, user guides, daily newspapers, weekly newspapers, and an index to publications. An especially useful feature is the designation of abstracting and indexing services where individual publications may be found.

@ ADDITIONAL RESOURCES

1428 Bartel, Julie. *From A to Zine: Building a Winning Zine Collection in Your Library.* Chicago: American Library Association, 2004. ISBN: 978-0-83890-886-0.

1429 Basch, N. Bernard, and Judy McQueen. *Buying Serials: A How-to-Do-It Manual for Librarians.* How-To-Do-It Manuals for Librarians 10. New York: Neal-Schuman, 1990. ISBN: 978-1-55570-058-4.

1430 Bluh, Pamela M., and Brad Eden, eds. *Managing Electronic Serials: Essays Based on the ALCTS Electronic Serials Institutes 1997–1999.* ALCTS Papers on Library Technical Services and Collections 9. Chicago: American Library Association, 2001. ISBN: 978-0-83893-510-1.

1431 Lightman, Harriet, and John P. Blosser, eds. *Perspectives on Serials in the Hybrid Environment.* ALCTS Papers on Library Technical Services and Collections 15. Chicago: American Library Association, 2007. ISBN: 978-0-83898-415-4.

1432 Nisonger, Thomas E. *Management of Serials in Libraries.* Englewood, CO: Libraries Unlimited, 1998. ISBN: 978-1-56308-213-9.

▤ PERIODICAL

1433 *The Serials Librarian.* Philadelphia: Routledge. Frequency: Four issues per year. ISSN: 0361-526X (print), 1541-1095 (online). URL: www.tandf.co.uk/journals/WSER/.

Articles cover serials management in any format (print, electronic, etc.), ranging from publication to abstracting and indexing by commercial services and collection and processing by libraries. The journal's main audience is librarians and other library staff working in collection development, acquisitions, cataloging/metadata, and information technology. All articles undergo editorial screening and double-blind review.

@ ADDITIONAL RESOURCE

1434 *Serials Review.* Amsterdam: Elsevier. Frequency: Four issues per year. ISSN: 0098-7913. URL: www.journals.elsevier.com/library-and-information-science-research/.

⬈ DATABASES

1435 *Academic Search Premier.*
www.ebscohost.com/academic/academic
-search-premier/.

Although designed specifically for college and university students and faculty, hence its name, this subscription database is equally useful in public library settings. An indexing/abstracting service, *Premier* provides full-text access to articles from about 4,600 journal titles representing a broad range of topics: chemistry, biology, mathematics, philosophy, and many others. The majority of these are peer-reviewed journals. There are about twice the number of journal titles for which only abstracts/summaries are provided. With a generous amount of content and a user-friendly interface for conducting searches, this is generally regarded as one of the better buys for the library dollar.

1436 *Directory of Open Access Journals (DOAJ).* www.doaj.org.

The phrase "open access" refers to publications with no copyright restrictions. They are, quite literally, "open," that is, free to access and copy by anyone, anywhere at any time. On the home page of this website, under the heading of "Aim and Scope," it is stated that "the aim of the Directory of Open Access Journals is to increase the visibility and ease of use of open access scientific and scholarly journals, thereby promoting their increased usage and impact. The Directory aims to be comprehensive and cover all open access scientific and scholarly journals that use a quality control system [read: peer reviewed] to guarantee the content. In short, a one-stop shop for users to Open Access Journals." As of this writing, there are approximately 7,000 journals available, 125 of which fall under the heading of "Library and Information Science." Because this site is international in scope, many of these periodicals appear in foreign languages. Links to individual journals include basic bibliographic information such as title of journal, ISSN, subject, country of origin, language of publication, and year the journal was founded.

SPECIAL, ACADEMIC, AND SCHOOL LIBRARIES AND LIBRARIANS

◆ BOOKS

1437 *A Basic Music Library: Essential Scores and Sound Recordings.* 4th ed. Chicago: American Library Association, 2014. ISBN: 978-0-83891-039-9.

The preface to the 1997 edition states that this work "is a selection and buying guide to printed musical scores and sound recordings, intended for use by librarians and others who are responsible for collecting music materials" (p. xi). Although published by ALA, this work, like its predecessor editions, has been compiled by a committee from the Music Library Association. Entries include CDs, DVDs, songbooks, printed scores, and sound performances, but not books and magazines. Individual entries include anthologies, study scores, performing renditions, vocal scores, and instrumental methods of studies. The classical music section is organized by genre, composer, and title. Popular music is organized according to genre and artist, and the world music section is organized by geographic area, genre, and artist. An index is provided for this 10,000-entry edition.

1438 Baumbach, Donna J., and Linda L. Miller. *Less Is More: A Practical Guide to Weeding School Library Collections.* Chicago: American Library Association, 2006. ISBN: 978-0-83890-919-5.

This comprehensive guide describes why weeding a collection is important, how to get started, weeding criteria, the impact automation brings, and future possibilities. Weeding resources on the web, weeding criteria by topic and Dewey number appendix, alphabetical index, and index by Dewey classification are included.

1439 Besnoy, Amy, ed. *Emerging Practices in Science and Technology Librarianship.* New York: Routledge, 2010. ISBN: 978-0-41560-432-1.

Contributors examine emerging practices of science and technology librarians through collection development and resource access in dire economic times. Targeted toward scholars and professional librarians, most of the discussion focuses on curriculum design and delivery, lifelong learning, information integration, and STEM curriculum. In addition, chapters address hidden costs, social networking, digital services, case studies, and the trend to merge information technology and library staff into one department. This book was originally published as a special issue of the *Journal of Library Administration*.

1440   Bishop, Kay. *Connecting Libraries with Classrooms: The Curricular Roles of the Media Specialist.* 2nd ed. Santa Barbara, CA: Linworth, 2011. ISBN: 978-1-59884-599-0 (print), 978-1-59884-600-3 (e-book).

This second edition covers collaboration and partnerships within the school setting along with the role of the librarian in K–12 curriculum development. Much of the book is spent looking at special audiences, such as reading in the elementary school, music in the middle school, English as a second language, autistic students, mobile students, and student with gay, lesbian, bisexual, or transgender orientation. Chapters are also devoted to educational trends including Web 2.0 and distance education. A bibliography and index are included.

1441   Brophy, Peter. *The Academic Library.* 2nd ed. London: Facet, ISBN: 978-1-85604-527-8; Chicago: American Library Association, ISBN: 978-1-85604-527-8. 2005.

This textbook looks at the changing missions of higher education libraries and the environment in which they operate. A wide range of topics—users, location, systems, networks, specialization, management, and professional behavior—provide a broad understanding targeted toward library science students and professionals entering the library field.

1442   Bush, Gail, and Jami Biles Jones, eds. *Tales out of the School Library: Developing Professional Dispositions.* Foreword by Theodore R. Sizer. Westport, CT: Libraries Unlimited, 2009. ISBN: 978-1-59158-832-0 (print), 978-1-59158-833-7 (e-book).

The authors create three fictional librarians with distinctive personalities, quirks, skill sets, and shortfalls; these composite figures borrow the traits of real-life elementary, middle, and high school librarians. In each chapter, the librarians face real-life problems with dispositions, basics, instructional strategies, assessment, diversity, literacy, communication, resilience, leadership, professional ethics, and more. Suggested actions in the follow-up to the dilemma connect to American Association of School Librarian (AASL) standards, and each chapter concludes with discussion questions. AASL standards, quotations, bibliography, information about the authors and contributors, and index are included.

1443   Coatney, Sharon, ed. *The Many Faces of School Library Leadership.* Westport, CT: Libraries Unlimited, 2010. ISBN: 978-1-59158-893-1 (print), 978-1-59158-894-8 (e-book).

Contributors discuss the multitude of opportunities available to implement change and provide guidance. The book opens with a discussion of specific competencies, behaviors, relationships, influence, and leadership for the modern-day librarian before moving on to discussion of roles, such as librarian as learning leader, advocacy leader, and curriculum leader. Several articles discuss librarians' influence in the preservation of minors' rights, promoting literacy, developing pride, and eliminating prejudice. Two chapters are devoted to staff development and participation in professional library association activities. An index and information about the editor and contributors are included.

1444   Copeland, Barbara S., and Patricia A. Messner. *Collaborative Library Lessons for the Primary Grades: Linking Research Skills to Curriculum Standards.* Westport, CT: Libraries Unlimited, 2005. ISBN: 978-1-59158-185-7.

This is a collection of lesson plans to be used in collaboration with classroom instructors to meet science and social studies curriculum standards. Each lesson plan uses standard reference material and includes patterns, worksheets, and all instructions necessary to implement the lesson.

Reference materials used are encyclopedias, almanacs, atlases, the online catalog, and the Internet. Themes cover biographies, animals, insects, state puzzles, scavenger hunts, and more. A bibliography and index are included.

1445 Doll, Carol A., and Beth Doll. *The Resilient School Library.* Westport, CT: Libraries Unlimited, 2010. ISBN: 978-1-59158-639-5.

Children must be resilient in order to grow up successful, content, and competent even though they may be exposed to violence, poverty, illness, or neglect. The authors dedicate a chapter to each of six elements of resilience before concluding with a chapter on educational strategies and instructional techniques librarians can use to support at-risk children. They provide examples, a copyrights survey instrument, a planning template, supplementary graphs, charts, and tables. An appendix includes ClassMaps for school libraries.

1446 Dugan, Robert E., Peter Hernon, and Danuta Nitecki. *Viewing Library Metrics from Different Perspectives: Inputs, Outputs, and Outcomes.* Westport, CT: Libraries Unlimited, 2010. ISBN: 978-1-59158-665-4.

"If it can't be measured, it can't be managed" is a favorite saying among administrative types. Metrics are all about measurement, and this volume gives the academic library manager about 100 different yardsticks to do so. The first three chapters introduce library metrics, related literature, and assessment and evaluation. The next four chapters look at library, customer, institutional, and stakeholder perspectives. Other chapters cover how metrics are used in benchmarking, best practices, marketing, public relations, management information systems, and, finally, presentations and communications. Numerous appendixes provided several examples of metrics—as numbers, ratios, and percentages for inputs, outputs, processes, trends, customers, infrastructure, and more. A bibliography and index are provided.

1447 Duke, Lynda M., and Andrew D. Asher, eds. *College Libraries and Student Culture: What We Now Know.* Chicago: American Library Association, 2011. ISBN: 978-0-83891-116-7.

The editors present the results of a Library Services and Technology Act grant awarded to five large Illinois universities to research how college students conduct research for class assignments. The user-centered approach to evaluating library services looked at ethnographic research, pragmatism, and idealism; learning for teaching faculty; student help-seeking behaviors; supporting academic success; first-generation student needs; and transformative changes in library thinking, services, and programs. Interview guide questions, bibliography, contributors, and index are included.

1448 Fontichiaro, Kristin, ed. *21st Century Learning in School Libraries.* Santa Barbara, CA: Libraries Unlimited, 2009. ISBN: 978-1-59158-895-5 (print), 978-1-59158-896-2 (e-book).

Contributors examine standards, learners, media programs, media specialists, reading, inquiry, assessment, and collaboration for the twenty-first-century learner. Each chapter includes an introduction, discussion questions, promotional ideas, and advocacy strategies for the theme under discussion. Ideas for building a toolkit of instructional strategies explore ways librarians can support curriculum activities. Elementary lesson plans cover reading, writing, social studies, and science, along with secondary lesson plans for language arts, government, social studies, and science that incorporate library services. References, recommended readings, and an index are provided.

1449 Forte, Eric, and Michael Oppenheim, eds. *The Basic Business Library: Core Resources and Services.* 5th ed. Westport, CT: Libraries Unlimited, 2011. ISBN: 978-1-59884-611-9 (print), 978-1-59884-612-6 (e-book).

Contributors focus on what the library's core collection must offer to meet business community demand. A range of topics includes resources for the accidental business librarian, accessing business literature, core business periodicals, government information sources, investment sources, marketing research, and advice and strategies for asking/answering business research and reference questions. Information about the editor and contributors and index are included.

1450 Gilmore-See, Janice. *Simply Indispensable: An Action Guide for School Librarians.* Santa Barbara, CA: Libraries Unlimited, 2010. ISBN: 978-1-59158-799-6 (print), 978-1-59158-800-9 (e-book).

Something of a survival guide for school librarians, this title takes the position that media specialists cannot assume that doing a good job will get administrators to sit up and take notice. With titles such as "The InterACTive Librarian," "The ProACTive Librarian," and so on, the message is clear: If you don't want to be a target for budget cuts, you must go on the offensive. In a word, this means advocacy, and it is up to the school librarian to do the advocating. The book covers such strategies for building a fan base as letter writing, using social media for spreading the good word, and collaborating/building relationships. Similar title alert: This book is not to be confused with *Being Indispensable* (see entry 60), which also deals with school librarianship.

1451 Hart, Thomas L. *The School Library Media Facilities Planner.* New York: Neal-Schuman, 2006. ISBN: 978-1-55570-503-9.

Hart covers pre-planning, planning, and designing a library media center in detail and accounts for the needs of elementary, middle, and secondary schools. Architectural styles, terminology, and floor plans are accompanied by organizational worksheets, planning documents, contracts, and example requests for bids. This volume includes a DVD that shows several Florida libraries and allows the viewer to hear librarians describe the pros and cons of their individual library designs.

1452 Hernon, Peter, and Ronald R. Powell, eds. *Convergence and Collaboration of Campus Information Services.* Westport, CT: Libraries Unlimited, 2008. ISBN: 978-1-59158-603-6.

This collection of articles examines how campus departments can partner with their libraries to provide a more comprehensive approach to teaching, research, and shared services. Contributors discuss organizational structure changes, allocation of resources, and service outcomes in eleven cases studies. Extensive notes provide insight into this academic approach to centers for teaching excellence, tutor and writing centers, centers for distance learning, and other student-focused delivery methods.

1453 Kelsey, Sigrid E., and Marjorie J. Porter, eds. *Best Practices for Corporate Libraries.* Westport, CT: Libraries Unlimited, 2011. ISBN: 978-1-59884-737-6 (print), 978-1-59884-738-3 (e-book).

Contributors emphasize return on investment, measurement and evaluation, collaboration, communication, and outreach services that are provided within a corporate structure. Case studies, surveys, interviews, and performance evaluation are some tools used to illustrate best practices for services and facilities, communication and networking, management, marketing, demonstrating value, change management, and reorganization. A chapter on the current state of libraries is intended to spur discussion among librarians on how to be more proactive and implement best practices in corporate libraries.

1454 MacDonald, Karen, and Hal Kirkwood, eds. *Business Librarianship and Entrepreneurship Outreach.* New York: Routledge, 2011. ISBN: 978-0-41568-976-2.

This slim volume looks at how business information needs create opportunities for librarians to be proactive and reach out to form partnerships in business development and entrepreneurship instruction. Case studies provide real-life examples of librarians providing value-added support for entrepreneurship education and local economic development. Contributors describe how to mine repositories of information to obtain and present business and economic data. This book was published as a special double issue of the *Journal of Business and Finance Librarianship*.

1455 Matthews, Joseph R. *The Bottom Line: Determining and Communicating the Value of the Special Library.* Library and Information Science Text Series. Westport, CT: Libraries Unlimited, 2002. ISBN: 978-1-59158-004-1.

Matthews tackles the age-old problem of too much to do and too little money to do it with. This book contains evaluation techniques, various input and output measurements, and how to build a balance scorecard while positioning the library as a "value center" to gain financial support. The appendixes include input measures and sample surveys.

1456 McCain, Mary Maude, and Martha Merrill. *Dictionary for School Library Media Specialists: A Practical and Comprehensive Guide.* Englewood, CO: Libraries Unlimited, 2001. ISBN: 978-1-56308-696-0.

The terms in this dictionary are listed in alphabetical order in the letter-by-letter style, which ignores spaces, punctuation, and numbers in the entry titles. Although there is no pronunciation guide, over 375 glossary descriptions have longer and more detailed explanations so school library professionals may more easily communicate with their colleagues.

1457 Messner, Patricia A., and Brenda S. Copeland. *School Library Spaces: Just the Basics.* Santa Barbara, CA: Libraries Unlimited, 2011. ISBN: 978-1-59884-805-2. EISBN: 978-1-59884-806-9.

The authors provide several diagrams, checklists, and resources to help the librarian with space organization, placement and labeling, and shelving. Topics covered include shelving and book arrangement, story corner, circulation desk, periodicals, decorations, signage, storage, bulletin boards, and furnishing. A resources list and index are included.

1458 Repman, Judi, and Gail K. Dickinson, eds. *School Library Management.* 6th ed. Columbus, OH: Linworth, 2007. ISBN: 978-1-58683-296-4.

Contributors cover the basics of running a successful school library in this fully updated edition. They begin with a discussion of librarianship before delving into ethics, collaboration, administration, professional growth, and staff development. Each section begins with a brief introduction that highlights key issues and technological challenges. Print and web-based resources and author/title/subject index are included.

1459 Smith, Geoffrey D., Steven K. Galbraith, and Joel B. Silver. *Rare Book Librarianship: An Introduction and Guide.* Westport, CT: Libraries Unlimited, 2012. ISBN: 978-1-59158-881-8 (print), 978-1-59158-882-5 (e-book).

Targeting practitioners in academic, large public, or specialty libraries, the authors describe the core skills and knowledge needed to be a successful rare book librarian. They cover topics such as handling, housing, and conserving rare materials along with collection development, user education, and outreach. The book also includes information on the role of digital technologies in a rare book collection.

1460 Steinberg, Avi. *Running the Books: The Adventures of an Accidental Prison Librarian.* New York: Anchor Books, 2011. ISBN: 978-0-76793-131-1.

Steinberg divides this part memoir, part exposé, part autobiography about working at a Boston prison into two parts, "Undelivered" and "Delivered." He describes his struggle not to cross a blurry line between providing library services and enabling unacceptable behavior. These tales illustrate the oft-told story of a person hired for a position because of his qualifications who then fails, not because of his work performance but through the organization's failure to provide sufficient training to deal with the face-to-face interaction with customers and expected appeasement by staff and supervisors.

1461 Zabel, Diane, ed. *Career Paths and Career Development of Business Librarians.* New York: Routledge, 2009. ISBN: 978-0-78903-794-7.

Traditional and nontraditional business librarianship in various environments follows different career paths and requires various skill sets and competencies. Contributors look at supply and demand to explore mentorships, succession planning, burnout strategies, academic pursuits, networking, business references, and career transitions. Some professional growth strategies include taking academic classes, working abroad, obtaining a fellowship, or teaching future librarians. This book was first published as a special issue of the *Journal of Business and Finance Librarianship.*

1462 Zmuda, Allison, and Violet H. Harada. *Librarians as Learning Specialists: Meeting the Learning Imperative for the 21st Century.* Foreword by Grant Wiggins. Westport, CT: Libraries Unlimited, 2008. ISBN: 978-1-59158-679-1 (print), 978-0313-36375-7 (e-book).

There is an increasing number of school job descriptions for learning specialist certified teachers that incorporate librarian core competences to increase the school's ability for improved student achievement. Zmuda and Harada integrate examples, quotes, and research results from mainstream and librarian-focused education literature to empower librarian learning specialists to take a leadership role by acquiring material, providing access to online resources, assessing performance, and sharing knowledge.

@ ADDITIONAL RESOURCES

1463 Bergart, Robin, and Vivian Lewis. *Sudden Selector's Guide to Business Resources.* ALCTS/CMDS Sudden Selector's Series. Chicago: American Library Association, 2007. ISBN: 978-0-83898-414-7.

1464 Bradbury, Judy. *The Read-Aloud Scaffold: Best Books to Enhance Content Area Curriculum, Grades Pre-K–3.* Santa Barbara, CA: Libraries

Unlimited, 2011. ISBN: 978-1-59884-684-3 (print), 978-1-59884-685-0 (e-book).

1465 Bell, Steven J., and John D. Shank. *Academic Librarianship by Design: A Blended Librarian's Guide to the Tools and Techniques.* Chicago: American Library Association, 2007. ISBN: 978-0-83890-939-3.

1466 Benedetti, Joan M., ed. *Art Museum Libraries and Librarianship.* Foreword by Michael Brand. Contributions by Ann B. Abid. Lanham, MD: Scarecrow Press, 2007. ISBN: 978-0-81085-918-0.

1467 Brake, Kate Vanda, ed. *Tips and Other Bright Ideas for Secondary School Libraries.* Vol. 4. Westport, CT: Libraries Unlimited, 2010. ISBN: 978-1-58683-418-0 (print), 978-1-58683-419-7 (e-book).

1468 Brettle, Alison, and Christine Urquhart, eds. *Changing Roles and Contexts for Health Library and Information Professionals.* London: Facet, 2011. ISBN: 978-1-85604-740-1.

1469 Budd, John M. *The Changing Academic Library: Operations, Culture, Environments.* ACRL Publications in Librarianship 56. Chicago: American Library Association, 2005. ISBN: 978-0-83898-318-8.

1470 Bush, Gail. *The School Buddy System: The Practice of Collaboration.* Chicago: American Library Association, 2003. ISBN: 978-0-83890-839-6.

1471 Cihak, Herbert E., Joan S. Howland, and American Association of Law Libraries, eds. *Leadership Roles for Librarians.* AALL Publication Series. Littleton, CO: Fred B. Rothman, 2002. ISBN: 978-0-83770-154-7.

1472 Coombs, James A. *Great Moments in Map Librarianship: Cartoons from the First 30 Years of Base Line.* Chicago: Map and Geography Round Table American Library Association, 2010. ISBN: 978-0-83898-555-7.

1473 Crowley, John D. *Developing a Vision: Strategic Planning for the School Librarian in the*

21st Century. 2nd ed. Libraries Unlimited Professional Guides in School Librarianship. Westport, CT: Libraries Unlimited, 2011. ISBN: 978-1-59158-891-7 (print), 978-1-59158-892-4 (e-book).

1474 Dawson, Heather. *Know It All: Find It Fast for Academic Libraries.* London: Facet, ISBN: 978-1-85604-759-3; Chicago: American Library Association, ISBN: 978-1-85604-759-3. 2011.

1475 Dickinson, Gail K. *Achieving National Board Certification for School Library Media Specialists: A Study Guide.* Chicago: American Library Association, 2006. ISBN: 978-0-83890-901-0.

1476 Donnelly, Christinea. *Know It All: Find It Fast for Youth Librarians and Teachers.* London: Facet, ISBN: 978-1-85604-761-6; Chicago: American Library Association, ISBN: 978-1-85604-761-6. 2011.

1477 *Empowering Learners: Guidelines for School Library Media Programs.* Chicago: American Library Association, 2009. ISBN: 978-0-83898-519-9.

1478 Fritts, Jack E., Jr., ed. *Mistakes in Academic Library Management: Grievous Errors and How to Avoid Them.* Lanham, MD: Scarecrow Press, 2012. ISBN: 978-0-81086-744-4.

1479 Gaskell, Carolyn C., and Allen S. Morrill, comps. *Travel, Sabbatical, and Study Leave Policies in College Libraries.* Clip Notes 30. Chicago: American Library Association, 2001. ISBN: 978-0-83898-164-1.

1480 Gavigan, Karen W., and Mindy Tomasevich. *Connecting Comics to Curriculum: Strategies for Grades 6–12.* Santa Barbara, CA: Libraries Unlimited, 2011. ISBN: 978-1-59884-768-0 (print), 978-1-59884-769-7 (e-book).

1481 Gibbons, Susan. *The Academic Library and the Net Gen Student: Making the Connections.* Chicago: American Library Association, 2007. ISBN: 978-0-83890-946-1.

1482 Gluibizzi, Amanda, and Paul Glassman, eds. *The Handbook of Art and Design*

Librarianship. London: Facet, ISBN: 978-1-85604-702-9; Chicago: American Library Association, ISBN: 978-1-85604-702-9. 2010.

1483 Hand, Dorcas, ed. *Independent School Libraries: Perspectives on Excellence.* Libraries Unlimited Professional Guides in School Librarianship. Westport, CT: Libraries Unlimited, 2010. ISBN: 978-1-59158-803-0 (print), 978-1-59158-812-2 (e-book).

1484 Hanson, Terry. *Managing Academic Support Services in Universities: The Convergence Experience.* London: Facet, 2005. ISBN: 978-1-85604-525-4.

1485 Hardesty, Larry L., ed. *Books, Bytes, and Bridges: Libraries and Computer Centers in Academic Institutions.* Chicago: American Library Association, 2000. ISBN: 978-0-83890-771-9.

1486 Harvey II, Carl A. *The 21st Century Elementary Library Media Program.* Westport, CT: Libraries Unlimited, 2010. ISBN: 978-1-58683-381-7. EISN: 978-1-58683-407-4.

1487 Herb, Steven, and Sara Willoughby-Herb. *Using Children's Books in Preschool Settings: A How-to-Do-It Manual.* How-to-Do-It Manuals for School and Public Librarians 14. New York: Neal-Schuman, 1994. ISBN: 978-1-55570-156-7.

1488 Hughes-Hassell, Sandra, and Violet H. Harada, eds. *School Reform and the School Library Media Specialist.* Westport, CT: Libraries Unlimited, 2007. ISBN: 978-1-59158-427-8.

1489 Johnson, Doug. *School Libraries Head for the Edge: Rants, Recommendations, and Reflections.* Westport, CT: Libraries Unlimited, 2009. ISBN: 978-1-58683-392-3 (print), 978-1-58683-408-1 (e-book).

1490 Jones, Jami Biles, and Alana M. Zambone. *The Power of the Media Specialist to Improve Academic Achievement and Strengthen At-Risk Students.* Westport, CT: Libraries Unlimited, 2008. ISBN: 978-1-58683-229-2 (print), 978-1-58683-354-1 (e-book).

1491 Karp, Jesse. *Graphic Novels in Your School Library.* Illustrations by Rush Kress. Chicago: American Library Association, 2011. ISBN: 978-0-83891-089-4.

1492 Kohrman, Rita, ed. *Curriculum Materials Collections and Centers: Legacies from the Past, Visions of the Future.* Chicago: Association of College and Research Libraries, American Library Association, 2012. ISBN: 978-0-83898-602-8.

1493 Levy, Philippa, and Sue Roberts, eds. *Developing the New Learning Environment: The Changing Role of the Academic Librarian.* London: Facet, ISBN: 978-1-85604-530-8; Chicago: American Library Association, ISBN: 978-1-85604-530-8. 2005.

1494 Lukenbill, W. Bernard, and Barbara Froling Immroth. *Health Information in a Changing World: Practical Approaches for Teachers, Schools, and School Librarians.* Westport, CT: Libraries Unlimited, 2010. ISBN: 978-1-59884-398-9 (print), 978-1-59884-399-6 (e-book).

1495 MacDonnell, Colleen. *Essential Documents for School Libraries.* 2nd ed. Westport, CT: Libraries Unlimited, 2010. ISBN: 978-1-58683-400-5 (print), 978-1-58683-411-1 (e-book).

1496 Macrea-Gibson, Rowena. *The Academic Librarian's Handbook.* London: Facet, ISBN: 978-1-85604-758-6; Chicago: American Library Association, ISBN: 978-1-85604-758-6. 2014.

1497 Markless, Sharon, ed. *Innovative School Librarian.* Contributions by Elizabeth Bentley, Sarah Pavey, Sue Shaper, Sally Todd, and Carol Webb. London: Facet, 2009. ISBN: 978-1-85604-653-4.

1498 Martin, Ann M. *Seven Steps to an Award Winning School Library Program.* 2nd ed. Westport, CT: Libraries Unlimited, 2012. ISBN: 978-1-59884-766-6 (print), 978-1-59884-767-3 (e-book).

1499 Matthews, Joseph R. *Library Assessment in Higher Education.* Westport, CT: Libraries Unlimited, 2007. ISBN: 978-1-59158-531-2.

1500 *Maximizing Law Library Productivity.* New York: Primary Research Group, 2008. ISBN: 978-1-57440-077-9.

1501 McAdoo, Monty L. *Building Bridges: Connecting Faculty, Students, and the College Library.* Chicago: American Library Association, 2010. ISBN: 978-0-83891-019-1.

1502 McKnight, Sue, ed. *Envisioning Future Academic Library Services: Initiatives, Ideas and Challenges.* London: Facet, ISBN: 978-1-85604-691-6; Chicago: American Library Association, ISBN: 978-1-85604-691-6. 2010.

1503 Mincic-Obradovic, Ksenija. *E-books in Academic Libraries.* Cambridge, UK: Woodhead, 2010. ISBN: 978-1-84334-586-2.

1504 Nabe, Jonathan A. *Starting, Strengthening, and Managing Institutional Repositories: A How-to-Do-It Manual.* How-To-Do-It Manuals for Libraries 69. New York: Neal-Schuman, 2009. ISBN: 978-1-55570-689-0.

1505 Nebraska Educational Media Association. *Guide for Developing and Evaluating School Library Programs.* 7th ed. Westport, CT: Libraries Unlimited, 2010. ISBN: 978-1-59158-717-0.

1506 Oakleaf, Megan, comp. *The Value of Academic Libraries: A Comprehensive Research Review and Report.* Chicago: American Library Association, 2010. ISBN: 978-0-83898-568-7.

1507 Oldroyd, Margaret, ed. *Developing Academic Library Staff for Future Success.* London: Facet, ISBN: 978-1-85604-478-3; Chicago: American Library Association, ISBN: 978-1-85604-478-3. 2004.

1508 Parry, Robert B., and C. R. Perkins, eds. *The Map Library in the New Millennium.* Chicago: American Library Association, 2001. ISBN: 978-0-83893-518-7.

1509 Peters, Diane E. *International Students and Academic Libraries: A Survey of Issues and Annotated Bibliography.* Lanham, MD: Scarecrow Press, 2012. ISBN: 978-0-81087-429-9.

1510   Rourke, James. *The Comic Book Curriculum: Using Comics to Enhance Learning and Life.* Santa Barbara, CA: Libraries Unlimited, 2010. ISBN: 978-1-59884-396-5 (print), 978-1-59884-397-2 (e-book).

1511   Safford, Barbara Ripp. *Guide to Reference Materials for School Library Media Centers.* 6th ed. Westport, CT: Libraries Unlimited, 2010. ISBN: 978-1-59158-277-9.

1512   Scheeren, William O. *Technology for the School Librarian: Theory and Practice.* Westport, CT: Libraries Unlimited, 2010. ISBN: 978-1-59158-900-6 (print), 978-1-59158-901-3 (e-book).

1513   Schopflin, Katharine, ed. *A Handbook for Media Librarians.* London: Facet, ISBN: 978-1-85604-630-5; Chicago: American Library Association, ISBN: 978-1-85604-630-5. 2004.

1514   Sinder, Janet, ed. *Law Librarians Abroad.* Copublished simultaneously as *Legal Reference Services Quarterly* 18, no. 3, 2000. New York: Haworth Press, 2000. ISBN: 978-0-78901-316-3.

1515   *Standards for the 21st Century Learner in Action.* Chicago: American Library Association, 2009. ISBN: 978-0-83898-507-6.

1516   Stein, Barbara L., and Risa W. Brown. *Running a School Library Media Center: A How-to-Do-It Manual for Librarians.* 2nd ed. How-To-Do-It Manuals for Libraries 121. New York: Neal-Schuman, 2002. ISBN: 978-1-55570-439-1.

1517   Stephens, Claire Gatrell, and Patricia Franklin. *Library 101: A Handbook for the School Library Media Specialist.* Westport, CT: Libraries Unlimited, 2007. ISBN: 978-1-59158-324-0.

1518   Torrans, Lee A. *Law for K–12 Libraries and Librarians.* Westport, CT: Libraries Unlimited, 2003. ISBN: 978-1-59158-036-2.

1519   *Training College Students in Information Literacy: Profiles of How Colleges Teach Their Students to Use Academic Libraries.* New York: Primary Research Group, 2012. ISBN: 978-1-57440-059-5.

1520   Tuten, Jane H., and Karen Junker, eds. *Appropriate Use Policies for Computers in College/University Libraries.* CLIP Notes 31. Chicago: Association of College and Research Libraries, American Library Association, 2002. ISBN: 978-0-83898-181-8.

1521   Woolls, Blanche, and David V. Loertscher, eds. *The Whole School Library Handbook.* Chicago: American Library Association, 2005. ISBN: 978-0-83890-883-9.

1522   Worley, Loyita, and British and Irish Association of Law Librarians, eds. *Biall Handbook of Legal Information Management.* Burlington, VT: Ashgate, 2006. ISBN: 978-0-75464-182-7.

1523   Zsravkovska, Nevenka. *Academic Branch Libraries in Changing Times.* New York: Neal-Schuman, 2011. ISBN: 978-1-84334-630-2.

📖 PERIODICALS

1524   *Behavioral and Social Sciences Librarian.* Philadelphia: Routledge. Frequency: Four issues per year. ISSN: 0613-9269 (print), 1544-4546 (online). URL: www.tandf.co.uk/journals/WBSS/.

This peer-reviewed journal focuses on the production, collection, organization, dissemination, retrieval, and use of social and behavioral science information. General topics include descriptive and critical analyses of information resources within particular fields; publishing trends; reference and bibliographic instruction; indexing and abstracting; and databases. Librarians and information specialists, collection development administrators, scholars, teachers, policymakers, publishers, and database producers make up the targeted audience.

1525   *Campus-Wide Information Systems.* Westport, CT: Emerald Group. Frequency: Five times per year. ISSN: 1065-0741. URL: www.emeraldinsight.com/products/journals/journals.htm?id=cwis&.

This magazine focuses on wide-ranging and independent coverage of the management, use, and integration of information resources and learning technologies. Topics include innovations in teaching and learning with technology, new technologies, information technology implementation and support, planning and administration, and more.

1526 *C&RL: College and Research Libraries.* Annapolis Junction, MD: Association of College and Research Libraries. Frequency: Bimonthly. ISSN: 0010-0870. URL: http://crl.acrl.org/.

C&RL is the official scholarly research journal of the Association of College and Research Libraries, division of ALA. Topics include all fields of interest and concern to academic and research libraries. Manuscripts are sent to a least two reviewers for comment prior to publication.

1527 *C&RL News.* Chicago: Annapolis Junction, MD: Association of College and Research Libraries. Frequency: Eleven times per year. ISSN: 0099-0086. URL: http://crln.acrl.org/site/misc/about.xhtml.

C&RL News serves as the official news magazine and publication of record for the Association of College and Research Libraries, an ALA subunit. Monthly columns cover Internet resources and reviews, preservation, "Washington Hotline," grants and acquisitions, people in the news, and new publications. Regular features are "Scholarly Communication," "Job of a Lifetime," and "The Way I See It."

1528 *Catholic Library World.* Chicago: Catholic Library Association. Frequency: Four issues per year. ISSN: 0008-820X. URL: www.cathla.org/catholic-library-world-clw.

The official journal of the Catholic Library Association (CLA), this publication has been continuously in print since 1929. As one would expect with such a title, the major audience is the librarian working in a Roman Catholic library or educational institution. That being said, the universal sense of *catholic* is evident in the contents, and librarians from other walks of professional life may find much of use here. For example, about half of each issue is devoted to book reviews, not only in the field of theology but in history, library science, philosophy, and general reference, among other subjects. Audiovisual materials are likewise evaluated. This journal is a membership benefit for CLA members, but nonmembers may purchase subscriptions.

1529 *Choice: Current Reviews for Academic Libraries.* Middleton, CT: Association of College and Research Libraries, American Library Association. Frequency: Twelve times per year. ISSN: 0009-4978. URL: www.ala.org/ala/mgrps/divs/acrl/publications/journalsandmagazines/choice/index.cfm.

Choice annually publishes approximately 7,000 critical reviews of current scholarly books and electronic resources within six months of their publication. Available in print formats (the magazine and *Choice Reviews on Cards*) and online (*Choice Reviews Online*), the reviews are primarily written by U.S. and Canadian teaching faculty active in the field.

1530 *Choice Reviews on Cards.* Middleton, CT: Association of College and Research Libraries, American Library Association. Frequency: Twelve times per year. URL: www.ala.org/ala/mgrps/divs/acrl/publications/journalsandmagazines/choice/howtoorder/howtoorder.cfm.

These convenient 4.25- by 5.5-inch card-size pages are a complete set of reviews from the corresponding issue of *Choice* magazine. There are approximately 600 reviews per set, or 6,500 review annually. *Reviews on Cards* is available only to current subscribers to *Choice* magazine or *Choice Reviews Online*.

1531 *College and Undergraduate Libraries.* Philadelphia: Routledge. Frequency: Four times per year. ISSN: 1069-1316 (print), 1545-2530 (online). URL: www.tandf.co.uk/journals/WCUL.

This journal focuses on library services, resources, and facilities that primarily serve undergraduate students along with staff professional development in higher education. Typical content includes research-based articles, case studies, reports of best practices, an occasional literature review or product review, and opinion pieces. Full-length articles are reviewed by the editor and then subject to anonymous double-blind review.

1532 *Community and Junior College Libraries.* Philadelphia: Routledge. Frequency: Four times per year. ISSN: 0276-3915 (print), 1545-2522 (online). URL: www.tandf.co.uk/journals/WJCL.

Articles provide theoretical research and practical studies dealing with the broad general topic of the delivery of information resources to lower-division undergraduate students. Topics commonly addressed are special relevant legislation, systems development, issues concerning community college libraries and learning resource centers, information literacy, collection development, programming initiatives, proven policies, conferences, and networks and consortia. Also included are book reviews, editorials, letters to the editor, and ongoing columns with specific focus. All review papers undergo editorial screening and peer review.

1533 *Information Outlook.* Alexandria, VA: Special Libraries Association. Frequency: Twelve issues per year. ISSN: 1091-0808. URL: www.sla.org/io/.

This is the current official publication of the Special Libraries Association (SLA). The former official publication, from 1910 to 1996, was *Special Libraries* (see Historic Interest sidebar). Articles are of a practical nature, with an emphasis on helping special librarians do better at their jobs. Typical fare includes case studies, reviews of websites, library management issues, and news and events concerning SLA. Themed issues are a recurring feature, taking an in-depth look at particular subjects such as government affairs and professional development.

HISTORIC INTEREST   FYI

Special Libraries. New York: Special Libraries Association. ISSN: 0038-6723

Once the official journal of the Special Libraries Association (SLA), *Special Libraries* saw print from January 1910 until fall of 1996 (it originally came out monthly; with volume 73 in 1981, it was changed to quarterly publication). Fortunately for library history researchers, every issue is freely available at www.sla.org/content/shop/speclibs.cfm. Besides reporting on association business, these issues focused on aspects of the profession unique to these types of libraries, always keeping in mind the organization's motto, "Putting knowledge to work." Early issues often had profile articles of individual facilities. The January 1912 number, for example, contained a review of the operations of the Library of the Bureau of Railway Economics. Later issues broadened the scope of this journal, with features on libraries in other countries and SLA's involvement with the International Federation of Library Associations and Institutions. Interestingly, throughout this publication's run there was an emphasis on technology, both as it applied to how special librarians performed their jobs and as it affected society at large. In any event, SLA's new official publication is *Information Outlook* (see entry 1539).

1534 *Journal of Academic Librarianship.* New York: Elsevier. Frequency: Six times per year. ISSN: 0099-1333. URL: www.journals.elsevier.com/the-journal-of-academic-librarianship/.

The *Journal of Academic Librarianship* is geared toward college and university librarians, academic administrators, educators, and students in LIS programs. Topics cover all aspects of academic libraries including management, acquisitions, relationships, alumni, managing technology, and book reviews.

1535 *Journal of Business and Finance Librarianship.* Philadelphia: Routledge. Frequency: Four times per year. ISSN: 0896-3568 (print), 1547-0644 (online). URL: www.tandf.co.uk/journals/WBFL/.

This journal provides practice-oriented and new empirical studies of business librarianship and business information needs of special libraries, academic libraries, public libraries, and other information centers outside the traditional library setting. Statistical and meeting reports, literature, and media reviews are included, along with website reviews and interviews. All research articles undergo rigorous peer review based on initial editor screening and vetting by two anonymous referees.

1536 *Journal of Electronic Resources in Medical Libraries.* Philadelphia: Routledge. Frequency: Four times per year. ISSN: 1542-4065 (print), 1542-4073 (online). URL: www.tandf.co.uk/journals/WERM/.

This is a source for practical, up-to-date information about important developments and issues related to the provision and use of electronic resources in medical libraries. Sample topics include electronic medicine and health care resources collection development and delivery; coping with electronic misinformation; fraudulence and shams on the Internet; "E-core" lists in medicine, allied health, nursing, pharmaceutical science, mental health, and other health care fields; the library's role in medical informatics; and the relationship between database/

journal publishers and medical libraries. Regular columns include "E-Journals Forum," which discusses all aspects of electronic journals; "Information Rx," reviews of databases and electronic resources in clinical practice; and "PDAs @ the Library," on all aspects of using personal digital assistants in medical libraries and clinical practice. All manuscripts undergo a rigorous, double-blind review; reviewers are assigned based on subject expertise.

1537 *Journal of Hospital Librarianship.* Philadelphia: Routledge. Frequency: Four times per year. ISSN: 1532-3269 (print), 1532-3277 (online). URL: www.tandf.co.uk/journals/WHOS/.

Articles focus on technical and administrative issues that most concern hospital librarians who organize and disseminate health information to both clinical care professionals and consumers. Topics may include research strategies, administrative assistance, managed care, financing, mergers, innovative strategies for transforming the health care environment, and new products and services reviews. All manuscripts are peer reviewed using a double-blind process; reviewers are assigned on the basis of subject expertise.

1538 *Journal of Map and Geography Libraries.* Philadelphia: Routledge. Frequency: Three times per year. ISSN: 1542-0353 (print), 1542-0361 (online). URL: www.tandf.co.uk/journals/WMGL.

This multidisciplinary journal covers international research and information on the production, procurement, processing, and utilization of geographic and cartographic materials and geospatial information. Articles and case studies run the gamut from the purely theoretical to practical concerns of those responsible for cartographic collections. All research articles undergo a rigorous double-blind peer review by professors, researchers, and practicing librarians with a passion for geography, cartographic materials, and the mapping and spatial sciences.

1539 *Journal of Religious and Theological Information.* Philadelphia: Routledge. Frequency:

Four times per year. ISSN: 1047-7845 (print), 1528-6924 (online). URL: www.tandf.co.uk/journals/WRTI/.

Articles are written by librarians, scholars, clergy, and others interested in the literature, publishing trends, and information-seeking behavior of the religious and theological community. Religious studies and related fields, including philosophy, ethnic studies, anthropology, sociology, and historical approaches to religion are examined as these topics relate to library and information studies. All articles undergo anonymous double-blind review.

1540 *Journal of Research on Libraries and Young Adults.* Chicago: Young Adult Library Services Association, American Library Association. Frequency: Four times per year. ISSN: 2157-3980. URL: www.ala.org/yalsa/products&publications/yalsapubs/jrlya/journal/.

This peer-reviewed, open-access online research journal published by the Young Adult Library Services Association (YALSA, a subunit of ALA) is intended to enhance the development of theory, research, and practices to support young adult library services. Articles may be based on original qualitative or quantitative research, an innovated conceptual framework, or a substantial literature review.

1541 *Knowledge Quest.* Chicago: American Association of School Librarians, American Library Association. Frequency: Six times per year. ISSN: 1094-9046. URL: www.ala.org/aasl/knowledge-quest/.

Knowledge Quest provides articles on new developments in education, learning theory, and relevant disciplines as they relate to the theory and practice of school librarianship. The target audience is building-level school librarians, supervisors, library educators, and others concerned with developing school library programs and services. Nonmember subscriptions are available.

1542 *Medical Reference Services Quarterly.* Philadelphia: Routledge. Frequency: Four times

per year. ISSN: 0276-3869 (print), 1540-9597 (online). URL: www.tandf.co.uk/journals/WMRS.

Articles are for professionals who provide reference and public services to health sciences personnel in clinical, educational, or research settings. Topics include current interest and practical value in the areas of reference in medicine and related specialties, the biomedical sciences, nursing, and allied health. All manuscripts undergo a rigorous, double-blind peer review; reviewers are assigned based on subject expertise. These areas are highlighted:

- Use of the Internet for providing medical information
- Utilization of biomedical databases
- Administration and management of medical reference services
- Continuing education of medical reference librarians and online search analysts
- Clinical medical librarians
- Marketing medical reference services
- Staffing for the medical reference department
- User education in health sciences libraries
- Legal aspects of medical reference
- Virtual (chat) reference
- Document delivery in health sciences libraries
- Patient education
- Ready reference in health sciences libraries
- Collection management of medical reference electronic and print resources
- PDAs and the medical library
- Evidence-based medical librarianship
- Use of blogs and RSS feeds by health sciences libraries

1543 *Music Reference Services Quarterly.* Philadelphia: Routledge. Frequency: Four times per year. ISSN: 1058-8167 (print), 1540-9503 (online). URL: www.tandf.co.uk/journals/WMUS/.

Articles submitted cover all management aspects and use of music collections and services in academic, orchestra, public, conservatory, and performing/fine arts libraries, as well as archives and museums. Emphasis is on administration and management research, bibliographic instruction, collection development, digital audio delivery, electronic resources, facilities, music librarianship education, preservation of music materials, reference services, cataloging, and bibliographies relating to printed music and audiovisual materials. Manuscripts undergo editorial screening and anonymous double-blind peer review.

1544 *New Review of Academic Librarianship.* Philadelphia: Routledge. Frequency: Two times per year. ISSN: 1361-4533 (print), 1740-7834 (online). URL: www.tandf.co.uk/journals/RACL/.

The target audience for this journal is academic librarians and educators involved with academic libraries. Content includes reviews, research, critiques, and case studies on topics relevant to those providing library and information services to academic communities. Emphasis is placed on theory, research, developments, and discussion of the future role of academic libraries and their services. Manuscripts undergo editorial screening and peer review by anonymous reviewers.

1545 *New Review of Children's Literature and Librarianship.* Frequency: Two times per year. Philadelphia: Routledge. ISSN: 1361-4541 (print), 1740-7885 (online). URL: www.tandf.co.uk/journals/RCLL/.

Articles cover library services to children and adolescents, education issues affecting library services, promotion of services and user education, staff education and training, collection development and management, children's and adolescent literature critical assessments, book and media selection, and research in literature and library services for children and adolescents. All review papers undergo editorial screening and anonymous peer review.

1546 *Public Services Quarterly.* Philadelphia: Routledge. Frequency: Four times per year. ISSN: 1522-8959 (print), 1522-9114 (online). URL: www.tandf.co.uk/journals/WPSQ/.

This journal covers a broad spectrum of public service issues in academic libraries. Research-based and theoretical articles and case studies reflect an understanding of public services. Topics include reference and research assistance, information literacy instruction, access and delivery services, and other services to patrons. All *Public Services Quarterly* regular issue articles undergo anonymous double-blind review. Thematic issues undergo double-blind review at the discretion of the special issue editor.

1547 *School Library Journal (SJL).* New York: Reed Business Information. Frequency: Twelve issues per year. ISSN: 0362-8930. URL: www.schoollibraryjournal.com.

Essentially, this is *Library Journal* for the K–12 librarian set (note that both are put out by Reed Business Information), although children's librarians in public libraries will also benefit from readership. The tagline is "The world's largest reviewer of books, multimedia, and technology for children and teens," and indeed reviews are a major reason to have access to this publication. A title of long standing, *SJL* first appeared on the scene in 1954 as *Junior Libraries*.

1548 *School Library Media Research.* Chicago: American Association of School Librarians, American Library Association. Frequency: Ongoing. ISSN: 1523-4320. URL: www.ala.org/aasl/aaslpubsandjournals/slmrb/schoollibrary.

Web-published, *School Library Media Research* is the official journal of the American Association of School Librarians (AASL, a subunit of ALA). The main focus of the journal is the publication of high-quality, original research regarding school library media programs. Topics may include research on instructional theory, teaching methods, critical issues, innovation, conceptual essays, and extensive research literature reviews. This journal is the successor to *School Library Media Quarterly Online*.

1549 *Science and Technology Libraries.* Philadelphia: Routledge. Frequency: Four times per year. ISSN: 0194-262X (print), 1541-1109 (online). URL: www.tandf.co.uk/journals/WSTL/.

This peer-reviewed, scholarly journal covers topics in science, engineering, clinical investigation, and agriculture. Typical content includes the following:

- Descriptions and analysis of emerging science and technology information needs
- New information products: features, coverage, and costs
- STMA information industry competition: publications, publishers, platforms, for-profit vs. nonprofit vs. open access sectors
- Scientific information resources and publications: accuracy and quality control
- Institutional repositories
- Specialized scientific and technical information: federated searching and retrieval
- Use of science libraries and their electronic resources in distance learning
- Science librarians professional training
- Science library users' education
- Evaluation of scientists and their grant proposals using bibliometric measures
- Building strategic alliances and advocacy groups
- "Profiles in Science": short biographies of distinguished scientists, engineers, clinical investigators, agricultural experts
- "Reviews of Science for Science Librarians": developments in science, engineering, clinical investigation, agriculture library services

1550   Young Adult Library Services (YALS). Chicago: Young Adult Library Services Association, American Library Association. Frequency: Four times per year. ISSN: 1541-4302. URL: www.ala.org/yalsa/products&publications/yalsapubs/yals/youngadultlibrary/.

Young Adults Library Services is the official journal of Young Adult Library Services Association (YALSA, a subunit of ALA). *YALS* provides articles of interest to librarians serving young adults ages 12–18, showcases best practices, provides news from related fields, highlights association events, and offers reviews of professional literature.

@ ADDITIONAL RESOURCES

1551   ALISS Quarterly. London: Association of Libraries and Information Professionals in Social Sciences. Frequency: Four times per year. ISSN: 1747-9258. URL: www.alissnet.org.uk/AlissQuarterly.aspx.

1552   ARL Bimonthly Report. Washington, DC: Association of Research Libraries. Frequency: Bimonthly. ISSN: 1050-6098. URL: www.arl.org/resources/pubs/br/index.shtml.

1553   Art Libraries Journal. Preston, England: Art Libraries Society in the United Kingdom and the Republic of Ireland. Frequency: Quarterly. ISSN: 0307-4722. URL: www.arlis.org.uk/documents/resources/alj_abstracts_list_2011.pdf.

1554   Christian Librarian. Ilford, Essex: Librarians' Christian Fellowship. Frequency: Four times per year. ISSN: 0309-4170. URL: www.librarianscf.org.uk/publications/index.html.

1555   Christian Librarian, The (TCL). Cedarville, OH: Association of Christian Librarians. Frequency: Annually. ISSN: 0412-3131. URL: www.acl.org/index.cfm/the-christian-librarian/.

1556   College and University Media Review. Ames, IA: Consortium of College and University Media Centers. Frequency: Once annually. ISSN: 1075-8496. URL: www.ccumc.org/media-review/.

1557   E-JASL: The Electronic Journal of Academic and Special Librarianship. Athabasca, AB: International Consortium for the Advancement of Academic Publication. Frequency: Four times per year. ISSN: 1704-8532. URL: http://southernlibrarianship.icaap.org.

1558   Government Information Quarterly. New York: Elsevier Science. Frequency: Four times per year. ISSN: 0740-624X. URL: www.journals.elsevier.com/government-information-quarterly/.

1559   Health Information and Libraries Journal. New York: Wiley-Blackwell. Frequency: Quarterly. ISSN: 1471-1834. URL: www.wiley.com/WileyCDA/WileyTitle/productCd-HIR.html.

1560 *Journal of the Canadian Health Libraries Association.* Toronto, ON: Canadian Health Libraries Association. Frequency: Three issues per year. ISSN: 1708-6892. URL: http://pubs .chla-absc.ca/journal/jchla/.

1561 *Journal of the Medical Library Association (JMLA).* Chicago: Medical Library Association. Frequency: Four times per year. ISSN: 1536-5050. URL: www.mlanet.org/publications/jmla/index .html.

1562 *Journal of Scholarly Publishing.* Toronto, ON: University of Toronto Press. Frequency: Four times per year. ISSN: 1198-9742. URL: www.utp journals.com/Journal-of-Scholarly-Publishing .html.

1563 *Judaica Librarianship.* New York: Associ-ation of Jewish Libraries. Frequency: Annually. ISSN: 0739-5086. URL: www.jewishlibraries.org/ ajlweb/publications/jl.htm.

1564 *Law Library Journal.* Chicago: American Association of Law Libraries. Frequency: Annually. ISSN: 0023-9283. URL: www.aallnet .org/main-menu/Publications/llj/.

1565 *Librarians' Christian Fellowship Newsletter.* Ilford, Essex: Librarians' Christian Fellowship. Frequency: Several times per year. ISSN: 0308-5473. URL: www.librarianscf.org.uk/ publications/enewsletter.html.

1566 *Library Issues: Briefings for Faculty and Administrators.* Ann Arbor, MI: Mountainside. Frequency: Six times per year. ISSN: 0734-3035. URL: www.libraryissues.com.

1567 *Notes.* Philadelphia, PA: Music Library Association. Frequency: Quarterly. ISSN: 0027-4380. URL: http://musiclibraryassoc.org/ publications.aspx?id=72.

1568 *Play Matters.* London: National Association of Toy and Leisure Libraries. Frequency: Three times per year. ISSN: 1352-7479. URL: www.natll .org.uk/index.php?page_id=16.

1569 *Private Library.* North Harrow, Greater London: Private Libraries Association. Frequency: Quarterly. ISSN: 0032-8898. URL: www.plabooks .org/journal.html.

1570 *Teacher Librarian: The Journal for School Library Professionals.* Seattle, WA: E. L. Kurdyla. Frequency: Five times per year. ISSN: 1481-1782. URL: www.teacherlibrarian.com.

1571 *Western Association of Map Libraries Information Bulletin.* Sacramento, CA: Western Association of Map Libraries. Frequency: Three times per year. ISSN: 0049-7282. URL: www .waml.org/wmlpubs.html.

☁ WEBSITE

1572 *Choice Reviews Online.* Middleton, CT: Association of College and Research Libraries. URL: www.ala.org/ala/mgrps/divs/acrl/ publications/journalsandmagazines/choice/ choicereviewsonline/cro2info.cfm.

Newly revised and updated, *Choice Reviews Online* now contains content not included in *Choice* mag-azine. The redesign allows one-click access to the current issue of *Choice*, advanced search, 2005 Outstanding Academic Titles (OAT) list, forth-coming titles, monthly reviews, and user lists. Users can browse, e-mail, print, and download reviews, bibliographic essays, forthcoming title lists, and OATs.

(1) Bibliometrics
(2) Information Science—Statistical Methods
(3) Library Statistics—United States

STATISTICS

◆ BOOKS

1573 Bertot, John Carlo, Charles R. McClure, and Joe Ryan. *Public Library Networked Services: A Guide for Using Statistics and Performance Measures.* Chicago: American Library Association, 2000. ISBN: 978-0-83890-796-2.

The authors show librarians how to measure and assess the quality of online/computer-based services that are provided to increasingly technology-savvy library patrons. The first chapter describes how the manual is used. The next six chapters focus on recommended statistics for general library usage, information technology service, instruction, user assessments, data collection and use, information collection and compilation, and environmental measurements. The appendixes are packed full of statistical calculations, data sources, vendors' statistics and usage reports, and tracking software. A bibliography, references, and index are included.

1574 Public Library Data Service Statistical Report 2012. Chicago: Public Library Association, 2012. ISBN: 978-0-83898-606-6.

Produced by the Public Library Association (PLA, a subunit of ALA), this volume represents data collected from more than 1,300 public libraries. The *Public Library Data Service Statistical Report* (PLDS) categories include financial information, library resources, per capita measures, annual use figures, technology usage, and library identification. This information can be used to identify top-performing libraries, compare service levels, and compile comparable statistics for performance review and funding requests. PLDS reports for 2010 and earlier are no longer in print.

✎ ADDITIONAL RESOURCES

1575 ACRL 2010 Academic Library Trends and Statistics for Carnegie Classification. ACRL Academic Library Trends and Statistics. Chicago: Association of College and Research Libraries, 2012. ISBN: 978-0-83898-599-1.

FYI

STATISTICS SOURCES

Statistics regarding libraries can be tough to track down, largely because there are so many surveys and reporting agencies. Here a few suggestions:

- ALA has an Office for Research and Statistics. According to its website (www.ala.org/offices/ors), its reason for being is to "provide leadership and expert advice . . . on all matters related to research and statistics about libraries, librarians and other library staff." Look for the "Resources" heading in the middle upper third of the web page, then click on the link for "Statistics about Libraries." This takes you to a page of further links for fact sheets regarding the number of libraries, the largest libraries, and other numerical goodies.
- *Statistics Sources,* 37th ed., 4 vols., published by Gale, 2012. ISBN: 978-1-41446-927-0. This alphabetically arranged dictionary covers 20,000 specific subjects, has more than 1,600 sources from more than 210 countries, and incorporates 20,000 more citations than the previous edition. It lists postal addresses, telephone numbers, fax numbers, and websites of organizations and agencies that supply statistics of all kinds. Two appendixes identify the sources of information used to compile this four-volume set.

1576 Smith, Mark. *Collecting and Using Public Library Statistics: A How-to-Do-It Manual for Librarians.* How-To-Do-It Manuals for Libraries 56. New York: Neal-Schuman, 1996. ISBN: 978-1-55570-206-9.

1577 Womack, Ryan. *Success by the Numbers: Statistics for Business Development.* Occasional Paper 28. Chicago: American Library Association, 2005. ISBN: 978-0-83898-327-0.

☁ WEBSITES

1578 Henderson, Everett. *Service Trends in U.S. Public Libraries, 1997–2007.* Research Brief 1. Washington, DC: Institute of Museum and Library Services, 2009. URL: www.imls.gov/assets/1/workflow_staging/AssetManager/695.PDF.

This report provides an overview of actual visitation and circulation figures for U.S. public libraries over a ten-year period. The figures are derived from statistical information compiled from the annual Public Library Survey data from FY1997 and FY2007. The report closely examines five key variables:

- Public library use, 1997–2007, per capita visits
- Public library use, 1997–2007, per capita circulation
- Public library use, 1997–2007, circulations per 1,000 visits
- Number of Internet PPCs in public libraries, 2000–2007, per 5,000 people
- Public library trends, 1997–2007, electronic materials as a percentage of all collection expenditures

1579 Henderson, Everett, and James Lonergan. *Majority of States Report Decline in Support for Library Services.* Research Brief 3. Washington, DC: Institute of Museum and Library Services, 2011. URL: www.imls.gov/assets/1/AssetManager/Brief2011_03.pdf.

This short brief provides an overview of the decline in support for state library administrative agencies (SLAAs) in the United States. Findings from the State Library Agency Survey released in March 2010 revealed significant and sudden reductions in budgets, staff, and revenues for many state agencies. The report closely examines four key statistical results:

- Real total SLAA revenue by source, FY2000–2009
- State revenue, FY2008–2009 change
- FTE staff by type of service, FY2005–2009
- Change in FTE staff, FY2008–2009

1580   Henderson, Everett, and Carlos Manjarrez. *State Library Agency Service Trends: 1999–2008.* Research Brief 2. Washington, DC: Institute of Museum and Library Services, 2010. URL: www .imls.gov/assets/1/workflow_staging/News/186 .PDF.

This report provides an overview of revenues, expenditures, and services provided by state library administrative agencies in the United States. The report closely examines provisions of the Library Services and Technology Act (LSTA) and the key statistical results:

- Total state library revenues by state, FY2008
- Number of states funding reading programs in public libraries by program type, FY1999–2008
- LSTA expenditures on hard-to-serve populations, FY1999–2008
- LSTA expenditures—financial aid to libraries, FY1999–2008
- Number of states providing statewide database licensing by recipient, FY1999–2008
- Total statewide database licensing expenditures, FY1999–2008
- Real spending on statewide database licensing by source, FY1999–2008
- Number of states providing library access to the Internet, by type of support, FY1999–2008
- Number of states providing selected collection maintenance services to public libraries by type, FY1999–2008
- State library agencies: number of continuing education events, FY1999–2008

- Attendance at continuing education programs, FY1999–2008
- Number of states utilizing LSTA to perform selected functions, FY2009
- Real total LSTA revenue, FY1999–2008
- Select LSTA expenditures by type, FY1999–2008
- Real total LSTA revenue by source, FY1999–2008

1581   Manjarrez, Carlos A., Joyce Ray, and Karment Bisher. "A Demographic Overview of the Current and Projected Library Workforce and Impact of Federal Funding." Library Trends 59, no. 1, Summer 2010. www.imls.gov/assets/1/ AssetManager/LibraryTrendsSummer2010.pdf.

This article examines the size of the U.S. library workforce and projects demand for librarians through an analysis of available statewide and national collection data. It includes references and a description of data sources used for these key tables and charts:

- Table 1. Estimates of Workforce Size and Growth Rate for Librarians, Library Technicians, and the Education, Training and Library Occupations Category, 2003–8
- Table 2. Estimated Number of Librarians and Library Technicians by State and as Percentage of the NAICS Educational Training, Library Employees Occupational Category, May 2008
- Table 3. Most Commonly Identified Industries for Librarians, 2008
- Table 4. Current Estimates and Projections of Librarians, Library Technicians and Library Assistants, 2008–18
- Table 5. Librarian Workforce Change by State and Population, 1998, 2003, and 2008
- Table 6. State Level Comparison of Librarian Estimates Across Three National Surveys, Circa 2000, Department of Education
- Chart 1. Gender Distribution of Librarians as a Percentage of All Librarians, Circa 2007
- Chart 2. Percentage of Librarians by Race/ Ethnicity, Circa 2007

1582 Manjarrez, Carlos A., and Kyle Schoembs. *Who's in the Queue? A Demographic Analysis of Public Access Computer Users and Uses in U.S. Public Libraries.* Research Brief 4. Washington, DC: Institute of Museum and Library Services, 2011. URL: www.imls.gov/assets/1/AssetManager/Brief2011_04.pdf.

This short demographic analysis shows that public libraries are providing more than basic technology access. Specific topics:

- Age categories of public access users compared to general public use
- Education attainment of public access computer uses compared to general population for persons over the age of 25
- Characteristics of public access users by home access
- Rank of public library Internet use by subject area
- Rank of public library Internet use by subject area and home access type
- Percentage of library public uses reporting social connections/communication use by age category
- Top substantive uses of public access computers by age category

1583 Pastore, Erica, and Everett Henderson. *Libraries Use Broadband Internet Service to Serve High Need Communities.* Data Note 1. Washington, DC: Institute of Museum and Library Services, 2009. URL: www.imls.gov/assets/1/workflow_staging/News/632.PDF.

This brief looks at the number of Internet-enabled PCs in public libraries per 5,000 people between 1998 and 2006 and the percentage of public libraries with broadband Internet access by area and connection speed (1.5 Mbps or greater) in 2007 to determine how libraries use this technology to provide content to meet the needs of patrons in the digital age.

VENDORS AND SUPPLIERS

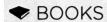 **BOOKS**

1584　Anderson, Rick. *Buying and Contracting for Resources and Services: A How-to-Do-It Manual for Librarians.* How-To-Do-It Manuals for Libraries 125. New York: Neal-Schuman, 2003. ISBN: 978-1-55570-480-3.

Processes, practical tips, and advice will help guide the librarian through the procurement process and vendor relations. Topics include identifying needs, writing requests for proposals/bids, negotiating terms, making awards, tracking vendor performance, and dealing with problems. "Standing Up for Yourself" and "Got Problems? Give Specifics" have sample dialogues between librarian and vendor and offer practical advice for dealing with unpleasant situations.

1585　Durrant, Fiona. *Negotiating Licenses for Digital Resources.* London: Facet, ISBN: 978-1-85604-586-5; Chicago: American Library Association, ISBN: 978-1-85604-586-5. 2008.

Durrant walks readers through the negotiation process for digital resources. In-depth coverage and advice are provided for preparation, the contract, negotiation, staff development, and communicating negotiation outcomes. The appendixes contain frequently asked questions, negotiation timeline, and personal negotiation experiences.

1586　Matthews, Joseph R. *Internet Outsourcing Using an Application Service Provider: A How-to-Do-It Manual for Librarians.* How-To-Do-It Manuals for Libraries 110. New York: Neal-Schuman, 2002. ISBN: 978-1-55570-422-3.

Matthews provides librarians with advice on eight factors to consider when using application service providers (ASPs) to outsource public Internet access, automated circulation, cataloguing, and business office functions. Chapters describe RFPs, service level agreements, functions, and advantages of using ASPs for various types and sizes of libraries.

1587 Wilkinson, Frances C., and Linda K. Lewis. *Writing RFPs for Acquisitions: A Guide to the Request for Proposal.* ACLTS Acquisitions Guides. Chicago: American Library Association, 2008. ISBN: 978-0-83898-483-3.

This slim volume walks readers through the steps for planning and writing RFPs, including evaluating vendor proposals, contracts, and contract management. Sample materials are provided.

@ ADDITIONAL RESOURCES

1588 Hirshon, Arnold, and Barbara Winters. *Outsourcing Library Technical Service: A How-to-Do-It Manual for Librarians.* How-To-Do-It Manuals for Libraries 69. New York: Neal-Schuman, 1996. ISBN: 978-1-55570-221-2.

1589 Wilkinson, Frances C., and Connie Capers Thorson. *The RFP Process: Effective Management of the Acquisition of Library Materials.* Westport, CT: Libraries Unlimited, 1998. ISBN: 978-1-56308-481-2.

▤ PERIODICAL

1590 *Against the Grain: Linking Publishers, Vendors and Librarians.* Charleston, SC: Against the Grain. ISSN: 1043-2094. Frequency: At least four times per year. URL: www.against-the-grain .com.

☁ WEBSITE

1591 *Librarian's Yellow Pages (LYP) 2012.* 18th ed. Library Resources Group. URL: www .librariansyellowpages.com.

LYP is a free online directory and buyer's guide for public, academic, special, and school libraries. The searchable PDF download covers audio, video, automation systems and services, books and periodicals, library furnishings (equipment, supplies, furniture, shelving, and display), library services, and online databases and resources. The search function accommodates keyword, company, and category. Information includes company profiles, detailed online listings, viewable demos, special offers, catalog requests, product information, and sales executives' e-mail addresses.

WRITING AND PUBLISHING

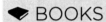 BOOKS

1592 Crawford, Walt. *First Have Something to Say: Writing for the Library Profession.* Chicago: American Library Association, 2003. ISBN: 978-0-83890-851-8.

Crawford walks librarians through many different avenues for writing and publishing works. He covers how to get started, journals, reports, copyrights, editors, ethics, discussion lists, blogs, zines, e-newsletters, books, columns, and series. Tips for dealing with editors, overwriting, second drafts, breaks, blocks, and presentations are found throughout. Resources, bibliography, and index are included.

1593 Hooper, Brad. *Writing Reviews for Readers' Advisory.* Contribution by Joyce Saricks. Chicago: American Library Association, 2010. ISBN: 978-0-83891-017-7.

This how-to guide includes tips on writing pertinent reviews for readers' advisory, collection development, and promotions. Hooper discusses marketing through reviewing, reviews versus criticism, before-publication reviews, after-publication reviews, book review contents, what makes good reviews and reviewers, and how to conduct a review-writing workshop. A chapter by Saricks covers writing audiobook reviews. Two appendixes—"Writing Annotations" and "My Favorite Reviewers"—bibliography, and index are included.

1594 Smallwood, Carol, ed. *Writing and Publishing: The Librarian's Handbook.* Chicago: American Library Association, 2010. ISBN: 978-0-83890-996-6.

Smallwood compiles a practical how-to collection of articles on writing fiction, poetry, children's book/magazine, self-publishing, literary agents, personal blogging, and more to help the librarians reach their inner writer. Part 1 covers why librarians write. Part 2 discusses the education of a writer and includes getting started, writing with others, the revision process, and lessons from publishing. Part 3 discusses print and online niche markets and offers writing advice about books, newsletters, reviewing, magazines, professional journals, essays, textbooks, children's book, blogs, online columns, and more. The final section addresses maximizing writing opportunities. A list of contributors and index are included.

AMERICAN LIBRARY ASSOCIATION DIVISIONS, CHAPTERS, AND AFFILIATES

The oldest and largest professional organization of its kind in the United States, the American Library Association was founded on October 6, 1876, to provide leadership for the development, promotion, and improvement of library and information services, funding, library use, and the profession of librarianship. ALA's guiding principles are diversity, equity of access, education and continuous learning, intellectual freedom, and twenty-first-century literacy. ALA divisions representing distinct types of libraries or library specializations publish journals, books, newsletters, and other material; provide continuing education opportunities; offer awards and scholarships; sponsor institutes and conferences; and maintain affiliates, chapters, and other collaborative relationship networks:

- American Association of School Librarians (AASL)
- Association for Library Collections and Technical Services (ALCTS)
- Association for Library Service to Children (ALSC)
- Association of College and Research Libraries (ACRL)
- Association of Library Trustees, Advocates, Friends and Foundations (ALTAFF)
- Association of Specialized and Cooperative Library Agencies (ASCLA)
- Library and Information Technology Association (LLAMA)
- Public Library Association (PLA)
- Reference and User Services Association (RUSA)
- Young Adult Library Services Association (YALSA)

American Association of School Librarians (AASL). www.ala.org/aasl/.

The AASL mission is to advocate excellence, facilitate change, and develop leaders in the school library field. Personal, retirement, and student memberships are available to ALA members. The association publishes three magazines—*AASL Hotlinks, Knowledge Quest,* and *School Library Media Research*—along with a variety of nonserial publications and products.

Association for Library Collections and Technical Services (ALCTS). www.ala.org/ala/mgrps/divs/alcts/index.cfm.

The ALCTS mission is to promote and guide selection, identification, acquisition, organization, management, retrieval, and preservation of recorded knowledge through education, publication, and collaboration. Personal, support staff, student, international, organizational, corporate, and life memberships are available to ALA members. The association publishes *Library Resources and Technical Services, ALCTS Newsletter Online,* and the *ALCTS Paper Series* along with publications on cataloging, collections, and preservation topics.

Association for Library Service to Children (ALSC). www.ala.org/alsc/.

The ALSC mission is to support and enhance library services to children. Student, personal, organizational, and corporate memberships are available to ALA members. ALSC administers several book and media awards (e.g., Newbery, Caldecott, Sibert, Wilder, Carnegie, Batchelder), the Children's Notable Lists, Bookapalooza Program, and several professional awards. ALSC publishes many award-related products and books.

Association for Library Trustees, Advocates, Friends and Foundations (ALTAFF). www.ala.org/altaff/.

The Friends of Libraries USA (FOLUSA) and the Association for Library Trustees and Advocates (ALTA) joined together on February 1, 2009, becoming ALTAFF. This division's mission is to support citizens who govern, promote, and raise funds for all types of libraries. Personal memberships are available to ALA members. Group memberships for non-ALA members are available to members of library boards of trustees, Friends groups, and foundations. Group members have access to member benefits and resources but have no voting privileges. ALTAFF offers a variety of products and services including publications, webinars, books for babies, literary landmarks, and training and consulting.

Association of College and Research Libraries (ACRL). www.ala.org/acrl/.

The ACRL mission is to enhance the ability of academic librarians and information specialists to serve the higher education community and improve learning, teaching, and research. Personal, international, retired, student, library support, and associate memberships are available to ALA members. ACRL publishes *College and Research Libraries News, College and Research Libraries, CHOICE: Current Reviews for Academic Libraries,* and *RBM: A Journal of Rare Books, Manuscripts, and Cultural Heritage* along with several books, monographs, digital publications, and resources for college libraries.

Association of Specialized and Cooperative Library Agencies (ASCLA). www.ala.org/ascla/.

The ASCLA mission is to represent specialized library agencies, state library agencies, library cooperatives, and independent librarians. Personal, student, retired, and organizational memberships are available to ALA members. The official ASCLA magazine is *Interface.* ASCLA offers several educational opportunities, publications, and guidelines.

Library and Information Technology Association (LITA). www.ala.org/lita/.

The LITA mission is to promote, develop, and aid the implementation of library and information technology. Personal, student, and organizational memberships are available to ALA members. LITA publishes *Information Technology and Libraries* and *ITALica* along with several other publications related to library and information technology.

Library Leadership, & Management Association (LLAMA). www.ala.org/llama/.

The LLAMA mission is to encourage and nurture current and future library leaders to develop and promote outstanding leadership and management practices. Personal, corporate, organizational, and student memberships are available to ALA members. LLAMA publishes *Library Leadership and Management, LL&M Editor's Blog,* and *Leads from LLAMA.*

Public Library Association (PLA). www.ala.org/pla/.

The PLA mission is to provide a diverse program of communication, publication, advocacy, continuing education, and programming for its members and others interested in the advancement of public library service. Regular, student, retired, inactive, unemployed, international, trustee and associates, and organizational memberships are available to ALA members. PLA publishes *Public Libraries* along with several publications on specific technologies, statistical reports, and other topics of interest to public librarians.

Reference and User Services Association (RUSA). www.ala.org/rusa/.

The RUSA mission is to stimulate and support excellence in the delivery of general library materials and the provision of reference and information services, collection development, readers' advisory, and resource sharing in every type of library for all users. RUSA memberships are available to any ALA member. RUSA is divided into several sections: Business Reference and Service Section (BRASS), Collection Development and Evaluation Section (CODES), History Section (HS), MARS: Emerging Technologies in Reference Section, Reference Services Section (RSS), and Sharing and Transforming Access to Resources Section (STARS). RUSA publishes *RUSQ, RUSA Blog,* and *RUSA Update.*

Young Adult Library Services Association (YALSA). www.ala.org/yalsa/yalsa/.

The YALSA mission is to expand and strengthen library services for teens (ages 12–18) and build the capacity of libraries and librarians to engage, serve, and empower teens. Regular, unemployed, nonsalaried, library support staff, retired, international, associate and advocate, trustee, organizational, and corporate memberships are available to ALA members. YALSA publishes the *Journal of Research on Libraries and Young Adults, Young Adults Library Services,* and *YALSA E-news,*

along with a variety of books to aid school and public librarians in their work.

ALA AFFILIATES

American Association of Law Libraries (AALL). 105 W. Adams Street, Suite 3300, Chicago, IL 60603. www.aallnet.org.

AALL was established in 1906 to promote the value of law librarians and become the premier resource for legal information and the law library professions. Besides offering numerous networking and educational programs, AALL publishes the *AALL E-newsletter* monthly, *AALL Spectrum* nine times per year, *Law Library Journal* quarterly, *AALL Price Index for Legal Publication* annually, and several other law and librarianship publications.

American Indian Library Association (AILA). 12 Highfield Rd. #2, Roslindale, MA 02131. www.ailanet.org.

AILA was founded in 1979 to address library-related needs of American Indians and Alaska Natives and disseminate information about their cultures, languages, values, and informational needs. Association members exchange information about grants, projects, programs, and sponsor the Joint Conference of Librarians of Color. They publish the *AILA Newsletter,* which contains information pertaining to Native Americans, and reviews of books on Native groups semiannually.

American Society for Information Science and Technology (ASIST). 1320 Fenwick Lane, Suite 510, Silver Springs, MD 20910. www.asist.org.

American Theological Library Association (ATLA). 300 South Wacker Drive, Suite 2100, Chicago, IL 60606-6701. www.atla.com/Pages/default.aspx.

ATLA provides support for theological and religious studies libraries and librarians. Besides the annual conference and professional development programs, ATLA publishes the *ATLA Newsletter,*

Summary of Proceedings of the annual conference, and *Theology Cataloging Bulletin.*

Art Libraries Society of North America (ARLIS/NA). 7044 South 13th Street, Oak Creek, WI 53154. www.arlisna.org.

Founded in 1972, ARLIS/NA fosters excellence in art and design librarianship and image management. The society offers meetings, networking, and sharing of ideas through conferences, forums, scholarships, and various publications. ARLIS/NA publishes *Art Documentation* twice annually; reviews on art, design, and architecture material; occasional papers; and other miscellaneous documents.

Asian/Pacific American Librarians Association (APALA). P.O. Box 1669, Goleta, CA 96113-1669. www.apalaweb.org.

APALA was founded in 1980 to provide a platform to discuss the needs of Asian Pacific American librarians and those who serve Asian Pacific American communities. The *APALA Newsletter* is published several times per year and the *APALA Listserv* is an ongoing effort to generate and promote communication among association members.

Association for Library and Information Science Education (ALISE). 65 West Wacker Place, Suite 1990, Chicago, IL 60601-7246. www.alise.org.

Originally founded in 1915 as the Association of American School Libraries, ALISE provides a forum for faculty, administrators, students, librarians, educational institutions, and others who want to share ideas, discuss issues, and seek solutions to common problems faced in library and information science education. Members have a subscription to the quarterly *Journal of Education for Library and Information Science,* quarterly *AILSE E-newsletter,* and ALISE *Membership Directory.*

Association for Rural and Small Libraries (ARSL). 201 E. Main Street, Suite 1405, Lexington, KY 40507. www.arsl.info/.

ARSL was established in 1982 to promote positive growth and development of rural and small libraries through networking, educational opportunities, partnerships, and advocacy and to serve as a source of current information about trends, issues, and strategies for librarians and others interested in rural and small libraries. The association publishes a quarterly newsletter and maintains communication through several media including Facebook, LinkedIn, Twitter, and wikis.

Association of Bookmobile and Outreach Services (ABOS). c/o MLNC, 13610 Barrett Office Drive, Suite 206, Ballwin, MO 63021. www.abos-outreach.org.

Formed to discuss activities, programs, challenges, and successes in the field of bookmobile and outreach services in libraries, ABOS represents library administrators, support staff, librarians, government officials, trustees, Friends groups, and other professionals interested in the library field. The association sponsors an annual conference and National Bookmobile Day along with related merchandise.

Association of Jewish Libraries (AJL). P.O. Box 1118, Teaneck, NJ 07666. www.jewishlibraries.org.

Established in 1966 when the Jewish Library Association and Jewish Librarians Association merged, AJL is dedicated to enhancing libraries and library resources through leadership for the profession and practitioners of Judaica librarianship by fostering access to information, learning, teaching, and research pertaining to Jews, Judaism, the Jewish experience, and Israel. AJL publishes the quarterly *AJL News,* scholarly journal *Judaica Librarianship,* *AJL Reviews,* AJL Convention proceedings, and monographs and pamphlets in the areas of Judaica librarianship and Jewish children's literature.

Association of Research Libraries (ARL). 21 Dupont Circle NW, Washington, DC 20036. www.arl.org.

ARL was created to advance the goals of its member research libraries, provide leadership in public and information policies, foster the exchange of ideas and expertise, facilitate the emergence of new roles for research libraries, and leverage its interests through partnership. Membership is limited to single research institutions that are willing to commit to common values, goals, interests, and needs shared between ARL and the research institution.

Beta Phi Mu (Library and Information Studies Honor Society). Beta Phi Mu Headquarters, Florida State University, 101H Louis Shores Building, 142 College Loop, P.O. Box 3062100, Tallahassee, FL 32306-2100. www.beta-phi-mu.org.

Founded in 1948 by a group of leading librarians and library educators, Beta Phi Mu recognizes and encourages scholastic achievement among library and information studies students. Regular membership is offered to students who have completed all requirements leading to a master's degree with a specified scholastic average or have completed a planned program of advanced study beyond the master's degree that requires full-time study for one or more academic years with a specified scholastic average.

Black Caucus of ALA (BCALA). Membership, Box 7493, 6985 Snow Way Blvd., St. Louis, MO 63130-4400. www.bcala.org.

BCALA is an advocate for the development, promotion, and improvement of library services and resources for African American communities and African American librarians. It offers professional development and networking and publishes the *BCALA Newsletter*.

Canadian Library Association (CLA). 1150 Morrison Drive, Suite 400, Ottawa, ON, K2H 8S9. www.cla.ca//AM/Template.cfm?Section=Home.

Founded in 1946, CLA comprises five units that represent the interests of academic libraries, public libraries, school libraries, special libraries, and library trustees to build the Canadian library and information community and advance its information professionals. The association sponsors an annual conference, Canadian Library Month, and several workshops and seminars. It

publishes *Feliciter* (national, six times per year), *CLA Digest* (biweekly), Libraries Canada (annually), and position statements.

Catholic Library Association (CLA). 205 W. Monroe Street, Suite 314, Chicago, IL 60606. www.cathla.org.

CLA was created in 1921 to provide its international membership with educational and networking experiences, publications, scholarships, and other services. CLA publishes *Catholic Library World* and the *Kapsner Cataloging and Classification Bulletin* (e-newsletter), along with *The Catholic Supplement to A Handbook for Church Librarians, Developing the Library Collection: A Workbook of Policies and Resources, Sinfully Good: Recipes from the Catholic Library Association,* and the *ATLA Catholic and Periodical Literature Index.*

Chinese-American Library Association (CALA). Lian Ruan, Director/Head Librarian, Illinois Fire Service Institute, University of Illinois at Urbana–Champaign, 11 Gerty Drive, Champaign, IL 61820. http://cala-web.org.

After expanding nationwide, the Chinese American Librarians Association (formerly Mid-West Chinese American Librarians Association) merged with the Chinese Librarian Association in 1983 to enhance communication among Chinese American librarians and other librarians, provide a forum to discuss mutual problems and professional concerns, promote Sino-American librarianship and library services, and provide a vehicle to form partnerships with other organizations with similar interests. CALA publishes the *CALA Newsletter* twice per year, the *CALA E-journal*, and, in partnership with National Taiwan Normal University, the *Journal of Library and Information Science* semiannually.

Medical Library Association (MLA). 65 East Wacker Place, Suite 1990, Chicago, IL 60601-7246. www.mlanet.org.

One of the earlier library associations, MLA was founded in 1898 to support professionals in the health sciences information field by providing educational opportunities, supporting health information research and access to international health sciences information, and working to increase access to high-quality health information. Besides publishing numerous books, Bib-Kits, DocKits, and standards, MLA publishes the quarterly, peer-reviewed scholarly *Journal of the Medical Library Association*, the bimonthly electronic newsletter *MLA-FOCUS*, and the monthly membership newsletter *MLA News*.

Music Library Association (MLA). 8551 Research Way, Suite 180, Middleton, WI 53562. www.musiclibraryassoc.org.

Devoted to music librarianship and all aspects of music materials in libraries, MLA, originally founded in 1931, became a branch of the International Association of Music Libraries in 2011. The association provides leadership for the collection and preservation of music and information about music through continuing education and professional development; contributes to codes, formats, and standards for bibliographic control of music; facilitates best practices for preservation; fosters information literacy; develops partnerships; and promotes music reference services, library instruction programs, and publications. MLA offers a variety of publications about the history and practice of music librarianship, including the monthly *Music Cataloging Bulletin,* which reports cataloging news relevant to music cataloging; *Notes: Quarterly Journal of the Music Library,* covering music librarianship, music bibliography and discography, and the music trade; the Basic Manual Series, designed to assist in the organization, administration, and use of a music library; Index and Bibliographic Series to all areas of music study; a quarterly newsletter with association news and upcoming events; and technical reports and online publications.

National Storytelling Network (NSN). P.O. Box 795, Jonesborough, TN 37659. www.storynet.org.

Formed after the first National Storytelling Festival in 1973, the National Association for the Preservation and Perpetuation of Storytelling changed its name to the present-day National Storytelling Network in 1994 to continue its advocacy of the preservation and growth of the art of storytelling. Published five times per year, *Storytelling Magazine* discusses important events, trends, people, and publications in the national storytelling community.

Online Audiovisual Catalogers (OLAC). Amy Weiss, Florida State University, Technical Services Division, 711 W. Madison Street, Tallahassee, FL 32306. http://olacinc.org/drupal/.

OLAC is an international organization that provides conferences, workshops, publications, e-mail lists, and expert and practical advice for catalogers who work with all types of nonprint materials. The association publishes the *OLAC Newsletter* quarterly along with cataloging tools and training documents, reports and informational papers, and archived historical publications and training materials.

Patent and Trademark Depository Library Association (PTDLA). Marian Armour-Gemmen, West Virginia University, Evansdale Library, 3 Evansdale Drive, P.O. Box 6105, Morgantown, WV 26506-6105. www.ptdla.org.

PTDLA was formed to advise the U.S. Patent and Trademark Office about the objectives, goals, interests, needs, and opinions of professionals working at Patent and Trademark Depository Libraries. The association publishes *Intellectual Property* and an annual membership newsletter.

ProLiteracy Worldwide. 104 Marcellus Street, Syracuse, NY 13204. www.proliteracy.org.

The Laubach Literacy International and Literacy Volunteers of America, Inc., merged in 2002 to form ProLiteracy, an organization that champions the power of literacy to improve the lives of adults and their families, communities, and societies. The group provides professional development and training, publications, and credentialing services. One of its most popular publications is the *ProLiteracy Annual Statistical Report.*

REFORMA (The National Association to Promote Library and Information Service to Latinos and the Spanish Speaking). P.O. Box 4386, Fresno, CA 93744. www.reforma.org.

REFORMA was established in 1971 as an ALA affiliate to promote the development of library collections to include Spanish-language and Latino-oriented materials, the recruitment of more bilingual and bicultural library professionals and support staff, and the development of library services and programs that meet the needs of the Latino community. The association newsletter contains articles, a president's column, chapter updates, book reviews, letters from the editor, and opinion pieces.

SALALM (Seminar on the Acquisition of Latin American Library Materials). SALALM Secretariat, Tulane University, Latin American Library, 422 Howard Tilton Memorial Library, 7001 Freret Street, New Orleans, LA 70118-5549. http://salalm.org.

Since 1956, SALAML has focused on the control and dissemination of bibliographic information about all types of Latin American publications, library collections of Latin Americana, and the special problems of librarians of Latin America and the Caribbean. The organization offers library materials for the Spanish- and Portuguese-speaking populations, compiles bibliographies for the field of study, conducts research of current and potential problems, and offers professional development opportunities for librarians.

Sociedad de Bibliotecarios de Puerto Rico. P.O. Box 22898. San Juan, PR 00931-2898. www.sociedadbibliotecarios.org.

This Spanish-language-based society is devoted to promoting library services, collections, best practices, partnerships, interlibrary loans, archives, and professional development for libraries, librarians, and staff in all types of libraries in the Caribbean.

Theatre Library Association (TLA). c/o New York Public Library for the Performing Arts, 40 Lincoln Center Plaza, New York, NY 10023. http://tla-online.org.

In 1937, TLA was formed to document theater as both an art form and a factor in a community's social and educational life. The association publishes *Performing Arts Resources*, a magazine that includes resource materials, essays on conservation and collection management, and information on public and private collections; along with *Broadside*, an online newsletter published about three times per year to update members on exhibits, collections, events, book reviews, and other items of interest that pertain to performing arts research, education, and production.

Urban Libraries Council (ULC). 125 South Wacker Drive, Suite 1050, Chicago, IL 60606. www.urbanlibraries.org.

ULC is dedicated to leadership, innovation, and the continuous transformation of public library systems and libraries to meet community needs. It serves as a forum for research used by public- and private-sector leaders through research papers, seminars, and council events. ULC's *e-News Weekly* and *eDiscussion Groups* electronic discussion lists allow library staff to network with peers to share problems and solutions and increase their libraries' effectiveness.

OTHER ALA GROUPS AND ORGANIZATIONS

ALA-Allied Professional Association (ALA-APA). 50 E. Huron, Chicago, IL 60611. http://ala-apa.org.

ALA-APA is a nonprofit professional organization established to promote the mutual professional interests of librarians and other library workers. Its two primary goals focus on verification of individuals in specialization beyond the initial professional degree and direct support of comparable worth and pay equity initiatives and other activities designed to improve the salaries and status of librarians and other library workers. ALA-APA produces Librarian and Library Worker Salary Surveys and publishes *Library Worklife: HR E-news for Today's Leaders*.

Freedom to Read Foundation (FTRF). 50 E. Huron, Chicago, IL 60611. www.ala.org/groups/affiliates/relatedgroups/freedomtoreadfoundation/.

Established in 1969 as a First Amendment legal defense organization, FTRF has a primary goal of protecting and promoting the First Amendment in libraries. It publishes *FTFR*, a quarterly newsletter that reports on current topics, court cases, state and federal legislation, upcoming events, and more.

Merritt Humanitarian Fund. Trustees, 50 East Huron, Chicago, IL, 60611. www.ala.org/groups/affiliates/relatedgroups/merrittfund/merritthumanitarian/.

The LeRoy C. Merritt Humanitarian Fund, established in 1970, is devoted to the support, maintenance, medical care, and welfare of librarians through individual grants. To qualify, an individual must have been denied employment rights or discriminated against on the basis of gender, sexual orientation, race, color, creed, religion, age, disability, or place of national origin; or denied employment rights because of defense of intellectual freedom; that is, threatened with loss of employment or discharged because of their stand for the cause of intellectual freedom, including promotion of freedom of the press, freedom of speech, the freedom of librarians to select items for their collections from all the world's written and recorded information, and defense of privacy rights.

Sister Libraries. International Relations Office, 50 Huron Street, Chicago, IL 60611-2795. http://wikis.ala.org/sisterlibraries/index.php/Main_Page/.

ALA created the Sister Libraries Program to encourage libraries to form relationships with libraries in other countries. Ideas, tips, and resources are available to help arrange this type of partnership. Potential partners are sorted by type of library (academic, national, public, school, special, or unspecified) or by geographic area (Africa, Americas, East Asia and the Pacific, Eurasia and Central Asia, Europe, Near East and South Asia, and the United States). The International Relations Round Table Sister Libraries Program maintains a wiki to help libraries find partners.

ALA STATE CHAPTERS

Alabama Library Association. 9154 East Chase Parkway, Suite 418, Montgomery, AL 36117. http://allanet.org.

Alaska Library Association. P.O. Box 81084, Fairbanks, AK 99708. www.akla.org.

Arizona Library Association. Association Managers of America, Inc., 950 E. Baseline Road, Ste. 104-1025, Tempe, AZ 85283, www.azla.org.

Arkansas Library Association. P.O. Box 958, Benton, AR 72018. www.arlib.org.

California Library Association. 2471 Flores Street, San Mateo, CA 94403-2273. www.cla-net.org.

Colorado Library Association. 3030 W. 81st Avenue, Westminster, CO 80031. http://cal-webs.org.

Connecticut Library Association. 234 Court Street, Middletown, CT 06457. www.ctlibraryassociation.org.

Delaware Library Association. P.O. Box 816, Dover, DE 19903-0816. www2.lib.udel.edu/dla/.

District of Columbia Library Association. P.O. Box 14177, Benjamin Franklin Station, Washington, DC 20044. www.dcla.org.

Florida Library Association. P.O. Box 1571, Lake City, FL 32056-1571. www.flalib.org.

Georgia Library Association. P.O. Box 793, Rex, GA 30273-0793. http://gla.georgialibraries.org.

Hawaii Library Association. P.O. Box 4441, Honolulu, HI 96814-4441. http://hla.chaminade.edu.

Idaho Library Association. P.O. Box 8533, Moscow, ID 83843. www.idaholibraries.org.

Illinois Library Association. 33 W. Grand Ave., Ste. 301, Chicago, IL 60654-6799. www.ila.org.

Indiana Library Association. 941 E. 86th Street, Suite 260, Indianapolis, IN 46240. www.ilfonline .org.

Iowa Library Association. 3636 Westown Pkwy, Suite 202, West Des Moines, IA 50266. www.iowalibraryassociation.org.

Kansas Library Association. 1020 SW Washburn, Topeka, KS 66604. http://kslibassoc.org/home/.

Kentucky Library Association. 1501 Twilight Tr., Frankfort, KY 40601. www.kylibasn.org.

Louisiana Library Association. 8550 United Plaza Boulevard, Suite 1001, Baton Rouge, LA 70809. www.llaonline.org.

Maine Library Association. P.O. Box 634, Augusta, ME 04332-0634. http://mainelibraries .org.

Maryland Library Association. 1401 Hollins St., Baltimore, MD 21223. www.mdlib.org.

Massachusetts Library Association. P.O. Box 535, Bedford, MA 01730. http://mla.memberlodge.org.

Michigan Library Association. 1407 Rensen St., Suite 2, Lansing, MI 48910. www.mla.lib.mi.us/ jobline/.

Minnesota Library Association. 1821 University Avenue West, Suite S256, St. Paul, MN 55104. www.mnlibraryassociation.org.

Mississippi Library Association. P.O. Box 13687, Jackson, MS 39236. www.misslib.org.

Missouri Library Association. c/o MLNC, 13610 Barrett Office Drive, Suite 206, Ballwin MO 63021. http://molib.org.

Montana Library Association. P.O. Box 1352, Three Forks, MT 59752. www.mtlib.org.

Nebraska Library Association. P.O. Box 21756 Lincoln, NE 68542-1756. http://nebraskalibraries .org.

Nevada Library Association. Paseo Verde Library, 280 S. Green Valley Parkway, Henderson, NV 89012. www.nevadalibraries.org.

New Hampshire Library Association. Portsmouth Public Library, 175 Parrott Avenue, Portsmouth, NH 03801. http://nhlibrarians.org.

New Jersey Library Association. P.O. Box 1534, Trenton, NJ 08607. www.njla.org.

New Mexico Library Association. c/o NMLA, P.O. Box 26074, Albuquerque, NM 87125. http://nmla .org.

New York Library Association. 6021 State Farm Road, Guilderland, NY 12084. www.nyla.org.

North Carolina Library Association. 1841 Capital Blvd., Raleigh, NC 27604. www.nclaonline.org.

North Dakota Library Association. P.O. Box 1595, Bismarck, ND 58502-1595. www.ndla.info/.

Ohio Library Association. 1105 Schrock Road, Suite 440, Columbus, OH 43229. www.olc.org.

Oklahoma Library Association. 300 Hardy Dr., Edmond, OK 73013. http://ola.oklibs.org.

Oregon Library Council. P.O. Box 3067, La Grande, OR 97850. www.olaweb.org/mc/page.

Pennsylvania Library Association. 220 Cumberland Parkway, Suite 10, Mechanicsburg, PA 17055. www.palibraries.org.

Rhode Island Library Association. P.O. Box 6765, Providence, RI 02940. http://rilibraries.org.

South Carolina Library Association. P.O, Box 1763, Columbia, SC 29202. www.scla.org.

South Dakota Library Association. 28363 472nd Ave., Worthing, SD 57077. www .sdlibraryassociation.org.

Tennessee Library Association. P.O. Box 241074, Memphis, TN 38124-1074. www.tnla.org.

Texas Library Association. 3355 Bee Cave Rd. #401, Austin, TX 78746-6763. www.txla.org.

Utah Library Association. P.O. Box 708155, Sandy, UT 84070. www.ula.org.

Vermont Library Association. P.O. Box 803, Burlington, VT 05402-0803. www .vermontlibraries.org.

Virginia Library Association. P.O. Box 56312, Virginia Beach, VA 23456. www.vla.org.

Washington Library Association. 23607 Highway 99 STE 2-C, Edmonds, WA 98026. http://wla.org.

West Virginia Library Association. P.O. Box 5221, Charleston, WV 25361. http://wvla.org.

Wisconsin Library Association. 4610 South Biltmore Lane, Suite 100, Madison, WI 53718-2153. www.wla.lib.wi.us.

Wyoming Library Association. P.O. Box 1387, Cheyenne, WY 82003-1387. www.wyla.org.

ALA REGIONAL CHAPTERS

Guam Library Association. P.O. Box 22515 GMF, Barrigada, GU 96921. http://sites.google.com/site/ guamlibraryassociation/home/.

Mountain Plains Library Association (MPLA). 14293 West Center Drive, Lakewood, CO 80228. Members: Arizona, Colorado, Kansas, Montana, Nebraska, New Mexico, Nevada, North Dakota, Oklahoma, South Dakota, Utah, and Wyoming. www.mpla.us/membership/index.html.

New England Library Association (NELA). 31 Connor Lane, Wilton, NH 03086. Members: Connecticut, Maine, Massachusetts, New Hampshire, Rhode Island, and Vermont. www.nelib.org.

Pacific Northwest Library Association (PNLA). 145 Whitemud Crossing Shopping Centre, 4211 106 Street, Edmonton, AB T6J 6L7. Members: Alaska, Idaho, Montana, Oregon, Washington, Alberta, and British Columbia. www.pnla.org.

Southeastern Library Association (SELA). P.O. Box 950, Rex, GA 30273. Members: Alabama, Arkansas, Florida, Georgia, Kentucky, Louisiana, Mississippi, North Carolina, Tennessee, Virginia, and West Virginia. http://selaonline.org.

Virgin Islands Library Association. P.O. Box 446, Kingshill, VI 00851-0446.

INTERNATIONAL AND NATIONAL PROFESSIONAL ASSOCIATIONS

INTERNATIONAL

★ SPOTLIGHT

International Federation of Library Associations and Institutions (IFLA). www.ifla.org.

Founded in Edinburgh, Scotland, in 1927, IFLA has over 1,600 members in 150 counties representing the interests of library and information services and their users. IFLA promotes high standards of provision and delivery of library services, encourages understanding of the value of good library and information services, and represents member interests worldwide. It publishes the *IFLA Journal*, IFLA Publication Series, IFLA Series on Bibliographic Control, and a variety of professional reports.

WEBSITES

Academy of Science. www.ukb.nl/index.html.

Asociación de Estados Iberoamericanos para el Desarrollo de las Bibliotecas Nacionales de Iberoamérica (ABINIA). www.abinia.org.

Association of Christian Librarians. www.acl.org.

Information for Social Change. http://libr.org/isc/.

International Association of Agricultural Information Specialist. www.iaald.org.

International Association of Law Libraries. www.iall.org.

International Association of Music Libraries, Archives and Documentation Centres. www.iaml.info/.

International Association of School Librarianship Libraries. www.iasl-slo.org.

International Association of Technological University Libraries. www.iatul.org.

International Council on Archives.
www.ica.org/3/homepage/home.html.

International Organization for Standardization.
www.iso.org/iso/home.html.

Librarians for Fairness.
www.librariansforfairness.org.

Special Libraries Association (SLA).
wwww.sla.org.

AFRICA

★ SPOTLIGHT

Association for Health Information and Libraries in Africa (AHILA). http://web.archive.org/web/20091026214532/http://geocities.com/HotSprings/Sauna/1910/.

AHILA promotes a high standard of library practices for health information services, education, and research in Africa through networking, professional development, and partnerships with the World Health Organization Regional Office for Africa and several national and international health organizations and learned societies.

Library and Information Association of South Africa (LIASA). www.liasa.org.za/.

Started in 1997, LIASA strives to unite and represent all institutions and staff working in South Africa's libraries and information services through networking, professional development, association events, publications and partnerships. The Association publishes *LIASA-in-Touch* four times per year, *SA Journal of Libraries and Information Science*, and an annual report.

☁ WEBSITES

Ghana Library Association. www.gla-net.org.

Nigerian Library Association. www.nla-ng.org.

Tanzania Library Association. www.tla.or.tz/.

Uganda Library Association. http://ugcla.org/.

ASIA

★ SPOTLIGHT

Japan Association of Private University Libraries.
www.jaspul.org/index-e.html

Since it was established in 1938, this group went through two reorganizations and name changes before becoming the Japan Association of Private University Libraries in 1943. The Association, which includes members from 90 percent of Japan's private university libraries, engages in investigation, research, seminars, lectures, publications, and professional development activities to improve and develop university libraries and related services.

☁ WEBSITES

Association of Special Libraries of the Philippines. http://aslpwiki.wikispaces.com.

Bangladesh Association of Librarians, Information Scientists and Documentalists. www.balid.org.

China Society for Library Science. www.nlc.gov.cn/old/old/newpages/english/org/index.htm.

East-Kazakhstan Librarians' Association.
www.pushkinlibrary.kz/index.php?lang=kz.

Hong Kong Library Association. www.hkla.org.

Library Association of Bangladesh.
www.lab.org.bd/.

Library Association of Singapore.
www.las.org.sg/wp/.

Medical and Health Librarians Association of the Philippines. http://mahlap.org.

Pakistan Library Automation Group. http://paklag.org.

Philippine Association of Academic and Research Librarians. www.dlsu.edu.ph/library/paarl/.

Pakistan Library Club. http://paklibcouncil.weebly.com.

Philippine Association of School Librarians. http://paslinews.wordpress.com.

Sri Lanka Library Association. www.slla.org.lk/.

EUROPE

★ SPOTLIGHT

Chartered Institute of Library and Information Professionals (CILIP). www.cilip.org.uk/Pages/default.aspx.

Reorganized on July 12, 2011, CILIP focuses on professional services, external relations and resources to provide advocacy and leadership, networking and creating communities, and continuing professional development for information, library, and knowledge practitioners. Branches have been established in East Midlands, East of England, Ireland, London, North East, North West, Scotland, South East Branch, South Western, Wales, West Midlands, and Yorkshire and Humberside. The association publishes *CILIP's Annual Buyer's Guide* to over 400 library suppliers and *CILIP Update* and *CILIP Update* digital monthly. Through Facet Publishing, its commercial publishing and bookselling arm, CILIP publishes over 200 titles on topics such as collection management, library management, library systems and technologies, information management, professional skills, and reference works.

Besides regional branches, CILIP has twenty-nine special-interest groups (see below). Each CILIP special-interest group member receives the newsletter and/or journals, publications, and invitation to relevant events.

✎ WEBSITES

Aerospace and Defence Librarians Group. www.cilip.org.uk/get-involved/special-interest-groups/aerospace-defence/.

Affiliated Members of CILIP. www.cilip.org.uk/get-involved/special-interest-groups/affiliated-members/.

Branch and Mobile Libraries. www.cilip.org.uk/get-involved/special-interest-groups/branch-mobile/.

Career Development Group. www.cilip.org.uk/get-involved/special-interest-groups/careerdevelopment/.

Cataloguing and Indexing. www.cilip.org.uk/get-involved/special-interest-groups/cataloguing-indexing/.

Colleges of Further and Higher Education. www.cilip.org.uk/get-involved/special-interest-groups/c-of-he/.

Commercial, Legal and Scientific Information Group (formerly ICLG). www.cilip.org.uk/get-involved/special-interest-groups/clsig/.

Community Services. www.cilip.org.uk/get-involved/special-interest-groups/community-services/.

Diversity Group. www.cilip.org.uk/get-involved/special-interest-groups/diversity/.

Education Librarians Group. www.cilip.org.uk/get-involved/special-interest-groups/education/.

Government Information Group. www.cilip.org.uk/get-involved/special-interest-groups/government/.

Health Libraries. www.cilip.org.uk/get-involved/special-interest-groups/health/.

Information Services. www.cilip.org.uk/get-involved/special-interest-groups/information-services/.

International Library and Information Group. www.cilip.org.uk/get-involved/special-interest-groups/international/.

Library and Information History. www.cilip.org.uk/get-involved/special-interest-groups/history/.

Library and Information Research Group. www.cilip.org.uk/get-involved/special-interest-groups/research/.

Local Studies. www.cilip.org.uk/get-involved/special-interest-groups/local-studies/.

Multimedia Information and Technology Group. www.cilip.org.uk/get-involved/special-interest-groups/multimedia/.

Patent and Trademark Group. www.cilip.org.uk/get-involved/special-interest-groups/patent/.

Personnel, Training and Education. www.cilip.org.uk/get-involved/special-interest-groups/personnel/.

Prison Libraries Group. www.cilip.org.uk/get-involved/special-interest-groups/prison/.

Public Libraries Group. www.cilip.org.uk/get-involved/special-interest-groups/public/.

Publicity and Public Relations. www.cilip.org.uk/get-involved/special-interest-groups/publicity/.

Rare Books and Special Collections Group. www.cilip.org.uk/get-involved/special-interest-groups/rare-books/.

Retired Members Guild. www.cilip.org.uk/get-involved/special-interest-groups/retired/.

School Libraries Group. www.cilip.org.uk/get-involved/special-interest-groups/school/.

UKeiG. www.cilip.org.uk/get-involved/special-interest-groups/ukeig/Pages/default.aspx/.

University, College and Research Group. www.cilip.org.uk/get-involved/special-interest-groups/ucr/.

Youth Libraries Group. www.cilip.org.uk/get-involved/special-interest-groups/youth/.

♠ OTHER EUROPEAN WEBSITES

Association for Information Management (formerly Association of Special Libraries and Information Bureaux, ASLIB). www.aslib.co.uk.

Association of European Research Libraries (LIBER). www.libereurope.eu.

Association of French Librarians. www.abf.asso.fr.

Association of Hungarian Librarians. http://mke.info.hu.

Association of Information and Documentation Professionals (ADBS) (formerly the Association of Specialized Librarians and Librarians). www.adbs.fr.

Association of Libraries of Czech Universities. www.akvs.cz.

Austrian Association of Librarians. www.univie.ac.at/voeb/php/.

Austrian Library Association. www.bvoe.at.

Belarusian Library Association. www.bla.by.

Belgian Association for Documentation. www.abd-bvd.be.

British and Irish Association of Law Librarians (BIALL). www.biall.org.uk.

Bulgarian Library Association. www.lib.bg.

Consortium of European Research Libraries. www.cerl.org/web/.

Consortium of Research Libraries (CURL). www.rluk.ac.uk.

Croatian Library Association. www.hkdrustvo.hr.

Danish Library Association. www.dbf.dk.

Dutch Association of University Libraries, the Royal Library and the Library of the Royal Dutch Academy of Science. www.ukb.nl/index.html.

Estonian Librarians Association. http://eru.lib.ee/joomla/.

European Association for Health Information and Libraries (EAHIL). www.eahil.net.

European Association of Libraries and Information Services on Addictions (ELISAD) (formerly the European Association of Libraries and Information Services on Alcohol and Other Drugs). www.elisad.eu.

European Bureau of Library, Information and Documentation Associations. www.eblida.org.

Federation Union of German Library and Information Associations. www.dgd.de.

Finnish Library Association. www.suomenkirjastoseura.fi.

Finnish Music Library Association. www.kaapeli.fi/~musakir/.

Finnish Research Library Association. www.stks.fi.

German Library Association. www.bibliotheksverband.de.

Greek Librarians Association. www.nlg.gr.

Italian Library Association. www.aib.it.

Netherlands Public Library Association. www.debibliotheken.nl.

Norwegian Library Association. www.norskbibliotekforening.no.

Polish Librarians Association. www.ebib.info/.

Private Libraries Association. www.plabooks.org (United Kingdom).

Russian Library Association. www.rba.ru.

School Library Association. www.sla.org.uk.

Slovenian Library Association. www.zbds-zveza.si.

Swedish Library Association. www.biblioteksforeningen.org.

Ukrainian Library Association. http://ula.org.ua.

Turkish University and Research Librarians' Association (UNAK). www.unak.org.tr.

LATIN AMERICA

★ SPOTLIGHT

LANIC. http://lanic.utexas.edu/la/region/library/.

Available in English, Spanish, and Portuguese, LANIC provides regional resources, including bibliographic databases, digital libraries, and information on libraries, collections, and associations. Country resources are included for Argentina, Aruba, Bahamas, Bolivia, Brazil, Chile, Colombia, Costa Rica, Cuba, Dominican Republic, Ecuador, El Salvador, Guatemala, Guyana, Haiti, Jamaica, Mexico, Nicaragua, Panama, Paraguay, Peru, Puerto Rico, Suriname, Trinidad and Tobago, Uruguay, Venezuela, and the Virgin Islands.

☁ WEBSITES

Argentinian Library Association.
www.abgra.org.ar.

Asociación Bibliotecológica de Guatemala.
http://web.archive.org/web/20091027170148/
http://es.geocities.com/asociaciondebiblio
tecarios/bibliotecario.htm.

Brazilian Federation of Librarians Associations, Information Scientists and Institutions.
www.febab.org.br.

Comité de Cooperación entre Bibliotecas Universitarias de Guatemala.
www-ccbu.blogspot.com.

Librarian Association of El Salvador.
www.ues.edu.sv/abes/.

Mexican Library Association.
http://ambac.org.mx.

NORTH AMERICA

★ SPOTLIGHT

Federal Library and Information Center Committee (FLICC). www.loc.gov/flicc/

Created in 1965 by the Library of Congress and the Bureau of Budget, FLICC comprises library leaders from all three branches of the federal government. The committee focuses on professional development, promotion of library and information services, and coordination of the available resources. FLICC publishes information alerts, service directories, the *Handbook of Federal Librarianship*, annual reports, and more. The committee is also responsible for making recommendations to federal agencies on library and information policies, programs, and procedures.

☁ WEBSITES

American Society for Information Science and Technology (ASIS&T). www.asis.org/about.html.

Association of Architecture School Librarians.
http://architecturelibrarians.org.

Association of Caribbean University, Research and Institutional Libraries. http://acuril.uprrp.edu.

Bibliographical Society of America.
www.bibsocamer.org.

Canadian Association for Information Science (CAIS-ACSI). www.cais-acsi.ca.

Canadian Association of Law Libraries.
www.callacbd.ca/en/content/home/.

Canadian Health Libraries Association.
www.chla-absc.ca/?q=en/.

Chief Officers of State Library Agencies (COSLA). www.cosla.org.

Church and Synagogue Library Association (CSLA). http://cslainfo.org.

Council on Library Resources (CLIR).
www.clir.org.

Evangelical Church Library Association.
www.eclalibraries.org.

Insurance Library Association of Boston.
www.insurancelibrary.org.

Library and Information Association of Jamaica (LIAJA). www.liaja.org.jm.

Library Association of Trinidad and Tobago.
www.latt.org.tt.

Manitoba Library Association (MLA).
www.mla.mb.ca.

Major Orchestra Librarians' Association.
www.mola-inc.org/index.html.

National Association of Government Archives and Records Administrators (NAGARA).
www.nagara.org.

National Church Library Association.
www.churchlibraries.org.

National Information Standards Organization.
www.niso.org/home/.

North American Serials Interest Group (NASIG).
www.nasig.org.

Polish American Librarians Association (PALA).
www.palalib.org/index.php?link=1.

Southeastern Library Association.
http://selaonline.org/about/index.htm.

Substance Abuse Librarians and Information Specialists (SALIS).
http://salis.org/about/about.html.

University Film and Video Association (UFVA).
www.ufva.org.

USA Toy Library Association (USATLA).
www.usatla.org/USA_Toy_Library_Association/Welcome.html.

OCEANIA

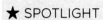 SPOTLIGHT

Australian Library and Information Association (ALIA). www.alia.org.au

1418 Established in 1937, this group has changed names and reorganized twice to keep up with developments in librarianship. *ALIA provides library and information professionals with career resources, discounts on events and professional development programs, access*

to services and publications, and networking opportunities. The forty-five ALIA groups consist of at least twenty-
five members and have a geographic, special-interest, special-purpose, issues, or sectoral basis. A link to an alphabetical listing of the groups and a description of group activities is at www.alia.org.au/groups/groups.html.

WEBSITES

Australian and New Zealand Theological Library Association. www.anztla.org.

Australian School Library Association.
www.asla.org.au.

Australian School Library Association.
www.aslansw.org.au (New South Wales).

Council of Australian University Librarians.
www.caul.edu.au.

Library and Information Association of New Zealand (LIANZA). www.lianza.org.nz.

Pacific Islands Association of Libraries and Archives. http://sites.google.com/site/pialaorg/.

Public Libraries Australia. www.pla.org.au.

School Library Association of New Zealand Aotearoa. www.slanza.org.nz.

School Library Association of South Australia (SLASA). www.slasa.asn.au/home.html.

School Library Association of Victoria.
www.slav.schools.net.au/slav.html.

AUTHOR AND TITLE INDEX

Locators refer to entry numbers.

Lightning Source UK Ltd.
Milton Keynes UK
UKOW02f0334130314

227992UK00001B/1/P